CRITICAL ESSAYS ON

MILTON

FROM *ELH*

CRITICAL ESSAYS ON
MILTON
FROM *ELH*

The Johns Hopkins Press
Baltimore and London

The Johns Hopkins Press, Baltimore, Maryland 21218
The Johns Hopkins Press Ltd., London

Library of Congress Catalog Card number 71-93296

Standard Book Number 8018-1094-9

Johns Hopkins Paperbacks edition, 1969

PUBLISHER'S NOTE

All of the essays in this volume have been reprinted from issues of *ELH* published between 1935 and 1968. Selected by the editors of *ELH*, they represent some of the finest modern criticism of Milton. The issue and year of original publication is noted on the opening page of each essay. Notes on the contributors are found on page ix. *ELH* is published by The Johns Hopkins Press and is issued quarterly in March, June, September, and December.

CONTENTS

ARNOLD STEIN (1915–   ) is professor of English literature at the University of Washington. His essay in *ELH* was followed by two books on Milton: *Answerable Style* (1953) and *Heroic Knowledge* (1957), and by two books on metaphysical poetry: *John Donne's Lyrics* (1962) and *George Herbert's Lyrics* (1968).

MARJORIE HOPE NICOLSON (1894–   ) is emeritus professor of English at Columbia University. Among her many books are *Voyages to the Moon* (1948), *Breaking of the Circle* (1950, 1960), *Science and Imagination* (1956), *Mountain Gloom* and *Mountain Glory* (1959), *John Milton: A Reader's Guide to His Poetry* (1963), and *Pepys' Diary and the New Science* (1965).

MERRITT Y. HUGHES (1893–   ) is emeritus professor of English at the University of Wisconsin. He edited *John Milton: Complete Poems and Major Prose* (1957) and Volume III of the *Complete Prose Works of John Milton* (1962), and is the author of *Ten Perspectives on Milton* (1965).

KINGSLEY WIDMER (1925–   ), professor of English at San Diego State College, has written *The Art of Perversity: D. H. Lawrence* (1962), *Henry Miller* (1963), *The Literary Rebel* (1965), a forthcoming book on Melville, and many articles on a wide range of literature. He is also an active social essayist and critic.

RICHARD NEUSE (1931–   ) has published articles on Spenser and Chaucer. He teaches at the University of Rhode Island.

GALE H. CARRITHERS, JR., (1932–   ), associate professor of English at State University of New York at Buffalo, has published on Donne and poetics. He is presently working on book-length studies of Donne's sermons and of seventeenth-century poetics.

ROGER B. WILKENFELD (1938–), visiting professor of English literature at Douglass College, Rutgers University, has published articles on Milton and Victorian literature. He is writing a monograph on *Lycidas* and is working on a study of Victorian irony.

Geoffrey H. Hartman (1929–   ), professor of English and comparative literature at Yale University, has published *The Unmediated Vision* (1954), *André Malraux* (1960), and *Wordsworth's Poetry* (1964). He is presently at work on a book tracing the transition from Renaissance to Romanticism.

Arthur O. Lovejoy (1873–1962) was professor of philosophy at The Johns Hopkins University. He was the author of many books, including *Essays in the History of Ideas* (1948), *The Great Chain of Being* (1936), *The Reason, the Understanding, and Time* (1961), *Reflections on Human Nature* (1961), and *The Thirteen Pragmatisms and Other Essays* (1963).

Russell E. Smith, Jr., (1940–   ) teaches English at Metropolitan State College, Denver. His article in *ELH* is the first he has published.

Mother Mary Christopher Pecheux, O. S. U. (1916–   ), professor of English at the College of New Rochelle, has published several articles on Milton in scholarly journals. She is especially interested in biblical, patristic, and seventeenth-century theological influences on Milton.

Albert R. Cirillo (1933–   ), associate professor of English literature at Northwestern University, has published articles on Milton, Spenser, and Donne, as well as a monograph on George Eliot's *Daniel Deronda* (1967).

Martin Mueller (1939–   ) teaches English and comparative literature at the University of Toronto. He has published articles on Milton and the epic tradition.

Lee Sheridan Cox, associate professor of English at The Ohio State University, is the author of articles on Milton, Shakespeare, and Chaucer. She has also published detective fiction, including a humorous narrative in that genre, *Andy and Willie* (1967).

William O. Harris (1923–   ) is the author of *Skelton's "Magnyfycence" and the Cardinal Virtue Tradition* (1965). He teaches at the University of California, Riverside.

CRITICAL ESSAYS ON

MILTON

FROM *ELH*

MILTON AND METAPHYSICAL ART:
AN EXPLORATION

BY ARNOLD STEIN

The traditional *Descriptio Rei* of Renaissance rhetoric was associated with painting. It was ideally a kind of speaking picture, to be presented, not simply, but with rhetorical " colors." It was meant to be looked at, and so executed that it should seem as if the writer had painted rather than told, and as if the reader had seen rather than read. When such descriptions had no strictly functional purpose, it was expected that the artist would make the most of his chance to luxuriate in a display of his craft—as Homer and Virgil had done.

I want to begin by looking at one such display of Milton's craft—or rather, at one aspect of that craft, the control of the tenses of the verbs. Satan has just ordered his standard raised.

> All in a moment through the gloom were seen
> Ten thousand Banners rise into the Air
> With Orient Colours waving: with them rose
> A Forrest huge of Spears: and thronging Helms
> Appear'd, and serried Shields in thick array
> Of depth immeasurable:
>
> > (*Paradise Lost*, I, 544 ff.)

It is in the past tense; *were seen* sets the time. But the effect of *rise* and *waving* is to move the action out of the past and make it seem out of time. (The infinitive *rise* dominates the passive *were seen*: partly because the preposition is omitted, and partly because *rise* is rhythmically the climax of its line and the preceding line.) Then the action returns definitely to the past with *rose*. One might look at it this way: the two verbs in the past tense are a kind of framework preceding and following the two verbs that give the impression of being in the present tense. Or look at it this way: all the details in a picture cannot be seen at once. The picture was there before the details could become discernible, so start it in the past

This essay first appeared in *ELH*, Vol. 16, No. 2 (June 1949).

tense, but tactfully. The banners rise with a kind of active immediacy that thrusts aside for the moment abstract logical time. For another moment time is suspended in the flutter of the orient colors waving. Then the next details come into focus; their approach to us is in the past tense. We must remember that the past tense *is* the real tense of these lines, and that the present tense *was* an illusion. To the eye, the first details perceived seem to be happening as they are seen. But the details that emerge later, since they are later, are more easily subject to logical order. What seemed to be happening all at once, assumes a pattern of sequence.

We have been considering the picture dramatically, in terms of the impact upon us of the details. But what we have seen so far is only the background of the picture. Once the details have made their impact, and have emerged " through the gloom," they move no longer. They are the static background, and quite properly in the past tense. For this picture, we are now able to observe, is a verbal one; and we must not expect to see the details in quite the same order that we should expect if this were an actual painting before our eyes. When the background is finished the tense changes:

> Anon they move
> In perfect *Phalanx* to the *Dorian* mood
> Of Flutes and soft Recorders; such as rais'd
> To highth of noblest temper Hero's old
> Arming to Battel, and in stead of rage
> Deliberate valour breath'd, firm and unmov'd
> With dread of death to flight or foul retreat,
> Nor wanting power to mitigate and swage
> With solemn touches, troubl'd thoughts, and chase
> Anguish and doubt and fear and sorrow and pain
> From mortal or immortal minds.

They and their music move towards us, in the active present. But the heroic mood suggests other pictures (and sounds and feelings) to the mind, and these rise from the past. Part of the richness of the present procession moving forward are these associations with things that are past, and yet, when evoked, seem more present than past, more intensely present because they bring with them the richness of the past. Perhaps one ought to think of this as part of the depth of the foreground, part also—for the poet as painter—of the past inextricably involved in the present. This sense of time, as we have already seen, works both ways. Some of the participles have, I think, a modifying effect that suggests the present. If this, together with my treatment of *rise* and *waving*, seems an unwarranted piece of subtlety, consider the following lines, which continue the quotation:

> Thus they
> Breathing united force with fixed thought
> Mov'd on in silence to soft Pipes that charm'd
> Thir painful steps o're the burnt soyle: and now
> Advanc't in view they stand, a horrid Front
> Of dreadful length and dazling Arms, in guise
> Of Warriers old with order'd Spear and Shield,
> Awaiting what command thir mighty Chief
> Had to impose:

This too appears to be following the same kind of pattern of sequence that we observed in the first passage. Once the detail has become fixed in focus, it is put in the past tense. But the effect is not quite so simple as that. Present and past are woven together. The present participle *breathing* (undefined in time) introduces the past verb *moved*; and then the past participle *advanced* (undefined in time) introduces the present verb *stand*. There they are, brought forward and motionless, awaiting the command their chief "*Had* to impose!" (In its magnificent defiance of mere logic *had* confirms the complex depth of the picture.)

Then, with the emergence of new details, the present tense is used unequivocally:

> He through the armed Files
> Darts his experienc't eye, and soon traverse
> The whole Battalion views, thir order due,
> Thir visages and statures as of Gods,
> Thir number last he summs. And now his heart
> Distends with pride, and hardning in his strength
> Glories: For never since created man,
> Met such imbodied force, as nam'd with these
> Could merit more then that small infantry
> Warr'd on by Cranes:

The historical allusions lead us once more into the past tense, and by the time we have wound our way through a dozen lines and returned to Satan the tense of the foreground has become definitely past. It remains so through a passage of extended description not concerned with motion. And then:

> He now prepar'd
> To speak; whereat their doubl'd Ranks they bend
> From Wing to Wing, and half enclose him round
> With all his Peers; attention held them mute.
> Thrice he assay'd. . . .

The device of the historical present is familiar enough in Milton, and in other writers. What I believe to be unusual is the shifting back to the past tense immediately after the present tense has been used to bring a part of the picture forward. But even this, in the example under consideration, is a piece of relatively simple technique compared with the complicated effects of the earlier passages.

To look backward then: the description is a painting, and plainly not a photographic one in its characteristics. It skilfully arranges depths and chiaroscuro; it is vague and sharp, suggestive and defined, real and unreal. It secures all these effects while it is obeying literary laws, and this though the final effects may approximate those of painting.

Something has been gained, I think, by isolating the verbs. But I do not want to sugggest that I have illuminated more than a single important device in this literary painting. Before proceeding to more important considerations, I want to comment briefly on some matters that I cannot settle but do not wish to ignore. For one thing, the phrase " Of depth immeasurable," in the first passage, confirms the effect of the verb tenses, and gives the impression of depth so frequent in the backgrounds of Renaissance paintings. Another phrase, " in guise/ Of Warriers old "—especially the *in guise*—brings in the note of strangeness, the imaginative unreality through which art achieves the real. Another observation that deserves note is the fact that for the poet a picture, however rich in details, need not be confined to one frame. The picture may move imperceptibly into a second picture and then into a third, the foreground of one becoming the background of the next, and so on. And yet the effect (except perhaps for the technique of the close-up) may remain closer to the effect of painting than of cinema.

Another, and more important, problem I have not considered is this: the way the art of music contributes to the verbal painting. I should say that, though there are special musical effects, in general the music is conveyed after the manner of painting. But some qualifications are necessary. It is true that the verse is delicately sensitive to the kinds of music being played by the " Flutes and soft Recorders ": a calm noble march at the beginning, a rhythm and verbal music more personal and tentative and consoling at the end. But though we have something of the immediate effect of " Flute and soft Recorders," the effect is less definite and less complete than some of the immediate effects of painting that we have already studied. Perhaps we have an approximation of the range and rhythm of the pipes, but little more. Another musical effect may be observed. The poetry, more in the manner of music than painting, can repeat the theme, altered and enriched:

> Mov'd on in silence to soft Pipes that charm'd
> Thir painful steps o're the burnt soyle. . . .

But this must be qualified too, for painting also can work by repetition, of color or line. The distinction I think I see is partly a matter of space: in music (as in literary picture) you cannot take in the whole outline at once; you must wait for development; and in this sense it is possible to arrange a longer interval for the ear than for the eye. At least this seems to be so in the lines under consideration, where the return to the original theme occurs after the long development has erected the implications into a kind of musical architecture. To me this musical enrichment of the theme is an effect parallel with the poetic richness of the procession that moves forward in the present while evoking associations with things that are past.

These, I think, are the chief effects that are close to the art of music. But the lines just quoted illustrate the really closer affinity with painting. The illusion of music is neither so immediate nor so complete in its details as the illusion of painting. In verbal painting we seem to be seeing the pictures, but we seem less to be hearing the music than to have heard it. A man with eyes, but no knowledge of painting, could still visualize these verbal paintings. But he could not, if he had not been a listener who had experienced music, imagine these musical effects; though *we* can, through the poet's mediation in these lines, hear music with our inner ear, by means of the esthetic memory. The painter could do most of this too. And Milton, in creating the illusion of music (though my qualifications are disproportionately long), has worked mostly in the visual manner of the painter. By the movement of his figures and by their faces, the painter could suggest the effects of the " Deliberate valour " and the power (perhaps on different faces) " to mitigate and swage." Also more available to the painter than to the composer of Milton's day is the art that can create the sensations of walking with painful steps over burnt soil—and all while being charmed by music.

II

So far I have been trying to convince myself and the reader that I have worked over these lines diligently. By mastering some of the externals I have been trying to earn the right—to qualify, as it were—to make statements about the internal qualities of the poetry. I want to say something about why I feel this to be great art and great poetry. Reasonable caution would avoid the word *great*. But I have gone almost as far as I can with reason and caution. I am reminded of the chronology of my experience with the passage: I *felt* it to be great poetry before I had much reasonable confirmation that it was even great art. (I am using the word *art* arbitrarily: to refer to the technique, the management of the materials, the form. I am quite aware that it is a critical error to separate form and content; but I am equally aware that it is a more serious distortion to act as if form were everything, and this is what often happens when critics reverentially refuse to consider content. Critics who insist that form and content are indissoluble— even for the temporary convenience of critical purposes— should stop talking about technique: which I do not propose to do.) Perhaps the preceding analysis helps confirm the feeling that the passage is great art. But I have no illusion that anything important has been said about the poetry.

Let us return to the art. One possible standard of greatness has been implicit in the discussion—the richness of the complexity; and more important, the degree to which one can significantly analyze the complexity and still not reach any essential mysteries. By this standard the first stanza of Mr. Wallace Stevens' *Sunday Morning* is great art.

> Complacencies of the peignoir, and late
> Coffee and oranges in a sunny chair,
> And the green freedom of a cockatoo
> Upon a rug mingle to dissipate
> The holy hush of ancient sacrifice.
> She dreams a little, and she feels the dark
> Encroachment of that old catastrophe,
> As a calm darkens among water-lights.
> The pungent oranges and bright, green wings
> Seem things in some procession of the dead,
> Winding across wide water, without sound.
> The day is like wide water, without sound,
> Stilled for the passing of her dreaming feet
> Over the seas, to silent Palestine,
> Dominion of the blood and sepulchre.

And so it is. The intricate complexity of attitudes is woven into its pattern of sounds, rhythms, meanings, and suggestions, with the essential attitude controlling all, yet allowing the other attitudes their due measure of freedom, but no more. I quote this stanza because of the attitudes, which give the significant depth to the complexity. Of course the attitudes cannot be separated from the suggestions in the words and rhythms. That is always true, but the reverse is not necessarily true: the words and rhythms can very easily be separated—they are in many poems—from any genuine and significant complexity of attitude. Then we have a surface complexity.

Let us look at an example, for the distinction is of course a relative one. This is the third and concluding stanza of a poem about the " perfect square " of a city block. It is one of Mr. Karl Shapiro's early poems.

> O neat, O dead, what feeling thing
> Could buy so bare! O dead, O neat,
> What beating heart could sink to buy
> The copy of the die complete.

It is certainly not just verbal in its complexity, and the ideas are inseparable from the expression—as in great art. But a principle of balance is violated. Here the expression flauntingly dominates the ideas, as in another kind of minor art the ideas dominate the expression. The complexity is meretricious; it annoys us when we see through it, for the contrivance is not justified by the results. In this sense all ingenuity, all complex art, runs a risk: it compels us to admiration and study. In these lines, once we have picked the rhetorical devices apart, we cannot recognize even the *disiecti membra poetae*; and somehow we cannot put the pieces together again, for there was no inviolable mystery that we could not get at. Everything came apart, for it was all surface; and what ingenuity and will can put together, ingenuity and will can take apart.

I am dwelling on this because there are kinds of complexity that must not be allowed to pass for great art. I am not discarding—I merely am not discussing—poetry that gets complicated effects through "simplicity." That is a great art which does not come within the scope of this discussion. I am, however, rejecting surface complexity. It is apparent that there are formulas for being complex; and many modern poets have mastered them, just as poets in every age have deceived themselves with formulas. One may, for instance, believe that poetry develops and enriches language without regarding that benefit as more than a kind of by-product of poetry. And though one certainly should not minimize the importance of medium, neither should one elevate the medium over the art. To push this a little further: there is a distinction between variations on a theme and variations on variations. It is plain enough which kind of complexity works by surface multiplication.

Milton's variations are on a theme, a traditional rhetorical theme. His basic method, though not necessarily better than Mr. Stevens' in *Sunday Morning*, is certainly different. The subtleties do not advertise themselves as subtleties, though they do, and quite rightfully, in *Sunday Morning*. Milton gets his great effects through making the ordinary extraordinary. The natural habits of the English language are made to yield miracles without seeming to. But, I repeat, that is only one method of art; it is not a standard. More significant is Milton's not really trying to paint or make music with words. It is true that he did not have easily available—as do modern poets—the techniques for such enterprises (though baroque artists were dabbling in that sort of thing). But it is clear that he had no major interest in such a performance. He wished to get some effects of painting and music, but for a purpose in poetry; and the other arts are perfectly subordinated to poetry. Could Milton have known the symbolists we might have had more and different musical effects; or from Mr. Stevens he might have learned some important devices for suggesting the effects of painting in verse. But would he have done much more in this passage? And would that have made the art greater?

These questions cannot of course be answered. But they are worth asking and, even indirectly, trying to answer. What *is* the purpose of this passage? To return to our rhetorical definition: it is a *descriptio rei*, not serving any immediate functional purpose and therefore an opportunity for the artist to display his skill. Milton has done this, though he has—if we wish to speak more precisely—rather displayed the effects of his skill and concealed the causes. He has, incidentally, been providing pleasure, not unimportant in a long poem. Part of the pleasure lies in our recognizing the concealed art, as the pleasure in another kind of art might lie in recognizing and apprehending the obscure, or in appreciating the brilliance of ingenious new tricks of style that say what has been unsayable. A value-judgment is not strictly relevant. Milton simply preferred certain kinds of technical triumph that suited his art and its purposes. But this passage is not merely a technical performance, a virtuoso piece. As Milton subordinated the arts of painting and music to the art of poetry—I risk the tedious—he subordinated the art of poetry to something else.

The immediate goal in this passage (it is really involved in the pleasure, for without Ciceronian "pleasing" there could be no "moving") is to create an important kind of realism—to make Satan and his cohorts real and credible antagonists. But a larger goal—the whole poem—helps free the poet from any over-anxiety to make the immediate goal a striking success in itself. He can work with a large hand that does not have to linger trembling over the fine effects, trying to make them finer. If Milton performs a minor miracle of craftsmanship, the reader is not invited to pause in admiration and study. Nor is the reader of Milton compelled to pause or else miss what is most important in the poem—a surface complexity which must be unraveled, and which, when unraveled, tells all, and so loses the newness that was indispensable to its charm. Such an art—the opposite, exaggerated, of Milton's—makes exquisite variations on itself, saying its few things over and over, perhaps beautifully, with no integral pattern of growth and enrichment, but only a peripheral growth, in shades of perception, in cobweb-fine nuances of words; it waxes old like a garment, and the disenchanted reader must, if his taste is that of the writer's, pass on in search of new newnesses.

Perhaps the most distinctive quality of this passage of Milton's is the sense of bigness that informs it. Subordination is one sign of the bigness. Painting and music, the miracles of craftsmanship—these are securely smaller than the part, and the part is smaller than the whole. It is a sense of the whole that makes for the bigness: that allows the poet to create the exquisite without stopping there, that allows him his free and reckless development of larger implications which pass beyond the immediate goal of achieving realism. Milton's realism needs further definition, but we can best approach that indirectly.

Consider two quite different poems that illustrate the same important kind of realism that distinguishes Milton's lines: One is immediate and sensual, Yeats' *Leda and the Swan*; the other is the fairy-tale reality of the child's world, Mr. John Crowe Ransom's *Bells for John Whiteside's Daughter*. They both have something very significant in common—a concern for more than the immediate, for more than the sensuous perception of things. Had Yeats' poem ended after the first half dozen lines, it would have been, not a greater poem, but a more surprising accomplishment in realism. Such realism—not photographic perceptions of the surfaces of things—seems to come from realizing the inner qualities of things; and such realization apparently cannot be gained from the things alone. It is the pattern, the framework, the larger meaning of Leda's experience—all this and chiefly this that permits Yeats to apprehend so greatly the brute immediate: for it is more than immediate.

If what I have said about *Leda and the Swan* holds, then the basic observation also applies to these stanzas from *Bells for John Whiteside's Daughter*:

Her wars were bruited in our high window.
We looked among orchard trees and beyond
Where she took arms against her shadow,
Or harried unto the pond

The lazy geese, like a snow cloud
Dripping their snow on the green grass,
Tricking and stopping, sleepy and proud,
Who cried in goose, Alas,

For the tireless heart within the little
Lady with rod that made them rise
From their noon apple-dreams and scuttle
Goose-fashion under the skies!

How did everything in this childish world come to be so real, so clear and sharp before us that it can quite disregard the realities of a grown-up world? Not because it is a pure fragmentary vision; but because it is the terrible memory of an adult, of one who is trying to find a way to deal with his grief over the death of the child. The pressure of his need gives him insight, though the insight cannot afterwards carry over completely into the grown-up world of death and funeral. He returns, from his memory, with some evidence of relief, but the special quality of his insight was part of the child's world, not of the adult's: only as an adult tormented by the mystery of the child's death could he enter the kingdom of the child. It was a painful seriousness (which, too easily, can blind the moralist to moral values in literature) that prevented Mr. Winters from recognizing the larger meaning of this poem. For it is not a lovely fragment but a perfect poem—and because of the mutual relationship between the larger meaning and the specific memory.

To return to Milton: his realism is distinguished by this same concern for more than the immediate. His subordination, with its sense of the whole, is one external sign of the bigness that can record the immediate and yet transcend it. The lines most directly concerned are these:

Anon they move
In perfect *Phalanx* to the *Dorian* mood
Of Flutes and soft Recorders; such as rais'd
To highth of noblest temper Hero's old
Arming to Battel, and in stead of rage
Deliberate valour breath'd, firm and unmov'd
With dread of death to flight or foul retreat,
Nor wanting power to mitigate and swage

With solemn touches, troubl'd thoughts, and chase
Anguish and doubt and fear and sorrow and pain
From mortal or immortal minds. Thus they
Breathing united force with fixed thought
Mov'd on in silence to soft pipes that charm'd
Thir painful steps o're the burnt soyle.

The opening lines are a noble expression of one powerful attitude towards life. It is an attitude of stern self-discipline, not
dependent upon the undisciplinable energy of rage. It is one
answer to the challenge of life, but it is an answer that affirms
its superiority by shutting out all alternatives and qualifications. It offers the discipline, complete: *deliberate valor, united
force, fixed thought*. It is noble, as superiority to self, as quiet
certainty, always are. Though it is an answer best maintained
while marching, it can shame into silence him who would argue
or qualify. For men marching under discipline towards a goal
are willing to sacrifice their lives; and that is an argument
difficult for other men to contradict, except by marching themselves. And yet, if we are not marching we recognize this
answer as a limited one. The lines, beginning " Nor wanting
power," and through " From mortal or immortal minds," express another attitude. This is not so much an answer as an
acceptance of what the earlier lines deny, by willed suppres-
sion: an acceptance, neither defiant nor submissive, of the
human condition.

This whole passage has an important purpose to fulfil. The
fallen angels, and their leader, are full of doubts and fears, but
they still desperately wish to be defiant. The only certainty
they are capable of feeling is that of marching men. Yet this
feeling is for fallen angels more a refuge than a strength. They
stiffen *in* this feeling; the verse tells us so through the fiction of
describing the music; and also tells us, with a wonderful indi-
rectness, that the music is not " wanting power to mitigate and
swage "—in the context a tremendous admission. Such comforts are necessary. The artist is great enough in his sympathy, and in his art, to feel his way into the villains of his
piece. Suddenly they are angels, though fallen; and like us,
underneath our various exteriors, they are dependent upon
comforts that are outside themselves. Satan and his legions
of devils, the fallen angels, all humanity—for a moment they

fuse and become one in their strength and weakness. It is only for a moment, but it is a bold moment.

I have some generalizations to make, some earned by the preceding discussion, some not. This passage of Milton's measures up to the most important standards of metaphysical art, and helps put some unimportant standards in their place.

It has the kind of complexity that counts—an inner and functional complexity. If it is not elliptical, compressed, and intense in every phrase, that does not matter much. For that is not an important standard—it may suit the strategy of *The Waste Land* very well, but not that of the *Four Quartets*. What is important is that this passage has genuine tension. Nor is irony the only possible test, the only means by which a poet can " earn " his vision. (I say this with sincere respect for the valuable work done by some of our modern critics. Perhaps they have done their work too well. There is point in Mr. Ransom's witty remark: " We should be so much in favor of tragedy and irony as not to think it good policy to require them in all our poems, for fear we might bring them into bad fame.") Milton's view of the way to earn a vision does not exclude irony, as we use the word today, but it is closer to what we call " the drama of structure ": " As therefore the state of man now is, what wisdom can there be to choose, what continuance to forbear, without the knowledge of evil? . . . that which purifies us is trial, and trial is by what is contrary."

Tension is like complexity: it can be inner tension, or it can be surface tension. In many a modern metaphysical poem every line has tension. And all the shocks and dissonances may, in Mr. Joseph Warren Beach's phrase, " cancel " each other out. An esthetic that puts a premium on small ironies may not follow the separate ironies far below the surface. And so all the lively variations will proceed from the one theme; the theme itself is just accepted: everything proceeds from it, lively and illuminating, but no more. The theme itself remains static, though the details may not. But the implications of the details do not really trouble and work the theme to make it a rich imaginative thing, greater and more significant by the suggestive evolvement of its implications. The difference is that between illustrating an idea and developing it with artistic imagination. It is the difference between using the esthetic of tension as a formula and using it as a standard.

The greater the faith perhaps the greater the challenge that can be afforded, the greater " recklessness," the greater tension. This faith, of course, is quite different from a settled commitment not earned *in* the work of art. Perhaps a settled core of belief is necessary for such tension. I do not know. But certainly essential is faith in the validity of the artist's view, and in the reality that can be reached through the ordered—yet miraculously independent—struggle of a dramatic structure. The poet who could produce his lines about music, and as accompaniment to the forward march of the legions of devils, achieved a great tension. Compared with it, the minor devices of irony make a tinkling sound.

MILTON AND THE TELESCOPE

BY MARJORIE NICOLSON

When Milton was born, in 1608, Tycho Brahe's " new star "
of 1572, whose appearance may well have startled his grand-
father, and Kepler's " new star " of 1604, the excitement over
which his father must have remembered, had already become
history.[1] Milton was only an infant when, in 1610, Galileo in
the *Sidereus Nuncius* gave the world the first intimation of the
greatest astronomical discoveries of the century, and revealed
to man the existence of countless new stars, a new conception
of the moon and the Milky Way, and the knowledge of four
new " planets " of Jupiter. Milton had therefore no such opportunity as John Donne[2] to realize at first hand the excitement
caused by these discoveries, or to experience the immediate
transformation of the imagination produced by the first " optic
tube." He grew up in a generation which gradually came to
take the telescope for granted; he lived into an age which
became familiar also with the wonders of the microscope,[3] and
which began to ponder on a world of life too minute for the
human eye, as Galileo's contemporaries had begun to ponder
anew on the possibility of life in other inhabited worlds beyond
sight. Although in youth, Milton undoubtedly knew of the tele-

---

[1] This paper is one of a series in which I attempt to deal with the effect of the
telescope upon poetic and religious imagination in the seventeenth century. In the
first — " The Telescope and Imagination," *Modern Philology*, February, 1935 —
I have discussed the discovery of " new stars," the invention of the telescope, and
the immediate effect in Italy of the *Sidereus Nuncius*. In the second — " The
Telescope and English Imagination," *Studies in Philology*, July, 1935 — I have
discussed the English invention of the telescope, its use by Hariot and others, and
the response to the *Sidereus Nuncius* on the part of various English writers.

[2] I have discussed the effect of the new telescopic discoveries upon Donne in the
second paper referred to above.

[3] I have given below my reasons for believing that Milton's blindness prohibited
him from understanding the real nature of the microscope; there is, so far as I can
see, no effect of it in his work.

This essay first appeared in *ELH*, Vol. 2, No. 1 (April 1935).   15

scope, and may even have read the *Sidereus Nuncius,* which was available in England, he was trained under a system of education which paid no attention to contemporary scientific theories and discoveries, and his own tastes and interests were for the world of letters. The astronomical background of his early works was a heritage from the classics, not from science. As a young man, he never knew the excitement of his older contemporaries who, in youth, had read of a new cosmos which almost overnight disrupted the immutable heavens of Aristotle.

Yet every reader of *Paradise Lost* is aware of the fact that Milton's imagination had been stimulated by astronomy, and more than one modern critic has pointed out the extent to which that astronomy was Copernican or Galilean. The problem of his astronomical references has been so frequently discussed [4] that it needs little repetition here, nor am I concerned with what we usually call "the astronomy" of Milton or any other poet — with his acceptance, that is, of the Ptolemaic, the Copernican, the Tychonic, or the Cartesian hypothesis. I am concerned rather with the stimulus of imagination which the telescope produced in the seventeenth century, and the transformation of imagination which resulted from that instrument. In such a study, Milton affords the most remarkable example of the century. Unlike Donne, whose mind also was clearly stirred by implications of the "perspective glass," Milton's imagination, I am persuaded, was stimulated less by *books about* the new astronomy than by the *actual sense experience* of celestial observation.[5] As almost in one night Galileo saw a

---

[4] See R. Owen, "Milton and Galileo," *Fraser's Magazine* 79 (1869). 678-84; E. S. Nadal, "The Cosmogony of *Paradise Lost*," *Harper's Magazine* 56 (1878). 137-40; Maria Mitchell, "Astronomical Science of Milton as Shown in *Paradise Lost*," *Poet-lore* 6 (1894). 313-23; A. S. Cook, "*Paradise Lost* VII. 364-6," *Modern Language Notes* 16 (1901). 202-5; T. N. Orchard, *Milton's Astronomy,* 1913; W. F. Warren, *The Universe as Pictured in Paradise Lost,* 1915; E. N. S. Thompson," "A Forerunner of Milton," *Modern Language Notes* 32 (1917).479-82; Katherine Morse, "Milton's Ideas of Science as Shown in *Paradise Lost*," *Scientific Monthly* 10 (1920). 150-6; Edwin Greenlaw, "Spenser's Influence on *Paradise Lost*," *Studies in Philology* 17 (1920). 320-59; Allan Gilbert, "Milton and Galileo," *Studies in Philology* 19 (1922). 152-85; "The Outside Shell of Milton's World," *Studies in Philology* 20 (1923). 444-7; "Milton's Textbook of Astronomy," *Publications of the Modern Language Association* 38 (1923). 297-307; Grant McColley, "Theory of a Plurality of Worlds as a Factor in Milton's Attitude toward the Copernical Hypothesis," *Modern Language Notes* 47 (1932). 319-23.

[5] As I have pointed out in the earlier article, I see no evidence in Donne that he had actually looked through a telescope. His was an intellectual interest in the

new universe, so Milton, having grown up in a world he had placidly accepted from the past, on some occasion " viewed all things at one view " through a telescope.⁶ Like his own Satan

> Before [his] eyes in sudden view appear
> The secrets of the hoary Deep — a dark
> Illimitable ocean, without bound,
> Without dimension. . . .

That experience he never forgot; it is reflected again and again in his mature work; it stimulated him to reading and to thought; and it made *Paradise Lost* the first modern cosmic poem, in which a drama is played against a background of interstellar space.

In my attempt to prove this contention, I shall, even at the risk of repetition, first examine Milton's early works, before his visit to Italy and — as I insist upon believing in spite of S. B. Liljegren! ⁷ — to Galileo; then I shall consider the possibility that his first telescopic observation occurred in Italy; and finally I shall attempt an analysis of those peculiarities of his mature work which seem to me to have been the result of his actual experience with the telescope.

I

The early poetry of Milton is the best evidence that before his journey to Italy there had occurred no stimulation of the imagination in astronomical matters such as may be found in Donne in 1611. Although astronomical references are common enough in the *Minor Poems*, there is no significant sentence, no awareness of the ideas of Galileo, Kepler, Bruno. Most of the early figures of speech are merely descriptive: the *sun* appears frequently, but in such lines as these:

> Now while the heaven, by the Sun's team untrod,
> Hath took no print of the approaching light.⁸

---

ideas of Galileo and Kepler. In Milton's case, as my later analysis will attempt to show, in addition to ideas gained from reading, there is a sense of *perspective* and an awareness of *cosmic space* which nothing in books alone could have produced.

⁶ An interesting modern study of the same psychological experience upon a different type of mind may be found in Wilbur Daniel Steele's story, *The Man Who Saw through Heaven.*

⁷ S. B. Liljegren, " Milton and Galileo," *Studies in Milton*, 1918, pp. 23-52. See below.

⁸ *Ode on the Morning of Christ's Nativity* 19-20.

The moon shines for him as for any poet of antiquity:

> the wandering moon
> Riding near her highest noon,
> Like one that had been led astray
> Through the heaven's wide pathless way.[9]

The stars that shine upon his youthful poetry are still the stars of Aristotle, undisturbed by the inruption of Tycho's or Kepler's *novae*. They are the "bright morning star, Day's harbinger";[10] "the star that rose at evening bright";[11] or the day star that sinks in the ocean bed.[12] Others of his references are to conventional astrology. His stars are found "bending one way their precious influence,"[13] such stars as in their malign aspect have influenced that "starred Ethiop Queen."[14] His planets are not the Medicean planets of Galileo, but the mediaeval planets which affected men's lives:

> Whose power hath a true consent
> With planet or with element.[15]

The cosmos of the youthful Milton, in fact, is that which he inherited from the past and apparently did not question. The "starry threshold of Jove's court" is still the boundary of man's world; "bright Spirits" hover "above that high first-moving sphere";[16] the "celestial Sirens" of Plato "sit upon the nine infolded spheres,"[17] so that the music of the spheres echoes not only in that poem, but even more clearly in others.[18] There is nothing, in short, in the early poems of Milton to suggest that his mind had been stirred by pondering upon the "new astronomy." Indeed, there is one clear piece of evidence that it had not. The long passage in *Comus*,[19] in which the Lady and Comus, like academic disputants, consider whether Nature is an evidence of superabundance, bidding man pour himself forth with lavish and unrestraining hand, or whether

[9] *Il Penseroso* 67-71.
[10] *Song on May Morning* 1.
[11] *Lycidas* 30.
[12] *Ibid.* 168.
[13] *Ode on the Morning of Christ's Nativity* 71.
[14] *Il Penseroso* 19.
[15] *Il Penseroso* 95-6.
[16] *Death of a Fair Infant* 39.
[17] *Arcades* 63-4.
[18] Cf. particularly *Ode on the Morning of Christ's Nativity*, stanzas 13-4.
[19] Lines 706-800.

she is a " good Cateress," who teaches frugality, restraint, proportion, anticipates to a remarkable degree the dialogue of Adam and the Angel in *Paradise Lost* on the same subject.[20] But while, as we shall see, the whole argument in the later poem is drawn from various astronomical hypotheses, no such proof occurred to Milton as he pondered the same problem in youth.[21] His illustrations in *Comus* are from Nature as she shows herself in this little world, Comus suggesting that wherever man looks, whether at the vegetation, the sea, or the earth, he perceives Nature pouring herself forth, the Lady replying with what is at best a mild form of ethical socialism, concerned only with the difference between " lewdly-pampered Luxury " and the " holy dictate of spare Temperance." In *Paradise Lost*, after astronomical conceptions have entered into Milton's imagination, and Adam finds himself confused between theories which, on the one hand, argue for disproportion and superfluity, on the other for moderation and restraint, the arguments are drawn entirely from current theories of astronomy. It is seldom that a poet has given us, in the work of his youth and his maturity, two passages which so clearly suggest the difference which years and experience brought in the seventeenth century.

But, while the early poems offer no evidence that Milton had pondered the " new astronomy," his early prose indicates that the soil was being prepared for new ideas on such matters.[22] Milton's college exercises, as his critics have realized, indicate that he was inclined toward at least a mild academic radicalism. He was among that group at Cambridge who, whether through the influence of Bacon or not, opposed the traditional philosophy. His *Third Academic Exercise*[23] is indeed an attack

[20] 8. 13-178.
[21] The only astronomical reference in the earlier poem is found in 2. 732-6. Since the argument is clearly in favor of the Lady, we may conclude that Milton is suggesting here what seemed incredible. The Lady does not even bother to reply to this rhetoric. There is certainly no suggestion of the " thousand thousand stars " of *Paradise Lost*.
[22] In Milton's *Sixth Academic Exercise* (*Private Correspondence and Academic Exercises*, translated by Phyllis B. Tillyard, Cambridge, 1932, p. 103) occurs what is evidently a reference to the telescope, in which Milton puns upon the popular title, " perspective-glass ":

> And in times long and dark Prospective Glass,
> Fore-saw what future dayes should bring to pass.

So far as I can see, there is no other reference in the early works to the telescope, and none to Galilean astronomy.
[23] *Private Correspondence*, etc., pp. 67-73.

on the scholastic philosophy and a defense of the sort of studies Bacon had advocated. Even in those exercises in which he is forced to argue in the accepted way,[24] one feels that he has little interest in the subject and less in the method. Since the adherents of the "new astronomy" were on the whole anti-Aristotelian rather than anti-Ptolemaic,[25] it is significant that Milton shows himself one with the anti-Aristotelians on various other aspects of the quarrel. But it is even more important to notice whom Milton defended than whom he attacked. The *De Idea Platonica* shows him not only cleverly satirizing the literal-minded Aristotelians of the day, but defending the Platonic philosophy. Even more important is his frequently expressed love of the Pythagorean philosophy, for it must be remembered that to many seventeenth-century minds, the discoveries of such men as Copernicus and Galileo were considered important less for novelty than because they brought back the beliefs of Pythagoras; even a cursory reading of such a man as Kepler will suggest the extent to which his mysticism was influenced by the supposed "mystick Mathematick" of the Pythagoreans. To Milton in youth Pythagoras seemed "a very god among philosophers" and his *Second Academic Exercise,* "On the Harmony of the Spheres,"[26] is filled with a defense of the philosopher against Aristotle, "the rival and constant detractor of Pythagoras and Plato."

There are other passages in the early exercises which are even more important as showing the direction of Milton's interests, and suggesting that his imagination was already prepared for the stimulus it was to receive. His *Oration in Defense of Learning*[27] contains many sentences which show his interest in the new arts and sciences which were attracting the thoughtful men of his day; the "Ignorance" he attacks is in part the "igno-

[24] *Fifth and Sixth Academic Exercises.*

[25] This is a significant point, and one which, in my opinion, has not been sufficiently stressed by those who have seen in the adherents of the "new astronomy" disciples of Copernicus ranged against disciples of Ptolemy. The student who reads the early work of Kepler, for instance, will observe that his arguments are against Aristotelian rather than Ptolemaic astronomy. The explanation is to be found in the fact that *philosophically* it was Aristotle, not Ptolemy — who was considered primarily as astronomer and mathematician, rather than as philosopher — who had established the conception of the heavens which dominated thought.

[26] *Private Correspondence,* etc., pp. 64-7.

[27] *Seventh Academic Exercise,* pp. 104-20.

rance of gownsmen," the " sluggish and languid " complacency of the past, which so satisfied men that they felt there was nothing new to learn, the complete dependence upon mediaeval logic and scholastic metaphysics which, declares Milton, is " not an Art at all, but a sinister rock, a quagmire of fallacies, devised to cause shipwreck and pestilence." Here, as in his later *Tractate on Education*, Milton urges the sort of learning which is not barren, which produces, as Bacon would have said, both "Fruit" and "Light." Among important branches of learning, Milton always mentions astronomy.[28] In one passage, indeed, even in these early works, Milton suggests the so-called "Copernican" point of view.[29] There is still another attitude of mind suggested in these academic exercises which, while not as yet specifically concerned with astronomical ideas, was to prove significant in Milton's thinking, and to make his mind even more receptive of certain implications in the new astronomy. "Let not your mind," he says, " rest content to be bounded and cabined by the limits which encompass the earth, but let it wander beyond the confines of the world."[30] In spite of the checks which he consciously put upon it, Milton's was indeed one of those minds of which he speaks in the *Areopagitica*, "minds that can wander beyond limit and satiety," can play with concepts of time and space, can deal in "those thoughts that wander through eternity."[31] Such minds were peculiarly receptive of the implications of the new philosophy of Galileo and Kepler.[32]

II

Until the last few years, there has been no question that Milton, during his Italian journey, visited Galileo, and conse-

[28] Cf. *Third Academic Exercise*, p. 72; *Seventh Academic Exercise*, p. 111.
[29] *Seventh Academic Exercise*, p. 108.
[30] *Third Academic Exercise*, p. 72.
[31] *Paradise Lost* 2.148.
[32] Psychologically it is evident that the most important adherents of the "new astronomy," particularly those who, like Campanella and Kepler, attempted to read important philosophical implications into it, possessed this type of imagination. The opposite type of imagination is to be seen in Bacon, who, as is well known, showed little interest in any of the conceptions of the new astronomy, and who indeed saw in this tendency of human minds which Milton praises, one of the *Idols of the Tribe.* Cf. the passage in the *Novum Organum*, Aphorism 48, beginning "The human understanding is unquiet; it cannot stop or rest, and still presses onward, but in vain. . . ."

quently no reason to doubt that it was Galileo's telescope which disclosed to him the new conception of the heavens and of space which is reflected in *Paradise Lost*. His own statement in the *Areopagitica* [33] that he " found and visited the famous Galileo, grown old a prisoner to the Inquisition," has always been considered sufficient to establish the fact of the visit. In 1918, however, that statement was challenged by S. B. Liljegren as a part of his general attack on Milton's veracity, and his attempt to build up a conception of Milton's character in which the chief characteristics of the poet were egocentricity and an unscrupulous desire for self-aggrandisement. While Liljegren has not succeeded in persuading most critics,[34] his argument cannot be passed over without some consideration. Liljegren's most important point is his evidence — based upon documents which he quotes from the great national edition of Galileo, edited by Antonio Favaro, — that during the period 1638-39 Galileo was so inaccessible, both because of the sentence of the Inquisition and because of his own health, that approach to him was difficult, almost impossible.[35] Perhaps the best single answer that can be made to this argument is that Signor Favaro himself, who has more intimate knowledge of this evidence than any other scholar, has found no reason to doubt

[33] *Areopagitica and Other Prose Works of Milton*, edited C. E. Vaughan, 1927, p. 25.

[34] See the article by Walter Fischer, *Englische Studien* 52. 390-6, with the reply, *ibid.* 54. 358-66; G. Hübener, *Deutsche Literaturzeitung* 40. 150-1; A. Brandl, *Archiv* 138. 246-7; H. Mutschmann, *Beiblatt* 29. 228-35; F. A. Pompen, *Neophilologus* 5. 88-96, with a continuation of the argument, *ibid.* 354-5. Most of these critics are concerned primarily with Liljegren's contention in regard to " Milton and the Pamela Prayer." His argument with regard to Milton and Galileo, a secondary point, has not occasioned much comment.

[35] Liljegren, pp. 25-34. It should be noticed that while Liljegren acknowledges the visit of D. Benedetto Castelli in the autumn of 1638, he lays his stress rather upon the difficulties which Castelli met than upon the fact that he succeeded in his request; he passes too easily over the visit of Padre Clement in January, 1639; see Favaro, *Le Opere* 18, p. 42. He omits entirely the visits of Vincenzo Viviani and Torricelli in 1639 and 1641; see *Le Opere* 18, pp. 126, 164. In his overemphasis upon the difficulties of Castelli, he neglects to point out sufficiently that the Inquisition may have had reasons for suspicion of Castelli which did not exist in Milton's case, particularly if Milton's visit occurred during his first stay in Florence. At that time Milton was completely unknown to the Inquisition; he was merely a young English traveller, who carried acceptable letters of introduction. Some of the Italian critics mentioned below agree that Milton would have found more difficulty in obtaining access to Galileo after his visit to Rome.

Milton's statement.[36] Nor have any of the other Italian critics who have considered the matter.[37] There is nothing in the other arguments of Liljegren which deserves or needs consideration — nothing which does not arise merely from his own conception of Milton's character. Against his purely hypothetical position, then, we still have the evidence of Milton's own statement — evidence which must remain conclusive until better proof is produced, and we may continue to believe in Milton's visit to Galileo, as have the poets and artists whose imagination has

[36] Favaro takes the meeting for granted in *Le Opere*, and evidently has found no reason since the publication of that work to doubt it, since in an article in *Il Giornale d'Italia*, 18 Giugno, 1922, " Galileo e Milton in Arcetri," he surveys some of the recent important work on Milton, and discusses the visits of Hobbes and Milton to Galileo; he apparently finds no difficulties in either visit.

[37] The chief Italian treatments of Milton in Italy are the following: Alfredo Reumont in *Archivo storico italiano* 26 (1902). 427 seqq.; Teresa Guazzaroni, " Giovanni Milton in Italia," Roma, 1902 (Estratto dal *Giornale Arcadio*, serie 3) ; Ettore Allodali, *Giovanni Milton e l'Italia*, 1907 (Chap. 2, " Questione della visita di Milton a Galileo "; cf. also J. G. Robertson, *Modern Langauge Review* 2, 1907, 376) ; Antoni Serao, *Giovanni Milton*, Salerno, 1907; (this work is not biographical, and does not discuss the matter) ; G. Ferrando, " Milton in Toscana," *Illustrazione Italiana*, October, 1925 ; Anon., " Milton a Firenze," *Marzocco*, November 9, 1925 ; G. N. Giordano-Orsini, *Milton e il suo poema*, 1928 ; D. Angeli, *Giovanni Milton*, 1928. The most recent Italian work on the subject is *Galileo Galilei* by Giovanni Lattanzi, which I have not seen, but Lattanzi's position on the subject is clear from a short article " Gli Ultimi anni di Galileo Galilei " in *Gli Astri*, Giugno-Luglio, 1924, pp. 210-4, for a copy of which I am indebted to Signor Abetti of Arcetri. Signor Abetti, who is in charge of the Galileo collections at Arcetri, has found no reason to doubt Milton's statement in regard to his visit, as I am informed by my colleague Miss Emma Detti, who was good enough to discuss the matter with him at my request. The only problem which is discussed by these Italian critics is whether Milton's visit occurred in the autumn or the spring. Reumont is inclined to believe that Milton would have found more difficulties after his visit to Rome, when his own political and religious views were known, but considers it certain that the visit took place (cf. p. 19). Signor Lattanzi in his article, p. 214, quotes a letter which he supposes to have been written by Milton to Grotius after his visit, in which he speaks of Galileo " tormentato com' è dalle sue malattie." The letter, however, was not written by Milton, but by Grotius to Vossius (*Epistola* 964). It is quoted, with correct attribution, by Teresa Guazzaroni, in her article, pp. 8-9. In this connection should be mentioned the series of letters published by R. Owen, " Milton and Galileo," *Fraser's Magazine* 79 (1869). 678-84, which, were they genuine, would afford conclusive evidence of Milton's visit. The letters, supposed to have been written by Milton, Galileo, and Louis XIV, were from the collection of M. Chasles, and were by him presented to the Académie des Sciences, and published in *Comptes rendus*, 28 Mars, 1869, with comments by Elie de Beaumont, *ibid.*, 5 Avril, 1869. Evidently their authenticity was not doubted at that time; Mr. Owen discusses them seriously, but there seems no reason to believe that they do not belong with other " Miltonic Myths " discussed by J. Churton Collins, *National Review* 43 (1904).

reconstructed the event.[38] Whether it was Galileo's telescope or not is of no consequence, however, to the main contention of this paper. Telescopes were common both in Italy and in England, as I have suggested elsewhere,[39] and Milton must have had many opportunities to survey the heavens at night, before his blindness made any sort of vision impossible. Since all his specific references in *Paradise Lost* are to the Florentine, not to the English instrument, one may still insist that, whether Galileo's or another, an Italian " optic glass " first made him conscious of realms of vision and of thought which his youth had never imagined.

Three of Milton's allusions to the telescope in *Paradise Lost* have been so frequently noted that they need little comment here: a specific reference to the " glass of Galileo ";[40] his comparison of Satan's shield to the " optic glass " of the "Tuscan artist " at evening " from the top of Fesole Or in Valdarno ";[41] and his suggestion that the Garden of Eden was

[38] For the benefit of other students who, like myself, may have had difficulty in tracing the effect of the Milton-Galileo meeting upon Italian imagination, I may refer to the valuable section on this subject by J. J. Fahie, *Memorials of Galileo Galilei*, 1929, and add the following information. In 1868 Giacomo Zanella wrote a poem on the subject, " Milton e Galileo," *Poesie di Giacomo Zanella*, Firenze, 1933, pp. 99-124, in which he reconstructed imaginatively the meeting. This poem served as inspiration to Annibale Gatti who *circa* 1877 painted a picture representing the meeting. The scene of the painting is laid in the Torre del Gallo, instead of Galileo's house in Arcetri where the meeting probably took place. Various copies are extant, some showing variations from the original (Fahie, pp. 97-100). For an edition of the original picture, see Giuseppe Palagi, " Milton e Galileo alla Torre del Gallo, quadretto a olio del Cav. Prof. Annibale Gatti; descritto e illustrato da Giuseppe Palagi," Firenze, 1877. In 1893 Tito Lessi produced a smaller picture, which, while less ambitious, is more nearly true to reality, " Milton e Galileo in Arcetri." A reproduction may be found in the issue of *Gli Astri* referred to above, p. 211; see also the note of Antonio Favaro in the same issue, p. 217. In 1880 the sculptor Cesare Aureli produced a marble composition, again following Zanella (Fahie, pp. 77-80). In his article in *Il Giornale d'Italia*, Professor Favaro describes this group and devotes a section of his paper to a plea that the statue may be moved to Arcetri, " la città scientifica fiorentina per sfolgorare al sole di Arcetri dove la storica visita ebbe luogo " as a consecration of friendship between England and Italy. See also " Galileo with Milton at Torre del Gallo," translated by Paul Selver from *The Apostles* of J. S. Machar, *Sewanee Review* 32 (1924). 30-1. I may also mention Solomon Alexander Hart's picture " Milton visiting Galileo in Prison," 1826, and in addition to the English works already well known on the subject, the modern imaginative picture given by Alfred Noyes in his *Watchers of the Sky*, 1922.

[39] See the two earlier papers in this series, referred to above.

[40] 5. 261-3.

[41] 1. 287-91.

> a spot like which perhaps
> Astronomer in the Sun's lucent orb
> Through his glazed optic tube yet never saw.[42]

There are, in addition, two references to the telescope in *Paradise Regained* less frequently noticed, both of them in the scenes in which Satan displays to Christ all the kingdoms of the world and the glory thereof. The means which Satan employed for that vision did not trouble the writer of the Gospels; but Milton, product of a scientific age, pauses to wonder, and concludes:

> By what strange parallax or optic skill
> Of vision, multiplied through air, or glass
> Of telescope, were curious to inquire.[43]

Satan returns to the same idea when, in the passage which follows, he suggests that Christ may see many things at one view because " so well I have disposed My aery microscope." [44]

In *Paradise Lost* are to be found all the discoveries which, from the time of the publication of the *Sidereus Nuncius* in 1610 enthralled poetic as well as scientific minds.[45] Here are the

[42] 3. 588-90. Since Milton seems to be referring here to such " sunspots " as those Galileo discovered, this reference also may be said to be associated in his mind with the Italian rather than the English instrument.

[43] *Paradise Regained* 4. 40-2.

[44] *Ibid.* 56-7. The use of the word *microscope* here is curious. The term *microscopium* or *microscopio* was used in Italy at least as early as 1625. While microscopes were known in England between 1625 and 1660, they did not come into common use until after 1660. The first microscopical observations reported to the Royal Society were those of Robert Hooke on March 25, 1663. Clearly, from the *Transactions* of the society, microscopes were still a novelty at that time. Since Milton was then totally blind, there is no possibility that he had seen a microscope, and I am inclined to believe that either he was using the word loosely, which would be remarkable at this time, or that from vague accounts of the new instrument, he misunderstood its function. In the passage in question, he seems to be suggesting a combination of a telescope and some supposed instrument which would show *interiors* as well as exteriors, since Satan says that by this means Christ may behold " Outside and inside both." This is an entirely possible interpretation, since the invention of the microscope and telescope precipitated a number of fantastic experiments with other instruments which were supposed to have strange powers.

[45] The *Sidereus Nuncius* was not particularly concerned with the problem of Copernicanism *versus* the Ptolemaic astronomy, as were the *Dialogues concerning Two Principal Systems of the World*, which, as Allan Gilbert has shown, Milton had in mind in the long discussion between Adam and the Angel in Book 8. Since Professor Gilbert has so carefully analyzed the similarities between the *Dialogues* and *Paradise Lost*, I am purposely omitting many technical references which may be found in his article, and limiting myself, as elsewhere in this series of articles, to references to those discoveries of Galileo which seem to me to have most stimulated poetic imagination.

" thousand thousand stars " [46] which the telescope had shown;
here the sun-spots of Galileo, and the Milky Way,[47] whose
nature the astronomer had proved in one night. The moon
which Galileo had discerned through his telescope in 1609 and
1610 appears in *Paradise Lost* as it had in Italy. This is no
longer the moon of conventional poetry — the moon of *Il Penseroso*.[48] It is a vastly larger moon — the largest circular body
which Milton could think of when he sought an apt comparison
with the shield of Satan.[49] The moon is to Milton as to Galileo
a world much like this earth in its appearance. There are " new
lands, Rivers or mountains in her spotty globe "; [50] there are
" imagined lands and regions in the moon." [51] The Angel ponders the same problem when he questions " if land be there,
Fields or inhabitants." [52] There are spots in the moon, the
Angel declares:

> Whence in her visage round those spots, unpurged
> Vapours not yet into her substance turned.[53]

And again the Angel suggests the significance of those spots as
the seventeenth century understood them:

[46] *Paradise Lost* 7. 383.

[47] *Ibid.* 7. 577-81.

[48] I do not mean to say that the conventional moon of poetry does not appear in
Paradise Lost. Cf. for example 4. 606-9. The moon seen by Adam and Eve is
the traditional moon of poetry, except in the scene in which Adam discusses
astronomy with the Angel; but the majority of Milton's own references are
Galilean.

[49] *Paradise Lost* 1. 287-91.

[50] *Ibid.* 1. 290-1. In discussing this passage, Allan Gilbert says (" Milton and
Galileo," p. 159) : " In mentioning ' rivers ' Milton is not following Galileo, who
held that there was no water on the moon." He bases this statement upon the
Dialogo intorno ai due massimi sistemi del mondo, Le Opere di Galilei, 1842, 1. 112.
But in the earlier *Sidereus Nuncius*, which as I have elsewhere tried to show was
the chief influence upon poetic imagination in the seventeenth century, Galileo said
(*Sidereal Messenger*, translated E. S. Carlos, 1880, pp. 19-20) : " If any one wishes
to revive the old opinion of the Pythagoreans, that the Moon is another Earth, so
to say, the brighter portion may very fitly represent the surface of the land, and
the darker the expanse of water. Indeed, I have never doubted that if the sphere
of the Earth were seen from a distance, when flooded with the Sun's rays, that part
of the surface which is land would present itself to view as brighter, and that which
is water as darker in comparison."

[51] *Paradise Lost* 5. 263.

[52] *Ibid.* 8. 144-5.

[53] *Ibid.* 5. 419-20.

> Her spots thou seest
> As clouds, and clouds may rain, and rain produce
> Fruit in her softened soil, for some to eat.[54]

Like the disciples of Galileo, also, Milton was impressed with the discovery of the planets of Jupiter, and by the possibility which Kepler had immediately suggested [55] that other planets might also be found to have their unknown attendants:

> and other Suns, perhaps
> With their attendant Moons, thou wilt descry,
> Communicating male and female light,
> Which two great sexes animate the World.[56]

In common with Galileo and many others of the century, too, Milton had been impressed by contemporary theories of meteors and comets and shooting stars. A nineteenth-century commentator has drawn attention to his observation that meteors are most common in autumn, as Milton suggests in his picture of Uriel's descent:

> Swift as a shooting star
> In autumn thwarts the night.[57]

Comets, too, had interested Milton, perhaps because of the various controversies to which Galileo's theories on comets gave rise, perhaps because he remembered in his childhood the comet of 1618, and had heard from others of the first appearance in the year before his birth of " Halley's comet," which startled the early seventeenth century, and was the cause of many pamphlets, ranging from direful prophecy to scientific theory.[58]

[54] *Ibid.* 8. 145-7.

[55] I have discussed this in " The Telescope and Imagination."

[56] 8. 148-51.   By Milton's time, however, the existence of other planets had come to be taken for granted to such an extent that there is little, as late as this, of the excitement which marks the work of earlier writers on this subject.

[57] This observation was made by Professor Mitchell, the astronomer, about 1857, and is reported in the paper by his sister, Maria Mitchell, referred to above.   Professor Mitchell comments, p. 319, " We of this age suppose this was first known since our recollections."   Cf. also Milton's figure, 1. 745-6.

[58] Milton speaks in the *Seventh Academic Exercise*, Tillyard, p. 111, of " fiery comets "; in the *Fourth Academic Exercise*, p. 72, he warns his hearers against alarm " when a huge and fearful comet threatens to set the heavens aflame." Gilbert in his article on " Milton and Galileo " thinks that the " comets and impressions of the air " in *Of Reformation in England (Works,* 1851, 3. 45) are a reflection of Galileo's ideas.

At least two fine figures of speech in *Paradise Lost* reflect this interest. Satan as he opposes the unknown Death

> like a comet burned,
> That fires the length of Ophiuchus huge
> In the arctic sky, and from his horrid hair
> Shakes pestilence and war.[59]

And the last of Milton's majestic figures in the poem is drawn from the same source. To the sad eyes of Adam and Eve

> The brandished sword of God before them blazed,
> Fierce as a comet.[60]

Yet it may be objected that these passages, though they clearly show that Milton had known and pondered upon the discoveries of Galileo — as what thoughtful man of his age had not? — might have been written by anyone who knew of them from books — that in themselves they do not exhibit actual personal experience with the telescope. There are, however, two characteristics which make *Paradise Lost* (and in the first instance *Paradise Regained*) unique, characteristics which critics and poets have always felt peculiarly " Miltonic," yet which have never, it seems to me, been satisfactorily explained. Even a casual reader of Milton is aware of the vast canvas with which Milton worked, and on which he displayed his cosmic pictures. We have spent our adjectives in admiration, yet have not seen the immediate source of Milton's imagination. I propose to analyze again some of those familiar passages, seeking to determine in how far Milton's imagination had been stirred by the extent of space of the new universe which the telescope had discovered to Galileo and his followers.

III

One of the peculiarities of Milton's technique is his sense of *perspective*. I shall here only raise, because I cannot pretend to answer the question: in how far was the new sense of perspective in seventeenth-century art, both pictorial and literary,

[59] 2. 708-11. W. T. Lynn, "Comet Referred to by Milton," *Notes and Queries*, series 7, no. 2 (1886), p. 66, suggests that this refers to the appearance of the comet of November, 1664.

[60] 12. 633-4.

the result of the telescope? Certainly during the period in which the telescope was first greatly impressing the minds of men, we feel the expansion of space on canvas and in poetry, as in the century that followed we can detect in descriptive technique in fiction a new feeling for distance. But this is intended for the present merely as a suggestion. So far as Milton is concerned, the case is clear. No preceding poet has been able to take us in imagination to such heights, such vantage points from which, like Satan or like God, we behold in one glance Heaven, Earth, Hell, and Space surrounding all. Even when he is not dealing with cosmic space, Milton in his mature poems loves far views. *Paradise Regained* contains a succession of them, all limited to this world alone, even though the scope of some of them is such as to stagger comprehension. The " high mountain " to which Satan led Christ offers at one view a perspective which includes " a spacious plain," two rivers, with their junction with the sea, huge cities; and, adds Milton, piling Pelion on Ossa indeed,

> so large
> The prospect was that here and there was room
> For barren desert fountainless and dry.[61]

The physiography of the scene is enough to give the needed impression of extensiveness; but, not content with that, Milton goes further, suggesting that " turning with easy eye, thou may'st behold " [62] Assyria, Araxes and the Caspian Lake, Indus, Euphrates, the Persian Bay, the Arabian Desert, Nineveh, Babylon, Persepolis, and half a dozen other real and fabulous places. This is the vastest prospect in *Paradise Regained*, yet the same general technique is evident, on a lesser scale, in the vision of Rome,[63] and of Athens.[64] That Milton himself clearly associated such views with the sense of distance and perspective given by the telescope is evident from his actual references in these passages to the " telescope " and the " aery microscope." [65]

[61] 3. 262-4. Cf. *Paradise Lost* 11. 377-411 for a similar prospect from a hill.
[62] 3. 293.   [63] 4. 31 ff.   [64] 4. 236 ff.
[65] It should be remembered that the seventeenth century was as deeply interested in telescopic views of scenes on earth as in observation of celestial phenomena. In " The Telescope and Imagination " I have described Galileo's first exhibitions of his telescope, which he considered at that time merely as an instrument valuable for war or for commercial observation. Many of his contemporaries ascended the tower in which the telescope was mounted in order to see ships at sea and buildings

The use of perspective in *Paradise Lost* is at once more difficult and more subtle. Geography has become cosmography. But because the scene of *Paradise Lost* is the cosmos, because much of the scene is laid in space, Milton has all the more reason to use the technique of the telescope, in order to describe the universe which the telescope had opened to the eyes of his century. Again and again we have a sensation of the sudden view of far distance, as with Satan we look " down with wonder at the sudden view Of all this World at once." [66] Uriel, explaining the scene to the Satan he does not recognize, sounds to our ears curiously like a seventeenth-century schoolmaster who combines, with a lesson in theory, practical demonstration through the telescope:

> Look downward on that globe, whose hither side
> With light from hence, though but reflected, shines:
> That place is Earth the seat of Man: that light
> His day, which else, as the other hemisphere,
> Night would invade; but there the neighbouring Moon
> (So call that opposite fair star) her aid
> Timely interposes, and, her monthly round
> Still ending, still renewing, through mid-heaven,
> With borrowed light her countenance triform
> Hence fills and empties, to enlighten the Earth,
> And in her pale dominion checks the night. [67]

In other scenes of cosmic perspective, however, Milton, for all the strangeness and novelty of the material with which he is dealing, forgets the teacher in the artist. Sometimes it is God himself whom we observe in far-off prospect of the universe:

> Now had the Almighty Father from above,
> From the pure Empyrean where he sits
> High-throned above all highth, bent down his eye,
> His own works and their works at once to view. [68]

More often it is Satan:

> upon the firm opacous globe
> Of this round World, whose first convex divides
> The luminous inferior Orbs, enclosed
> From Chaos, and the inroad of Darkness old,

---

not visible to the naked eye. The telescopes mounted in public parks in both Italy and England, which attracted the public, were more often used for such displays than for observation of the heavens. I am persuaded that some such observations as these were in Milton's mind when he wrote *Paradise Regained*.

[66] 3. 542-3.   [67] 3. 722-32.   [68] 3. 56-9.

> Satan alighted walks. A globe far off
> It seemed; now seems a boundless continent
> Dark, waste, and wild, under the frown of Night
> Starless expos'd.[69]

It is Satan again who, in prospect of Eden, looks sadly from the earth:

> Sometimes towards Eden, which now in his view
> Lay pleasant, his grieved look he fixes sad;
> Sometimes towards Heaven and the full-blazing Sun,
> Which now sat high in his meridian Tower.[70]

It is through Satan's eyes that we view the most telescopic of all the scenes in *Paradise Lost*: as Satan

> Looks down with wonder at the sudden view
> Of all this World at once . . .
> Round he surveys, (and well might, where he stood
> So high above the circling canopy
> Of Night's extended shade) from eastern point
> Of Libra to the fleecy star that bears
> Andromeda far off Atlantic seas
> Beyond the horizon; then from pole to pole
> He views his breadth, — and, without longer pause,
> Down right into the World's first region throws
> His flight precipitant, and winds with ease
> Through the pure marble air his oblique way
> Amongst innumerable stars that shone,
> Stars distant, but nigh-hand seemed other worlds.[71]

It is, too, through Satan's eyes that we observe far off this tiny universe of ours, once so great, which has become to imagination like the other planets which Galileo had discovered —

> This pendent World, in bigness as a star
> Of smallest magnitude close by the moon.[72]

Such a sense of cosmic perspective is as characteristic of Milton as is the so-called " Miltonic style " — for which, indeed, it is in part responsible; yet it is also characteristic of his generation. We do not find it a century before; and though we may find it frequently enough in the century which follows, in the cosmic poems of the eighteenth century familiarity has lost something of the amazement and fascination with which this

---

[69] 3. 418-25.   [70] 4. 27-30.   [71] 3. 542-66.   [72] 2. 1052-3.

first generation of men surveyed the new cosmos. Yet even this magnificent sense of perspective was not Milton's greatst heritage from Galileo and his telescope.

IV

" Shakespeare," Professor David Masson used to declare in his lectures at Edinburgh, " lived in a world of time, Milton in a universe of space." [73] The distinction which Professor Masson felt is the distinction between two worlds — the old and the new; and the profound difference arises from the seventeenth-century awareness of the immensity of space.[74] How valid the distinction is will be clear to any student of Shakespeare and Milton, who, considering them merely as reflectors of the thought of their respective periods, observes their obsession with certain dominant conceptions. Of Milton's fascination with *space*, to which *Paradise Lost* bears witness in nearly every book, there is no indication in Shakespeare. And yet that was not because Shakespeare's imagination was not influenced by abstract conceptions. *Time* with Shakespeare is equally an obsession. The use of actual words is perhaps misleading; yet it is at least interesting to observe that the word *space* — according to concordances [75] — occurs in Shakespeare only thirty-two times, always with an obviously limited meaning;

[73] This sentence was quoted to me by President William Allan Neilson, who was one of Masson's students. Masson only suggests the idea in his *Life of Milton.* See the 1875 edition, 6.532 and note.

[74] The new conception of space may be said to have begun with Bruno in the sixteenth century. English theories, on the whole, were more directly influenced by telescopic discoveries than by the philosophy of Bruno, though, as I shall later attempt to show, Bruno's ideas were not so unfamiliar to some of the theorists as certain critics have suggested. Fundamentally, the chief spatial theories of the seventeenth century — at least those of the Cambridge Platonists, Barrow, and Newton — were based on Plato and neo-Platonism; but telescopic astronomy played a large part in their development. While Platonic ideas played a part in Milton's imaginative conception of space, there are other elements, as will be seen, which are peculiar to his century. John Tull Baker in *An Historical and Critical Examination of English Space and Time Theories from Henry More to Bishop Berkeley*, 1930, considers many of the important theories, but fails to take into account their relationship to Galilean and Keplerian astronomy.

[75] Mrs. H. H. Furness in her *Concordance to Shakespeare's Poems*, 1875, lists only four uses of *space* and one of *spacious.* Mrs. Cowden-Clarke, in the *Complete Concordance to Shakespeare*, 1881, lists twenty-eight uses of *space*, some of which refer only to a " space of time." The latter concordance lists eight columns showing the use of *time*, averaging roughly 1200 instances.

32   *Milton and the Telescope*

space to him was little more than "the distance between two objects." The same concordances list more than eight columns of the use of *time*. An *Index to Shakespeare's Thought* [76] makes no reference to his thoughts about space; yet the same index devotes page after page to his thoughts about time, from Rosalind and Orlando's light dialogues on the relativity of time, through familiar references to the "whirligig of time" which brings in its revenges, to the constant reflections on time on the part of more serious characters. Time is to Shakespeare, "the king of men, He's both their parent, and he is their grave." [77] There are the fine lines in the *Rape of Lucrece* beginning: "Time's glory is to calm contending kings," and there are, as everyone knows, many of Shakespeare's most familiar sonnets which deal with the poet's insistent awareness of time.[78] But with the exception of a few dubious lines,[79] there are no passages in Shakespeare which show his mind playing with concepts of space. His world is still bounded by the sphere of the fixed stars, and, indeed, the orb of the moon is the customary limit of space in his plays. Though travellers' tales could hold Desdemona spellbound, and the geographical world had grown immensely, Puck still could "put a girdle round about the earth in forty minutes." Shakespeare's astronomy is still largely astrology; his conception of the order and relation of the heavenly bodies, when suggested at all, still conventional mediaevalism. There is no interest here in "other worlds," as there is no interest in the "new stars" which had enthralled Galileo, Kepler, Donne.[80] Certainly no vision through a telescope had disturbed his placid cosmos; nor had he heard, as had Milton's generation

> A shout that tore Hell's concave, and beyond
> Frighted the reign of Chaos and old Night.

[76] Cecil Arnold, *An Index to Shakespeare's Thought*, 1880.
[77] *Pericles* 2.3.45-6. It is interesting to notice that as to Shakespeare *time* is the "breeder," the "parent," and the "grave," so to Milton (*Paradise Lost* 2.911) *space* is "the womb of Nature and perhaps her grave."
[78] Cf. especially Sonnets 5, 15, 60.
[79] As for example, *Hamlet* 2.2.260-1: "O God, I could be bounded in a nutshell and count myself a king of infinite space, were it not that I have bad dreams."
[80] A possible exception is to be found in *King Lear*, which I have mentioned in "The Introduction of the 'New Astronomy' into England."

No reader of *Paradise Lost,* on the other hand, can fail to be aware of the tremendous scale on which it is conceived, or the part which the concept of space plays in its structure.[81] One explanation of the way in which Milton produces this effect is to be found in his conception of the *world,* which, when compared with earlier cosmic poems, indicates the effect of the new astronomy. It must be remembered — a point which is too frequently neglected — that when Milton uses the term *world* he customarily means not the " little world of man " but the universe.[82] Milton makes much of the difference between this earth as it seems to those who dwell upon it and to those who survey it from afar, to whom it shows its relative unimportance in the cosmic scheme. To Adam and Eve, as to man at all times, earth seems fixed and secure, the center of the universe. At night they survey from their peaceful bower " this fair Moon, And these the gems of Heaven, her starry train." [83] In the morning, they praise in conventional Biblical language " this universal frame, Thus wondrous fair." [84] Satan perceives the difference between the earth as it appears to the angels and to its inhabitants, for, when he finally reaches it, after his first vision from a distance, he finds

A globe far off
It seemed; now seems a boundless continent.[85]

But to those who view it from far off — whether God or Satan — and see it in its relation to the vast expanse of space, " this world that seemed Firm land imbosom'd " [86] is but a " punctual spot," a tiny body, merely one of many stars " not

---

[81] A striking illustration of the extent to which the conception of space developed during the seventeenth century is to be found by comparing passages in Milton with corresponding ones in *Du Bartas His Divine Weekes and Workes,* 1608. Professor George Coffin Taylor in *Milton's Use of Du Bartas,* 1924, has made an interesting and illuminating comparison of many passages in which the two authors treat the same ideas, and builds up a strong case for the influence of Du Bartas on Milton. Yet there is nothing in Du Bartas which approaches the magnificent conception of *space* which is constant in *Paradise Lost;* even when actual verbal parallels can be established in the passages which I here quote, Milton introduces an imaginative conception which is lacking, so far as I can see, in the earlier writer.

[82] This was pointed out by Masson, and by Nadal, in his " Cosmogony of *Paradise Lost,*" and has been reiterated by Gilbert in " The Outside Shell of Milton's World." Nevertheless many critics, since Addison, interpret such a line as, " This little world in bigness as a star " as referring merely to the globe which human beings know.

[83] 4. 648-9. [84] 5. 154-5. [85] 3. 422-6. [86] 3. 74-5.

unconform to other shining globes." [87] It has shrunk to minute proportions, " a spot, a grain, An atom, with the Firmament compared." [88] It is, " in comparison of Heaven, so small, nor glistering." [89] The Angel, who has experienced both the world of man and the great cosmos of which it is a tiny part, explains to Adam the vastness of the universe beyond:

> regions to which
> All thy dominion, Adam, is no more
> Than what this garden is to all the earth,
> And all the sea, from one entire globose
> Stretched into longitude.[90]

Beyond the universe of man — even the vastly expanded universe of the telescope which Milton himself had beheld — there stretched in his imagination space, and it is *space* which dominates *Paradise Lost*. We begin to perceive it first through the eyes of Satan as, astounded and momentarily appalled, he gazes into the Chaos which opens beyond the gates of Hell. This is not, we must recall, Satan's first awareness of the extent of the universe. When earlier he warned his followers in Hell of the herculean task which awaited them, he remembered " the dark, unbottomed, infinite Abyss," the " uncouth way," the " vast Abrupt," the " dreadful voyage " [91] as Belial remembered " the wide womb of uncreated Night " in which the fallen angels had so nearly been " swallowed up and lost." [92] There is no exaggeration in Satan's warning of the " void profound Of unessential Night . . . Wide-gaping" which threatens even angelic natures " with utter loss of being . . . plunged in that abortive gulf." [93] His memory is even less than the actuality he faces as he sets out

> with lonely steps to tread
> The unfounded Deep, and through the void immense
> To search, with wandering quest,[94]

and the passage in which Milton shows Chaos to his readers reflects in its vocabulary the *new space* of telescopic astronomy. There was as yet no vocabulary which could express it, and Milton, in common with the astronomers of his day, was driven to a succession of negatives as

[87] 5. 259.   [89] 8. 92.   [91] 2. 405-10; 426.   [93] 2. 438-41.
[88] 8. 17-8.   [90] 5. 750-4.   [92] 2. 150-1.   [94] 2. 828-30.

> Before their eyes in sudden view appear
> The secrets of the hoary Deep — a dark
> Illimitable ocean, without bound,
> Without dimension; where length, breadth, and highth,
> And time, and place, are lost.[95]

The " wild Abyss " before him, " the womb of Nature and perhaps her grave," is " neither Sea, nor Shore, nor Air, nor Fire." [96] Again and again Milton searches for terms to describe Chaos as Satan " with head, hands, wings, or feet, pursues his way." He meets " a vast vacuity "; [97] he springs upward into the " wild expanse "; [98] he forces his way over the " boiling gulf " of the " dark Abyss," [99] until after immense labor he finally approaches the " sacred influence Of Light " where " Nature first begins Her farthest verge." [100] Milton's description of Chaos, both in its vocabulary and its conception, is the first great attempt of English poetry to picture to man the vision which the telescope had shown. Many of its details are classical, some are mediaeval, but fundamentally it is a modern Chaos which no mind had conceived before Galileo.

But the description of Chaos is only the beginning of Milton's attempt to depict the new space. We see it through the eyes of God as he " bent down his eye His own works and their works at once to view," [101] and saw in one glance the sanctities of Heaven close about Him, the " Happy Garden " upon earth, " Hell and the gulf between." We realize it again in the further voyages of Satan — voyages, one may suspect, which were inherited from and which were to influence that group of " voyages to the moon " in which the seventeenth century delighted.[102] At one time Satan beholds " Far off the empyreal Heaven "; [103] at another he wanders in the Paradise of Fools in which strong cross winds are to blow fools " ten thousand leagues awry." [104] Finding at last an entrance to earth, Satan upon the lower stair of Heaven's steps " Looks down with wonder at the sudden view Of all this World at once," [105] and " from

---

[95] 2. 890-4. [97] 2. 932.
[96] 2. 910-2. [98] 2. 1014.

[99] 2. 1027. Cf. also the passages which describe Satan's return, 10. 282-8; 300, 366-71; 397; 470-7. [100] 2. 1034-8. [101] 3. 58-9.

[102] I am treating in a separate study the vogue of " moon voyages " and voyages to other planets, and attempting to show the effect which the new science had upon an old motif.
[103] 2. 1047. [104] 3. 488. [105] 4. 542-3.

Milton and the Telescope

pole to pole He views his breadth," [106] before he " throws His flight precipitant " downward. Milton's idea of other worlds adds greatly to the expanse of the universe in such passages as these, for we watch Satan at one time winding his " oblique way Amongst innumerable stars " [107] which to men below seemed distant " but nigh hand seemed other worlds." [108] At another time " through the vast ethereal sky " he " sails between worlds and worlds." [109]

It is not alone Satan's voyages which give the reader the sense of space which prevades the whole poem. One need only compare Milton's story of the creation with its original in *Genesis* to realize the expansion of imagination which astronomy had produced. Milton's is, in truth, an account of

> the rising birth
> Of Nature from the unapparent deep.[110]

It is significant that the passages to which he has added non-Scriptural details are particularly those which show the creation of the universe rather than those which have to do with earth and man. As Christ and his attendant angels survey the Chaos upon which Deity is to impose order, they see it as had Satan at the gates of Hell:

> On Heavenly ground they stood, and from the shore
> They viewed the vast immeasurable Abyss,
> Outrageous as a sea, dark, wasteful, wild,
> Up from the bottom turned by furious winds
> And surging waves.[111]

The first Creation produces the earth as Galileo conceived it, " And Earth, self-balanced, on her centre hung." [112] The firmament which follows the creation of light is diffused

> In circuit to the uttermost convex
> Of this great round.

The Sun and Moon follow, together with the " thousand lesser lights," many of them, even to the phases of Venus and the Milky Way, in accordance with the new astronomy.[113] The

---

[106] 2. 560-1. [108] 3. 566. [110] 7. 102-3.
[107] 3. 563-5. [109] 5. 267-8. [111] 7. 210-4. [112] 7. 242.
[113] There is perhaps no more charming example of the conjunction of old and new in this age than Milton's introduction into his expansion of *Genesis* of his beautiful passage on the phases of Venus, discovered by Galileo (7. 364-9), followed not long afterwards by a Galilean description of the Milky Way (7. 577-81).

greatness of the descriptive technique in the passage becomes apparent when we realize the subtlety with which Milton suggests the vastness of Space by stressing the *limitation* which Deity imposed " to circumscribe the universe." As the mystic compasses turn " through the vast profundity obscure," [114] the mystic words are spoken:

> ' Thus far extend, thus far thy bounds;
> This be thy just circumference, O World ! ' [115]

Vast as seems the world, with its light, its firmament, its " thousand, thousand stars," it is yet only a small portion of space, as earlier God had circumscribed for the rebel angels a portion of space which seemed to those still angelic beings to confine them, in spite of the fact that their " adventurous bands " were to discover vast continents of ice and snow, dark and dreary vales, " a gulf profound as that Serbonian bog." [116] The " new-made World," to the angels who beheld its emergence, might seem " of amplitude almost immense," but beyond the world, beyond Hell, even beyond Heaven, in Milton's imagination stretched still the " vast unbounded Deep " of Space.

Important as are the scenes of Creation, Milton is still too bound by reverence for the Scriptures to read into them some of the profound ideas which the new concept of space was bringing to men's minds. It remained for the inquiring mind of Adam to raise — if the Angel could not answer — other problems. The long astronomical conversation between Adam and the Angel [117] is concerned with Copernicanism, to be sure, but it also shows the awareness of a vast universe which is post-Copernican. Even to Adam, it is now clear that this Earth is minute in comparison with heaven, an atom when compared with the Firmament:

> And all her numbered stars, that seem to roll
> Spaces incomprehensible, (for such
> Their distance argues, and their swift return.[118]

He ponders, as had the century, the incredible speed at which these vast bodies must move in incredible space, " incorporeal

[114] 7. 229.   [116] 2. 592.   [118] 8. 19-21.
[115] 7. 230-1.   [117] 8. 13-178.

speed . . . Speed, to describe whose swiftness number fails." [119]
The Angel speaks of this also:

> The swiftness of those Circles attribute,
> Though numberless, to his omnipotence,
> That to corporeal substances could add
> Speed almost spiritual.[120]

The vastness of the universe which both the Angel and Adam
feel is increased by an idea which the Angel introduces in this
particular scene, but which has been recurrent in Milton's mind
throughout the poem, as we have already seen — the idea of
other inhabited worlds.[121] In this particular passage, it is the
Moon which may conceivably be inhabited — " if land be there,
Fields and inhabitants." [122] But in other lines in *Paradise Lost,*
Milton shows that his mind, as earlier Campanella's,[123] had
lingered on the possible existence of other worlds in other stars
and planets. Satan considers the possibility as he wends his
way

> Amongst innumerable stars, that shone
> Stars distant, but nigh-hand seemed other worlds,
> Or other worlds they seemed, or happy isles,
> Like those Hesperian Gardens famed of old,
> Fortunate fields, and groves, and flowering vales;
> Thrice happy isles ! But who dwelt happy there
> He staid not to inquire.[124]

Some such idea is in Satan's mind when, close to Heaven, he
pauses to inquire of Uriel, as both of them survey the myriad
worlds before them:

[119] 8. 37-8. Cf. 4. 592-5, " The Prime Orb, Incredible how swift."
[120] 8. 107-10.
[121] This aspect of Milton's thought has been discussed briefly by Grant McColley,
" Theory of a Plurality of Worlds," *Modern Language Notes* 47. 319-23.
[122] 8. 144-5.
[123] I have mentioned Campanella's immediate interest in this possibility after his
first reading of Galileo in " The Telescope and Imagination."
[124] 3. 565-71. Such a passage as 3. 459-62 is probably of no significance, since the
idea that " translated Saints, or middle Spirits " might dwell in the moon is common
in older literature. Cf. Edward Chauncey Baldwin, " Milton and Plato's *Timaeus*,"
Publications of the Modern Language Association 35 (1920). 210-7; J. B. Fletcher,
" The Comedy of Dante," *Studies in Philology* 18 (1921). 400 ff. While some of
these other passages may legitimately be called " Platonic," as one reads them in
the light of many other passages on the moon and stars written by disciples of
Galileo, it is clear that they reflect also the new astronomy.

> In which of all these shining orbs hath Man
> His fixed seat — or fixed seat hath none,
> But all these shining orbs his choice to dwell . . .
> On whom the great Creator hath bestowed
> Worlds. . . .[125]

Such a universe of habitable worlds is hymned, too, by the chorus of angels on the seventh day when, creation accomplished, they sing not of one world but of many:

> stars
> Numerous, and every star perhaps a world
> Of destined habitation.[126]

True, the Angel, at the end of his astronomical discussion, adds to his suggestions to Adam:

> Dream not of other worlds, what creatures there
> Live, in what state, condition, or degree,[127]

in the same mood in which he assures him that the knowledge of the true astronomical hypothesis is not essential to man. As if in obedience to the command of the Angel, the theme of "other worlds" disappears from *Paradise Lost* from this moment, nor does it enter again into any of Milton's works. Yet Milton's mind being what it was — like Adam's, curious in regard to the world about him — we may justly conclude that the apparent coincidence is due less to angelic behest than to the fact that from this time on, he dealt almost exclusively with matters of this world, in the remaining books of *Paradise Lost* and in his last two poems.

Not only are there other existing worlds in Milton's cosmic scheme, but he suggests a still more far-reaching conception which in the age which followed was to develop implications more profound than Milton himself read into it. "Space may produce new worlds," declared Satan to his despondent host upon the lake of Hell.[128] Though Milton did not further develop the suggestion in Satan's speech — for Satan, after all, was little concerned with metaphysics and much with expediency!— the idea lies behind several passages in *Paradise Lost*. The "wild Abyss" is "The womb of Nature, and perhaps her grave,"[129] an expression which may or may not hold profound

---

[125] 3. 668-74.
[126] 7. 620-2.
[127] 8. 175-6.
[128] 1. 650.
[129] 2. 911.

Milton and the Telescope

mystical interpretation.[130] The Angel, who, unlike Satan, is concerned with metaphysical ponderings, goes a step farther, after having suggested to Adam the possibility of life upon the moon. As the telescope of Galileo had discovered satellites around Jupiter, so, the Angel, as we have seen, suggests, there may well be " other Suns with their attendant Moons "

> Communicating male and female light,
> Which two great sexes animate the World,
> Stores in each Orb perhaps with some that live.[131]

Thus having prodigally filled the expanded firmament with suns and stars, having filled the moon with life, and surrounded the suns with attendant moons, the Angel suggests the possibility of future creation, in order that there may not be

> such vast room in Nature unpossessed
> By living soul, desert and desolate.[132]

This is the superabundance and the fertility of Nature which the century was coming to realize, as their conception of life expanded with the expansion of the universe. The development of imagination which has occurred between *Comus* and *Paradise Lost* is obvious. In the youthful poem " Nature " was confined to this earth. Though she might " pour her bounties forth with such a full and unwithdrawing hand," she was still only the productive force which governs the " odours, fruits, and flocks," the " spawn innumerable," the " millions of spinning worms." Her possible " waste fertility " would be shown only in the " earth cumbered and the winged air darked with plumes," and the last possibility which Comus can conceive is that, unrestrained, she should " bestud with stars " the firmament. The older Milton perceives not only without dismay but even with a certain exultation the vast expansion of a world into a bewildering universe, the possible existence of other inhabited worlds, even the possibility of production of worlds to come.

Yet these are exceptional passages, and no one of them is developed to its full implications. Milton did not in *Paradise Lost* reach such a conception of the infinity of space as Bruno,

---

[130] Cf. Greenlaw, " Spenser's Influence on *Paradise Lost*," *Studies in Philology* 17 (1920). 328-9.   [131] 8. 148-52.   [132] 8. 153-4.

nearly a century earlier, nor such an idea of infinite fullness as evidence of Deity as did Leibniz, not much later.[133] Though we may justly say that in comparison with Dante's, Milton's universe has become indefinite, there is here no such conception of *indefiniteness* as we find, for example, in Descartes. Indeed, one of the most remarkable characteristics of Milton's conception of space is his combination of definiteness and indefiniteness. Like his Christ, in the scene of creation, he seems on the one hand enthralled by the " vast immeasurable Abyss," on the other, laboring " to circumscribe This universe." If his " rising World " is " won from the void and formless Infinite," it is nevertheless a measurable world, in which Hell is

> As far removed from God and light of Heaven
> As from the centre thrice to the utmost pole.[134]

True, Milton's angel warns us that in speaking of things infinite, he must speak, as it were, Platonically, and must describe " what surmounts the reach Of human sense " in such terms " as may express them best." [135] Nevertheless, even in his conception of that immeasurable Space which continues beyond the world already created and the worlds to come, Milton does not approach the problem of absolute space as did his Cambridge contemporary Henry More, for example, who at almost the same time was introducing into English thought new concepts of space which were to influence Barrow, Newton, and others.[136] Only at one point in *Paradise Lost* does Milton suggest the problem of Infinite Space and Infinite Deity, the problem which motivates so much of the philosophy of Henry More and of Malebranche. It is tempting to read the words of Milton's Deity

[133] One invention which profoundly influenced this conception of Leibniz's — the microscope — came, as I have shown, too late to stir Milton's imagination.

[134] 1. 73-4. In this particular passage Milton *is*, of course, referring to the created universe, which is circumscribed and measurable. It is, as it appears to the angels (7. 620) " of amplitude *almost* immense," but, as a created thing, it still possesses limits and boundaries. Yet throughout Milton's treatment of space, there is the same combination of infiniteness and finiteness.

[135] 5. 570-6; cf. 7. 112-4.

[136] I am not suggesting here a comparison between *Paradise Lost* and More's philosophical works; More first approached this problem in a poem, *Democritus Platonissans: or an Essay upon the Infinitie of Worlds*, 1646, following a poem in which he had refused to accept the idea of infinity. I shall discuss both these works in a later paper in this series.

> Boundless the Deep, because I am who fill
> Infinitude; nor vacuous the space. . . .[137]

in the light of contemporary spatial conceptions; and, indeed, considered with More and Malebranche, they may seem to take on new meaning. But so much has already been made of this passage [138] that any Milton student must be aware of the dangers of seeking in any one source the origin of what was probably in Milton's mind a conventional, though complex, theological idea. There is no question that to Milton, God, not Space, was infinite; and no one was more conscious than he of the logical and theological fallacy of making

> Strange contradiction; which to God himself
> Impossible is held, as argument
> Of weakness, not of power.[139]

It is significant that in the *Treatise of Christian Doctrine,* in which Milton, as theologian, might well have discussed further implications of the *idea of infinity* which were being reflected in contemporary philosophical works, he avoids the whole problem of the nature of space in his discussion both of the creation and of the nature of God.[140] Milton's theology, on the whole, as has been pointed out,[141] draws from a tradition which is antithetic to that tradition which was at least temporarily to triumph in establishing in the seventeenth century a theory of infinite universe as the inevitable expression of infinite Deity, the essence of whose Nature is the overflowing goodness which must show itself in the creation of all possible forms of existence in the created universe. Had he expressed himself on the subject in the *Treatise of Christian Doctrine,* there is little

[137] 7. 168-9.
[138] Since the publication of Denis Saurat's "Milton and the Zohar," *Studies in Philology* 19 (1922). 136 ff., and Saurat's later *Milton: Man and Thinker,* 1925, this passage has been the subject of much dispute. Saurat was primarily concerned with the idea of "retraction" which he found in the passage, but various other conceptions which may enter into it have been discussed. General bibliography on the passage may be found in the latest discussion of it by George Coffin Taylor, *Milton's Use of Du Bartas,* 1934, pp. 16-7, 38-45, and *passim.*
[139] 10. 799-801. Cf. *Treatise of Christian Doctrine,* Chapter 2, section 9.
[140] In Chapter 2, "Of God," Milton lists as the third of the attributes of Deity "Immensity and Infinity"; they are among the few attributes which he does not further develop.
[141] See A. O. Lovejoy, "Optimism and Romanticism," *Publications of the Modern Language Association* 42 (1927), particularly pp. 928-31.

doubt that he would have denied the possibility of infinite space. Yet Milton was first of all a poet; and as poet he shows in *Paradise Lost* a momentary imaginative response to certain impressions of the "new astronomy," which, had they been carried to their ultimate conclusion, were inconsistent with his own theological premises.[142] But Milton in *Paradise Lost* was concerned much more deeply with ethics than with metaphysics. Like his own Angel, he turns from astronomical implications and from metaphysical considerations of space, to bid Adam, "Think only what concerns thee and thy being." It is enough for him that the expanded universe suggests an expansion of Deity; vast though the universe has become, "Heaven's wide circuit" bespeaks for Milton, as for the Psalmist and the Prophets,

> The Maker's high magnificence, who built
> So spacious, and his line stretched out so far,
> That Man may know he dwells not in his own —
> An edifice too large for him to fill.[143]

Although Milton's mature prose and poetry, then, will offer little to the philosopher seeking new concepts of absolute or infinite space which were stimulated by the new astronomy, yet *Paradise Lost* still affords a remarkable example of the extent to which telescopic astronomy effected in an imaginative mind a vast expansion of the idea of space. Sensitive men of the seventeenth century, who by actual physical experience of the night sky seen through an "optic glass," had become aware of "stars that seem to roll Spaces incomprehensible" did not return to the limited conception of the universe which they had

[142] While Milton was a clearer and more consistent thinker than King and Law, whom Professor Lovejoy discusses in the section referred to above, it seems to me that there are in him also indications of the "curious waverings and . . . self-contradiction" which Professor Lovejoy finds in them (p. 929 n.), not only in the contradiction between some of the imaginative passages on astronomy in *Paradise Lost* and their ultimate implications, but between his expressed conception of Deity in the *Treatise of Christian Doctrine* and his imaginative treatment of Deity in some of the implications in *Paradise Lost*. These are to be explained in part, as in the case of King, Law, and others by the attempt to make older orthodox theological ideas consistent with implications which the new science was bringing to men's minds, and, in Milton's case at least, by the fact that he *was* primarily a poet rather than a theologian and that in some instances—to use his own terminology— "imagination" or "fancy" triumphs over "reason"—or, rather, "reasoning"!
[143] 8. 100-4.

once taken for granted. As *Paradise Lost* was affected by the new astronomy, so in its turn it affected other poets. The impression of space which Milton achieved is imitated with more or less success by many poets of the later and the next century. The " sublimity " of Milton to them was not a matter only of his language, and his lofty conception of God and Satan, Heaven and Hell, but even more of his sense of space, the vast reaches of his cosmic imagination—

> Et sine fine Chaos, et sine fine Deus,
> Et sine fine magis, si quid magis est sine fine. . . . [144]

The eighteenth-century growing " delight in wide views " of which critics have so often spoken,[145] has usually been associated with growing interest in mountains and in mountainous scenery; but in this delight, as well as in the sense of perspective and the awareness of space which enters English writing after *Paradise Lost*, there is in part a direct heritage from Galileo's telescope, and in part a heritage from Milton, whose patron goddess was, as he so truly felt, " Urania," and who, even more truly than we have realized, succeeded in portraying in *Paradise Lost*, " things unattempted yet in prose or rhyme."

---

[144] Barrow's commendatory verses, prefixed to the second edition. While I have purposely read into the second line — by omitting the next — an implication which the poet did not intend, the whole poem indicates the impression which Barrow had received of Milton's boundless conceptions. I shall consider in a later paper some of the cosmic poems which followed *Paradise Lost*, less as imitating Milton than as showing the great interest of the poets in the new sense of space.

[145] Cf., for example, Myra Reynolds, *Nature in English Poetry*, 1909, p. 344: " One of the interesting characteristics of the love of Nature in the eighteenth century is a delight in wide views. What had in the classical period 'tired the travelling eye,' with the dawning of the new spirit gave satisfaction. It was in accord with the mental revolt against close boundaries of any sort." Many of Miss Reynold's quotations, particularly those which suggest " far views " of the ocean and the sky at night, take on new meaning if read as the result of telescopic awareness of distance.

MILTON AS A REVOLUTIONARY *

BY MERRITT Y. HUGHES

Since the end of World War I there has been a growing doubt
of Milton's rank among the leaders of the Puritan revolution.
In part, as we shall see, it has taken the form of discontent like
Mr. Don Wolfe's with his failure to anticipate the proletarian
gospels of the twentieth century as well as he did the liberal
faith of the nineteenth. In part it has taken the form of sub-
mergence of Milton in the growing doubt of the economic wisdom and disinterestedness of Puritan religion among historians
like Max Weber and R. H. Tawney.[1] And in part it has paradoxically arisen from the research of Miltonists in the pamphlet
literature of the English Civil War. For a time after Professor
Haller's publication of his volumes of *Tracts on Liberty in the
Puritan Revolution*[2] it seemed that Milton's preeminence as a
thinker among the spokesmen of his party might, from our
point of view, suffer some loss of apparent originality and
courage, and that from the point of view of his own contemporaries he might have to yield his claim to have seriously influenced public opinion with any of his tracts earlier than the
Defence of the English People. Professor Parker's Introduction
to the pamphlets which he has published in *Milton's Contemporary Reputation*, and their evidence as corroborated by the
tract called *The Dignity of Kingship Asserted*[3] have in part
restored our belief in Milton's increasing influence from 1649,
if not earlier, until 1660. The question of the influence of
Areopagitica, the tracts on divorce, and the anti-episcopal tracts

* Lecture before the Tudor and Stuart Club, Jan. 25, 1943.
[1] Max Weber, *The Protestant Ethic and the Spirit of Capitalism*, translated by
Talcott Parsons, with a Foreword by R. H. Tawney (New York, 1930); and R. H.
Tawney, *Religion and the Rise of Capitalism. A Historical Study* (London, 1929).
[2] Three volumes, edited by William Haller (New York, 1934).
[3] W. R. Parker, *Milton's Contemporary Reputation* (Columbus, 1940) and W. R.
Parker, editor of *The Dignity of Kingship Asserted* (New York, 1942).

    This essay first appeared in *ELH*, Vol. 10, No. 2 (June 1943).

may never be answered to the satisfaction of historians. For us, however, that question may not be crucial. Whatever its answer may be, no one is likely to deny Milton a place among the world's typical revolutionists—" Hampden, Sir Harry Vane, . . . , Sam Adams, John Hancock, Washington, Thomas Paine, Lafayette, Marat, Talleyrand, Hebert, Miliukov, Konavalov, Kerensky, Chichirin, Lenin "—a list in which Professor Brinton places [4] him third.

Perhaps at bottom our modern dissatisfaction with Milton as a revolutionary thinker springs from the fact that he himself habitually regarded the Puritan Revolution as a late and perhaps final stage in the Protestant Reformation; that his first political tracts, the five anti-episcopal pamphlets, were ecclesiastical; that his supposedly antifeminist defence [5] of free divorce rested mainly on biblical grounds; that *Areopagitica*—though it is still the literary charter of freedom of conscience and of the press—is full of religious passion and fails to grant toleration to Roman Catholics and atheists; and that—as Macaulay pointed out over a century ago—the 'Arianism' of his great theological work, the *Christian Doctrine,* has distracted attention from his really more ' startling' opinions " respecting the nature of the Deity, the eternity of matter, and the observation of the Sabbath." [6] In various ways we all find the Protestantism of Milton's Protestant religion a little hard to swallow. For Catholics like Mr. Belloc his 'Arianism' is still a stumbling-block, and it is refreshing to find a theologian like Mr. G. Wilson Knight correcting Mr. Belloc about Milton's ' unitarianism' and quoting the *Christian Doctrine* itself to prove that for Milton " the nature of the Son " was " indeed divine." [7] Yet, as is inevitable from his general position in *Chariot of Wrath,* Mr. Knight simply cannot recognize the sterner, historical, ȿevolutionary implications of Milton's demand in the *Christian Doctrine* and in the *Likeliest Means to Remove Hirelings out of the Church* for separation of Church and State. Mr. Knight's

[4] Crane Brinton, *The Anatomy of Revolution* (New York, 1938), p. 116.

[5] The case for Milton as continuator of the revolutionary thought of the sixteenth century about divorce is admirably made by Allan H. Gilbert in " Milton on the Position of Women," *Modern Language Review* 15 (1920). 240-64.

[6] *Critical and Historical Essays by Thomas Babington Macaulay* (London and Toronto, 1924) I. 151.

[7] G. Wilson Knight, *Chariot of Wrath* (London, 1942), p. 114.

Chariot will engage us more than once in the course of this discussion, and its robust transvaluations of parts of Milton's political thought, while we may not sympathize with them, will help to throw its true, revolutionary character into high relief. Mr. Knight's case seems to be somewhat like that of the late Paul Elmer More, who, as Mr. Alfred Kazin has just said,[8] had the paradoxical gift of combining a " passionate love of Milton's poetry " with a fondness for Dr. Johnson's " strictures on Milton's politics." Although Mr. Knight quotes [9] Dr. Johnson's charge that " Milton's republicanism was . . . founded in an envious hatred of greatness, and a sullen desire of independence, in petulant impatience of control, and pride disdainful of superiority," and even "half-subscribes" to it, *Chariot of Wrath* in the main treats Milton's politics in a very unrevolutionary though fulgurously apocalyptic light. Although some of his historical interpretation of Milton's political thought must be challenged, Mr. Knight's more than Wordsworthian faith that Milton should be with us at this hour is a corrective for those who study him only in the light of the prevailing Marxian view of Protestantism as a mere ' reflex ' of a " society based upon the production of commodities," for which " the most fitting form of religion " is " Christianity with its *cultus* of abstract man, more especially in its bourgeois developments, Protestantism, Deism, &c." [10]

In *Chariot of Wrath* Milton's Protestantism is transformed into a messianic faith of the most urgent application to both the Puritan Revolution and World War II. Since Mr. Knight's main interest is in the contemporary scene, while ours primarily is in Milton's part in the historic drama of the Puritan Revolution, the importance of his book for us lies in its treatment of Milton's stand in such crucial questions of the Revolution as the relation of Church to State and the value of monarchy, both as represented by Charles I and as an institution abstractly regarded. On those matters and on Milton's treatment of the questions of freedom, discipline, and the choice and function of an aristocracy, and above all on the idea of truth in

[8] *On Native Grounds* (New York, 1942), p. 309. [9] *Chariot of Wrath*, p. 32.
[10] Karl Marx, *Capital, A Critique of Political Economy*, edited by Frederick Engels, revised and amplified according to the fourth German edition by Ernest Untermann, Modern Library, New York, p. 91.

Areopagitica as related to the 'dynamics' of the Revolution Mr. Knight has much to say that is pertinent to our view of Milton as a revolutionist. What we find on these topics in *Chariot of Wrath* inevitably challenges attention, yet none of these secondary features of the book can fairly be discussed apart from its main, messianic theme.

In *Areopagitica*, the *Defences of the English People*, and to some extent in all Milton's political writing Mr. Knight sees a prophetic message to England, both in the seventeenth and in the twentieth centuries, which culminates in *Paradise Lost*. Briefly, it consisted in an apocalyptic vision of " England, or Great Britain, . . . as . . . a Messiah-nation." [11] That, Mr. Knight tells us, was Milton's view of his country, and it is his own also. For Mr. Knight sees " Great Britain in the Renaissance era (in which we live) as having assumed the power-content of the medieval Christian Church," and as laboring, " without any conscious recognition (outside her greater poets) of this destiny, . . . on the whole, . . . to curb lust for power and tyrannic ambition " [12] in a world of strife. The Christ of *Paradise Regained* and *Paradise Lost* seems to Mr. Knight a symbol of " some great, vice-gerent (to use Milton's habitual phrase) responsibility, under God," [13] which is England's destiny. He sees the " Cromwellian revolution " less as social and political than as military and religious, and as a part of a continuous defence of the " Christian structure " of the world which " Great Britain is today defending." [14]

It is hardly necessary to follow Mr. Knight to the end of his interpretation of contemporary events in the light of the role of Messiah in *Paradise Lost*. The drama in Book V will not gain much in artistic value even if we assent to the suggestion that " Satan's sense of injustice under the enthronement of Messiah as God's vice-gerent exactly reflects Germany's view of Great Britain's ascendency " ; [15] nor will the English constitutional monarchy gain much prestige from Mr. Knight's view of the Messiah who vanquishes Satan with thunder and lightning in Book VI as " an especially *constitutional monarch*, in its [*sic*] more divine, upreaching aspect, as a carrier of God's grace into the domain of secular action." [16] What Mr. Knight

[11] *Chariot of Wrath*, p. 20.
[12] *Ibid.*, p. 140.
[13] *Ibid.*, p. 141.
[14] *Ibid.*, p. 143.
[15] *Ibid.*
[16] *Ibid.*, p. 150.

Merritt Y. Hughes

means, he explains, is that the English conception of both royal and national character is " an incarnation of that royalty blending justice and mercy defined once and for all by Portia's speech in *The Merchant of Venice*." [17] The Shakespearian parallel may seem far-fetched; it is one of many, all of which are due to Mr. Knight's conviction that the Puritan Revolution itself was a spiritual, though violent, process of " re-creation " of the British constitution and " a fulfillment in actuality and through long time of the Shakespearian vision." [18]

In essence this belief in Milton (though hardly in Shakespeare) as a political prophet with something like an Old Testament seer's inspiration, and with something like the charisma which Lenin's disciples recognize in their master, is nothing new under the sun. Mr. Knight finds some encouragement for it in Sir Herbert Grierson's study of the poet as prophet in *Milton and Wordsworth*. He finds very much more encouragement in Mr. Middleton Murry's *Heaven and Earth* though the concern of that book with Milton is hardly vital. If his faith in the working of the leaven of the Puritan Revolution beyond British bounds had been wide enough to admit Russia and the United States further into his book than the footnote on pages 184-5, his faith in the contemporary power of Milton's vision might be greater than it is. Without sacrificing his fondness for an apocalyptic attitude toward Milton, he might have looked at the Puritan Revolution as an international thing, with its roots far in the past, even the pagan past, as Shelley did in *A Philosophical View of Reform*; or he might have seen it in the image of Shelley's eagle in *Hellas*, sweeping down all recorded time and across at least all Europe:

> From age to age, from man to man,
> It lived, and lit from land to land—
> Florence, Albion, Switzerland.

It is worth while to remember that to most historians—and even to a revolutionary historian like Prince Kropotkin, whose work on the French Revolution set the example of going behind constitutional changes to economic upheavals as the central factor in such movements—the movement in England " between 1648 and 1688 " [19] has been spiritually linked to every

---

[17] *Ibid.* [18] *Ibid.*, p. 171.
[19] *The Great French Revolution*, translated by N. F. Dryhurst (1909), p. 3.

subsequent revolutionary attempt on the continent. Mr. Knight's chauvinistically messianic view of Milton in the Puritan revolution obscures the full value of his political thought. To understand that we must go to the magnificent analysis of his sympathy with Sir Henry Vane and the Fifth Monarchists of another Canadian, Mr. Arthur Barker, in *Milton and the Puritan Dilemma.*[20] Mr. Knight's effort in *Chariot of Wrath* to make Milton a figure whose leadership we can follow today is too far removed both from sound historical scholarship and modern political faith to be as moving as Macaulay's picture of Milton's active years as " the very crisis of the great conflict between Oromasdes and Arimanes, liberty and despotism, reason and prejudice." If Milton's principles have " worked their way into the depths of the American forests, . . . and, from one end of Europe to another, . . . kindled an unquenchable fire in the hearts of the oppressed, and loosed the knees of the oppressors with an unwonted fear," it is mainly on account of the prophetic force of the controversial works. Macaulay ranked the best of Milton's prose with the first two books of *Paradise Lost.* His admiration for the " devotional and lyric rapture " of Milton's controversial writing could treat it as describable only in the poet's " own majestic language [as] a sevenfold chorus of hallelujahs and harping symphonies."[21] Macaulay yields nothing in appreciation of the apocalyptic and prophetic element in Milton to Mr. Knight; and he may remind us that the more we know of the inward history of modern liberty, the greater must become our interest in Milton.

Our habit of regarding the Puritan Revolution as the beginning of civil liberty and modern constitutional government in England makes us forget its originally ecclesiastical, and perhaps genuinely religious, nature. In this country we are most accustomed to think of the Revolution in terms of the civil liberties that we associate with *Areopagitica.* In England it is regarded mainly as a landmark in constitutional history. English historians lay greatest stress, as a recent biographer of John Pym[22] does, upon the clarity with which the final constitutional issues of the Civil War were understood and stated as early as

[20] University of Toronto Press, 1943. See particularly chapter 12.
[21] *Critical and Historical Essays by T B. Macaulay* I. 171 and 192.
[22] S. Reed Brett in *John Pym* (London, 1940), pp. 222-3.

Merritt Y. Hughes   51

June, 1642, in " The Nineteen Propositions " of Parliament to Charles. They included, it will be remembered, the demands that the chief Ministers of State should be " such as shall be approved by both Houses of Parliament "; that the government and liturgy of the Church should be reformed " as both Houses of Parliament shall advise "; that the King should accept Parliament's control of the militia, and that he should agree " by act of Parliament, to clear . . . the five members of the House of Commons [whose privilege he had violated by causing their arrest on the floor of the House], in such manner that future Parliaments may be secured from the consequence of that evil precedent." If we are to understand Milton's mixed role as both religious prophet and political philosopher to the Puritan Revolution, we have to relate him alike to its religious and political sides. To understand him fully we need to be reminded, as we are by Professor Merriman, writing from the point of view of a comparison of the Puritan Revolution with its five contemporary revolts—the Fronde, the struggle between the Stadtholders and the Estates in Holland, and the revolts in Naples, Portugal and Catalonia,—that the Puritan movement was unique in being centrally religious, or at least ecclesiastical. Disregarding the force of the physical and rhetorical support that rallied around Charles after the break with Parliament in 1642, Dr. Merriman thinks that, before the quarrel of the Commons with Archbishop Laud confused the issues, Charles could find no supporters willing to fight " for the royal prerogative as he conceived it." " The Church issue," he adds, " in the last analysis, was the fundamental cause of the Great Civil War. 'Let religion be our *primum quaerite*,' declared Sir Benjamin Rudyerd in 1642, ' for all things are bot etceteras to it.' " [23]

As a revolutionist Milton ought first to be known as a volunteer in the attack by the sects, with the Presbyterians in the lead, upon the bishops. Except for their autobiographical passages, such as the famous resolve in the Preface to the second book of *The Reason of Church Government* to write something, someday, that would be the fruit of " devout prayers to that eternal Spirit, who can enrich with all utterance and knowledge,

[23] Roger Bigelow Merriman, *Six Contemporary Revolutions* (Oxford, 1938), p. 38.

and sends out his seraphim, with the hallowed fire of his altar, to touch and purify the lips of whom he pleases," [24] those pamphlets are too little read to contribute to the popular view of Milton. Even their scattered bits of autobiography are too seldom understood as the writer's response to the conventional expectation of his public that he should prove his right to be heard by ' ethical argument ' or vindication of his own character. The apocalyptic note in this passage is more easily interpreted today as evidence of morbid egotism or hypocrisy than as a logical part of the selfjustification that readers trained in Aristotelian rhetoric expected.[25] What seemed to the seventeenth century audience a rather casual and probably convincing proof of sincerity now excites suspicion, and we need the word of a scholar like Sir Herbert Grierson to assure us that Mr. Hilaire Belloc is wrong in saying that " the first prelatical tracts mark no new experience, no awakening in Milton." [26] So disingenuous do the five anti-episcopal tracts seem to a Miltonophobe like the late Heinrich Mutschmann that he convinced himself [27] that they were the cowardly attempt of a man just returned to England after seeking refuge from ecclesiastical censorship in Italy, to take advantage of the defeat of Archbishop Laud and Charles in the Second Bishops' War. It *is* true that Milton began to write his anti-episcopal tracts about the time that the Root-and-Branch Bill in the House of Commons indicated the rising strength of the opposition to the bishops. It is also true, however, that there is no more reason for doubting the sincerity of Milton's work in the five tracts against them than there is to doubt his sincerity in his attack on the "blind mouths " in *Lycidas*. Of the perfect harmony of that passage in thought and imagery with the anti-episcopal pamphlets of Milton and his Smectymnuan friends there is abundant evidence in Professor Haller's analysis of that literature in *The Rise of Puritanism*. " Milton's poem, with its extraordinary denunciation of the prelatical church, . . . was an

[24] The Columbia *Milton* (hereafter cited as *CM*) 3. 241.
[25] The point is well made in *Milton's Rhetoric* (Columbia, Missouri, 1939) *passim*, by Dr. Wilbur E. Gilman.
[26] *Milton and Wordsworth* (London, 1937), p. 32.
[27] In "Die Beweggrunde zu Miltons Festlandreise," *Beiblatt zur Anglia* 50 (1939). 278-82.

expression of the same spirit which . . . was at the moment clamoring in the reckless pamphlets of Prynne and Lilburne." [28]

Milton's quarrel with the bishops is sometimes explained as a personal affair arising out of his differences with the authorities at Cambridge and his fancy of himself as "church-outed by the prelates." [29] It was, of course, something very much larger than any personal interest of his or than any professional interest of the Presbyterian clergy represented by the five Smectymnuan divines. It rallied men of many professions—not only Lilburne and Prynne, but the lawyers and merchants in the Long Parliament who in 1641 pushed the Root-and-Branch Bill against the resistance of cooler men, such as Henry Robinson,[30] who were bent on the reform of episcopacy, though not on its destruction. Instead of regarding Milton's contempt for the bishops as either a personal or a sectarian prejudice, we should recognize it as something deeply involved in the social life of his time. As the constant, perhaps naive, glimpses in the anti-episcopal tracts of a better world to be had simply by erasing the courts and exactions and secular ambitions of the bishops would indicate, there was something utopian in the revolt against them. There was something utopian not only in the ordinary sense of the word, but also in Karl Mannheim's sense, as he defines it in *Ideology and Utopia*. The bitter, indiscriminate attack on episcopacy by "the ascendant bourgeosie" to which Milton belonged was a part of their ideal of 'freedom,' which Mannheim acknowledges as "in part a real utopia, *i. e.*, it contained elements orientated toward the realization of a new social order which were instrumental in disintegrating the previously existing order, and which, after their realization, did become translated into reality." [31] Certainly it is not fantastic to see the anti-episcopal tracts as a part of a wide-spread thrust against the "static guild and cast order" inherited by Milton's England from the "status-bound, feudal society" of the past, and as contributing to the sense of "political freedom and freedom of the unhampered development of the personality" which Mann-

[28] William Haller, *The Rise of Puritanism* (New York, 1938), p. 288.
[29] *CM* 3. 242.
[30] See W. K. Jordan, *Men of Substance* (Chicago, 1942), pp. 107-8.
[31] Karl Mannheim, *Ideology and Utopia* (London, 1936), p. 183.

heim makes central in the conception of liberty that the nineteenth century inherited from the seventeenth.

On the whole, discussion of Milton's anti-episcopal tracts ignores or depreciates their importance as expressions of a revolutionary mind. Few commentators have been enough excited by the spirit of the controversy to accept the ' scurrility ' of the liveliest onslaughts against Bishop Hall and to judge the lampooning passages, as Professor French does,[32] objectively, and simply from the point of view of their fitness for their controversial ends. Less urbane than Bishop Hall Milton certainly was; and he made no pretense of writing with the philosophic scope of Richard Hooker's *Law of Ecclesiastical Polity*, with which his *Reason of Church Government* and *Of Reformation in England* have recently been unfavorably compared.[33] His tracts are to be judged by rhetorical standards such as apply to Tom Paine's *Common Sense*, not by those by which we measure Burke's *Reflections on the French Revolution* or Hooker's treatise. And we should not be misled by the immaturity of their thought. If it is true that in the anti-episcopal tracts he accepted—implicity or explicity—the Calvinistic doctrine of predestination which he repudiated in a famous passage in *Areopagitica* and condemned in the *Christian Doctrine*; it is also true that at the end of the first book of *The Reason of Church Government* he anticipated the ground of his charter of the freedom of the press and of conscience, as well as of the human will, in *Areopagitica*, by answering those who argued that episcopacy was necessary to keep the warring Protestant sects in order in a sentence which reads as if it had been written in 1644 rather than two years earlier:

No wonder then in the reforming of a church, which is never brought to effect without the fierce encounter of truth and falsehood together, if, as it were the splinters and shares of so violent a jousting, there fall from between the shock many fond errors and fanatic opinions, which, when truth has the upper hand, and the reformation shall be perfected, will easily be rid out of the way,

[32] See John Milton French, " Milton as Satirist," *PMLA* 51 (1936). 414-29; and Haller, *Rise of Puritanism*, pp. 358-61.

[33] See E. N. S. Thompson, " Richard Hooker among the Controversialists," *Philological Quarterly* 20 (1941). 263-4.

or kept so low, as that they shall be only the exercise of our knowledge, not the disturbance or interruption of our faith.[34]

The man who wrote these words was already a tolerationist in religion. At the core of his willingness to encourage theological discussion was the respect for "the dignity and importance of the individual" which Mr. Tillyard sees as animating "the whole discussion about the episcopacy."[35] And in that respect for the individual's dignity there was bound up the implicit utopianism (in Mannheim's sense of the word) which had inspired the emotionally valid part of the attack on the bishops from the days of the old Martin Marprelate in Queen Elizabeth's times to the appearance of the new Marprelate tracts at the height of the controversy against Archbishop Laud. Without reading long and widely in the literature of attack upon the prelates between the two Marprelates it is impossible to understand its tremendous utopian drive. The puritan conscience was not only convinced, as Sir Herbert Grierson says,[36] that the quarrel was one "between the ethical in religion and the magical." The revolt was not only against the liturgy and against the whole inheritance of the English Church from Rome which the Puritans stigmatized as idolatry; it was against the interference of the bishops' authority and of their ecclesiastical courts with private lives, private studies, and private beliefs.

A good example of this almost traditional anti-episcopal literature, which happens to date from the year 1614, when the tract found a publisher in Amsterdam, is Leonard Busher's *Religions Peace, or a Reconciliation, between Princes and Peoples, and Nations.* The writer, who described himself as a citizen of London and also "of the Country of Gloucester, of the Town of Wotton," wrote in a style and orthography quaint even for the time; and he wrote with a humble man's sense of his own presumption in speaking at all, but with an apostle's certainty of what he had to say. The tract is less liberal than Milton's *Reason of Church Government,* but it has quite as utopian a faith in the better world to be easily and instantly attained by the liquidation of the bishops. Busher saw them as responsible by their interference with men's consciences for all the religious hypocrisy in the world. He saw them as responsible

[34] *CM* 3. 224.   [35] E. M. W. Tillyard, *Milton* (New York, 1930), p. 127.
[36] *Milton and Wordsworth,* p. 42.

by their administration of canon law in their courts for all the domestic unhappiness in England, and he was as naively convinced as Milton was in *The Doctrine and Discipline of Divorce* that with the disappearance of canon law there would not be an unhappy husband or wife, or a single case of adultery in the land. And of course he was profoundly certain that all of England's political woes came from the interference of the prelates at court.

That last thesis Milton takes for granted in a way which modern readers can hardly understand, and which indeed can hardly be understood, either intellectually or emotionally, without an acquaintance with William Prynne's amazing indictment of ambitious churchmen from the very beginning of the Archbishopric of Canterbury under Augustine at the end of the sixth century down to the contemporary encroachments on the rights of both the crown and its subjects by Archbishop Laud. Milton's accusations (some of them resting on a mistaken attribution of the commentary of the Frenchman, Herveus Burgidolensis, to St. Anselm of Canterbury) [37] against the bishops were recognized by his more learned readers as a kind of popularization of the mass of historical ' evidence ' against them which William Prynne had published in 1641 in *The Antipathie of the English Lordly Prelacie both to regall monarchy, and civill unity*. In 1641 and still in 1642, of course, when Charles, it was hoped, might yet be weaned away from Laud, there seemed to be good ground for Prynne's strategy; that is why, in the latter year, Milton thought fit to end the *Reason of Church Government* with his famous appeal to Charles to assert his prerogative as head of the English Church against the ' innovations ' which Laud was making in its liturgy. In the light of Prynne's theory and in that of its curious appeal to the laws of the realm as a veiled but shrewd threat, if the king will not come to terms with the anti-episcopal party, to constrain him by legal pressure to do so, the passage is worth quoting. In *Chariot of Wrath* [38] Mr. Knight is attracted by Milton's identification of Charles with Samson in this passage, and he parallels it with some other places in the prose works where Milton uses Samson, as Mr.

[37] I am indebted for this explanation of Milton's mistake (which is found in *CM* 3. 208) to Dom Anselm Strittmatter of St. Anselm's Priory, Brookland, D. C.
[38] P. 96.

Knight sees him doing again in *Samson Agonistes*, as a symbol of "Nietzschean 'chastity' and power. In Milton's comparison of Samson's hair to the laws of England, which ought to be the king's glory, and which he cannot harm without losing his strength, it is perhaps more instructive to see, as Mr. Don Wolfe does,[39] the beginning of the open charge of tyranny against Charles which was to be pressed home years later in *The Tenure of Kings and Magistrates* and the First *Defence of the English People*. Although Mr. Knight says nothing about the significance of Milton's comparisons of the king's flowing locks to the laws, he fully understands the importance of the Puritans' faith that they had law on their side against Charles, and when it comes to the legal issue between the king and Parliament he roundly contradicts[40] Mr. Belloc's "contention that the doctrine concerned was 'wholly new' and to Englishmen 'unnatural.'" Milton's words, it must be acknowledged, do suggest the unction of *Thus Spake Zarathustra*:

I cannot better liken the state and person of a king than to that mighty Nazarite Samson, who being disciplined from his birth in the precepts and practice of temperance and sobriety, without the strong drink of injurious and excessive desires, grows up to a noble strength and perfection with those his illustrious and sunny locks, the laws, waving and curling about his godlike shoulders. And while he keeps them about him undiminished and unshorn, he may with the jawbone of an ass, that is, with the word of his meanest officer, suppress and put to confusion thousands of those that rise against his just power. But laying down his head among the strumpet flatteries of prelates, while he sleeps and thinks no harm, they wickedly shaving off those bright and weighty tresses of his laws, and just prerogatives, which were his ornament and strength, deliver him over to indirect and violent counsels, which, as those Philistines, put out the fair and far-sighted eyes of his natural discerning, and make him grind in the prison-house of their sinister ends; . . . till he, knowing this prelatical razor to have bereft him of his wonted might, nourish again his puissant hair, the golden beams of law and right; and they sternly shook, thunder with ruin upon the heads of those his evil counsellors, but not without great affliction to himself.[41]

II

Few passages are more significant of the working of Milton's mind as he thought about the Puritan Revolution in Church

[39] Don Wolfe, *Milton in the Puritan Revolution* (New York, 1941), pp. 46-7.
[40] *Chariot of Wrath*, p. 48.
[41] *CM* 3. 276.

and State than is this one from the close of *The Reason of Church Government Urged against Prelaty*. If we look at it in the light of Mannheim's distinction between ideological and utopian thinking, we find the strong elements of both types, which his analysis would lead us to expect. Nothing is more characteristic of the ' ideologies ' of ascendant classes than the sincere, or canting, or cynical notion that the law is on their side, and the first act of a class which is translating its 'utopian' thinking into reality is to make sure that the law *is* interpreted as being on its side. When Milton wrote these words in 1642, just such a translation of 'utopian' intentions was visibly beginning in the ecclesiastical realm, and it was soon to begin in politics. In the opening duel between the crown and parliament it was not yet clear which party would find the common and constitutional law on its side. And it is worth while to remember that for many historians in the twentieth century it is no longer possible to give Macaulay's confident answer to the question; " Had Charles the First broken the fundamental laws of England? "[42]

Charles, of course, was blind enough to identify the law with his own prerogative, and in *Eikon Basilike* he (or Bishop Gauden, or whoever it was that wrote the passage) was fatuous enough to compare his resistance of Parliament's demands to the replies of Christ to the Devil in the temptation on the pinnacle of the Temple in Jerusalem. To such an impertinent and unflattering analogy Parliament's advocate could only answer as Milton did in *Eikonoklastes*[43] by recalling the " zeal to justice and their native liberty, against the proud contempt and misrule of their kings," of the lords who brought Richard II to book for his tyranny and of all the other champions of the liberties which Englishmen were supposed once for all to have secured from the crown in *Magna Charta*.

The story of the reply of Charles's clerical supporters to such sharp, two-edged, legal reasoning as this by their appeal to the principle of the king's divine right[44] is too well known to need repeating, and so is that of the support of absolutist principles later by writers like Robert Filmer and Hobbes. To both theological and philosophical absolutism the reply, as Professor

[42] *Op. cit.*, p. 174.   [43] *CM* 5. 125.
[44] See John N. Figgis, *The Divine Right of Kings*, second edition (Cambridge, 1922).

Merritt Y. Hughes

Woodhouse points out in his exceedingly able discussion of the service of Puritanism to the cause of liberty,[45] had to be in terms of something still more absolute. "Nothing could dissipate the divinity that hedged a king save the divinity of religion itself when religion was ranged against him." Because Charles chose to make common cause with Archbishop Laud and the more reactionary bishops, it was easy to represent what Milton regarded as the completing or 'reforming' of the Reformation in England as vitally involved with Parliament's case against the king. Charles made the mistake of solidifying everything that was revoltuionary in the English Church against himself. At the same time his own very religious nature and the religious position of many of his supporters at the outset of the struggle finally threw most liberal thinkers, such as John Selden, into opposition to him. Among educated readers the royalists soon had reason to fear the influence of Selden's theory [46] of natural law as more favorable to human rights than to royal prerogative. The royalist John Bramhall, defending the monarchical principle in 1644, in *The Serpent Salve; or, A Remedy for the biting of an Aspe*, warned against the "far-fetched conclusions drawn by empirics from the law of Nature and Nations." What was this Charter of Nature? Whatever it was, Bramhall replied, "it might be limited by the King, his title being not election but conquest." [47] Against this claim the first line of defence was the stand taken by Milton in *The Tenure of Kings and Magistrates* when he asserted that, beginning with William the so-called Conqueror himself, every king of England since Saxon times had sworn in his coronation oath to abide by the laws of the realm.[48] The second and perhaps for both sides the more dangerous line of defence, however, was

[45] A. S. P. Woodhouse, Introduction to *The Army Debates*, edited from the Clarke Manuscripts as *Puritanism and Liberty* (London, 1938), p. 61.

[46] In *De Jure Naturale*, Book I, especially chapters 8, 98, and 99.

[47] Quoted by G. P. Gooch and H. J. Laski in *English Democratic Ideas in the Seventeenth Century* (Cambridge, 1927), p. 93. A typical challange to the royalist claim to absolute rights of power by virtue of the Norman conquest occurs in an anonymous tract, published in 1642, *The Unlimited Prerogative of Kings subverted* (p. B 2r), where the reader learns that William obtained the throne only by the conditional submission of the Saxons, who agreed to serve him " as our Liege Lord, and Sovereigne, so that he would promise to govern us, according to these Laws and Customes to which covenant he consented, as all the Kings of *England* have done since."

[48] *CM* 5. 10.

the Puritan and liberal assertion against royalist claims to divine right and every kind of absolute prerogative for the king of the essentially religious law of nature. In *A Ready and Easy Way to Establish a Free Commonwealth* in 1660 Milton recalled his many past appeals to it in a passage calling it the " only law of laws, . . . fundamental to mankind," and " the beginning and end of government." [49] In his most characteristic thinking the law of nature became simply the law of the intellectual and moral integrity of the individual: The " light of nature," he wrote in the *Commonwealth*, equals " right reason," [50] and the latter is the former's best interpreter. In saying this Milton spoke a language which had been familiar to his countrymen since Robert Greville, Lord Brooke, had appealed against the bishops in 1642 to " Right Reason, the Candle of God, which He hath lighted in man." [51] Already in that tract humanistically trained Puritans found their sanction of the originally Stoic conception of Right Reason interpreting natural law raised by one of the most intellectual and aristocratic of their leaders to a level of philosophical authority that seemed more commanding to Christian idealists than the doctrine of divine right could ever hope to seem. Greville, they knew, was but recalling Seneca's dictum that, " Right Reason is nothing else than a portion of the divine spirit set in a human body." [52] With him they were convinced that "All philosophers yeeld, (and it needeth no dispute) that the *Understanding* rectified still dictates to the *Will*, Optimum faciendum." The Ultimately Socratic principle of right reason, " the understanding rectified," or conscience—call it what you will—is the key to the conception of liberty in the Puritan Revolution. It is the key to the best thinking of the time in both religion and politics; just as the key to most of the less disciplined thought of the period is to be found in such popular, quasi-religious shibboleths as the Truth to which Milton appealed in *Areopagitica*, and which he seems, once or twice, there to idetify with Christ—the ' Christwithin ' of the Fifth Monarchy men.[53] One thing is certain:

---

[49] *CM* 6. 158.   [50] *Ibid.*

[51] Greville's *Episcopacie* is reprinted in William Haller's *Tracts on Liberty*, Vol. 2. References are to pp. 25 and 22.

[52] *Epistulae*, LXVI (Lodge's translation).

[53] The association of Milton with the Fifth Monarchy men was made by Pease in *The Leveller Movement* (New York, 1917), p. 154, and is explored by Barker in *Milton and the Puritan Dilemma.*

in all of Milton's religious and political thinking—from his appeal to 'regenerate reason' in the anti-episcopal tracts, on down through the *Tenure*, the *Commonwealth* and *De Doctrina Christiana*, to almost his last word in the little tract *Of True Religion, Heresy, Schism, Toleration* in 1673—he was dominated by his confidence in the power of a half-divine Right Reason to find out the *Truth*.

The passage in all of Milton's writing where his faith in the final discoverability of Truth comes to climactic expression is the famous myth of Osiris in *Areopagitica*. It should be read in the light of many parallels in his own work and in that of his contemporaries, and it should also be read in the light of the two most telling and damaging criticisms which have been leveled at Milton by his many modern critics. With both of those criticisms in mind, let us read the passage against a very small segment of its literary background. The first of them is Mr. Ernest Boyd's objection (in *Literary Blasphemies*) that *Areopagitica* is quintessentially platitudinous and therefore insignificant; the second is Mr. Leavis's complaint (in *Revaluations*, pp. 58-9) that Milton is, "for purposes of the understanding, disastrously single-minded and simple-minded. . . . This defect," he says, "is a defect of imagination." The charge is brought against Milton as a poet, but it is worth checking against his use of the Osiris myth in his plea for liberty of conscience, for Mr. Leavis thinks that Milton's "inadequacy to myth" (in the structural sense in which the word is used in *Revaluations*) makes "the routine eulogy of his 'architectonic' power (in *Paradise Lost*) plainly a matter of mere inert convention." If our subject warranted such a digression, it would be a temptation to explore the structural significance for *Areopagitica* of this myth of Osiris which comes at its climax and is a symbol of its central theme of the search for Truth:

Truth indeed came once into the world with her divine Master, and was a perfect shape most glorious to look on: but when he ascended, and his apostles after him were laid asleep, then straight arose a wicked race of deceivers, who, as that story goes of the Egyptian Typhon with his conspirators, how they dealt with the good Osiris, took the virgin Truth, hewed her lovely form into a thousand pieces, and scattered them to the four winds. From that time ever since, the sad friends of Truth, such as durst appear, imitating the careful search that Isis made for the mangled body of Osiris, went up and down gathering up limb by limb still as they could find them. 'We have not yet found them all, lords and commons, nor ever shall do, till her Master's second coming, he shall bring together every joint and member, and shall mold them into an immortal feature of loveliness and perfection.[54]

The myth of Osiris, as Milton expected his readers as a matter of course to know, is found in Plutarch's *Moralia*. He expected them to be familiar also with some of the many interpretations of the myth [55] in just his sense by his contemporaries. He expected them also to be familiar with the kindred Renaissance conception of Truth as the Daughter of Time, the prevalence of which in literature and many of the pictorial arts has been studied for us by Professor Saxl.[56] The two ideas of truth are perhaps confused in Milton's condemnation in *Of Prelatical Episcopacy* of the search for Truth " among the verminous and polluted rags dropped overworn from the toiling shoulders of Time," to which he contrasted " the spotless and undecaying robe of Truth, the daughter, not of Time, but of Heaven, only bred up below here in Christian hearts, between two grave and holy nurses, the doctrine and discipline of the gospel." [57] Milton's experience of Presbyterian discipline within two years of the writing of these words was to confirm his notion that Time's shoulders dropped many verminous and polluted rags, but his faith in the quest for Truth never faltered—" Truth which," he said in *The Tenure of Kings and Magistrates*,[58] " among mortal men is always in her progress."

Of course, the progress was also a battle, and a winning one. When in *Areopagitica* Milton proposed to let Truth and Falsehood grapple, he was using the most platitudinous of all the images that had been consecrated in the Puritan struggle with the bishops. In countless Puritan pamphlets Truth strode invincibly into battle while the godly looked on with the serene faith that her strength was " sufficient for vanquishing the most artificial, sophisticall errour that ever was in the world." [59] The

---

[54] *CM* 4. 337.

[55] Some of these are paralleled with this passage in my forthcoming edition of Selections from Milton's prose (Odyssey Press).

[56] In *Truth the Daughter of Time* (Publications of the Warburg Institute 4.).

[57] *CM* III. 91.   [58] *CM* 5. 57.

[59] See Haller's *Tracts on Liberty* 2. 278. Compare William Dell on Truth's invincibility in a speech in the Army Debates preserved in Woodhouse's *Puritanism and Liberty*, p. 315.

words are William Walwyn's in his *Power of Love*, a tract inspired far more by an enlightened visionary's prospect of a really democratic commonwealth to be established in England than by sectarian religious fervor. To the still more worldly-minded Henry Robinson, Truth's triumph in the politico-ecclesiastical battle seemed no less certain, and in *Liberty of Conscience* (1643) he asked, ". . . doe we suspect that errour shall vanquish truth? This is so vaine that no man will confesse so much; but for their full conviction if they were so conceited, let them take notice what *St. Paul* saith to the *Corinthians, We cannot do anything against the truth but for the truth*." [60] Indeed in the Whitehall debates, when the Army leaders were talking and praying themselves into the resolution to show Charles I no mercy and to take the step which would inevitably turn England into a Republic, no figure of speech was commoner in their violent and whirling speeches than that of Truth as wrestling victoriously against Error and at the same time as somehow—both emotionally and philosophically—to be identified with the Christ for whose speedy second coming they prayed. When Ireton proposed a censorship on ' atheistical ' publications and beliefs (not unlike that which Milton proposed in *Areopagitica*) Sprigge, supported by Lilburne, was prompt in condemning such lack of confidence in the ultimate victory of truth, and in " the breaking forth of him who is the Truth, the breaking forth of Christ, in the minds and spirits of men." [61] When Milton wrote *Areopagitica*, he knew that his public was conditioned to respond with either an enlighened, philosophical belief in Truth as symbolized by the Osiris myth, or with a fanatical faith in Truth the invincible champion; and he knew that both the belief and the faith were merged in many minds in the image of " her Master's second coming."

It is as easy for modern readers as it was for Milton's contemporaries to sentimentalize about the notion of Truth that found its classical expression in *Areopagitica*. It is closely bound up with the ' prophetic ' side of the man in which Sir Herbert Grierson has interested us,[62] and it undoubtedly was related to his poetic gift. Indeed, Mr. G. Wilson Knight roundly

---

[60] Henry Robinson, *Liberty of Conscience* (London, 1643), p. 59.
[61] *Puritanism and Liberty*, p. 144.
[62] *Milton and Wordsworth*, p. 47.

identifies that poetic gift with Milton's passionate determination that " truth was to enter politics. This truth, (which Milton sometimes calls 'right reason') " he thinks,[63] "corresponds to ' faith ' in St. Paul's epistles or the Church fathers and to ' imagination ' as conceived by Coleridge and Shelley." As an antidote to Mr. Knight's impliedly sweeping and uncritical acceptance of Milton's political propaganda in the name of Truth it is worth while to remember that most of the political crimes of the Puritans were committed—perhaps quite sincerely —in the service of Truth. In our times the semanticists love to dissect the word, not greatly to the credit of its loudest devotees. With the aid of the Great Tom Fuller—speaking as he did in a sermon in honor of the anniversary of Charles's coronation in 1643—we may profitably pause to notice what a seventeenth century semanticist could do with the word and its abuse by the Puritans.

" Know," he said to his doubtless sympathetic courtly audience, " then that the word *Truth* is subject to much *Homonymie*, and is taken in several senses, according to the opinions, or rather humours of those that use it. Aske the Anabaptist what is truth, and he will tell you, Truth is . . . that all goods should be common, that there should be no civill Magistrate, that there ought to be no warres but what they make themselves, for which they pretend inspiration. . . . Againe, Aske the Separatists what is Truth, and they will tell you, that the further from all ceremonies (though ancient and decent), the nearer to God. . . . Aske the Schismaticks of these times what is Truth, and they will bring in abundance of their own opinions, which I spare at this time to recite.[64]

Fuller, like all his party, was aware as no modern reader of *Areopagitica* can be of the anarchy and hypocrisy that lurked behind the idol of Truth, but his intolerance was the very thing that validated the faith of all the sects, and of liberals who were above the sectarian mêlée, in the divinity of Truth. Yet even Fuller, after declaring all the truths of the sectaries to be " flat falsities," professed his willingness to submit all differences of opinion to the fair debate for which the Puritans clamored. He had only one condition to lay down, but that was

[63] *Chariot of Wrath*, p. 74.
[64] " A Sermon Preached at the Collegiat Church of S. Peter in *Westminster*, on the 27 of March, being the day of His Majesties Inauguration, by Thomas Fuller, B. D. (London, 1643), p. 18.

a betrayal of his own and his party's failure to comprehend the utopian energy of the "new Gospell" of the Puritans, which he insisted should not "be given as the Law, with thundering and lightning of Cannon, fire and sword." [65]

It is a nice question whether the kind of passion and thought which went into Milton's willingness to tolerate all kinds of heresies in *Areopagitica* can be regarded as evidence of imaginative power either in the political or in the Coleridgean sense. Perhaps most readers of *Ideology and Utopia* will grant the 'utopian' power of Milton's conception of truth (in Mannheim's sense of the word 'utopian'), as readers of Ortega y Gasset's *The Revolt of the Masses* may see a perfect correspondence between the successful imposition of Milton's notion of Truth as it shaped the emergent liberalism of the Puritan Revolution and Gasset's view that the "Imagination is the liberating power possessed by man. A people is capable of becoming a State in the degree to which it is able to imagine." [66] In a very vague and perhaps not highly significant sense there can be no doubt that, if not in the activity of the political imagination of the Puritans, then certainly in the shaping of the popular poetic imagination, the idea of the defeat of falsehood in open battle by truth was what Rebecca West has called "a potent image"; certainly it gave rise to many subsidiary images which were beautiful, if not very potent. For example, after a picture of embattled Truth in conflict with Error, Leonard Busher, in *Religions Peace*, changed the image and assured his audience that they should "understand that, errors being brought to the light of the word of God, [they would] vanish as darkness before the light of a torch." [67] And Robert Greville, in a great passage on the Understanding as "a Ray of the Divine Nature, warming and enlivening the Creature, and conforming it to the likeness of the Creator," in the little essay called *The Nature of Truth*, which is cited in *Areopagitica*, wrote finally of Truth in a style that suggests the invocation to light at the opening of the third book of *Paradise Lost*:

[65] *Ibid.*, p. 19.

[66] Ortega y Gasset, *The Revolt of the Masses* (London, 1932), p. 62.

[67] Quoted by Wolfe in *Milton in the Puritan Revolution*, p. 27. Cf. the close of the Humble Petition of 1641: "That which is erroneous vill in time appeare, and the professors of it will bee ashamed, and it will perish and wither as a flower, vanish as smoke, and pass as a shadow." (Quoted by Wolfe on p. 70.)

For the Beauty of Truths character is, that she is a shadow, a resemblance of the first, the best forme; that she is light, the species, the sparkling of primitive *light*; that she is *life*, the sublimation of *light*, that she may reflect upon herself.[68]

Against the account of the diabolic parliament in Books One and Two of *Paradise Lost*, and in view of the following, contrasting debate in heaven, from which the Son of God emerges as leader of the states of heaven as Satan is leader of those of hell, it may not be forced to see some political intention in the seemingly purely metaphysical glories of the famous invocation to light at the beginning of Book III. Certainly it is as much a possibility as is Mr. Knight's interpretation of the Son in Book VI as a pattern of an English constitutional monarch. While feeling far less certain of any political significance in the invocation to light than Mr. Knight is of his view of the Son, we do have one very good reason for supposing that the Son is intended as a political symbol and a revolutionary one at his first appearance in the third book. If the suspicion of most readers that the diabolic parliament is a portrait of the Long Parliament can be confirmed, then the Son can hardly be regarded otherwise than a symbol of whatever it is that makes parliaments good. In that case it may be easy to see him as a symbol of a British constitutional king (though Milton's antipathy to kings and kingship from the days when he wrote his Commonplace Book to the time when he wrote the *Commonwealth* hardly encourages that opinion) ; or it may be easy to look upon him as a symbol of the Cromwellian leader, the god-commissioned superman, as Professor Liljegren is inclined ironically to do. Neither of these positions is easy to defend, but neither is it easy to disbelieve that Milton's treatment of his infernal and heavenly parliaments was in some sense an attempt to solve the political and moral problem of the failure of the Long Parliament, which he dissected so severely in *The History of Britain*.

If the Son of God in the third book of *Paradise Lost* has any political significance, it is simply as the force of good and effective leadership without which parliaments are worse than helpless. Milton's impatience with the impotence of the Long Parliament to act rightly and independently on questions like

<hr>

[68] *The Nature of Truth* (1641), pp. 3-4.

the freedom of the press, the divorce law, and the great problem of disposing of the King, must have given him many moments when his disgust with representative governments was as great as Lenin's with the Russian Douma. As a young man at the beginning of his political career, writing his anti-episcopal tracts, Milton could sincerely describe Parliament as " so much united excellence, (met) in one globe of brightness and efficacy, . . . encountering the dazzled resistance of tyranny." [69] In *Of Reformation in England* [70] he wrote of " the indiminishable majesty of our highest court, the law-giving and sacred parliament." That was " our time of parliament, the very jubilee and resurrection of the state." [71] Perhaps there was no fundamental loss of faith in connection with Parliament's neglect of the divorce pamphlets and *Areopagitica*; but when, after the execution of Charles, he declared that " the parliament is above all positive law, whether civil or common," [72] and said that the " Law of England " was " but the reason of Parliament," [73] he was beginning to be aware of what Lenin was to call the ' disease of parliamentarism.' He had, with reason, lost faith in the power of Parliament to act without the spur of Cromwell's will. Bitter experience was teaching him the need of strong leadership in representative government, and the wonder is that at no time does he seem to have succumbed to the remedy of the single, strong leader.[74] At the fall of the Commonwealth in 1660, when he was writing his *Ready and Easy Way* to establish a better one, his contempt for government by " a single person " was uncompromising. Even the sonnet to Cromwell in 1652 accepts him only as the champion of truth who is to save England, if he proves worthy, from foes who were " Threatening to bind our souls with secular chains." Significantly, in his eulogy in *The Second Defence*, he is presented only as one of the soldiers whom England has used in her own liberation, and his greatest distinction is that he is a man who has mastered

[69] *CM* 3. 337.
[70] *CM* 3. 58.   [72] *CM* 5. 115.
[71] *CM* 3. 127.   [73] *CM* 5. 83.
[74] In " The Theory of the Mixed State and the Development of Milton's Political Thought " (*PMLA* 57 [1942]. 721-2), Professor Z. S. Fink acknowledges that for a time Milton believed in . . . divinely appointed . . . leaders " who were law givers like Lycurgus and Solon and, presumably, Cromwell. In *A Ready and Easy Way*, however, Milton abandoned that faith.

the passions which beset the soul. And when in 1660 final defeat for the Commonwealth came, Milton proved his fidelity to the parliamentary principle by grappling in *The Ready and Easy Way* with the ' disease of parliamentarism ' and trying to devise means to prevent the Grand Council which he proposed should govern the realm from being one of the " mere ' talking shops ' " that Lenin condemned in modern Europe. Like Lenin, he thought that a Parliament should be " a working corporation, legislative and executive at the same time," [75] and it is perhaps the best claim of both men to have been honest and clear-headed leaders in their respective revolutions that they both tried to make parliaments responsive to strong leadership and capable of producing it. And this is true even though Lenin's notion, which looked forward to the Russian soviets, had as little to do with Milton's Grand Council as it did with the heavenly parliament in the third book of *Paradise Lost*.

III

To compare Milton with Lenin in any respect is to invite a challenge of his right to rank at all as a revolutionist in the modern democratic and economic sense. That he was no democrat in the modern sense needs no demonstration. The " popular assembly of upward of a thousand " which he provided for in *A Ready and Easy Way to Establish a Free Commonwealth*, as Professor Fink has shown,[76] however, had a genuine, though rather negative and contemptible part to play in Milton's theory of state sovereignty as best if ' mixed ' and unevenly divided among "magisterial, aristocratic and democratic elements." It is the uncompromisingly aristocratic cast of Milton's political thinking that is hard for the modern world to accept. We forget how radically consistent his aristocratic thinking was, and what a social and economic revolution it entailed. We forget how bitterly the abolition of the House of Lords under the Cromwellian Commonwealth had been resented, and what an economic upheaval was involved in the nationalization of the estates of the royalist nobles. No one supported the abolition of the House of Lords more cordially than did Milton, and no one deplored the dishonest resale of

[75] Nikolai Lenin, *The State and Revolution* (New York, 1929), p. 153.
[76] *PMLA* 67. 716.

what might have largely remained public land by Parliament to the favored grandees of the Parliamentary Party more sincerely than he did. The extent of the economic revolution under the Protectorate is amusingly exploited in the reply to Milton's *Ready and Easy Way* by George Starkey, *The Dignity of Kingship Asserted*.[77] The whole country, and especially the gentry and the merchant classes, are represented as having been robbed by the Rump's expropriations of nobility and churchmen, and by its "monstrous taxes, (which they extorted to maintain their *Janisaries* the *Apostate Souldiers* by whose *mutiny* and *Rebellion* they were first *constituted*) ."[78]

Yet what interested Milton in the attack on the hereditary nobility in the Puritan Revolution, it is plain, was the emergence of the principle that was to play so large a part in the French Revolution—the principle that honor should go to men of talent rather than to men of family. If rank and property could be cleared of snobbery, Milton had no quarrel with the landed families. That much seems clear from his refusal in the *Way* to accept the principle of the periodic return of all the land in the realm to small or comparatively small holders, which Harrington had made a basic part of his constitution in his *Oceana*. In spite of Harrington's weighty authority for the principle in the laws of Moses and the example of the agrarian proposals of the Gracchi in republican Rome, Milton said that, if he could be assured that in his commonwealth there would be no temporal or spiritual lords, he was confident that no individual or group could " attain to such wealth or vast possessions as will need the hedge of an agrarian law." Such laws, he added, had never been successful, " but the cause rather of sedition, save only where it began seasonably with first possession."[79] Milton's commonwealth would hardly have been levelled down economically any more than the England in which he actually lived. If he shared in the middle-class hatred of a privileged nobility which Professor Brinton says in *The Anatomy of Revolution*[80] is a part of every revolutionary movement, it was less because he was envious of the nobles, as Dr.

[77] *The Dignity of Kingship Asserted*, edited for the Facsimile Text Society by W. R. Parker (New York, 1941).
[78] *Ibid.*, p. 148.
[79] *CM* 6. 134.
[80] Pp. 72 and 286-7.

Milton as a Revolutionary

Johnson said that he was, than because, as George Starkey said,[81] he believed that a commonwealth was the best kind of government to secure " *Civil Freedome*, which consists in Civil Rights and the advancement of every person according to his *merit*."

Probably none of Milton's twentieth-century readers outside of Germany will dislike him a whit for being guilty of an interest in civil rights. His interest in the mutual claims of society and the meritorious individual smack too much of ' rugged individualism ' and the Aristotelian " concept of natural slavery and the Christian doctrine of sin," [82] however, to be acceptable to Mr. Don Wolfe. Because " in *Paradise Lost*, as in the pamphlets, Milton identified sin with political ignorance," [83] Mr. Wolfe regrets the severity of Milton's verdict on his countrymen for throwing away (or seeming to throw away) the hard-won liberties that were sacrificed to recall Charles II in 1660. By implication, he would disapprove of the characteristic entries under the heading of *Libertas* in the Commonplace Book which declare that nations get the governments that they deserve, that Brutus and Cassius erred in thinking that Rome was capable of liberty,[84] and that liberty once lost is irrecoverable.[85] He looks askance at the psychology which led Milton to preach the subjection of passion to reason in some of the speeches of Michael and Raphael in *Paradise Lost*, and at the extension of that psychology into the political principle of the rule of good men. The Christ of *Paradise Regained*, who says that God and Nature approve

> When he who rules is worthiest, and excells
> Them whom he governs,

smacks to Mr. Wolfe of the tyrant that Professor Liljegren saw in the Christ of *Paradise Lost*, and in " the stern judgments " of that poem he sees " the boundless charity of the Christ, glimpsed by . . . Saltmarsh and Walwyn and Roger Williams (fluttering) helplessly in the offing." [86] Altogether, Mr. Wolfe

[81] *Dignity of Kingship*, p. 25.
[82] *Milton in the Puritan Revolution*, p. 346.
[83] *Ibid.*, p. 347.
[84] *CM* 18. 163.
[85] *CM* 18. 193-4.
[86] *Milton in the Puritan Revolution*, pp. 346 and 349.

Merritt Y. Hughes 71

finds that " Milton's portrayal of Christ . . . shows his lack of sympathy with the full measure of love and forgiveness that the extreme Puritan revolutionists emphasized in their characterizations." [87] The upshot is that for Mr. Wolfe the peak of Milton's effectiveness as a political thinker is the "revolutionary fervor that would open all creeds to pitiless criticism " in *Areopagitica*, and " the democratic arguments of *The Tenure* and *The Defence*." [88]

Probably most of Mr. Wolfe's readers will concur with him in rating *Areopagitica* and *The Tenure of Kings and Magistrates* above *The Ready and Easy Way to establish a Free Commonwealth*. Doubtless Milton would not agree with him. In the equal stress upon the evils of royal tyranny and mob rule in the *Way* he spoke out of his experience of the Puritan Revolution. From his silence about the extremely liberal humanitarian and theological views of men like Walwyn, Williams, and Winstanley it is hardly fair to conclude that he had a hard heart. Winstanley's *Law of Freedom*, the communistic manifesto of the Diggers of St. George's hill in February, 1652, with its Marxian conviction that wealth is produced only by labor, its annual turnover of all public offices, its principle of exchange by barter, and above all with its proposal of free and technical education for everyone, seems to anticipate the economic ' dialectic ' of Marx and his followers. No one can deny the interest of Winstanley's communistic conception of a commonwealth for his own time as well as for ours.[89] Yet in general it is true, as Professor Jordan believes, that " the thought of the incendiary political groups—the Fifth Monarchy men, the Levellers, the Diggers, and the more violent republicans—was quite as divorced from the economic realities of the age as it was from the political necessities of the period. Moreover, the economic and social thinking of the more radical sectaries, animated as it was by the vision of the Kingdom of God on earth, was in most instances so detached from the trend of English development as to be without great significance for the period." [90] Certainly there was some radically democratic

[87] *Ibid.*, p. 350.

[88] *Ibid.*, p. 351.

[89] Cf. Professor Sabine's Introduction to his edition of *The Works of Winstanley*, pp. 54-8.

[90] *Men of Substance*, pp. 203-4.

interpretation of the law of nature by men like Rainborough in the Army debates, but in general " even the Levellers were against interference with property," [91] and men like Ireton, who defended property rights, carried the argument. Mr. Jordan points out that the most unsparing attacks on the Levellers' leaders were made by one of the most effective political writers of the Revolution, Henry Parker,[92] and it is surely true that in his attack on John Lilburne, Parker proclaimed the principle that " liberty cannot be permitted to degenerate into anarchy " [93] with far greater controversial bitterness than Milton ever showed.

Argument of this kind, however, will never reconcile Mr. Wolfe and those of his way of thinking to Milton as a political thinker in the Puritan Revolution. They are hardly likely to be impressed by even the most liberal and far-seeing of his political views, like his recommendation of strong local governments with independent courts and good schools throughout England.[94] Nor are they to be silenced by M. Saurat's condescending warning not to " forget too easily that Milton was not only a critic of kings and tyrants," or by his approval of Milton's " vital observations on the essential principles on which democracies should be worked." Mr. Wolfe is not likely to agree with M. Saurat that the practice of " explaining everything by economic factors " is a " craze," or that the " older . . . method of blaming and somewhat regulating human nature . . . in Milton's pamphlets " [95] is the right way to face either political or ethical problems.

Perhaps those problems need not be faced before justice is done to Milton as a political thinker. Perhaps we may understand him best if, like Mr. Barker, we regard him as an idealist who thought that " the function of the revolution was to achieve civil liberty through the inward laws of true religion," [96] and if

[91] Margaret James in *Social Problems and Policy during the Puritan Revolution* (London, 1930), p. 119.

[92] *Men of Substance*, p. 156.

[93] *Ibid.*, p. 176.

[94] The significance of this suggestion and of Milton's support for it from the value of local institutions in the Dutch struggle for liberty, becomes clear in the light of Starkey's violent reply in *The Dignity of Kingship*, pp. 107-9.

[95] Denis Saurat in a review of the Columbia Milton, Vol. 5 to 10, in *The Review of English Studies* 10. 230.

[96] *Milton and the Puritan Dilemma*, p. 192.

we study his political pamphlets as " the not altogether successful attempt of an idealist . . . to read in the chaotic events of
the revoltuion a pattern which would justify both the ways of
God and men." [97] The effort to account for his faith in private
reason and natural law as capable of finding the way to the City
of God has a more than literary-historical value. It is not merely
a matter of showing that his political thought in both his poetry
and prose was essentially Platonic. It is a matter of finding
where to place him in the revolutionary process of the past four
centuries. His part in the Puritan revolution is a landmark in
the transition from the religious culture of the Middle Ages to
the materialistic world of today. In that movement he appears
not exactly as a Platonist, but as an ' idealist ' in the sense
that Professor Sorokin regards [98] Plato as an idealist whose
development was governed by an historical principle which
makes the appearance of idealistic thought inevitable when-
ever religious civilizations begin to move toward a materialistic
or " sensate " culture. Although Milton's political idealism involved faith in the City of God, it was not reactionary, for it
not only made the individual free; it made his salvation and
that that of society rest upon his use of his critical faculties.
Today it can hardly be admired or understood because it was
more concerned with social discipline than it was with the
social justice of humanitarian democracy. Milton's prime concern was with the perfection of the state and of the individual.
That is why, in his first burst of revolutionary writing, in the
anti-episcopal tracts, he was more of a reformer than a revolutionist; and that is why, as he explored what Christian liberty
meant to him in the divorce tracts, *Areopagitica*, the *Tenure*
and the later political pamphlets, he became more and more
of a radical idealist—a revolutionist without a party and with
only the faith of the champion of a lost cause in revolution
itself.

[97] *Ibid.*, p. 213.
[98] The use made of Platonic concepts and of Aristotle's theory of kingship and
tyranny in *The Tenure of Kings and Magistrates* may be recognized as one of the
" Idealistic motives " by which Professor Sorokin explains " the theories of Plato "
and " Aristotle's three good forms of government (monarchy, aristocracy, and
polity) in contradistinction to the three wrong or bad forms of government and
leadership, where the Idealistic values are absent (tyranny, oligarchy, and mob
rule)." *Social and Cultural Dynamics* 3 (1937). 145-6.

THE ICONOGRAPHY OF RENUNCIATION:
THE MILTONIC SIMILE

BY KINGSLEY WIDMER

The conception of Milton as primarily a Renaissance or Christian humanist, a view perhaps inevitably associated with the skillful study of Milton's historical and intellectual relationships, raises difficulties when applied to Milton's major poems. Humanistic emphasis upon the positive values of classical learning, religious and ethical moderation, and general reasonableness, may not do justice either to Milton's radical religious commitment or to some of the distinguishing qualities of his poetry. The conception of Milton which in large part is contrary to the humanistic view approaches him as " an absolutist, an all-or-none man." [1] If the problem be confined to Milton's longer poems, the questions might thus be posed: Is the tone and texture of Milton's poetry reasonable or absolutist? And, consequently, does the Miltonic valuation of the world lead to acceptance or renunciation?

Milton's figurative language, particularly the similes, provides a vantage point for such discussion, not only because of its felicity but because it shows Milton's peculiar use of traditional materials. The similes have also been the focus for adverse judgments of Milton's poetic texture (Eliot, Leavis, Bell, Pound and Rajan). However, the criticism that " Milton's similes don't focus one's perception of the relevant, or sharpen definition in any way . . .",[2] does not appear to have gone below the surface relationships or recognized the principled peculiarity that governs the work.

A simile from *Paradise Regained* (IV, 562-71) may suggest some of the relevant complexity. Satan, falling from the pinnacle upon which he has, as a final threat, placed Christ, is compared to a giant (Antaeus) defeated in physical combat

---

[1] William Empson, *The Structure of Complex Words*, p. 101.
[2] F. R. Leavis, *The Common Pursuit*, p. 22.

This essay first appeared in *ELH*, Vol. 25, No. 4 (December 1958).   75

by a herculean Christ (Alcides). Milton self-consciously helps define the function of the simile by a parenthetical comment: " to compare/ Small things with greatest." It is, then, the disparity as much as the similitude of the comparison which is important.

The principle of the disparate simile requires application both to Christ and to Satan in order to achieve the full realization of Milton's dialectical poetry. Clearly, there is an ironic disproportion in the comparison of Christ with Hercules: Hercules' victory was an active assertion of the flesh whereas Christ's victory is a renunciation of all fleshly action. The simile directs attention to Milton's point that Christian renunciation is the " greatest " heroism. Furthermore, in comparing " Small things with greatest," we see that Milton intends Satan to be viewed as far superior to a classical giant. This simile— and its method is repeated in other similes in both *Paradise Lost* and *Paradise Regained*—both exalts Christian renunciation and Milton's ironic view of classical virtue. For Milton, the heroic pagan image is appropriate, yet insufficient, for the dramatization of evil.

There is also another dimension to the Antaeus-Alcides simile. Earlier in *Paradise Regained* Milton has made his vehement attack on classical learning. In this simile he returns to the learning he has previously denigrated. A contradiction? The burden of proof must rest on those readers who would insist that an explicitly self-conscious poet has forgotten his own passionate criticism of two-hundred lines earlier. It is more coherent to understand Milton as mocking the pagan comparison; the classical similitude is, even for Satan, mean and belittling. The emphasized disparity between the combat of Satan and Christ and the combat of the classical heroes is a final fillip against classical learning. The negation of classical knowledge and myth is a defense of the single-revelation and an exaltation of the myth of Satan and Christ. Contrary to the Leavis view, then, the Miltonic simile focuses the relevant and sharpens definition, not only for the particular Satan-Christ combat but for the larger Miltonic insistence on the incommensurability of the Christian and classical views of heroism and evil.

Some such fuller perspective of the texture of Milton's

poetry, rather than an emphasis upon local scenic effects, is necessary if we are to relate the particulars of Milton's verse to his commanding ideas and values. Most of Milton's similes require an awareness of ironic disparity as well as the more obvious sense of comparison. Two similes which depend for their larger coherence on Milton's evaluation of the pastoral tradition may provide further illustration of this procedure. Satan in the Garden of Eden (*Paradise Lost*, IX, 455 ff.) appears " as one who long in populous city pent." Satan in *Paradise Regained* (II, 300 ff.), though on the whole a considerably lesser dramatic figure because of his more purely dialectical function, is the same urban type—" as one in City, or Court, or Palace bred." Some critics (Watkins and Tillyard) might direct attention here to Milton's personal distaste for urban sophistication, but the recurrent relation of evil to the urban has a significance beyond the biographical. The association of Satan with the urban in these two scenes prepares for a pastoral outfoxing of the rustics, Christ and Eve, by the villainously sophisticated gentleman. Milton then develops the dramatic reversal in which the natural goodness of the rustic overcomes the villain: in *Paradise Lost* it is because of Eve's natural beauty that Satan remains " stupidly good " (IX, 465) for the moment; in *Paradise Regained* the sophisticated villain's comic stupidity consists of tempting a good and ascetic man with food (I, 337-56). Then the easy pastoral victory of natural goodness is reversed because Eve is tempted and Christ is forced to reveal his other (divine) nature. Only by divine miracle is the defeated natural virtue of the pastoral figure finally redeemed and made victorious.

In *Paradise Lost*, Satan's sly victory with the apple in the pastoral garden is revealed as illusory by the ashen apples in the infernal garden (X, 547-72). In *Paradise Regained* Satan " forces " Christ to reveal his divinity and save himself from falling from the pinnacle, but the illusory success of violence is revealed in Satan's own fall (IV, 551-71). This extensive ironic parallelism binds together an elaborate theological paradigm which reverses the significance of the pastoral similes. Natural goodness (the rustic figure) momentarily wins in the conflict with sophisticated evil, then loses, and is finally superseded and redeemed by the revelation of divine power.

Kingsley Widmer   77

The pastoral machinery, of course, has a much larger scope in the two poems than its function in the similes; Milton may be inverting the classical idea of Elysium in the Garden of Eden when he emphasizes the pastoral as the starting scene for the heroism of human redemption, rather than its reward. The pastoral antithesis, the world as represented by the city, is also a recurrent image of evil in Milton. We find this in Gaza and Pandemonium, and in such distinguishing (and Protestant) religious metaphors as the contrast between the reign over " cities of men " and the " reign within." But, repeatedly, Milton's use of the pastoral machinery appears to dramatize the momentary adequacy, and final inadequacy, of natural goodness, and the necessity for all natural goodness to be redeemed by Christian divinity.

While Milton is writing a literary epic and thus has a wide range of figurative material, he most often follows traditional usage in the materials for his similes. The insect simile (bees, hornets, locusts and flies) appears repeatedly in Homer, Virgil and Tasso. The use of the insect simile in Milton and in later poetry (see particularly the examples cited in Haven's *The Influence of Milton*) appears to have a tone which can be distinguished from the classical usage in that the bee image is didactically positive and the fly and grasshopper didactically negative. The glorification of work in the Protestant ethos may well have influenced the tone of the insect similes. Milton's self-conscious adaption of traditional epic formulae to Christian themes and meanings would seem to require the reader's constant awareness of the Miltonic variances from the classical.

In *Samson Agonistes* Milton utilizes traditional classical imagery when Samson's " restless thoughts " are " like a deadly swarm of hornets " (19-20). However, Milton's comparison is to inward torments which in classical literature would have been presented as external torments. When Samson refuses to " sit idle . . . a burdensome drone " (567-8), the insect image does not appear to have an adequate parallel in classical literature. Even more revealing of the Miltonic tone is the simile by the Chorus in *Samson Agonistes* in which the " common rout " of men are they who " grow up and perish, as the summer fly." Has not Milton added a sense of Protes-

The Iconography of Renunciation

tant vocation and dedicated duty to the traditional classical insect comparison?

Another example of the flies simile appears in *Paradise Regained* (IV, 15-24) where Satan is compared to a " swarm of flies " annoying a Christ who is likened to a " wine press." (While Satan is ostensibly tempting Christ, the simile of the flies and the wine press suggests that, paradoxically, Christ is tempting Satan). A connected simile transforms the swarming of the flies to a " vain battery," like that of waves upon a rock. The hyper-logical critic, one supposes, might ask how the two similes can provides a coherent image of the action; how, that is, puny flies can be powerful waves, how a wine press can also be a rock, how buzzing can also be battery, and how the single person of Satan can reasonably be compared to a swarm of flies and a series of waves. Milton's similes, however, do not attempt to elaborate the visual logic of a scene or character. The coherence of the Miltonic texture requires the application of a dialectical rather than a visual principle. The two similes might thus be paraphrased: Satan's parasitic and futile temptations—actually self-tempting to further acts of evil—are properly compared to a swarm of flies in their trivial plenitude; but evil's assaults upon goodness (Christ) have a persistence through all natural time which requires that Satan's action also be compared, more threateningly, to the battery of waves. The action of evil is both trivial and immense, and it is the linkage of disparate similes which reveals the significant duality. Similarly, the apparently rich and seasonable energy of Christ (the wine press) is really the principle of immutability (a rock).

As is appropriate in a theological poem, each surface effect has a deeper, ultimate, quality. William Blake noted in " The Marriage of Heaven and Hell " that Milton's Satan demonstrated the principles of " desire " and " energy " (such as flies and waves). But Milton's deity is a machine, a rock (" Or as a stone that shall to pieces dash/ All monarchies . . . ." *Paradise Regained*, IV, 149), an immutable absolute which defeats all natural desires and energies. Though the surface images shift, Milton's Satan—and his deity, too—has a coherent principle. Therefore he is not to be understood as a " personified self-contradiction " (C. S. Lewis) but as a " passionate paradox " (E. E. Stoll). The similes for Satan and Christ help define the recurrent and central Miltonic dialectic of the eternal conflict of energy and immutability.

Puzzling qualties of Milton's poetic texture frequently reveal a deeper coherence if read as part of Milton's theological polarity between a dynamic and plenitudinous evil and an unchanging and absolute good. That this has not always been recognized in discussions of Milton's similes may be due to a misapplied esthetic. Not only the classical use of the simile but the classical theory of the simile, as in Quintilian, Samuel Johnson and T. S. Eliot, has held the simile to be digressive, ornamental, and not essentially related to the structure of the poem. Milton's use of the simile, however, appears to diverge from the classical view as inevitably as the conception of rhetoric in a logos-believing Protestant would diverge from the classical precepts of persuasion. The Word of the simile must also be part of the truth.

That the poetic details must be understood in consistent terms with the underlying poetic-theological principles of the work can be suggested by another historical vantage point. In Milton's Protestant baroque style we may look for the usual baroque resolution in which the apparent disparity and flourish of detail re-enforces rather than dissolves the underlying equilibrium and logic of the art work.

The recurrent patterns of imagery, of which the similes are but a part, are also related to the principles of energy and immutability. Satan's natural state is that of flux: the waves beating against the rock of Christ and the " Port of Despair " in *Paradise Regained*; the ship similes for Satan in books I, II and IX of *Paradise Lost*; Satan's repeated motion of sailing or swimming through liquid and chaotic materials, as in the Lake of Hell, part of his journey through Chaos, and the river and mist by which he enters the Garden of Eden. There are also similitudes made between Satan and water monsters (Leviathan) and classical voyages. The major significance of individual comparisons of this sort has been noted by various critics. William Empson, for example, has commented on one of the ship-similes for Satan in *Paradise Lost* (IX, 510-18): " Satan is like a merchant [ship] because Eve is exchanging these goods for her innocence; and like a fleet rather than one ship because of the imaginative wealth of polytheism and the variety of the world." [3]

Then, too, one may suggest that the "boundless deep" of Satanic despair in *Paradise Lost* is essentially related to the "remorseless deep" and "perilous flood" of "Lycidas." One comes to expect cruel evil to be related to the liquid state in Milton. Thus Dalila is compared to a ship in *Samson Agonistes* (714-19). One possible connection between these negative images associated with the liquid state is the Miltonic rejection of the flux which constitutes the essential evil of natural and worldly activity, in contrast to the permanence of the divine.

Thus the pilot of the small boat, in the first major comparison in *Paradise Lost* (I, 196 ff.), is wise in mistaking the Satanic Leviathan for an island, a natural part of the sea. Those commentators (Eliot and Leavis) who have found a narrative confusion in the pilot's being "night foundered" may have failed to appreciate that the scene constitutes a metaphysical as well as an actual sea. The lost single pilot in his small boat perhaps anchors himself to the illusory island of a monster in a traditional dark night of the soul. The similitudes of this state for the experience of Hell are rather more significant than scenic logic.

Milton's similes appear frequently to have multiple functions, rather than single comparisons, and the Leviathan simile discussed above explores both the qualities of Hell and Satan. The comparison of Satan to Leviathan, of course, is one of a series that provides a gigantic image of Satan. He is further magnified by a contrasting series of similes which provide a diminshed view of the other fiends. The principle of evil, Satan, dominates all of evil's multitudinous forms, the other fallen angels. Where Satan is compared to a sea monster, and his spear to a Norway pine that will "be the mast of some great ammiral" (I, 294), the other fiends are compared to "autumnal leaves" (instead of monsters and trees) "that strow the brooks" (instead of seas). (The autumnal leaves comparison was a favorite with Virgil and also appears in Dante, Tasso and Marlowe.) By further reduction, the fiends are compared to "scattered sedge" on the "Red-Sea Coast." Apparently an associational movement from the color of the

[3] *Some Versions of Pastoral*, p. 171.

flaming lake of Hell has led into the Red-Sea allusion, which immediately brings to Milton's mind the Biblic exodus from Egypt. The fiends develop in the comparisons from autumnal leaves to Red-Sea sedge to Pharaoh's drowned cavalry. The movement in association from the melancholy of dead vegetable matter to the evil of dead human nature is perhaps also the transformation of the classical epic simile into the Biblical moral simile.

The Egyptian abjectness of the fiends fuses with the dramatic action of the poem in Statan's angry demand that the fiends arise (310-30). In a sense the action itself is but a culmination of the similes since the fall of Pharaoh's mighty legions is parallel to the fall of the angels. The concluding comparison of the verse paragraph is the contrast of the now lowly fiends to their former station as " Cherub and Seraph." A pattern of comparisons, running from vegetable to human to angelic, ends in the dramatic intellection of evil and Satan's awareness of the fallen state. The dramatic pathos resides in the repeated disparities, which the comparisons call forth, between what the fiends are and what they previously were. The same poetic technique of the double view is applied all through books I and II in the alternating expansion and deflation of the fiends. In viewing evil here as both trivial and immense, and as both multitudinous and unified, we have an essential Miltonic dialectic. The very means for presenting the dual nature of evil—the cycles of comparison, the traditional nature images, the emphasis upon heroic combat and temporal fortunes—provide evil with classical characteristics. Evil is the subject for most of the classical allusions. It achieves its fullest embodiment in Satan as the classical hero, not only as warrior but as a classical reasoner (by parody in book II, by simile in IX, 670-6, and implicitly by defending Greek wisdom in *Paradise Regained*). It is the fallen, not the good, which must be understood in pagan, cyclic and heroic terms. The good, on the contrary, is not part of natural forces nor heroic cycles of temporal fate.

When the fallen angels heed Satan's command and rise from the lake (337-43) for a new cycle of rise and fall, they are as " a pitchy cloud of locusts." Although this is a traditional epic simile it is neither digressive in function nor classical in meaning. Milton declassicizes the comparison by relating it, once again, to the Biblical Red-Sea story. The locusts, which in *Exodus* preceded the Red Sea defeat of Pharaoh, are not, therefore, the natural evil of classical epic; they are a divine scourge that appears and disappears at the command of God's chosen prophet and his " potent rod." Classical misfortune is but the disguise of Biblic chastisement in Milton's epic technique. Thus it frequently appears that when Milton is being most classical, his tone is most Miltonic and Christian. The dialéctic of subtly subsuming the pagan mythology under the Christian revelation is a major aspect of Milton's poetic texture, and thus becomes a major qualification of what might otherwise appear as a humanistic fusion of classical and Christian materials.

We might briefly follow several of the poetic strategies indicated above through some of the other similes of book I of *Paradise Lost*. From the hordes of insects, Milton's comparisons move to the hordes of barbarians " of Rhene or Danaw," and then to the " godlike Shapes " of pagan deities. The progression in size is also a progression in degree of evil ravaging a land (locusts to barbarians to false gods) and repeats the pattern of enlargement of the similes in the preceding verse paragraphs, (fallen leaves to fallen men to fallen angels). The following verse paragraphs, the catalogue of the fallen angels as pagan gods and the building of a pagan temple as the infernal capital, elaborately develop the equation of paganism and evil, and constitute a thorough renunciation of classical knowledge for the single myth of Christian revelation.

In the final verse paragraph of book I (752 ff.) a rich compound of similes suggests more fully Milton's view of evil. One ironic simile compares the infernal gathering place to that for chivalric " champions "—ironic because the champions " Defied the best of Paynim chivalry " while the fallen angels are the very source of pagan chivalry. (Besides, we know that the fiends are really quite unchivalric 17th century soldiers, as indicated by their " squared regiment.") Then follows one of the classical insect similes: "As bees in springtime . . . ." The relations of this simile would seem to be complex. The replacement of the earlier ravaging locusts by hardworking bees suggests a positive tone to the fiends. This has been prepared for by the work of the " industrious crew " building Pandemonium. The Protestant virtue of dutiful hard work pervades even Hell; Belial is wrong, Milton later comments, for advising the fallen angels to " ignoble ease and peaceful sloth " (II, 227). As with Samson's acceptance of laboring for the enemy at Gaza ("labour/ Honest and lawful to deserve my food," *Samson Agonistes*, 1365-6) , and with Adam and Eve laboring even in the Garden of Eden (IX) , dutiful work is a good in itself. However, Milton reverses the positive quality of the simile in at least three ways; the beehive, the golden " Straw bilt citadel," reveals the moral impermanence of the " precious bane " from which Pandemonium has been built; secondly, the end of the simile emphasizes the thickly swarming mass-insect quality (negative) rather than the industry (positive) ; and, finally, there is the satiric political touch of the insects engaged in " state affairs." In larger terms, the positive qualities given to the fiends reveal not the absence of virtue but the power of active evil, whether as the constructed falsity of Pandemonium, military discipline, hard work, or any other heroic or natural attractiveness turned to bad purposes. Evil is not so much sin as false virtue, as in Satan's principle, " Evil, be thou my Good." The various positive and heroic qualities given the fallen angels in *Paradise Lost* (work, discipline, ambition, intelligence, bravery, energy) are, of course, undercut by irony; but, in addition, they emphasize the rich variety of evil and the single nature of goodness as faith in and submission to divine authority. Neither virtues nor good works are redemptive for Protestant Milton; any and all activity may be evil if it is not at one with the immutable authority for the universe. The true antithesis of the infernal crew is not different activity than that of Hell, but the will and the faith beyond all activity: the anti-hero, the immutable Lord, the untemptable Christ, the renunciatory Samson, the poetic mind fixed only on the single revelation.

The bee simile also prepares the way for the fantastic reduction of the giant fiends to " smallest dwarfs," " Pigmean race " and " Fairy Elves." These similitudes partly reverse the heroic emphasis of previous images, thus maintaining the trivial-immense Miltonic dialectic about evil. Nor should we take the elaboration of the fairy elves simile (781-8) as simply the light and fanciful touch of the poet, for this identification of moonlight magic (and its mirth and dance and music) with

The Iconography of Renunciation

the fiends is but another element in the consistent denigration of paganism. The reduction in size has been applied to the spacious scene as well, which is now a " narrow room." The penultimate reduction of the fiends—" incorporeal Spirits to smallest forms reduced "—is a humorously fantastic touch (the formless given smallest form) which by its very logical absurdity casts doubt on the process of reduction, and thus prepares for the reversal. Book I concludes with the Satanic crew in all their ominously heroic largeness: the " great Seraphic Lords and Cherubim," " the thousand Demi-Gods " in " their own dimensions like themselves." That final simile is no simile, but the essential Miltonic fact of the immense and self-defining nature of evil.

In the pattern of tropes that conclude this section, both dramatic commonsense and theological principle dictate that the proportions of evil must rise above all ironic reductions and must still retain not only the power but much of the virtuous appearance which makes evil significant. The dialectic of the similes re-enforces rather than obscures the Miltonic principle of the richly varied, multitudinous, and substantial actuality of evil.

If we may leave the discussion at this point of suggestiveness rather than exhaustiveness, several general considerations might be raised. Rajan, in arguing the popular view that the essential weakness of *Paradise Lost* was Milton's inability to make Heaven " poetically preferable " to the richness of Hell, points to the " drab legalities of Milton's celestial style," including the absence of a single complex simile in the speeches in Heaven.[4] But this is to miss the point and fight the cohering principle of the work. (The same charge could repeatedly be made against esthetic-religious works, such as the ethical section of Soren Kierkegaard's *Either/Or* as contrasted with the esthetic section.) The problem of the disparity between Heaven and Hell is sometimes ignored (C. S. Lewis and Arnold Stein); more often it is acknowledged but explained away as historically conditioned (Douglas Bush and E. M. W. Tillyard); or it is viewed as the peculiar limitation of Milton's personality (Ezra Pound and William Empson); or it is seen as a basic difficulty in 17th century Christian mythology (A. J. A.

[4] *Paradise Lost and the Seventeenth Century Reader*, pp. 129 and 164.

Waldock). But why should we ignore, or suggest biographical and historical conditions as an adequate explanation of a major and principled characteristic of Milton's poetry? The entire Miltonic view, and thus much of Protestant Christian mythology, is involved in the stylistic antithesis between Heaven and Hell. Milton's Heaven may have Reason and certain traditional images of hierarchy and harmony which elaborate the Revelation and the Word, but most other similitudes simply do not belong there. Immutable transcendent authority is the center of the poem; it is harsh and stark; it could not be otherwise.

The texture of reality and plenitudinous human actuality is not, for Milton (as it is for much of romanticism), part of the divine. The similes, from the obscene smell of flesh to that of the pagan hero, could only belong with Satan. The rich range of natural and mythical comparisons are part of the infernal, not just as ornament but in the deepest sense. Pagan wisdom, the qualities of the natural fallen world, sensory experience, the desires and mutabilities of times, pagan and secular codes of heroism, and even certain appearances of Christian work and virtue are more likely to be appropriate to the fallen state than to the immutable absolute. Satan, we might even suggest, is the hero, but the hero in a poetic vision in which heroism is rejected for a radical religious submission to transcendental authority.

The traditional modern question about the hero is hardly adequate. Satan, as so many of the similes emphasize, is not a person but a multiplicity, a poetic refraction of the iconography of the ultimately transitory immanent values and virtues which are worshipped in life but not in Heaven. It has often been noted that such paradoxes as the *felix culpa* and the assertion of " good from evil " are at the heart of Milton's longer poems. Perhaps we can also add to these paradoxes those of anti-heroic heroic poetry and the inversion of a mythology of regeneration into a mythology of renunciation. In any case, a subtle and dialectical reading of the Miltonic texture and tone suggests a fascinating and shocking master simile: the world as evil, and virtue as renunciation.

METAMORPHOSIS AND SYMBOLIC ACTION
IN *COMUS*

BY RICHARD NEUSE

It no longer seems necessary to conclude that because he was no Royalist Milton was Port-Royalist in his poetry. And quite aside from the fact that Milton was never a doctrinaire Puritan in the manner of William Prynne, say, increasing evidence has been presented lately to show that seventeenth-century Puritanism was by no means unalterably opposed to the realm of the aesthetic either in theory or practice. All the same, enough discordant strains continue to be heard at least in the criticism of what D. C. Allen has happily called the "harmonious vision" of Milton's verse, to make one realize that at certain crucial points the quality of that vision is still in doubt. In particular *Comus*, the concern of this essay, has seemed to many the product of a sensibility divided against itself. The delicate flower of the masque, it is often implied, withers under the icy blast of the poet's Puritan or simply youthful idealism.

Almost forty years ago Enid Welsford, in her admirable book on *The Court Masque*, expressed such a view, which in its essentials is, I believe, still prevalent today. "The essential moment" in *Comus*, she wrote,

> is not the presentation of the young people to their parents, but it is the steadfast refusal of the Lady to partake of the enchanted cup.... The hinge therefore on which *Comus* turns is not the solution of a riddle, not a sudden metamorphosis or revelation, but an act of free choice. This is most important, for it shows that difference in structure corresponds to a difference in spirit between *Comus* and the Court Masque; the masque is a dramatised dance, *Comus* is a dramatised debate.[1]

[1] *The Court Masque*: A Study in the Relationship Between Poetry and the Revels (Cambridge, 1927), p. 318. (For a recent view that *Comus* fulfills perfectly the demands of the Jonsonian masque form, see S. Orgel, *The Jonsonian Masque* [Harvard University Press, 1965], p. 102 f.) A. S. P. Woodhouse's well-known interpretation, "The Argument of Milton's *Comus*," *UTQ*, 11 (1941), 46-71, does recognize a certain complication in the Lady's enchantment but sees it as resolved by a progressive

This essay first appeared in *ELH*, Vol. 34, No. 1 (March 1967).

This idea of the poem's structure seems to me, if not incorrect, at least drastically incomplete. In concentrating on the overtly dramatic part it virtually ignores the sequel. The Lady's enchantment and release, that is, are treated here and in most subsequent interpretations as a mere concluding flourish to her refusal of the cup, or else as its fairly straightforward conclusion by the intervention of a superior power. Instead, I shall argue that the symbolic and ritual scenes of the Lady's paralysis and liberation by Sabrina present a genuine complication and resolution initiated by the original clash between the Lady and Comus.

It may well be that this clash reflects one that agitated Milton personally. In her idealism the Lady surely mirrors the erstwhile "Lady of Christ's." But it must be reemphasized that she does not have the last word in the poem, which means that Milton does not impose an abstract, arbitrary conclusion on the conflict but develops instead a resolution in the manner distinctive to the masque. This also seems truer to the probable biographical facts: it seems unlikely that Milton's "late spring" at Horton was a period of sublime self-assurance. What evidence we have points the other way; if nothing else, the problem of choosing a career must have involved a real struggle among competing ideals.

Is there a connection between that struggle and the conflict in *Comus*? I venture to suggest that there is. Roy Daniells in his discussion of the poem has a statement that seems to me beautifully apt in this connection and also anticipates a major part of my own conclusion:

Release and relief [he writes] from the clash between the sensuous world and the world of straining idealism comes from unconscious sources, from underneath the waters, from the flowery banks, from music and poetry and memory, and all the deep wells of nature's purity and innocence.[2]

How conscious Milton was of these implications as relevant to himself when he wrote the masque in 1634 it is impossible to say. But I believe that the anonymous publication of *Comus* in 1637, with the self-conscious Virgilian epigraph [3] marks his tacit ac-

---

removal from the human, natural realm to that of supernatural grace. As my discussion will indicate, this idea seems to me very questionable.

   [2] Cf. *Milton, Mannerism and Baroque* (Toronto, 1963), p. 37.

   [3] *Eheu quid volui misero mihi! floribus austrum / Perditus—*(Virgil, *Ecloques*, II, 58-9). The wind to which the poet has exposed his garden of verses is scarcely the trumpet of a prophecy, but the line does mark a moment of transition, of psychic metamorphosis. As I shall try to show, there is a like moment in *Comus*.

knowledgment of his love-affair with the Muse and of her relevance to his personal concerns: namely that precisely in and through poetry conflicting claims are reconciled. Despite its anonymity, therefore, I suggest that the publication of this " entertainment " should be viewed as his first publicly avowed commitment to the career of a poet.[4]

The foregoing is admittedly speculative. In what follows I shall strive to show that the theme of *Comus* is close to " pleasure reconciled to virtue " and involves the poet's traditional concern with the life of the senses rather than the exaltation of an ideal like virginity as a vehicle to the divine. This theme will be seen to spring, it is to be hoped, from a dramatic-symbolic structure that in true masque fashion, as Rosemond Tuve's fine essay has insisted,[5] always maintains an intimate relationship to a particular place and time. A recent tendency, therefore to read the poem as radical spiritual allegory of the Neoplatonic variety, does not seem to do justice to its particular mode of symbolization.[6] Sears Jayne, for instance, sees the Lady's imprisonment as in fact the triumphant climax of her flight from the flesh:

So long as she merely rejects Comus's attentions, she is merely fastened to the chair; thus innate human reason, uninstructed, is able temporarily to reject the passions; but ... [it] is still subject to temptation. Only when Comus has been banished by the haemony, that is, when reason is fortified by philosophic knowledge, does the soul banish temptation entirely; at the same time the departing Comus waves his wand and paralyzes the Lady completely, symbolizing the fact that only in this final rejection, both rational and philosophic, does the soul lose entirely its motion toward the flesh.[7]

[4] The nature of Milton's ' early development ' is still debated; the question of when he decided to become a poet has recently revolved around the problem of dating *Ad Patrem*; cf., e. g., J. Shawcross, " The Date of Milton's ' Ad Patrem,' " *N & Q*, 204 (1959), 358-9 [" around March 1638 "] D. Bush, " The date of Milton's *Ad Patrem*," *MP*, 61 (1964), 204-8 [1631-2]; J. Carey, " Milton's *Ad Patrem*, 35-37," *RES*, 15 (1964), 180-4 [possibly " as late as 1640 "].

[5] Cf. " Image, Form, and Theme in A MASK," *Images and Themes in Five Poems by Milton* (Cambridge, Mass., 1957), esp. pp. 112-20.

[6] Cf. J. Arthos, " Milton, Ficino, and the *Charmides*," *SR*, 6 (1959), 261-74; the same author's *On A MASK Presented at Ludlow Castle* (Ann Arbor, 1954); and S. Jayne, " The Subject of Milton's Ludlow Mask," *PMLA*, 74 (1959), 533-542.

[7] Jayne, p. 539. Jayne divides the action into three stages " corresponding to the three motions of the soul, descending, stopped, and ascending. We first see the soul moving away from God in the physical world. . . . Second we see the Soul halt its downward (or outward) motion; third we see it with the help of *mens* begin its upward (or inward) motion. . . . The human soul is represented jointly by the Lady

It is difficult to see how Comus' action of paralyzing the Lady can come to represent *her* act of rejecting him. Assuming haemony symbolizes ' philosophic knowledge,' who uses it, the Lady or her Brothers? The whole interpretation, moreover, ignores the Lady's soaring speech in answer to Comus' sophistries (ll. 762-99), and glosses over the fact that her paralysis appears to the Brothers and the Attendant Spirit as an unforeseen contretemps. Finally, it treats the saving appearance of Sabrina—identified without argument as symbol of the Neoplatonic *mens*—as the logical conclusion of a spiritual process, instead of a *peripeteia* that frees the captive and her would-be rescuers from perplexity.

Neoplatonic *allegoresis* that identifies man with his soul and treats the soul and its destiny as the only realities, tends perhaps inevitably to be cavalier in its treatment of narrative probabilities. In *Comus*, Milton is writing, I think, allegory of a different kind, Spenserian might be the word for it, that points both to the realm of spirit and to the realms of nature and history. (Sabrina is an example: she points to the historical past as daughter of Locrine; topographically, she points to the river Severn; and as mythical figure she has allegorical, spiritual significance.)

In this second kind of allegory, the figures are determined by, and remain imbedded in the dramatic context, so that we can never quite isolate them as conceptual counters derived from a stock of ready-made allegorical equivalents. Now, one feature of *Comus* on which a vast amount of exegetical effort has been expended is the haemony that the Attendant Spirit recommends as a protection against Comus. It has been defined principally as grace or philosophic knowledge, especially on the basis of Renaissance allegorizations of moly.[8] But it would be well to look closely at the actual description of the plant, which seems to have been largely ignored by the exegetes.

(Reason) or Sabrina (*mens*)" (pp. 538-39). To begin with, it seems unreasonable to interpret the Lady's journey to her father's house—even through a *selva oscura*—as an image of " the soul moving away from God." As regards the Lady's paralysis, Gregory the Great has an extremely suggestive analysis of the psychology of temptation, *Moralia in Iob*, II, 49; cf. the bilingual text, *Morales Sur Job*, Livres 1 et 2, tr. Dom André de Gaudemaris (Sources Chrétiennes; Paris, 1950), esp. pp. 237-38.

[8] Cf. Roger Ascham, *The Scholemaster* (London, 1895), pp. 74, 76-77, for a characteristically broad Renaissance interpretation. For " grace " cf. E. LeComte, " New Light on Milton's ' Haemony ' Passage in *Comus*," *PQ*, 21 (1942), 283-98. For " philosophic knowledge " see, e. g., J. Steadman, " Milton's *Haemony*: Etymology and Allegory," *PMLA*, 77 (1962), 200-207.

The Attendant Spirit tells how the dangers of Comus' magic reminded him of the plant's virtues:

> Care and utmost shifts
> How to secure the Lady from surprisal,
> Brought to my mind a certain Shepherd Lad
> Of small regard to see to, yet well skill'd
> In every vertuous plant and healing herb
> That spreads her verdant leaf to th'morning ray,
> He lov'd me well, and oft would beg me sing,
> Which when I did, he on the tender grass
> Would sit, and hearken even to extasie,
> And in requitall ope his leather'n scrip,
> And shew me simples of a thousand names
> Telling their strange and vigorous faculties;
> Amongst the rest a small unsightly root,
> But of divine effect, he cull'd me out;
> The leaf was darkish, and had prickles on it,
> But in another Countrey, as he said,
> Bore a bright golden flowre, but not in this soyle:
> Unknown, and like esteem'd, and the dull swayn
> Treads on it daily with his clouted shoon,
> And yet more med'cinal is it then that *Moly*
> That *Hermes* once to wise *Ulysses* gave;
> He called it *Haemony*, and gave it me,
> And bad me keep it as of soveran use
> 'Gainst all inchantments, mildew blast, or damp
> Or gastly furies apparition;
> I purs't it up, but little reck'ning made,
> Till now that this extremity compell'd, ...   (617-43)

The first point to notice is that haemony has undergone a metamorphosis from bright golden *flower* to unsightly *root*; and that in this metamorphosis it has yet maintained, at the base of life itself, within the dark soil, its divine or paradisal efficacy. Haemony thus illustrates the pastoral spirit of humility in its etymological sense of what is close to the soil (*humus*). At its lowliest, most fundamental level, where it is "unsightly" or of "small regard to see to," Nature preserves God's grandeur incorrupt, with "strange and vigorous faculties."

It seems to me the Spirit's language points us towards such a distinctively pastoral idea. For support of this interpretation we can refer to a tradition of root symbolism that has been superbly elucidated by Hugo Rahner and would certainly be known to Milton, for it extends from antiquity through the

Church Fathers to Renaissance alchemy.[9] In the words of Gregory the Great, by the root was understood

the nature of man, that nature that is the essential part of him. Even as a root ages in the ground and gradually begins to die, so it is with man, who, according to the nature of his flesh, resolves himself at the last into ashes. . . .[10]

Thus moly and mandragora are merely the most famous of the plants that were felt to express man's doubleness as both root and flower, product of the dark earth and yet able to " spread before heaven the white flower . . . of his conscious mind." This doubleness at the same time was felt as an antithesis or spiritual division in man that moly and mandragora, preeminently, had the power to heal. And so there are " rhizotomists " or

herbalists of the spiritual life who show us how to change ourselves from the black root into the white blossom, . . . [and] warn us that even in the flower which Helios has kissed awake that primal power still has dominion, which, in accordance with the mysterious law of spirit, has ascended out of the root.[11]

One side of man's dual nature is symbolized in *Comus* by the metamorphosis of the Attendant Spirit into the shepherd Thyrsis (parallel to that of haemony from golden flower to dark root). But significantly this metamorphosis or descent of Spirit does not resolve the perplexity of the Lady's enchantment. The solution lies, in pastoral fashion, at a lower level prefigured by the haemony root: Sabrina, the nymph within the river's waters, to whom the Attendant Spirit now makes his appeal.

The scene involving Sabrina might therefore be regarded as an express denial of the Neoplatonic notion of a *progressive* trans-

[9] Cf. H. Rahner, *Greek Myths and Christian Mystery*, tr. B. Battershaw (New York and Evanston, 1963), Ch. V, ' Moly and Mandragora in Pagan and Christian Symbolism.'

[10] *Moralia in Iob*, XII, 5, 7, cited by Rahner, p. 248. Cf. Augustine, *Enarrationes in Psalmos*, 51, 12, cited *ibid.*, p. 181.

[11] Rahner, p. 179. For classical sources connecting human beings with the earth (via the seed-soul), see E. M. Cornford, *From Religion to Philosophy* (Harper Torchbooks, New York, 1957), p. 165 f. (citing Plato, *Statesman*, 272E; *Timaeus*, 42D). For the traditional Biblical image of man as plant, cf. John Donne, *The Sermons*, ed. E. M. Simpson and G. R. Potter, Vol. IX, Sermon No. 5, p. 132: " God plants us, and waters, and weeds us, and gives the increase; and so God is *Hortulanus*, our Gardiner." In the medieval-Renaissance scientific tradition man is linked with plant-life by such concepts as ' vegetative soul,' ' radical humor,' etc. Cf. K. Svendsen, *Milton and Science* (Harvard University Press, 1956), pp. 180 f., 178, 115 ff.

substantiation. In the earthly dark forest spirit and matter, soul and body, maintain their dual claims upon the human person, and in the Lady's paralysis we seem to glimpse the *limitations* of pure spirit. For even as the Lady rightly repudiates Comus' temptation, she is held captive by him and cannot free herself by an effort of will or spirit. The latter, in the form of the Attendant Spirit, must turn elsewhere for help.

As we have seen, he calls upon Sabrina as an exemplary figure who in some ways is a parallel to the Lady. More importantly, Sabrina symbolizes a virtue or force in nature analogous to the haemony we have discussed. She likewise has undergone a metamorphosis: subjected to the threat of murder, like an Ovidian heroine she

> Commended her fair innocence to the flood
> That stay'd her flight with his cross-flowing course.
>
> (831-2)

After drowning and being bathed "[in] nectar'd lavers strew'd with Asphodil," she

> reviv'd
> And underwent a quick immortal change
> Made Goddess of the River. (840-42)

This divinization involves a sudden death and equally sudden rebirth, in a process as mysterious as it is beyond the conscious will. By way of contrast there are the Elder Brother's words about the chaste soul's "oft convers with heav'nly habitants" which casts

> a beam on th'outward shape,
> The unpolluted temple of the mind,
> And turns it by degrees to the soul's essence,
> Till all be made immortal. (459-63)

They imply a divinization that is deliberate, proceeding "by degrees" and not involving loss of conscious control or unforeseen catastrophe to the self.

After her divine rebirth in the waters, Sabrina—like the Attendant Spirit in this respect—henceforth performs her saving mission:

> still she retains
> Her maid'n gentlenes, and oft at Eeve
> Visits the herds along the twilight meadows,

Helping all urchin blasts, and ill luck signes
That the shrewd medling Elfe delights to make,
Which she with pretious viold liquors heals.
For which the Shepherds at their festivals
Carrol her goodnes lowd in rustick layes. . . .   (842-49)

By entrusting herself to the waters it would seem that Sabrina
comes to symbolize spirit at the other end of the scale from the
Attendant Spirit.[12] In the realm of flux she manifests through it
that spirit which in the intellectualist Platonic view is reserved
for a realm of transcendental fixity and permanence. As river
goddess she represents, not *mens,* but the ' lower,' unconscious
life of nature [13]—in a sacramental order. She rises in response
to the Spirit's appeal, and when she descends again, " the Lady
rises out of her seat " redeemed or healed.[14]

[12] The water-nymph Leucothea, mentioned in l. 875, represents a striking parallel
to Sabrina. C. G. Osgood, *The Classical Mythology of Milton's English Poems* (New
York, 1900), s. n., cites Homer, *Od.* 5. 333: ' Ino of the fair ankles, Leucothea, who
in time past was a maiden of mortal speech, but now in the depths of the salt sea
she had gotten her share of worship from the gods.' Also: Ovid, *Met.* 4. 513-41;
Fasti 6. 541 ff.

[13] The psychological symbolism of water and river is familiar; a couple of somewhat
random instances will suffice: Ficino, *in Phaedrum Commentaria et Argumenta*, Cap. I
(*Opera Omnia* [Basel, 1576], Vol. II, Tom. L, p. 1363):

Sed dum ad definiendum [Socrates] pergit, duo nobis tribuit duces, unum quidem
appetitum voluptati ingenitum: Alterum uerò legitimum quandam opinionem
acquisitam paulatim per disciplinam, & ad honesta ducentem. Verum hos nobis
intrinsecos duces extrinseci duo monent. *Daemon quidem aereus opinionem. Aqueus
uerò libidinem.*

In Donne's sermon on Genesis 1. 2, "And the Spirit of God moved upon the face
of the waters " (*The Sermons,* ed. Simpson and Potter, IX, No. 3), the waters represent
the unconscious source of man's regenerated existence (see esp. p. 103). There is
a tradition in which the lower, ' corporeal ' faculties are seen as the source of
illumination of the soul. In the *Timaeus* (70D-72D) the idea is primarily mantic,
religious: the lower faculties ' reflect ' divinely inspired images in dreams, ecstasy,
etc. Cf. M. W. Bundy, *The Theory of Imagination in Classical and Mediaeval Thought*
(Univ. of Illinois Studies in Language and Literature, 12 [1927], Nos. 2 and 3),
pp. 51 ff. For the subsequent development of this idea, up to the Middle Ages and
Dante, see the later chapters of Bundy's monograph, and for the Renaissance see
esp. R. Klein, " L'imagination comme vêtement de l'âme chez Marsile Ficin et
Giordano Bruno," *Revue de Métaphysique et de Morale* (1956, No. 1), pp. 18-39.
Under the influence of Aristotelian psychology, there develops a shift from the Platonic
rational-irrational dualism (and all that it implies) to a view of the potentially
harmonious and dynamic union of body and soul through the mediation of the
imagination-phantasy; cf. esp. Hugh of St. Victor, *De Unione Corporis et Spiritus,*
PL, 177, cos. 285-89; also Boehme, who uses both the water and flower imagery:
The Works of Jacob Behmen, the Teutonic Theosopher, trans. William Law (London,
1763-1781), I, p. 77.

[14] Stage direction following l. 920. Vertical movement is of great significance in the
poem, especially because the latter embodies a qualitatively structured world-picture

For just as haemony is " of soveran use / 'Gainst all inchant-
ments, mildew blast, or damp, / Or gastly furies apparition," so
Sabrina's " pretious viold liquors " heal all nature, including the
human, affected by " the shrewd medling Elfe." " Brightest Lady,"
Sabrina says,

> look on me,
> Thus I sprinkle on thy brest
> Drops that from my fountain pure,
> I have kept of pretious *cure*.   (910-13)

The Lady's encounter with Comus must, then, be seen from
more than an intellectual perspective, as an encounter with the
side of her nature below the threshold of rational consciousness.
Traditionally, indeed, Comus was conceived as an instinctual god
or *daimon*, and this aspect is suggested in Milton's masque by his
parentage (Bacchus and Circe) and his realm of operation (the
forest). It is his sophisticated rhetorical pretense to be a spokes-
man of natural principle that the Lady is bound to repudiate.[15]
But the point is that in the very moment of her own rhetorical
triumph she is paralyzed by the *daimon's* magic.

Hence there seems to be deliberate dramatic irony in the Elder
Brother's statement about the power of chastity:

> What was that snaky-headed *Gorgon* shield
> That wise *Minerva* wore, unconquer'd Virgin,
> Wherwith she freez'd her foes to congeal'd stone?
> But rigid looks of Chast austerity,
> And noble grace that dash't brute violence
> With sudden adoration, and blank aw.   (447-52)

Here is a fairly precise image, not of what the Lady does—she
does not meet with brute violence in any case—but rather of
what happens to her. In the clash of sensual nature and chaste
austerity (so I would take the allegorical meaning), there comes

---

in which place, above and below, has metaphysical significance, so that movement
upwards or downwards implies metaphysical change or metamorphosis. This is made
clear in the Spirit's descent through the spheres, down the Great Chain of Being.
The Spirit descends, Sabrina ascends, but at the end of the masque the Spirit's ascent
is an oblique one.

[15] Cf. W. G. Madsen, *The Idea of Nature in Milton's Poetry* in *Three Studies in
the Renaissance* (New Haven, 1958), "Comus and the Libertine Idea of Nature,"
pp. 186 ff. For sources and references on Comus as daimon in antiquity and the
Renaissance, cf. Arthos, *On A MASK*, p. 42. In the Trinity MS the Attendant Spirit
is called a daemon: hence the Lady is precisely situated between higher and lower,
celestial and earthly daemon.

about a paralysis. Sabrina's liberation of the Lady thus involves what is most profoundly natural in her, in that it is drawn up and presented to consciousness, as it were.

In this view Sabrina becomes a symbolic expression of man's lower nature seen truly in a new light, transformed, namely as no longer in conflict with spirit and reason, but as harmoniously responsive to them. It would seem that Milton envisioned the essential harmony and continuity between the sensual and spiritual faculties long before he wrote the Tree of Life passage in Book V of *Paradise Lost*:

> So from the root
> Springs lighter the green stalk, from thence the leaves
> More aerie, last the bright consummat floure
> Spirits odorous breathes: flours and thir fruit
> Mans nourishment, by gradual scale sublim'd
> To vital spirits aspire, to animal,
> To intellectual, give both life and sense,
> Fansie and understanding, whence the Soule
> Reason receives, and reason is her being.   (479-87) [16]

What in the Garden state is an unbroken continuity, however, must be recovered as such in the ' dark forest ' of this world. But even here a profound analogy between spirit and nature remains, which sometimes imperceptibly fuses into a metaphoric or emblematic identity, as in George Herbert's " The Flower ":

> Who would have thought my shrivl'd heart
> Could have recover'd greenesse? It was gone
> Quite under ground; as flow'rs depart
> To see their mother-root, when they have blown,
> Where they together
> All the hard weather,
> Dead to the world, keep house unknown.   (stanza 2)

Haemony and Sabrina undergo a death and a transfiguration, and this is paradigmatic for the human spirit that must find its roots, its own instinctual basis.

This paradigm in *Comus* is encompassed and reinforced by a seasonal pattern whose outlines can be traced in the poem. It is generally assumed that masques had their origin in the rituals of an agricultural people, and some scholars believe that the masque

---

[16] In this connection it is interesting to note that DuBartas links the Tree of Life with moly; cf. La Seconde Semaine, Premier Jour, l. 207 f. in U. T. Holmes, *et. al.*, eds., *The Works of Guillaume de Salluste Sieur Du Bartas*, Vol. III (Chapel Hill, 1940), p. 8.

never entirely lost sight of this origin.[17] The particular seasonal rite implicit in *Comus* would seem to be that of thanksgiving for the bounty of the soil. The idea is introduced obliquely when the Lady mistakes Comus' revelry—heard from a distance—for a harvest festival:

> This way the noise was, if mine ear be true,
> My best guide now, me thought it was the sound
> Of Riot, and ill manag'd Merriment,
> Such as the jocond Flute, or gamesom Pipe
> Stirs up among the loose unletter'd Hinds,
> When for their teeming Flocks, and granges full
> In wanton dance they praise the bounteous *Pan*,
> And thank the gods amiss.   (170-79)

Though Comus is of course not celebrating a harvest festival, his parodistic ritual does bear certain resemblances to it:

> We that are of purer fire
> Imitate the Starry Quire,
> Who in their nightly watchfull Sphears,
> Lead in swift round the Months and Years.   (111-14)

Finally, however, we do have a band of authentic country dancers appearing before the Lord President at the end of the poem (and it is tempting to see them as Comus' crew re-metamorphosed). "[N]ot many furlongs thence," says the Attendant Spirit to his young charges, "Is your Fathers residence,"

> Where this night are met in state
> Many a friend to gratulate
> His wish't presence, and beside
> All the Swains that there abide,
> With Jiggs, and rural dance resort,
> We shall catch them at their sport. . . .   (946 ff.)

And after the shepherds have danced for the benefit of the Earl— as to their Pan—the Spirit addresses them:

> Back Shepherds, back, enough your play,
> Till next Sun-shine holiday,
> Here be without duck or not
> Other trippings to be trod. . . .   (958 ff.)

[17] Cf. Ch. 1 of Welsford, *The Court Masque*, p. 8 and *passim*; also E. K. Chambers, *The Mediaeval Stage*, I, 203.

[18] According to the title-page of the 1637 edition, the masque was held "On Michaelmas night" (Michaelmas marking the beginning of winter), and Miss Tuve

Framed by the two dances, *Comus* firmly establishes its ritual occasion. The shepherds are celebrating both the Earl's investiture and the Michaelmas holiday: the munificence of nature and man's basic affinity with the rhythm of the seasons, the fruition, death, and longed-for rebirth of vegetation. And if the antimasque represents a profanation of the main masque's central rite,[19] then the dance of Comus and his crew is precisely a profane parody of the shepherds' concluding dance as well as of the courtly dance that follows. For though the shepherds' is prologue to the court's dancing, this *is* a pastoral masque that projects a harmony between them.

Comus, accordingly, is a threat just because he represents a nature really disjoined from spirit. A variant of the Lord of Misrule, he symbolizes the anarchic urge that recognizes no season, *mesure* or rhythm other than the rhythm of his own self-intoxication. At the same time, however, there turns out to be an affinity between Comus and Attendant Spirit after all: both are leaders of revels and by the end of the poem the Spirit speaks in the same tetrameter rhythm reserved earlier for Comus.[20] With the dispersal of Comus and his crew, therefore, the true *kōmos* can take place as the Attendant Spirit invites all

> To triumph in victorious dance
> O're sensual Folly, and Intemperance.   (974-75)

Furthermore, in the Epilogue the Spirit depicts a realm of perpetual youth that stands in direct contrast to the make-believe world of seasonless " waste fertility " into which Comus lures his followers.

The Spirit's timeless realm represents the completion of the seasonal cycle, in the manner of Spenser's Garden of Adonis, to which it is an extended allusion. In the Gardens of Hesperus,

> young *Adonis* oft reposes,
> Waxing well of his deep wound
> In slumber soft, and on the ground

---

states flatly that the late wassailers " are the Shropshire drunks of Michaelmas 1634 " (p. 129). Cf. Broadbent, p. 10, for further implications of Michaelmas, mention of which is omitted in the title of the 1645 and 1673 editions.

[19] Cf. W. T. Furniss, *Ben Jonson's Masques* in *Three Studies in the Renaissance*, p. 160.

[20] For further parallels between the two see Madsen, p. 179, Broadbent, p. 30. The kinship between Mercury and Attendant Spirit has often been remarked, and the latter names Mercury as the inventor of courtly revels (ll. 962-3).

> Sadly sits th'Assyrian Queen;
> But farr above in spangled sheen
> Celestial *Cupid* her fam'd Son advanc't,
> Holds his dear *Psyche* sweet intranc't
> After her wandring labours long. . . .   (999-1006)

Adonis, embodiment of the vegetative cycle, killed by the boar (of winter), revives or is reborn during a healing sleep: the scene reminds us of the Lady's trance in Comus' enchanted chair. And just as Adonis owes his recovery, in the Spenserian version of the myth, to the solicitous care of the goddess of earthly beauty— "th'Assyrian Queen" sitting "on the ground"—, so the Lady is saved from the 'wound' of Comus' rod by Sabrina rising from the river's waters.

Like Adonis, Psyche is presented as about to awaken in the arms of Cupid from the deathlike trance that overcame her when, having descended to the underworld, she looked into Proserpina's cask. And like Psyche, the Lady has undergone a trial (cf. ll. 970 ff.), her "wandring labours long" through the forest. This, then, implies the *active* side of her nature, which does more than passively suffer or undergo transformation, is indeed a precondition for it. We remember that the Spirit presents his golden world as the goal of the soul's active aspirations.

The psyche, awakening from its final ordeal, is reborn into a new and fuller existence—in the arms of celestial Cupid. It has become worthy of, and united with, the love which was its motive power and goal. Now it also holds the promise of fruitfulness, for

> from her fair unspotted side
> Two blissful twins are to be born,
> Youth and Joy; so *Jove* hath sworn.   (1009-11)

In substituting Youth and Joy for Apuleius' (and Spenser's) Pleasure, Milton is, I think, among other things adapting the myth to his own fable of youth. The youthfulness of the Lady and her Brothers needs no emphasis, and yet it is often forgotten in discussions which consequently miss a good deal of the poet's gentle irony in the treatment of his characters. At any rate, I would read much of the Epilogue's imagery as a great emblem of youth, and the coupling of youth and joy as implying an increased inner ripeness which the Lady has now achieved.

Youth at the same time may be conceived as a state rather than a stage of life, the state of joy which is ageless youth, so to speak. As such, it calls up erotic allegory like the *Romance of the Rose*, where Youth is inside the garden of love and Eld outside.[21] In this perspective, the " Gardens fair / Of *Hesperus*, and his daughters three / That sing about the golden tree " (981-3) become a vision of the soul that recognizes the source of its vitality and revels in the possession of its freedom.

In the Epilogue we may be supposed to see the Spirit in his "ambrosiall weeds" again as he is poised for renewed flight. Another metamorphosis he has certainly undergone: his couplets are reminiscent not only of Comus' but also of Ariel's and Puck's. No longer the stage magician, he turns into the aerial spirit who has discovered, or recovered, the playful sense of boundless possibility characteristic of the poetic imagination:

> . . . now my task is smoothly done,
> I can fly or I can run
> Quickly to the grean earth's end,
> Where the bow'd welkin slow doth bend
> And from there can soar as soon
> To the corners of the Moon.   (1012-17)

And the significant point, as the language here suggests, is that the Spirit appears humanized, almost naturalized now, as the result of a changed attitude to the earth. By way of contrast, here is the stern perspective of his opening speech on

> this dim spot
> Which men call Earth, and with low-thoughted care
> Confin'd and pester'd in this pinfold here. . . .   (5. ff.)

Heaven and earth, which there seemed unimaginably remote from each other, now come together at " the *green earth*'s end, / Where the bow'd welkin slow doth bend." And the Spirit is returning, not to the Platonic halfway house at an unearthly height (" Before the starry threshold of Jove's court "), but to the ocean and the earthly paradise whose names are legion.

Hence " those happy climes that lie / Where day never shuts his eye, / Up in the broad fields of the sky " (977-79), are both a pattern of celestial bliss and a promise of what the real world can be, as heaven and earth meet, virtue and pleasure are reconciled, and all seasons temperately join:

[21] A tradition going back to Claudian's *Epithalamium for Honorius*; see C. S. Lewis, *The Allegory of Love* (Oxford, 1936), p. 75. Comus also excludes " Strict Age [= Eld], and sour Severity " (109) from his world of midnight revelry.

> Iris there with humid bow,
> Waters the odorous banks that blow
> Flowers of more mingled hue
> Than the purfl'd scarf can shew. . . .   (992 ff.)

The rainbow is a promise of the joining of heaven and earth, and
symbol of its fulfillment. More significantly, perhaps, to and in
the soul that loves virtue and follows the call of spirit, heaven
and earth will meet even " within the navel " (520) of the dark
forest—as the Lady states in lines, fortunately concelled, in the
Trinity MS, where she addresses the Platonic forms of Faith,
Hope, and Chastity:

> I see ye visibly, & while I see yee
> this dusky hollow is a paradise
> & heaven gates ore my head now I beleeve.[22]

Here is indicated the possibility of a transforming imaginative
vision. But as the cancellation of the lines indicates, this possibility had to be reserved to the end as something only realized
through the experience or ritual of the masque. And it is appropriate that it should be expressed by the Spirit, who comes to be
seen as a representation, almost a definition, of the functions and
limits of poetry, in particular of the kind of poetry represented
by the masque. For an assumption of the masque is that its
Platonic forms, enacting a ritual drama, can transform the (social)
reality which they serve.

Thus there is a dual metamorphosis in the masque's ' program '
to restore the golden age or world: the metamorphosis of the
Platonic forms into active participants in the realm of human
trial and error, the " seeming show of things "; and the metamorphosis of the social world, as represented by masquers and
audience, when the two come together and mingle in the final
dance. There we have a heightened reality where make-believe
and actuality, fiction and ' real life ' are momentarily indis-
tinguishable.

By its very hyperbole, then, the masque could insist on a kind
of magic, a magic mediating between the world of ideal forms
and the world of social fact. For in a highly significant strand
of Renaissance esthetics, the Platonic Idea, brought down to earth

---

[22] Ll. 44 ff. in the transcription in *John Milton's Complete Poetical Works* Reproduced in Photographic Facsimile, compiled and edited by H. F. Fletcher, Vol. 1
(Urbana, 1943), p. 404.

and given poetic, visible form, had incalculable powers of operation and of stimulating imaginative-philosophic insight.[23] Consequently, those critics who see the realm of the Epilogue as altogether transcendental, otherworldly,[24] seem to me mistaken; like Spenser's Garden of Adonis it is "on earth," though where "I wote not well":

> But well I wote by tryall, that this same
> All other pleasant places doth excell. . . .   (FQ 3. 6. 29)

Just as Hesperus' garden could serve Jonson as a symbol of James I and his court, so the Gardens of Hesperus in the Epilogue can serve as an archetype of the 'true' England or even of "all this tract that fronts the falling Sun" which "A noble Peer of mickle trust and power / Has in his charge" (30-32).

Finally, however, the Epilogue is to be seen, I think, as itself a form of (verbal) action. And in this respect it passes beyond the realm of social ritual and magic to something that antecedes it: the personal, the individual human soul. In the pictured flight to the earthly paradises of the imagination, the Spirit becomes a dramatic image or projection of the human spirit realizing this condition of flight within itself. The Spirit has the last word, after the dancing, to point up that the other, golden world presented by the masque has its true origins deep within the mind, in the motions of the poetic spirit imitable by all mortals. And so, with the final injunction to "Mortals that would follow me," and the image of heaven stooping down to earth, the Spirit dissolves into pure spirit and the revels are ended.

---

[23] Cf. E. H. Gombrich, "*Icones Symbolicae*: The Visual Image in Neo-Platonic Thought," *JWCI*, 11 (1948), 163-92; also E. Panofsky, *Idea*: Ein Beitrag zur Begriffsgeschichte der älteren Kunsttheorie (Leipzig, 1924). For the masque, see esp. Ch. 6, "Court Hieroglyphicks," in A. Nicoll, *Stuart Masques and the Renaissance Stage* (London, 1937).

[24] Cf., e. g., J. Arthos, "The Realms of Being in the Epilogue of *Comus*," *MLN*, 86 (1961), 321-24; Broadbent, p. 31.

MILTON'S LUDLOW *MASK*:
FROM CHAOS TO COMMUNITY

BY GALE H. CARRITHERS, JR.

In the dark a bit ourselves, we recognize two boys groping in unfamiliar surroundings, speaking at length not so much to each other as each to recruit his own distracted spirits. The first speech, by Elder Brother (like the earlier and more familiar entry-speeches of Spirit and Lady), sketches a great deal of the realm of discourse and general dramatic situation in the first part of this resonantly poetic masque:

> Unmuffle ye faint stars, and thou fair moon
> That wontst to love the travailers benizon,
> Stoop thy pale visage through an amber cloud,
> And disinherit *Chaos*, that raigns heer
> In double night of darknes, and of shades;
>
> (331-335)[1]

The very title stuck so misleadingly on this masque by eighteenth century adapters prompts us to mutter 'not Chaos, but Comus,' and it was no faint personage from " before the starry threshold of *Joves* court " we saw unmuffled as the action began. And before long we will see neither fair moon nor allegorical Cynthia but the better and more remarkable Sabrina lovingly earning " travailers benizon." But the boys' terms, their perplexity, the inadequacy of their apprehension, and the changfulness of their situation from antecedent action to conclusion, all invite us to scrutinize what is going on, and frame a new, more nearly exact and inclusive appraisal.

A densely poetic masque must be one of the most difficult artifacts for this generation's criticism to take coherent account of. Published criticism of Milton's Ludlow *Mask*, for all its erudition and acuity, has tended to move back and forth on single steps

---

[1] " A Mask " (based on 1645 text), in *The Complete English Poetry of John Milton*, ed. John T. Shawcross (New York, Doubleday, 1963); all quotations are from this edition.

This essay first appeared in *ELH*, Vol. 33, No. 1 (March 1966).   103

half-way or so up the stairs that extend from particular lines and events of the masque to its most general implications and significances. These " steps "—such as light and dark, or virginity, chastity, trial, and the like—have their place in the working of this masque, and all of us who take Milton seriously will be greatly in debt to Miss Tuve, to Messers Jayne, Madsen, Tillyard, Brooks and Hardy, Woodhouse, Allen, and others. On the other hand, criticism attentive to the dramatic way of this poem has tended to collapse into minutely particular, usually biographical, facts of the initial presentation; clearly we must live with those facts, but this lively masque does not entirely live by them, so neither need we. This exercise in definition aims, then, to promote discussion of this poignantly lyrical masque in terms less static, stratified, and piece-meal. A good poem is not a flight of stairs; it is at least more like an escalator. This masque-poem appears to me to be animated by an ideal of community, more particularly a lively established community reinforcing itself by a significantly precarious process of recruitment. This ideal of community, explicitely stated nowhere but actuating speech and action everywhere, appears to be no less a conviction than that the true earthly fulfillment of man is free participation in loving, God-seeking society. Such loving concord, permitting orientation and aspiration towards " the Palace of Eternity," would seem to be the cosmos to " disinherit *Chaos.*" And the two appear to be concurrently available, never far apart.

Refinements might be urged on this definition, perhaps in the direction of more traditional formulations such as " the household of faith " or " the city of God." But something of the kind seems indispensable if we are to assimilate the thematic sense of the boys' large roles, of lines reading " Mortals . . . Love vertue, she alone is free " (instead of ' Girls, love chastity, she alone is wise.') , of why Thyrsis " Longer . . . durst not stay " (577) , of the dynamism in this least tableau-like masque.

The bulk of the action involves three young people moving from threatened isolation and from relative passivity, to relative activity and charitable commitment, attending " their Father's state." They are like all men, " confin'd and pester'd in this pinfold " but can serve in special exemplary ways partly because " nurs't in princely lore " to be mindful of crowns and partly because of their own aspiration " by due steps . . . To lay thir just hands on that golden key/That opes the palace of Eternity."

We might call the two brothers and the sister children, knowing as we do that the young Egertons were only nine, eleven, and fifteen years old in 1634; but the 17th century like earlier centuries tended to regard children as compact adults, and this poem does not really treat them as small children. In any case, they move out of the tutorial closet into the woods, and finally to an earthly counterpart of heavenly mansion.[2] Doing so, they learn needful lessons which are complex, mysterious, and above all social, and they learn as recruits to a free world's work. Since we were early told that most "tast through fond intemperate thirst" (67), we are further obliged to see them as the surviving minority in a tremendously costly battle, a fact which poignantly qualifies Elder Brother's premature announcement that "virtue may be assail'd but never hurt."

The Spirit defines the danger impending from Comus and his rout not as a breach of reason (or of virginity) but of charitable community: the beguiled ones

> . . . all thir freinds and native home forget
> To roul with pleasure in a sensual stie.
>
> (76-77)

Appropriately, figures in the rout, albeit a sort of group, are visibly disaffiliated by heads resembling *disparate* beasts. With more clearly Christian conviction,[3] the Spirit notes that those sinners' sins are, in orthodox fashion, self-blinding, even ludicrously so: they

> Not once perceave thir foul disfigurement,
> But boast themselves more comely then before
>
> (74-75)

[2] Cleanth Brooks and John E. Hardy, "Essays in Analysis," in *Poems of Mr. John Milton; The 1645 Edition* (New York, Harcourt, Brace and Co., 1951), p. 191. I have noted some positive debts to this essay (hereafter as "Brooks and Hardy"), and those familiar with it will notice here many divergences of emphasis and interpretation which (being sometimes conscious disagreement) make a kind of general witness to the stimulating quality the essay still has. See also Sears Jayne, "The Subject of Milton's Ludlow *Mask*," *PMLA* LXXIV (1959), 533-543, p. 542, where the Earl has to be less an agent than a figure of God; but the article is the most substantial argument for the masque as a Platonic allegory of chastity.

[3] Don Cameron Allen observes that some of its "characters are uncertain about their theology and their chronology." Exactly; most children and adolescents do not often *feel* themselves to be living in a world other than pagan, or in the years of our Lord. See "Milton's *Comus* as a Failure in Artistic Compromise," *ELH* XVI (1949), 104-119, pp. 117-118.

These things hold true or threaten significantly even for the young three. Their apparent community does not bear inspection: it shows itself to be centrifugal, idiosyncratic, extremist.

The symbolic and psychological landscape permits the unfolding action to show very quickly the relationships of the three not only to one another and to other characters, but to various components of reality.[4]

The Elder Brother begins authoritatively with the lines first quoted, all part of an adjuration to stars, moon, or even "a rush candle" to "disinherit *Chaos*" and "usurping mists" or to provide at least a "long levell'd rule of streaming light" (340). *Disinherit, usurping*, and the doubly meaningful *rule* bespeak a lively sense in him of issues which animate the action. Such notions are present to him in a categorical, rational fashion that serves well a moment later when he sanely cautions the Second Brother against "over-exquisite" (albeit valid) conjectures of "Savage hunger, or of Savage heat" (358). But he quickly betrays a speculative and quasi-philosophical egotism which disables him for dealing with the world around him. Brooks and Hardy rightly emphasize both the possibility and the unawareness on his part that the real world may not "square with the ideal one which he has constructed for himself" (p. 205). But more than that, his style as he *thinks* he appraises the real world veers from distortion to distortion in a way which may seem at first simply to jumble abstraction and concreteness. Always, though, his style depersonalizes his subject and favors the conceptual. He dismisses what he takes to be only literal and material: the "single want of light and noise" (369) should indeed *not* "stir the constant mood" of his sister's thoughts—*if* light and noise were totally unsymbolic, a presupposition valid presumably only if she were a stone. But as her situation (like modern brain-washing and experimental evidence) shows, sense-deprivation usually disorients

[4] We might expect from the young poet who proclaimed his admiration for Spenser that characters in the woods may be ethically in the shade. And Spenser's currency with that audience argues for the plausibility and dramatic viability of the poetic density I shall outline. Readers who do have the *Faerie Queene* fresh in the mind will readily see kinships between the Mask and elements in the stories of Florimell (besieged by Proteus), Amoret (by Busyrane), Belphoebe, even Britomart, Acrasia's bower; but readers who do not have that in mind would be helped not at all by definitions in terms which would in any case take more space. William Madsen makes briefly the basic point about the landscape: "The Idea of Nature in Milton's Poetry," in *Three Studies in the Renaissance* (New Haven, Yale, 1958), p. 197.

a person and unsettlingly confronts him with fantasy, with figures from memory and imagination. Elder Brother magnifies the conceptual: virtue seeing " to do what virtue would," automatically, as a quasi-personified virtue by definition might see, but less diversely than the Lady and any whole person does see, " wisdoms self " with " nurse Contemplation " and feathers (" to ruffl'd " feathers, at that), an unspecified *he* with a by-now-symbolic light " within his own cleer breast " (381). By the time Elder Brother comes with avuncular roundness to " 'Tis chastity, my brother, chastity " (420), he is endowing his conceptual heritage from more or less Biblical traditions of the armor of righteousness with " complete steel " and " sacred rays " more substantial than the material world. Accordingly, we are given as dependent clause of logical concession, " Be it not done in pride or in presumption " (431), what is a practical focus of the play.

He executes dramatically a kind of rising turn into inanity continuing full circle into the interchange with " Thyrsis " before subsiding into step with that guide's wisdom. In the speech beginning with the sober practicality of " Peace brother, be not over-exquisite " (359) he quickly launches into elevations, circumlocutions, slippery equivalences, quasi-philosophical verbosities as if words were magic enough without community association. In this context, even if wisdom " lets grow her wings," would not the growth be the less-than-natural fecundity of mere verbosity? The " to ruffl'd " feathers are a vehicle without a tenor, their condition " sometimes impair'd " a generality without any particulars. Thence, within a few lines, to a catalogue of static counters— *virgin purity, unblench't majesty, congeal'd stone, rigid looks, a soul . . . found* (427-454) and on to the building-block construction of a romance landscape charming, surely, in its over-exquisiteness: " defilement to the inward parts . . . clotted by contagion . . . shadows damp . . . in charnel vaults " (466-471). By another half-turn in a following speech he comes to a practical suggestion about the immediate situation which by its arbitrary and fanciful impracticality (it is a quasi-epic boast) puts Thyrsis to his best courtesy:

> Ile . . . drag him by the curls and cleave his scalp
> Down to the hipps.
>
> (606-609)

On the other hand there could of course be no heroic tradition or legacy of philosophy such as those genuflected to in the masque —or even any society to make the masque possible, meaningful, and gratifying—without the words and verbal structures Elder Brother relishes.

The Second Brother's style generally complements his elder's. He deals in materiality. His sense of the outside world and processes does not assess realities welling from within which have directed that world or might re-direct it. In a variation on the masque's pervasive theme of freedom, he posits an external, material " dungeon " of " innumerous bows " (349). Elder Brother posits an internal, negative " dungeon " (384), prison-like because unfurnished with his compendious abstractions " Virtue " and " Wisdom." Elder Brother pooh-poohs " the single want of light and noise " (369). Second Brother avers:

> Of night or lonelines it recks me not,
> I fear the dred *events* that *dog* them both
>
> (404-405; my italics)

Second Brother has his abstractions—beauty, incontinence, Danger, opportunity—but they sink in a redolence of depersonalizing *things*: " her blossoms," " her fruit," " rash hand," and the like. And what dare we expect from the lad who says " unsun'd heaps of misers treasure " when those words indirectly label the virginity of that prim Lady who says " Faith . . . Hope . . . Chastity," and who speaks more impressively of the " Sun-clad power of Chastity." But he rises to a new style, a change of heart, personal and humbly concerned: " I fear . . . Lest some ill greeting touch attempt the person/Of our unowned sister " (405-407). And in any case the *Mask* does insist that those who would go to heaven must tread on the ground.

Elder Brother needs external prompting. Thyrsis, by voice and person and associations with madrigals, chastens him (slightly) with benign reminders of aesthetic, graceful communication in a natural and humane world. The Shepherd's very greeting invokes relationships of affection, civic order, lineage, and calling in one, two, three, four order:

> O my lov'd maisters heir, and his next joy
>
> (501)

He asks " O my virgin Lady, where is she? " She is in trouble, we know. But criticism has sometimes noticed only the outward side of that trouble. For her neither Elder Brother's conceptualizing detachment, nor Second Brother's unassimilated outwardness. She has the strengths of both tendencies, perhaps, with little of the related weakness. Moreover, her predicament has acute poignancy. Her opening lines are surely no simple rehearsal of a Renaissance hierarchy of the senses:

> This way the noise was, if mine ear be true,
> My best guide now;

A word stressed by metrics and situation is *now*. Her eye may have been a better guide before, but the whole poem asks whether either was or is now *adequate*. She has moved out of the study and into a world of " Riot " and conversation and summons. She continues scornfully on themes of " ill manag'd merriment " supposedly by " loose unlettr'd hinds " who are assumed " in wanton dance " to " thank the gods amiss." The play would seem to define these sentiments as uncharitable, Shepherds and " swains " carol and dance acceptably enough in the description by Thrysis late in the play (849), and at the festival at her " Fathers residence " near the end (947).

Her soliloquy in this peculiar landscape unfolds more of her misorientations and indispositions toward the world. Milton has formulated a domain which shows good and ill partly by externalizing them and which tends to make equally material those things taken to be more or less equally real. In this landscape, chastity manifests itself to Comus as a " different pace," " footing " on its more purposeful journey in contrast to his " light fantastick round " (144-146). This would seem not so much a case of ' the order of grace *versus* the order of nature ' as a matter of less and more *inclusive*, less or more orderly modes of reality in nature. " Good is as visible as green," as Donne said in a differently ironic context (" Communitie," 14). Goodness and greenness have a roughly equal materiality in two ways, of course: within the mind, as notions, and in the external world, in some of their consequences. The Lady externalizes, disengages, and fragments good and ill.

She errs, even if somewhat engagingly, in thinking the woods " kind " and " hospitable " (187; unless one takes *kind* also in its other sense, ' having blood relationship,' and hence as ironic truth). She errs by thinking the sylvan world in seeming "palmers weeds " of evening will provide for her and her brothers in the way she herself would prescribe, the naively flashy way of golden wings and " glistring " guardians (214, 219). The " quaint habits " of Comus when he does appear are supposed to look " glistring " to the audience, but not to her bleared and beguiled eye (153-167). The poignant element in this deepens presently in her plaintive comment on eye and ear at odds:

> . . . mirth
> Was rife and perfet in my list'ning ear,
> Yet nought but single darknes do I find.
>
> (202-204)

The pettish egotism deepens in her attributing to " envious darkness " and " theevish night " a " fellonious end," as if the travellers were only " mis-led and lonely," were altogether passive and unresponsible.

Darkness here is neutral, of course, save insofar as it is a projection of the observer's self. In that character it quickly appears: " A thousand fantasies/Begin to throng into my memory . . . pure-ey'd Faith, white-handed Hope . . . And thou unblemish't form of Chastity,/I see ye visibly " (205-216). Roundabout genealogies from neoplatonism, and Bacon on the attractiveness of virtue if visible, obscure the point. Surely the most relevant source and influence is the most immediate one, the familiar Pauline passage at I Corinthians 13:13, and the wit here turns on diverted expectation, and invites a smile of benevolent seniority. The Lady's disproportionate concern with the negative—with *un-blemished* chastity (instead of, say, resplendent charity), with pure-eyed faith not explicitly viewing anything, with white-handed hope not explicitly offering or receiving, with a " Supreme good " noteworthy for " officers of vengeance," with even " love-lorn " nightingale (234)—all this comes out of her own mind. That it comes naturally in the dramatic situation is just the point: showing and educating her natural self is the double work underway. Something must fuse, liberalize, make benevolent the elements of her being and the world she takes—comically or fatally but all too crisply—as separate, like the thoughts and walking mind (210-211), or " mind " and " corporal rind " (a jarring jingle; 663-664). She briefly figures as the Manichaean in the group.

If Second Brother was in an inchoate sense the perennial Lucretian (and hence the most novelistic character), Comus stands further in that line as the being who has committed his will to the materialistic, deterministic round, is thereby demonic and closer to romance or to tragedy. Elder Brother's will churns actively enough so that the possibility of tragedy (like that of burlesque) just begins to show (as in his arrogant proclamation " if this fail,/The pillar'd firmament is rott'nness " 598). But, as suggested earlier, his naive version of the perennial conviction that 'the world is my idea' does offer entries to redemptive ideas, whereas Comus's representation to himself and the Lady of reality appears in diction and image as a tissue of reductive ideas. In his first speech he offers *Joy, feast, shout, dance* without *Rigor, Advice, age, severity*. Light and dark are less cosmic than appetitive alterations (" gilded car of day/His glowing axle doth allay . . . slope sun his upward beam/Shoots *against* the dusky pole ") which in turn control values: " 'Tis only daylight that makes sin " (93-144). In his second speech (244-265), he expresses surprise, after the Lady's song, that " somthing holy " might lodge in " Earths mould " and master brute nature, as testified by " vocal air "; he immediately himself longs to subdue this strange mixture to his brute-natural will. His seduction speeches propose imagistically an interior life dominated by naturalistic, exterior forms:

> . . . all the pleasures
> That fancy can *beget* on youthful thoughts
> (668-669; my italics)

His exterior life puts the goddess Natura in charge (" dainty limms which nature lent ") and lets " mortal frailty " subsist along with " shops " and consumption and something like a death-wish (see 715-736), but not 'mortal strength,' still less 'immortality.'

He does not simply personify a sexual license antithetical to a narrowly, negatively conceived chastity; his remarks point toward a rejection of the work of daylight, of nature, nurture, and the *polis*, toward chaos. Brothers and Lady have made no such rejection, but only by the end have they moved and been moved to harmonious commitment to night, day, nature, nurture, and *polis*.[5]

[5] David Wilkinson asserts the poem concerns itself primarily with chastity and secondarily with family solidarity, but denies that the sub-theme works independently of the special factors involved in the first performance. See " The Escape from

Movement and a journey dramatic, literal, and symbolic loom large in the play.[6] "Where else shall I inform my unacquainted feet" asks the Lady (180), who later speaks of "this leavy Labyrinth." The Spirit begins by adverting to "due steps" of virtuous travellers; he later describes his encounter with Comus in terms of a bird on earth:

> I knew the foul inchanter though disguis'd,
> Enter'd the very lime-twigs of his spells,
> And yet came off
>
> (645-647)

At the end he says "follow me, Love vertue . . . She can teach ye how to clime" (1018-1020). In similar vein are various references to the travels of "wise Ulysses." Comus participates in this pattern of describing the human condition, but with a difference. He will attempt to lie, but will ironically speak truth:

> I can conduct you Lady . . .
> . . . where you *may* be safe
> Till furder *quest*.
>
> (319-321; my italics)

Or he will introduce some relatively inharmonious note, like the fruitless roundy-go-round of

> Com, knit hands, and beat the ground,
> In a light fantastick round.
>
> (143-144)

All this is as it should be for aesthetic and thematic unity. Milton is no Manichaean, and Comus cannot create, work, even propose things, *ex nihilo*. He testifies to cosmos over chaos sometimes even when trying to lie (like Chaucer's Pardoner):

> It were a journey like the path to Heav'n,
> To help you find them.
>
> (303-304)

He self-disqualifyingly pictures as bad (even if it were possible) something clearly good in terms of Renaissance iconography (if only it were possible):

Pollution. A Comment on *Comus*," *Essays in Criticism* X (1960), 32-43, and rejoinders by Geoffrey Rans, pp. 364-369, and William Leahy, *EIC* XI (1961), 111.

[6] For a recent and convenient compendium illustrating the journey as a commonplace in Renaissance art and literature, see Samuel C. Chew's *The Pilgrimage of Life* (New Haven, Yale Univ., 1962), especially chaps. 6 and 7.

To gaze upon the sun with shameless brows.

(736)

Comus participates in that reciprocal definition of outer and inner life already introduced. The Spirit later proclaims that " unbeleif is blind " (519), a kind of night akin to that materialized on stage as a setting for the young three's set of ignorances, non-affiliations, misbeliefs, and presumptions. In a way symbolic " daylight " does " make sin " in making it apprehensible. To describe hearing the Lady's song, the Spirit invokes " drowsy-flighted steeds " which seemingly figure languid rhythmic progressions alike of night and sleep, and " breathing sound " like perfumes (possibly the most internal and intimate of sense apprehensions), and a creaturely " Silence," soothed, " took e're she was ware " (558). He " took in strains that might create a soul/Under the ribs of Death." Silence is " took " rather than ended, and the fruitful union of song and silence " might create a soul." Comus heard the song as a like fusion of externality and internality, and activity and passivity, but he, in contrast, orients the experience hedonistically; of " these raptures " he exclaims:

> How sweetly did they float upon the wings
> Of silence, through the empty-vaulted night,
> At every fall smoothing the raven down
> Of darknes till she smil'd:
>
> (249-252)

Darkness, not an element of social communication, is titillated; silence buoys up speech, is simply an inert medium, not a dynamic counterpart. The whole configuration diverges markedly in coordination, purposiveness, and fertility from the analysis proposed by the spirit. Elder Brother's ears might be presumed to have taken in the strains had his tongue not been so engaged in spinning out variations on the figures of bird/communication[7] and daylight/virtue:

> And wisdoms self
> Oft seeks to sweet retired solitude,
> Where with her best nurse Contemplation
> She plumes her feathers, and lets grow her wings
> That in the various bustle of resort

---

[7] Worth reiterating in this connection: the Lady sings of " love-lorn nightingale," and the Spirit characterizes her as " poor hapless nightingale " (566). She likens the brothers to Narcissus. And the " spungy air " (154) which is the medium for Comus's " dazzling Spells " seems significantly unfit for graceful flight or sound.

Were all to ruffl'd, and somtimes impair'd.
He that has light within his own cleer breast
May sit i'th center, and enjoy bright day,

(375-382)

But although the Lady herself comes to sit fixedly i'th'centre,
" freez'd . . . to congeal'd stone " (449; astounded, despite her
contrary expectation in 210) while her foes remain mobile, neither
she nor her brothers enjoy bright day. Her trial and her brothers'
constitute the second phase of the action. The opening three hundred lines or so have shown in the main an apparently close-knit
group which disintegrates. The second phase, not enough looked
at coherently, shows the effects under trial of the nurtures already
defined as strong but not strong enough.

The Lady goes off-stage, beginning the part of her journey to be
made in the company of Comus, with remarks which are a significant overture to the trial. She speaks in terms which subsume
and go beyond even a large concept of chastity:

> Shepherd, I take thy word
> And trust thy honest offer'd courtesie,
> Which oft is sooner found in lowly sheds
> With smoaky rafters, then in tapstry halls
> And courts of princes, where it first was nam'd
> And yet is most pretended: In a place
> Less warranted than this, or less secure
> I cannot be, that I should fear to change it;
> Eye me blest providence, and square my triall
> To my proportion'd strength. Shepherd lead on.—
>
> (321-330)

Several things invite comment here. Her imagery restlessly implies
one kind of sensory experience after another, as if pointing up the
question of which shall be primary in revealing truth.[8] Shall it be
the primarily auditory taken word or named name of courtesy,
the primarily visual " tapstry " or " Eye me," the odorous, eye-
smarting tactile smoky rafters, the kinesthetic *lowly* (or squared
trial or proportioned strength) or shepherd leading. She shows
obvious hubris in her basic assumption that she can apprehend
truly. Her conventional paean to pastoralism shows irony both
general and immediate, ending as it does in the most ironic mis-
placement of trust since " Honest Iago." If she is right about the

---

[8] Similarly Second Brother, at lines 342-349, has implored that an earful of mobile
associations amid appropriate frames of order serve in the place of habitual vision.

location of true courtesy, then what is to fear in woods most likely peopled with low shed-dwellers? The projections of her own mind? The play moves ultimately by song, dance, and story to establish the stylistic, aesthetic, intellectual, moral primacy of something contrasting with pastoral and broader than "courtly," the superiority of—call it—the civic, or the communal.

Simple justice here demands careful righting of the balance and clarification. If we consider the three young people as regularly in situation, speech, and action a bit wide of the full truth, and in ways uneasily mixed as to emotional and evaluative implications, then we have smelled out irony. But ascribing irony seems to summon up for most of the people likely to be reading the *Mask* a motley parade of knaves and fools, the remembered figures of their literary touchstones. Clearly Milton has not drawn any Egerton child parallel to a Shylock exultantly croacking "A Daniel, come to judgment" nor to a Malvolio, cross-gartered in *his* inordinate hopes, nor to a cynical manipulator of language like Mark Antony in the forum, nor to those worshippers of false deity Othello and Desdemona. Milton has presented brothers and Lady as never quite oriented towards a bad or self-seeking cause, and mistaken in ways which often would be less mistaken in a better world. The ironies invite the wry or rueful chuckle a little heart-burnishly kept from condescension by the knowledge of having in some sense been there, or invite the twinge of recognition that naive mis-steps can entail hurt that must humanly seem large in proportion. And we, the viewers of masque, by definition do not want the heroes and heroines of masque hurt at all, although we may in comedic vein want them reformed or married.[9]

Within that broad, partly ironic scope of the communal, the largeness of Comus's challenge and of the Lady's faulty response should be remembered. His wand is a threat not just to her but to the boys. That which in the normal course of things can "unthred . . . joints . . . crumble . . . sinews" (613-614) and chain up nerves in (monumental?) alabaster (660) would seem to be that old familiar Renaissance natural triad of time, decay, and death. This threat to the brothers if they do not employ "Farr other arms, and other weapons," and the seeming variation threat-

---

[9] Dr. Tillyard, for example, affirms "She must take her place in society." *Studies in Milton* (London & New York, Chatto and Windus & Barnes and Noble, 1951), p. 95.

ening the Lady, to be " as *Daphne* was/Root-bound " both work
to the same end. The wand is a symbol of natural process in its
mechanistic, graceless, uncreative aspects. To live by this nature
would be to die by it, as the Spirit warns, in effect; to retreat into
its lesser consciousness and vegetable determinism would come
to much the same thing. Hence Comus has unobtrusively been
made to involve himself in a contradiction which reveals his own
plight: ' be in tune with nature by joining me, or be in tune with
nature as punishment.' The two look alike because neither sex
nor anything else in nature can ever be more than natural for him,
can ever be articulated and oriented by something larger or of
absolute value. He must urge that being alive and conscious
always involves sexual consciousness without ever involving faith,
hope, and charity or community, or patience. Indeed, in his extra-
ordinarily vivid lines about " green shops " and the like, he views
the whole cosmos in consumer-technocratic terms, and sees no
ruling Father but only a weltering race between appetites and the
occasions and fruits of appetite.

Her rejoinders to all this, upon sober inspection, are apt to
appear somewhat amazing. Her logic falters even more conspicu-
ously than his:

none
But such as are good men can give good things

(702-703)

This apparent converse of the Pauline notion that the good man
from the good treasures of his heart brings forth the good, this
endorsement of integrity is formally invalid as logic. Moreover,
its congruence is uncertain with the disparagement of integrity
seemingly involved in rejecting the cup *even* " Were it a draught
for *Juno* when she banquets " (701). Yet paradoxically these first
disordered recognitions—a precarious one of saving division,
" Thou canst not touch the freedom of my mind " (663), the
abstract one of an ideal integrity (" that which is not good is not
delicious/To a well-govern'd and wise appetite " 704-705), the
immediately telling one of a damning division, " false traitor,"
(690 ff.)—are the untidy margin on which her constructive destiny
develops. It develops, not surprisingly, in an intermittent note,
a counterpoint of humble tones:

. . . while Heav'n sees good

(665)

Mercy guard me!
(695)
swinish gluttony
Ne're looks to Heav'n amidst his gorgeous feast
(776-777)

With the humility goes a developing sense of ongoing process, of life as more dynamic than categorical. She herself dramatizes this in response to his challenge by acting, even if sometimes presumptuously or erroneously, to style her role and self as representative of a " Chastity " now associated with " Virginity " but —she has yet to understand—also " Sun-clad " (782) and so associated not only with enlightenment but with creativity and the works of daylight.[10]

The counter-force endowing this movement with dramatic vitality and with some of its symbolic resonance appears not only in the externalized and rationalized element of Comus's argument, but, as Brooks and Hardy have intimated, in the subrational but not unnatural sexual instinct suggested by her fixity in " this marble venom'd seat/Smear'd with gumms of glutenous heat," a state counteracted by Sabrina's " chast palms moist and cold " (916-918).

The fixity exemplies captivity, which everywhere in the poem is insisted upon as a condition of any life not sufficiently graced by love. Comus himself, for another example, feels that which he does " fear," " Her words set off by som superior power " (801), and he " *must* dissemble " (my italics, but on a metrical stress). He remains master of the wood (Brooks and Hardy, p. 226), but his rounds are compulsively and predictably patterned. As C. S. Lewis observed about *Paradise Lost*, Hell is locked on the inside.

Like Brooks and Hardy, David Wilkinson has contended that the Lady's arguments do not fully answer Comus's. But how this and the other characters' behavior bear on themes of virtuous society, power, and liability, repay further attention.[11]

---

[10] That the doctrine of virginity has not yet " entered fully into her experience " and become " a positive virtue, or principle of action," A. S. P. Woodhouse some time ago urged as a reason for her fixity. But his treatment seems to me overshifted in the direction of static category and abstraction. See " *Comus* Once More," *UTQ* XIX (1950), 218-223, p. 221. In any case, emphatic dissent has occurred; see Geoffrey Rans, *EIC* X (1960), p. 367.

[11] Professor Madsen, after citing the Faith-Hope-Chastity passage from 500 lines earlier in the masque, claims " Her [Platonic idealist] equipment is more than adequate to counter the all-dissolving skepticism of her tempter." Apart from questions of

Her final deliverance, melodramatically begun with the on-stage charge of the brothers, illuminates, extends, and intensifies the goings on. The Spirit cannot rescue her or completely effect her rescue; this does not, I think, leave him simply as a stage-prop in the masque nor leave the masque aground on difficulties connected with presenting mystery. The Spirit's flight ("Longer I durst not stay" 577) to find the brothers, and his lagging backstage until they have rushed on and "driven in" the rout alike signal that the Spirit's gifts must work through the ties of human commitment and human relationship, as human nature comes to adequate and social terms with itself. The dramatic facts might be taken as a corollary of Milton's Incarnation-centered Christianity. In any case, the Spirit's gifts of discernment are god-like in a way that makes him look like an attendant on the Holy Ghost, a way that makes his uncoercive comings and goings like inspirations in the mind. He "knew the foul inchanter though disguis'd"[12] (645). And his advice to reverse the rod/re-orient natural powers parallels what must later be done by special agencies of God's grace.

The brothers cannot be any more coercive than he, and their failure says things about broader concerns than boyish foibles. The heedlessness which, apparently, makes their apprehension of the Spirit's directions impatient and incomplete and their performance of them faulty seems an apt particular instance of ordinary self-absorption. Theologically it may even exemplify the Augustinian dictum that not to love someone for God's sake is necessarily to love that person for one's own sake. If they at this juncture perfectly loved her for God's sake, with no trace of vainglory attending the rescue, they theoretically should resent the wand as much as any other element of the scene. They can quite well recognize the rights and wrongs and desiderata in the

whether Comus has the universal solvent or she the container for it, this could only be true if this masque were merely a tableau. See "The Idea of Nature in Milton's Poetry," p. 190. The whole study is indispensable, despite what seems to me this inattention to dramatic elements.

[12] That haemony signifies knowledge I take to be convincingly shown by John Steadman, "Milton's *Haemony*: Etymology and Allegory," *PMLA* LXXVII (1962), 200-207. John Arthos usefully raises the question of conventions of magic, folktale, and romance, but does not prove or try to prove that we should demand perfect consistency in Milton's handling of these resources (any more than in his handling of epic conventions elsewhere). See *On "A Mask Presented at Ludlow-Castle"* (Ann Arbor, Univ. of Michigan, 1954). Haemony can symbolize knowledge without the necessity arising for Comus's wand or glass to symbolize entities equally clear-cut.

situation intellectually; that is, in a way real and valid but as external to their living as the leaves of haemony. The anguish latent in the situation, indicated and then (in line 820) superseded, resides in the inability of intellectually valid wishes, strongly felt by those who love her, to make the Lady free.

There she sits, then, in a stasis of confused or immature negation, becoming gradually conditioned and responsive (even if mostly in distaste) to the obsessions of her adversary. "Shall I go on?" she says, "Or have I said anough?" (779-780). Alas, she had said "false traitor," quite enough, some forty of her own lines earlier, and much better had not "unlockt" her lips further "In this unhallow'd air" (757). A not impossible she, demure and of chaste upbringing, whose logic is unreliable and whose instincts are, well, instinctive. So far Milton might almost be giving in Comus and his wood local habitations and names to Martin Luther's thesis on Satan: "On earth is not his equal."

But one would not, I think, find much satisfaction in citing Luther in connection with the Lady's redemption, which "More witnesseth than fancy's images/And grows to something of great constancy." Sabrina emerges from her pastoral river as both a second-generation classical grace and a noncanonical saint, a combination precarious in a naturalistic external landscape no doubt, but stable enough in an internal, imaginative and psychological one, and an able combatant there with various demonic forces and "shrewd medling" elves (846).

Not that she is wholly internal; the daughter of Locrine may be thought of generally (in Milton's retelling) as having experienced a transformation outside the realm of human life, and a fulfillment in history. History is the simultaneously external and internal, public and private medium in which she can function as a species of grace (presumably vivified by the Giver of all Grace). She is associated with "smooth Severn stream," which water-imagery, pastoralism, and neo-Ovidian metamorphosis associate with natural vitality, fertility, and reasonably benign process. Her own song emphasizes these things. The shepherds by their "carol" to her goodness, the Spirit by his "adjuring verse" and effectively invocative "warbled Song," Sabrina herself by her sympathetic listening to him and her loving pronouncements to the Lady— all acquit her of bloodless abstraction and associate her with the dynamic, mutually involved world of vocal communication.[13] The names in the Spirit's invocation apparently all involve Sabrina in a variously maternal company, all except four, which are significant in other relevant ways: Ligea's presence in this context seems to accent beauty, Proteus's presence stewardship, the presence of Triton and Glaucus authoritative communication in groups. She leaves, hastening " To wait in *Amphitrite's* bowr." No " huntress *Dian* " she (441). Service to the wife of the sea-god would seem a considerable endorsement of society and fertility.

The Spirit's two long final speeches, and the concluding action, gloss Sabrina's role and the preceding action of the whole play in ways not always recognized. He begins with a reminder of lineage, using diction emphasizing the vitality of generation: " daughter of Locrine/*Sprung* of old Anchises line " (922-923; my italics: Milton's italics for names omitted). This leads, by a turn on due rule and order, to an anatomy of perennial distortions, abstractions, and disorders afflicting her clear " brimmed waves ": freezing, drying, turbidity, silt. Her crown is on the contrary to be abundance either pastoral (" Groves of myrrh, and cinnamon," with connotations rich and surely in part Biblical), *or urban* (" many a tower and terrace round ").

Thyrsis enjoins the three to fly, by the grace of Heaven, " this cursed place " which the Lady first thought benign. Their arrival at " holier ground " means stepping into a festive paradigm of country, town, and (" President's ") castle with gabby brothers at last shaken into the heedful decorum of reinforcements to the godly *civitas*. The Spirit further defines this dynamic situation of reunion, familial initiation, and social responsibility by announcing his own destination as another kind of ideal, the world of noncyclical but benignly near-static, all-but-perfected labors of love. At the same time, his immensely associative and sensory description of the paradoxical and hence mysterious plenitude where " eternal Summer dwells " (988) provides the final, commensurately weighty answer to the sensory vividness of Comus. Now, moreover, he can counterpoint closely and explicitly the complex and dominant motifs of love, reproduction, regeneration, and communication in an emblematic tableau of ideal integrity (1003-1011).

[13] Juno, a relevant figure to whom the Lady alludes, never becomes so variously real as Sabrina.

In this context his injunction to "List mortals, if your ears be true" should make us surer than ever that the concern with noises, songs, and valid and reliable hearing throughout the poem has been a concern with the harmonization of appearance and reality, matter and spirit, vehicle and tenor, substance and structure, self and society. Lastly, his mobility, from President's Castle to "green earth's end" to "corners of the Moon" figures the freedom which for mortals attends love of virtue and only love of virtue. This last speech he directs forthrightly towards the *conventional* (and at the first performance literal) audience of the masque which conventionally merged with the dramatis personae.

His formulation implies some decisive conclusion in any auditor who hears so intently as to engage in a dialogue of affirmation or dissent with the poet. That auditor must realize retrospectively that the Lady fettered must have been Lady with virtue imperfect, that the touch of "chaste palms moist and cold" manifested to the Lady's consciousness some inclusive and positive ideal, that the Lady's release and status in her family and society figure an achieved love of virtue, a love of virtue achieved in not-too-closely definable part by the miracle of grace.

The play's extraordinary reach embraces a pastoral-romantic landscape which is both exterior and interior,[14] a movement from pastoral exclusions and simplifications in the leafy maze to the inclusions and possibilities and cosmic affinities of masque and godly *civitas*. These endeavors come at us in a set of thematic cruxes which summon to dialogue, and a mode of comedy which stems from a vision of society as somewhat precariously viable (or perhaps *narrowly*, if Milton's Christian optimism is to be emphasized). The auditor may well arrive with the youthful three at a some sense of contemplating and celebrating not simply a small miracle of feminine chastity transformed from passive and negative to active and positive, but more intricately a large exploration of large mysteries of freedom and necessity and grace

---

[14] I have a general debt to Northrop Frye's remarks on "The Four Forms of Fiction," in *Anatomy of Criticism* (Princeton, Princeton Univ., 1957), and a general debt to Walter J. Ong, "Voice as Summons to Belief" in *Literature and Belief* (English Institute Essays, 1957), ed. M. H. Abrams (New York, Columbia, 1958). The social rationale defined in this essay, like the signification of 'knowledge' adopted for haemony, would seem to agree generally (though not in some particulars) with the penetrating remarks about temperance in Robert Martin Adams, *Ikon: John Milton and the Modern Critics* (Ithaca, Cornell, 1955), pp. 13-16.

elusively and inextricably bound, of large paradoxes of love in society as freedom in order.

An observer in the classrooms of academe or in its dubiously hallowed groves may sense certain variations of the human comedy more intently and bitter-sweetly perhaps for the actions in which Milton explores the Lady's resonant question

> yet O where els
> Shall I inform my unacquainted feet
> In the blind maze of this tangl'd Wood?
>
> (179-181)

Ultimately this Miltonic human comedy of a thousand-odd lines assumes the shape of a parable of society, of its tilth and husbandry so poignantly less simple and straightforward than the green fertility around it or than the assurance of the spirits accompanying it, its sources of replenishment and inspiration of profound depth, its catechumens (and hence its future) proceeding always through the valley of the shadow, handed on by care and forethought and a continuing miracle.[15]

---

[15] An earlier version of this paper was read to the English Institute, September, 1964.

Milton's Ludlow " Mask "

THE SEAT AT THE CENTER:
AN INTERPRETATION OF *COMUS*

BY ROGER B. WILKENFELD

I. The Device in Motion

In his preface to *Chloridia*, Ben Jonson describes the construction of his masque in some detail:

It was agreed, it should be the celebration of some rites, done to the Goddesse Chloris, who in generall counsell of the Gods was proclaimed Goddesse of the flowers, according to that of *Ovid* in the *Fasti*.

And was to be stellified on Earth, by an absolute decree from *Jupiter*, who would have the Earth to be adorn'd with starres, as well as the Heaven.

Upon this hinge, the whole Invention moov'd.[1]

Jonson sometimes substitutes the term " device " for " invention " but what he seems to be describing is that sudden change in the masque's action which transforms the entire scene and releases or discovers the masquers.

Since there are no masquers, in the orthodox sense, in *Comus*, identifying its " hinge " has remained an elusive problem. Rosemond Tuve states that " upon the great hinge of the Circe-Comus myth Milton's whole invention moves; out of its known connoted meanings the pervading imagery of light and darkness springs quite naturally, and this is elaborated with the greatest originality by Milton, with conceptual refinements and extensions impossible to a lesser genius." [2] Alternatively, Enid Welsford states that " the hinge on which *Comus* turns is not the solution of a riddle, not a sudden metamorphosis or revelation, but an *act* of free choice." [3] As opposed to these views, I believe that the " hinge " in *Comus* is neither a " myth " nor an " act " but an

---

[1] *Ben Jonson*, ed. C. H. Herford and Percy and Evelyn Simpson (Oxford, 1925-52), VII, 749-750.

[2] Rosemond Tuve, *Images and Themes in Five Poems by Milton* (Cambridge, Mass., 1955), 116.

[3] Enid Welsford, *The Court Masque* (Cambridge, 1927), 318.

This essay first appeared in *ELH*, Vol. 33, No. 2 (June 1966).   123

emblem, the concrete, visual, dramatically viable emblem of the Lady paralyzed in the seat of Comus.[4] As I hope to show, the whole verbal mechanism of *Comus* is geared *to* this emblem and *from* this emblem devolves the " turn " of Milton's " device."

Milton chose as his central figures an Attendant Spirit, a Lost Virtuous Lady, a Vile Enchanter, and two Errant Brothers. Because he recognized that fully developed characters were neither possible nor desirable in the stylized masque, Milton knew that no part of his plot would seem either " necessary " or " probable." He also knew that the dramatic void left by the lack of concatenation in the plot had, somehow, to be filled. Jonson's usual practice was to fill this inevitable void with spectacle, allegorical personages, music and revels. Rather than clutter his stage with a multiplicity of portentous, visually symbolic figures as Jonson did in, for example, *Pleasure Reconcil'd to Vertue*, Milton chose to simplify and at the same time to dramatically engage the otherwise disparate actions of his masque by concentrating spectator and reader attention on one and only one concrete image. Jonson had to encumber the printed texts of his masques with learned notes and elaborate descriptions just because his masques moved from emblem to emblem. Milton, on the contrary, could present his readers with a " clean " literary text of his poem precisely because he had used his emblematic imagery with such masterful economy.[5]

In many other ways *Comus* compares favorably with the masques of Jonson. The Jonsonian masque, for example, was so constructed that the forces of chaos had to be defeated before the representatives of order could be discovered to complete the contrast. As opposed to this, Milton built right into the structure of his masque the forces of order and virtue and set them in direct conflict with the forces of disorder and sensuality throughout the work instead of in a single climactic scene. By introduc-

[4] The only other critic to discuss this aspect of the masque in any detail is Northrop Frye in *The Anatomy of Criticism* (Princeton, 1957), but his purposes markedly diverge from those of the present study. Frye sets up a scheme in which " the two nodes of the scriptural play are Christmas and Easter: the latter presents the triumphant god, the former the quiet virgin mother who gathers to herself the processional masque of the kings and shepherds. This figure is at the opposite end of the masque from the watching peeress of an ideal masque with the virtuous but paralyzed Lady of *Comus* halfway between " (292). Frye continues to discuss *Comus* tangentially, but never comes back to the significance of the Lady's paralyzed condition.

[5] That we read today a literary text is explained by Miss Tuve and by J. B. Broadbent in *Comus and Samson Agonistes* (New York, 1961).

ing the adversaries at the beginning of *Comus* Milton expanded the possibilities for direct and oblique verbal confrontations throughout the poem and at the same time enlarged the dramatic potential of the anti-masque.

Milton also handled the spatial coordinates of his " device " more effectively than Jonson, for he constructed a plot with two movements, one horizontal and the other vertical. The horizontal movement concerns the passage of the Lady and her Brothers through the drear wood to the safety of their home. This is the literal movement of the masque, and when *Comus* was first performed, it was the elegant method by which Milton " presented " Alice Egerton and her brothers, Lord Brackley and Thomas Egerton, to their father, the Earl of Bridgewater. On the other hand, Milton used the vertical movement of *Comus* to explore symbolically the central theme of his masque: the nature of freedom. The economy of Milton's craftsmanship is nowhere more evident than in the fact that the central dramatic emblem, the paralyzed Lady in the seat of Comus, is at the center of a framing series of vertical and horizontal movements. Through his manipulation of these movements, Milton contrasts the heights of the sky and the depths of the sea to that middle state in which a virtuous Lady can encounter an Enchanter and his monster rout. Furthermore, unlike Jonson, whose work is permeated by mythological designs, impresses and devices, Milton makes use of the informing Circe myth in a dramatically concentrated manner. He effects a balanced contrast between the natural and prosaic activity of the journey and the exciting, mythopoeic activity in Comus' palace. By using his spatial coordinates most effectively at the climax of his masque, Milton perfectly couples his complex verbal design to a stylized dramatic form which lends itself with particular grace to the conjunction of natural and supernatural events.

Comus opens with the immediate conjunction of the natural and supernatural worlds. The Attendant Spirit " descends onto a wild wood. This descent is the first of a series of vertical movements which culminates with the ascent and descent of Sabrina and the ascent of the Lady in the masque's central scene, and symmetrically concludes with the Spirit's ascent at the end of the masque. These vertical movements constitute the dramatic highlights of *Comus*. Milton organized the whole of his device in the following pattern:

Vertical Movement	— The descent of the Spirit.
Horizontal Movement	— The wanderings through the drear wood of Comus, the Lady, the Brothers, and Thyrsis.
Vertical Movement	— The ascent of Sabrina; the Lady's ascent out of Comus' seat; the descent of Sabrina.
Horizontal Movement	— The journey of the Lady, the Brothers, and Thyrsis to the palace of the President of Wales.
Vertical Movement	— The ascent of the Spirit.

The Spirit's prologue plays a crucial role in Milton's development of the masque's verbal mechanism. As Miss Welsford has shown, the ficelle of the opening speech is not at all uncommon in many of the masques of the period. The Attendant Spirit is a dramatic character in the masque and the traditional " presenter " of the device.[6] What is uncommon is Milton's functional handling of the opening speech, for through it he outlines the shape and direction of his device in seventeen lines.

> Before the starry threshold of Jove's Court
> My mansion is, where those immortal shapes
> Of bright aerial Spirits live inspher'd
> In Regions mild of calm and serene Air,
> Above the smoke and stir of this dim spot,
> Which men call Earth, and with low-thoughted care
> Confin'd and pester'd in this pinfold here,
> Strive to keep up a frail and feverish being,
> Unmindful of the crown that Virtue gives
> After this mortal change to her true Servants
> Amongst the enthron'd gods on Sainted seats.
> Yet some there be that by due steps aspire
> To lay their just hands on that Golden Key
> That opes the Palace of Eternity:
> To such my errand is, and but for such,
> I would not soil these pure Ambrosial weeds
> With the rank vapors of this Sin-worn mold.   (1-17)

The first eleven lines of the Spirit's prologue, while ostensibly merely a description of his residence, actually present in a concentrated form the thematic and verbal framework within which all the characters in the masque will be placed by the future action. The Spirit's " mansion " will serve as the coulisse by

---

[6] See Miss Welsford for a full discussion of the " presenter's " role.

which all the other " places " in the masque's physical and moral geography are placed in perspective. His description of the " calm and serene Air " will have important reverberations as the masque turns on its hinge in Comus' palace of pleasure. His image of the earth as a " pinfold " where men are " confin'd " and " pester'd " verbally establishes the masque's concern with the varieties of restraint and confinement which mark the natural and the supernatural world, and projects the action of the masque forward to the entrance of the Brothers. " Pinfold " also internally contrasts with the " inspher'd " Spirits and the " enthron'd " gods on Sainted seats." These latter images are expansive. They describe the gloriously circumscribed life of the virtuous, and contrast not only with " pinfold " but also with that seat of Comus in which the Lady will find herself paralyzed at the masque's climax. This cluster of related " seat " images is just one part of the masque's complex design of verbal repetitions, a design through which Milton explores the essential distinctions between a virtuous stability and a monstrous fixity, between restraint and constraint. Through his phrase " this mortal change," the Spirit rings the first modulation on the masque's further concern with the process of transformation, and in his reference to " due steps " he introduces the concept of an ordered movement with a serious objective (" aspire "), a concept which will be dramatically resolved only at the end of the masque when the Lady's dance of freedom finally sets the wild and " tipsie " steps of the " solemn " dance of Comus and his rout of monsters into the most appropriate perspective. The perspective thus established is an important means through which Milton, yet once more, contrasts the stability of restrained movement with the instability of apparently unrestrained but actually deeply constrained movement, a contrast which involves the paradoxical relationships of freedom to restraint and slavery to unrestraint.

Milton's technique in the first lines of the prologue reflects, then, his procedure throughout *Comus*. The power of the masque ultimately derives from the closely textured, dramatically compact verbal design which provides weight, support, and energy for the serious ends of the poem.

Milton's handling of the " compliment " is particularly masterful. As all the commentators on the orthodox masque have pointed out, together with the discovery of the masquers, the

" compliment " is the most important aspect of the form.[7]   Not only does Milton use the element of conventional praise thematically, but freed from the restrictions of a compliment to the King or Queen, he is able, in an unconventional way, to suggest ascending patterns of behavior and at the same time retain the conventional grace of the compliment.

In *Comus* the compliment to the President of Wales is preceded by the description of the world as it is split between Jove and Neptune. This is not a gratuitous mythological formulation. It narratively prepares for the dramatic conjunction of the surrogate of Neptune, Sabrina, with the surrogate of Jove, the Attendant Spirit, in the masque's climactic scene. Furthermore, the Spirit's narration of Neptune's " presentation " of his domain to the " tributory gods " (" And give them leave to wear their Sapphire crowns . . .") indirectly relates to the " crown " of Virtue and the " Golden Key," and directly leads to the compliment:

> And all this tract that fronts the falling Sun
> A noble Peer of mickle trust and power
> Has in his charge, with temper'd awe to guide
> An old and haughty Nation proud in Arms;
> Where his fair offspring nurs't in Princely lore,
> Are coming to attend their Father's state
> And new-entrusted Scepter.   (30-36)

This compliment is multi-functional:

1. It sets the fable in motion.
2. It suggests the linear direction of the plot at its literal level.
3. It looks forward in the phrase " princely lore " to the Brothers' subsequent discussion.
4. It prepares the verbal texture of the masque through the phrase " proud in Arms " for the important image of Diana to be subsequently introduced.
5. It describes a secular power which is effectively handled for virtuous ends precisely because it is restrained or " temper'd."

The Spirit's prologue continues with a picture of the " drear wood," " the nodding horror of whose shady brows/Threats the

[7] See Frye, *op. cit.*, 287: " The masque . . . is usually a compliment to the audience, or an important member of it, and leads up to an idealization of the society represented by that audience." See also Dolora Cunningham, " The Jonsonian Masque as a Literary Form," *ELH*, XXII (1955), 108-123, and E. H. Gombrich, " *Icones Symbolicae*," *JWCI*, XI (1948), 163-192.

forlorn and wand'ring Passenger" (38-39). This description contributes an ominous perspective to the horizontal direction which each of the masque's characters will take, as well as an image of a world in which the powers of good and evil are ranged against one another. It is in the context of this vision of a sacramental world that the Spirit introduces (50-53) Circe's name into the masque's complicated mythological equation. This is the first name to be introduced. Many more will allusively appear before Circe's power is finally neutralized.

The final words of the prologue serve to contrast the Spirit and Comus, and Comus and the Lady in terms of their appearance, manner of movement and mode of discourse. The description of Comus' dark domain contrasts with the light domain of the Lady's father and also sets the stage for the more dramatic (because direct) conflicts between Lady and Enchanter. But the verbal associations in *Comus* are usually not in the simple order of a one-to-one correspondence, and so too here the sense of the malevolence and benevolence of place is further reinforced by the disparity between Comus' dreary domain and the Spirit's starry mansion. This is an especially important comparison for Comus is an "imitator" yet his native haunts are, descriptively, a grotesque distortion of those heavenly realms he seeks to imitate. We also learn that after "roving the Celtic and Iberian fields" Comus:

> At last betakes him to this ominous Wood
> And in the thick shelter of black shades imbow'r'd
> Excels his Mother at her mighty Art.   (60-62)

The description not only identifies Comus himself as a horizontal wanderer, but also reintroduces into the masque the suggestion of "prison" and "prisoners" that will appear again and again until the climactic scene. All of the verbal references to varieties of prisons will ultimately be consolidated in the central dramatic emblem of the paralyzed Lady. Through the complex verbal design of his masque Milton systematically builds up a pervasive sense of the imminence of "prison" so that the paralyzed condition of the Lady, and her eventual freedom of movement, will appear as the logical climax of the masque.

As the Spirit's narration ends and the dramatic action begins, the Spirit decides on a plan of attack. He will put off his "sky robes,"

> And take the Weeds and likeness of a Swain
> That to the service of this house belongs,
> Who with his soft Pipe and smooth-dittied Song
> Well knows to still the wild winds when they roar,
> And hush the waving Woods. . . .   (84-88)

This is the prelude to those active transformations anticipated in the first lines of the prologue; moreover, it is the effective beginning of what will become a constant emphasis on the power of song as well as the beginning of a catalogue of kinds of singers and songs, a catalogue with far-reaching implications for the turn of the device.

We can see, then, how masterfully Milton has handled a conventional feature of the masque. It is through the prologue that the device is set verbally and dramatically in motion, only to be stopped by the formal epilogue of the Attendant Spirit himself after the masque has turned full circle on its hinge.

As Comus arrives on the scene, the Spirit hears " the tread/Of hateful steps." Comus' movements contrast, for all his imitative skill, with the movements of those " that by due steps aspire." This verbal clarification of Comus' position in the moral hierarchy of the poem is dramatically reinforced by the complementary appearance of the anti-masquers:

A rout of Monsters. . . . They come in making a riotous and unruly noise.

It is the special providence of Milton's masque, and one of the chief sources of its dramatic energy, that the anti-masquers and their noise are not dispelled either literally or symbolically until the dances and the songs of freedom at the poem's conclusion. In this way Milton relates " step " to " noise " and dance to song. The anti-masquers are consistent. Their verbal gestures (" noise ") and their physical gestures (riotous dances) have the same inherent form: they are both untempered. This untempered form will not be dissolved by song alone. It will finally be dissolved only by the effective combination of Sabrina's song and the Lady's dance of freedom and subsequent song.

In his welcome rite of Night and his exorcism of Day Comus cries:

> We that are of purer fire
> Imitate the Starry Choir

> Who, in their nightly watchful Spheres,
> Lead in swift round the Months and Years.
>
> (111-114)

He has just previously welcomed "midnight shout and revelry/ Tipsie dance and jollity" (103-104). This call for untempered noise and movement is in direct contrast to the "mild of calm and serene air" which the Spirit has already described as the nature of the heavenly atmosphere. Comus also calls for the nymphs to "braid your locks with rosy twine." This is a beautifully designed anticipatory irony, for through his description Comus unconsciously relates himself to his future nemesis, Sabrina, who will be described at the climax of the masque as preferring to "braid her locks with flowers." Furthermore, the "shout" and "revelry" contrast not only with the heavenly choir's harmonic music, but also with Sabrina's purely ordered songs, and with the songs of the Attendant Spirit as Thyrsis and the Lady. The "noise" of Comus and his rout are, therefore, placed in two perspectives: one is established by the various verbal references to singers and kinds of song in the masque, while the other is established by the actual songs which are sung, songs which constitute one of the masque's traditional elements. In each case the perspectives reveal the distinctions between the monstrous imitations of a virtuous reality and that virtuous reality itself.

Milton integrates the traditional masque dances into the overall movement of *Comus* in the same way that he makes the traditional songs structurally and thematically significant. The complex verbal framework, once again, insures this integration. Comus sees Night in terms of the "wavering Morris" and the tripping of the "pert Fairies," but he is ironically undercut by the inevitable movements of his rout of monsters. His words suggest that the dance movements in his world are ordered, while the actual dance movements of his rout make it clear that in his world all movement is emphatically disordered. The appearance of the rout is a concrete, dramatic presentation which serves to destroy any illusion of dance as "form" that might be implicit in Comus' description of the activities in his enchanted world. For all his verbal display, Comus cannot mask his true nature and the true nature of his rout. Despite his elaborately sustained images, the total impression which he makes is not of serene order, but of frenzied disorder.

The self-expressive aspect of dance as gesture is heightened, conventionalized and rendered significant by the masque. Anti-masquers have no choice; they must dance as a rout. Milton used the anti-masque as he inherited it to formally reflect his theme. The appearance of the antimasque is visual proof that life with Comus is a life of imprisonment. Despite their apparent freedom of movement, the anti-masquers are deeply constrained. Through the traditional anti-masque, then, Milton explores the paradoxical relationship of slavery to movement, for despite their frenzied activity, the anti-masquers are paralyzed without knowing it. The anti-masquers constitute a herd. Although they appear to be physically free, they are morally paralyzed. Their dance is the dance of slaves. They dance only at Comus' call. The full significance of this first antimasque will emerge, however, only when the Lady delicately executes her freedom dance at the end of the masque.

Comus himself does not stand outside this system of perspectives, for after his invocation to the " Goddess of Nocturnal Sport," " Dark veil'd Cotytto," he links himself with the monsters. This linkage is, as he says himself, made " in Solemnity."

> Come knit hands, and beat the ground,
> In a light fantastic round. (143-144)

Comus then cries:

> Break off, break off, I feel the different pace
> Of some chaste footing near about this ground.
> (145-146)

This crystallizes that implied relationship between Comus' " tread of hateful steps " and the " aspiring " steps defined by the Spirit by interposing a third set of steps. These are the Lady's and they stop the anti-masquers' dance. The Lady's ability to effect such an interruption in the opening moments of the masque dramatically foreshadows the power of her final and triumphant dance of freedom. Yet there is a potential danger in the Lady's situation, a danger suggested not only by the fact that she is lost in a dark wood, but also, and more powerfully, by the language of her opening speech.

> This way the noise was, if mine ear be true,
> My best guide now; methought it was the sound
> Of Riot and ill-manag'd Merriment,

Such as the jocund Flute or gamesome Pipe
Stirs up among the loose unletter'd Hinds,
When for their teeming Flocks and granges full
In wanton dance they praise the bounteous Pan,
And thank the gods amiss. I should be loath
To meet the rudeness and swill'd insolence
Of such late Wassailers. . . .   (170-179)

As Comus has said, this is a time when the " eye " can be deluded
with " blear illusion," and although the reference to the shepherd's
" wanton dance " anticipates the Lady's easy triumph over the
second anti-masque, at this moment, the Lady mistakes her potential enemy. For the Lady is here thinking of a natural opponent;
she does not entertain the possibility of a supernatural opponent,
and while Pan may be dangerous for the virtuous, Comus and the
anti-masquers were invoking in their ritual the fearsome Hecate
and Cotytto. Furthermore, the Lady's conception of Night, " the
gray-hooded Ev'n/Like a sad Votarist in Palmer's weed," (188-
189) ironically contrasts with the religious " mysteries " of Night
in which Comus and his rout are initiates.
   The Lady's own invocation actively contrasts with Comus'
invocation uttered moments before her arrival.

        O welcome pure-ey'd Faith, white-handed Hope,
        Thou hov'ring Angel girt with golden wings,
        And thou unblemish't form of Chastity,
        I see ye visibly, and now believe
        That he, the Supreme good, t'whom all things ill
        Are but as slavish officers of vengeance
        Would send a glist'ring Guardian, if need were,
        To keep my life and honor unassail'd.   (213-220)

The Lady's " pure-ey'd Faith " matches Comus' " dark-veil'd
Cotytto." The " unblemish't " form of Chastity takes on addi-
tional significance because of its connection with Comus' celebration of " the thickest gloom spit by Stygian darkness " (132);
and the " glist'ring Guardian " looks forward to Comus as the
helping stranger and subsequently to the arrival of the Attendant
Spirit, as well as backward to Comus and his rout in their guise
of " vow'd priests."
   With her invocation completed, the Lady's spirits are " en-
liv'n'd " and she sings. This first song of the masque, " to Echo,"
introduces color and delicacy into the world of the poem. We
have been subjected to the melodramatic antipodes of night and

day, black and white. The innocent and virtuous Lady (even though her innocence is not unfallen) knows another world, and her song with its aerial perspectives and fresh, flowering landscapes concretely projects a sense of her enlivened spirits and frees the action for a moment from the constrained closeness of the "blind mazes of a tangled wood." The song also suggests, in its development and projection of "Heav'n's Harmonies," the serene air of the Spirit as opposed to the "imitated" starry choir of Comus. Milton's assured handling of the dramatic requirements of his work becomes even more apparent when we recognize that with the appearance of Comus as a villager, the world of black and white returns, only to be lifted again when Sabrina with her song is invoked, through song, by the Attendant Spirit as Thyrsis. Milton uses the songs of the Lady and Sabrina as delicately formed antiphonal responses between which he suspends the principal dramatic actions of his masque.

Milton integrally relates the first anti-masque to the movement of the device, for it is the Lady's song which finally dissipates the antimasquers' "noise." The differences between the Lady's song and the rout's "noise" dramatically represent the differences between order and chaos, virtue and sensuality. Yet while the Lady's song serves as a direct contrast to Comus' sentiments, it also brings Comus out into the open, and Comus is a figure whose nature is the very antithesis of Echo's. Through the song, then, Milton makes it clear that the initial scattering of the riotous anti-masquers has not been of sufficient potency to reconstitute the disorder which Comus has effected. The world Milton images in *Comus* is dangerous; a simple and beautiful song is not powerful enough to permanently remove its roving agents. The momentary solace the Lady achieves with her song is about to be shattered as Comus makes his wily advances. The rout has been scattered, but Comus remains on the scene to try the Lady's experience. Only with Sabrina's appearance at the climax of the poem will Comus, even for a moment, give up his eminent domain.

The contrasting chords of harmony and disorder struck in the opening scenes of the poem continue to sound as Comus and the Lady confront one another. Comus is affected by the Lady's song, and his response seems, at first, to be a momentary easing of the tension, but as he adds another singer and kind of song to the growing catalogue of singers and songs, the verbal implications of his speech belie the ease of his delivery. Comus translates the freedoms implicit in the Lady's song into the language of the prisoner and his prison:

> I have oft heard
> My mother Circe with the sirens three . . .
> Who as they sung would take the prison'd soul
> And lap it in Elysium. . . .   (252-257)

The minute structural level at which Milton worked to insure a sense of symmetry in the plot can be clearly seen in Comus' dramatic answer, " Hail foreign wonder," to the Lady's " Hail " to Echo. And whatever easing of the tension may have resulted from Comus' gentle reply, the tenseness of the actual situation is quickly re-established through the tone of his replies, as the easy-flowing lines of the Lady's " blest song " are soon followed by the disjunctive *stichomythia* (277-290) .

The scene between Comus and the Lady ends when the Lady takes Comus at his word and accepts his offer of a " lowly shed " at the same time that she disparages the courts of princes. The ironies are still operating against the Lady, for her statement involves an obvious ironic foreshadowing of the palace of the priest of darkness to which she will be summarily taken. Comus has successfully obscured her vision. Her inexperience with the world of a " drear wood " has made it impossible for her to penetrate Comus' imitation of beneficence. With the conclusion of this scene, the masque has moved half-way to its hinge.

The speeches of the two Brothers and Thyrsis serve as a commentary on the preceding scene between Comus and the Lady and as a forecast of the Lady's career.[8] The Brothers' entrance is verbally bound to the entrances of Comus and the Lady through their reactions to Night. The world imaged in the Elder Brother's words is constrained too. He enjoins the stars to " unmuffle." They do not " unmuffle " and will not " unmuffle " until the action in Comus' palace is completed and the Lady's freedom is restored. By dramatically presenting three distinct reactions to Night, Milton economically employs his language to characterize the various personages of the plot at the same time that he builds up a sense of the prison-world from which the Lady must be extricated.

---

[8] See Miss Welsford, *op. cit.*, 318, who does not see that the debate is subordinated to the larger structure of the masque. See also the negative criticism of David Wilkinson in " The Escape from Pollution," *EIC*, X (1960), 32-43.

When the Second Brother speaks, we seem to move closer to the real world and away from the sacramental world with its mythological constructions, but this is only superficially true. The Second Brother's acknowledgment that to hear

> The folded flocks penn'd in their wattled cotes
> Or sound of pastoral reed with oaten stops,
> Or whistle from the lodge, . . .
> Twould be some solace yet, some little cheering
> In this close dungeon of innumerous boughs . . .
>
> (344-349)

recalls the Attendant Spirit's observation that from the perspective of Heaven, the earth of men is nothing more than a " pinfold," and this reminiscence leads directly to a verbal conjunction with the image of the " close dungeon." Comus' world is becoming explicitly more clear as the world of prisons, the world of constraints. Furthermore, the pastoral sounds which the Brother wishes to hear have been (or are being) heard by the Lady " perfect " in her " List'ning ear " and they have boded ill for her. The Second Brother's insight into his sister's position is limited precisely because he (like her) thinks in terms of the likely dangers of the natural world rather than the potential dangers of the supernatural world. Thus the Second Brother only considers the physical discomforts that might afflict his lost sister. He talks of " savage hunger " and " savage heat," but we have already been exposed to the " savage " in a different and far more dangerous guise, that of the transformed Enchanter.

The Elder Brother continues:

> He that has light within his own clear breast
> May sit i'th' center, and enjoy bright day,
> But he that hides a dark soul and foul thoughts
> Benighted walks under the midday Sun;
> Himself is his own dungeon.   (381-385)

This beautifully articulated statement makes the relationships of light to dungeon, of the " immur'd " Comus to the prison of the self, explicit, although the Elder Brother does not as yet know the precision of his utterance. The economy of Milton's technique is demonstrated by the fact that in so many instances the Brothers' speeches relate directly to Comus so that their position may be contrasted with his without direct verbal confrontation. This is important because the action of the masque is rapidly moving toward the confrontation of antithetical positions, but this must be reserved for the dramatic, face-to-face conflict between Comus and the Lady. The verbal patterns in *Comus* are so concentrated that these particular lines also relate to the Spirit's opening statement on Virtue and the enthroned saints after " this mortal change." Through this connection, the speech helps to clarify the relationship between the accumulating " seat " images and the " prison " motif, a relationship which Milton dramatically resolves in Comus' palace.

Although, as a general rule, the writers of masques tend to avoid elaborate differentiations of character, in *Comus* Milton partially distinguishes the two Brothers through the language they use. The most overt example of this is the Second Brother's habit of speaking alliteratively:

> Tis most true
> That musing meditation most affects
> The Pensive secrecy of desert cell,
> Far from the cheerful haunt of men and herds,
> And sits as safe as in a Senate-house.   (385-389)

It is significant that the most alliterative line is that which carries the imagery of " seats." As the masque moves closer and closer to the central dramatic emblem of the paralyzed Lady, the verbal patterns accentuate the possibility of such a condition through a series of ironic foreshadowings. Another example of this kind of foreshadowing appears in the Elder Brother's discourse on " chastity " or " true virginity."

> Some say no evil thing that walks by night
> In fog or fire, by lake or moorish fen,
> Blue meager Hag or stubborn unlaid ghost
> That breaks his magic chains at curfew time,
> No goblin or swart Faery of the mine,
> Hath hurtful power o'er true virginity.   (432-437)

Here Milton means us to feel a disparity between the " unlaid ghost " and the Lady who will also try, in the climactic scene, to break her " magic chains." In addition, Comus' earlier invocation to Cotytto serves to set on edge the Elder Brother's (comparatively) mild impression of the night-world.

The Elder Brother then introduces three new names into the masque's mythological equation. First he puts the conflict between " Chastity " and " Vice " in terms of the story of Diana

and Cupid, a story which looks forward to the different relationship between Psyche and Cupid described by the Spirit in his
epilogue, and then he turns to Minerva:

> What was that snaky-headed Gorgon shield
> That wise Minerva wore, unconquer'd Virgin,
> Wherewith she freez'd her foes to congeal'd stone,
> But rigid looks of chaste austerity
> And noble grace that dash't brute violence
> With sudden adoration and blank awe?　　(447-452)

Although the Elder Brother does not know it, this statement
represents a partial formulation of Comus' first reaction to the
Lady's song and Comus' later reaction to the Lady's position in
their debate, but the central image of " congeal'd stone " only
serves to ironically reinforce the continuing motif of imprisonment.　For the Brother has inverted the correct application of
his image.　" Congeal'd " and " rigid " will refer directly to the
Lady's position, not to that of her enemy.　It is Comus and not
the Lady who holds Minerva's power.

　　The parallels and echoes that crisscross through the poem do
not exist only at the verbal level.　They exist, as well, at the level
of the poem's action.　Thus when the Elder Brother says that he
hears " some far-off hallo break the silent Air," (481) the tension
inherent in his statement derives from the fact that the Lady's
" Hail " has already been heard and answered.　Yet the Brothers
do not think of their sister who has also sent her voice into the
" silent Air " to make it the " vocal Air " heard by Comus.　Rather,
they think of the " hallo " in terms of someone like themselves—
a woodman or perhaps a " roving robber."　All of this contributes
to the continuity of actions in the silent night.　It is at this point
in the action that the Attendant Spirit makes his appearance as
Thyrsis.

　　Afer Thyrsis greets the Brothers, he launches into a long narrative in which he recounts what we already know but what the
Brothers do not know.　In *Comus* Milton effected an exact fit of
the dramatic and narrative sections.　It is partially through the
balance of dramatic and narrative passages that he sustains the
kind of formal design typical of the genre.　The pattern can be
schematized as follows:

> Narrative Exposition (Prologue)
> Dramatic Confrontation (Lady and Comus)
> Debate (Brothers)

Narrative Exposition (Thyrsis)
Debate (Lady and Comus)
Dramatic Confrontation (Sabrina and Comus)
Narrative Exposition (Epilogue)

Although Thyrsis goes over known information in his second exposition, his presentation reinforces the basic motifs that have moved contrapuntally through the masque to this point. The close relationship between the interior verbal motifs and the exterior balance and symmetry of the poem reflects the great care Milton took to make of *Comus* a consistent and uniform work of art.

The image of the wood as dungeon continues to develop, when, for example, Thyrsis describes Comus as " immur'd " (a word which now recalls " imbrute," " imbodied," and " imbow'r'd ") " within the navel of this hideous wood." And when Thyrsis discusses his own music he sets into perspective the various music of the drear wood as it has been heard and talked about to this moment in the action. The catalogue of singers and kinds of song includes:

1. Thyrsis' meditated minstrelsy.
2. Comus' barbarous dissonance.
3. The Lady's song to Echo.

Thyrsis then describes the sublimity of harmonious song (560-562) and tells the Brothers that he fears for the " poor hapless Nightingale." The Lady singing about the nightingale in her Echo song is now identified as the nightingale by a friendly ear that heard her song, and this identification throws a deep shadow on Comus' current possession of the Lady. Thus only with Thyrsis' narration are all the ironies implicit in the Lady's song finally revealed.

The masque's songs function in the same way as its verbal motifs. Each song sets all the others into perspective and all of the songs before the " hinge " look forward to the songs which accumulate after the device has turned.

Thyrsis' narration gives the Elder Brother another opportunity to expostulate on the defensive powers of virtue:

> Gather'd like scum and settl'd to itself,
> It shall be in eternal restless change
> Self-fed and self-consum'd.   (595-597)

These lines play yet another variation on the masque's continuing interest in transformation, a variation that leads directly to the climactic scene in which the Lady is twice transformed.

II. The Hinge and the Turn

The change of scene incorporates the hinge of the masque. It is in the central episode in Comus' palace that all the motifs that have informed the masque to this point are resolved in terms of the dramatically concrete emblem of the paralyzed Lady. As the verbal framework has made emphatically clear, music and place will be thematically operative in this scene. The stage direction is of particular importance:

. . . the Lady set in an enchanted Chair to whom he offers his Glass, which she puts by, and goes about to rise.

With all pretenses dissolved, Comus immediately suggests his ability to effectively constrain:

> Nay Lady sit; if I but wave this wand,
> Your nerves are all chain'd up in Alabaster,
> And you a statue; or as Daphne was,
> Rootbound, that fled Apollo.   (659-662)

Comus intrudes into the masque's mythological world a new and far more serious equation than has yet appeared. Minerva, Diana, and Echo are now threateningly replaced by the rigid Daphne. All through the masque the overt stress has been laid on the power of Comus' liquor, but as we have seen, the interior verbal patterns continually looked forward to the more dreadful possibilities inherent in " congeal'd " stone. This scene is the dramatic resolution and emblematic representation of those verbal projections.

In her reply to Comus the Lady emphasizes the difference between restraint and constraint:

> Thou canst not touch the freedom of my mind
> With all thy charms, although this corporal rind
> Thou hast immanacl'd, while Heaven sees good.
> (663-665)

In three lines the Lady compresses the most important motifs that have been operative in the work. The seminal motif of " prison " and the specific problem of the Lady's personal freedom are now, in this scene, conjoined.

The manner of dramatic conflict between the Lady and Comus—a debate—follows naturally upon the Brothers' debate. Just as the " prison " motif is afforded its ultimate perspective by the Lady's condition in Comus' palace, so too the debate of the Brothers gathers its ironic strength primarily from this central scene. The context of the debate between the Lady and Comus is one of practical menace, not one of hypothetical injury.

The cup that Comus offers with the Julep that " dances in his crystal bounds " suggests the coming importance of the formal dance of freedom over against the constrained dance of the antimasquers. Comus calls for the Lady to restore her body with its tired needs. He offers " refreshment," " ease," and " timely rest." The grotesque nature of these propositions is rendered emblematically by the Lady's " rooted " position. Everything Comus says must be reinterpreted in terms of the Lady's condition. The fact that she is a visual presence on the stage makes such reinterpretation direct and simple.

The Lady still has the freedom of speech and she counters Comus' offer with an appeal to the restorative quality of spiritual goods at the same time that she points out that Comus has been rather heavy-handed in his temptation. For he has offered material goods while the recipients of his previous goods stand by as visual testimonials to his good faith and power:

> What grim aspects are these,
> These ugly-headed Monsters? (694-695)

The Lady re-emphasizes the brutish nature of the appeal and its customary result:

> wouldst thou seek again to trap me here
> With lickerish baits fit to ensnare a brute? (699-700)

She has, unlike the monster rout, a " well-govern'd " appetite. Furthermore, her direct apprehension of the true nature of Comus' herd completely undercuts Comus' conception that he and his rout, in their ritual incantations to Cotytto, can imitate the " starry choir." It is significant that the " soft music " of the palace is totally artificial. The monster herd remains mute.

Comus' famous appeal to nature loses touch with all sense of harmony. He describes nature's riot, " thronging the seas with spawn innumerable," (713) and his subject is reflected in the frenzy of his speech (720-729). His position is one of subjunctive potentiality. His speech is continually intercepted by the "shoulds" and "woulds" of desire. Using the rhetoric of deceit, Comus tries to persuade with superficially gorgeous images but his own material concerns are egregiously present in his verbal declarations. When he describes nature "strangl'd with her waste fertility," the principle of plenitude becomes a principle of license. It is through such verbal transpositions that the theme of transformation ultimately embraces, in this debate scene, Comus himself. This is the Comus who wants to add more sheep to his stock and who views the conflict with temperance in the most overtly mundane way. He describes the "riches" of nature in such grossly materialistic terms that his argument undercuts itself: "Beauty is nature's coin, must not be hoarded/But must be current (739-740).

His discussion of the nature, uses and adversities of beauty takes place in the hostile context of the "grim-aspects" of his palace. The disjunction between the physical appearance of the palace, itself "stately," and the grotesque configurations of its inhabitants is an emblematic reminder of the disjunction between the gorgeousness of Comus' rhetorical display and the "monstrous" sense of his pronouncements.

The Lady's response shows that she understands the situation perfectly:

> I hate when vice can bolt her arguments,
> Obtruding false rules prankt in reason's garb.   (759-760)

Her response derives added force from the fact that it is a direct echo of the Elder Brother's discussion of "the frivolous bolt of Cupid." Through the verbal echoes, the mythological allusions refine the dramatic action and render it more meaningful. The Lady responds to Comus' hypothetical formulations by clearly stating the realities of excess. She calls for an "even proportion" of Nature's bounty. Her sense of context makes her observations quietly exact:

> for swinish gluttony
> Ne'er looks to Heav'n amidst his gorgeous feast,
> But with besotted base ingratitude
> Crams and blasphemes his feeder.   (776-779)

The Lady's "argument" ends here; the rest is a threat and a promise as she describes the power of the sublime and mysterious aspects of virginity, a description which recalls the Elder Brother's conception of chastity's defensive armor (421-427). Her comment also points up the falsity of Comus' desire to consecrate his "conceal'd solemnity."

> To him that dares
> Arm his profane tongue with contemptuous words
> Against the Sun-clad power of Chastity
> Fain would I something say, yet to what end?
> Thou hast nor Ear nor Soul to apprehend
> The sublime notion and high mystery
> That must be utter'd to unfold the sage
> And serious doctrine of Virginity,
> And thou art worthy that thou shouldst not know
> More happiness than this thy present lot. . . .
> Thou art not fit to hear thyself convinc't.   (780-792)

The power the Lady defines is far more strong than the Elder Brother's conceptual "complete steel" (421), and what she says proves dramatically true with Sabrina's appearance, for Sabrina's offensive weapons do not consist of material armament or logical argument, but the power and mystery of song.

Finally the Lady ends her statement with an image more powerful than anything in Comus' mincing conclusion. Its dramatic effect is to be seen in a duplication of pattern. Comus reacts to her again as he did when she first sang her song to Echo. To the Lady's threat (798-799), Comus, thinking aloud, says:

> I must dissemble
> And try her yet more strongly.   (805-806)

His argument has dwindled into a trivial temptation. Milton clearly distinguishes the apparent power of Comus and the sublime power of the Lady in the contrast between the "flames" of Comus' "cordial julep" and the "flame of sacred vehemence" of the Lady's "pure cause." Comus' final statement indicates the direction in which the debate has turned: "I must not suffer this" (809). He has moved from the imperative "you must" to the imperative "I must not." He is now on the verbal defensive; ultimately, with Sabrina's arrival, he will lose his voice entirely. The powers of virtue will descend onto the scene and Comus will have no further opportunity to try his "dear Wit and gay Rhetoric."

The masque's device is now *turning* on its hinge. After the rout of Comus, the spirit enters but discovers that he cannot

" free the Lady that sits here/In stony fetters fixt and motion-less " (818-819). This is the visual climax of the masque. All the verbal foreshadowings of this dire event have now collapsed into the event itself. Milton dramatically resolves all the varia-tions he has played on prisons and imprisonment, on rigid stances and seats, at this moment. It is in terms of the emblematic pres-ence of the paralyzed Lady that the complex verbal structure of *Comus* makes most sense, and all of those motifs that are not resolved by the emblem of the paralyzed Lady are about to be resolved with the appearance of Sabrina and in the action which follows her appearance. There is very little action in *Comus* before the turning of the device, but the masque remains vital and energetic in its first half precisely because Milton translates all of the *language* of the device in motion into the *actions* of the device turned.

In his opening lines the Spirit described the conjunction of the powers of the sea and the powers of the sky. This description becomes realized in dramatic terms when the Spirit, recognizing his own deficiencies in sympathetic magic, narrates the history of Sabrina. The story is brief. However, it fits naturally into the masque's verbal design, for it reinforces many of the motifs that have been initially resolved by the emblem of the paralyzed Lady. We learn, for example, that in Nereus' Hall Sabrina was " im-bath'd " " in nectar'd lavers strew'd with Asphodel." The trans-lation of Sabrina's countenance and the directional movement of that change stand in direct contrast to the kinds of transpositions effected by Comus' wand.

Milton strikes his final variation on the subject of transforma-tion when we learn that Sabrina underwent a " quick immortal change." This aspect of her story recalls all the changes, both real and hypothetical that have been established through the verbal framework and the dramatic action of the masque. Each of these " changes " provides perspective for, and is afforded per-spective by, all the others. They include:

1. The transformation experienced by those who after " this mortal change " are embraced by the " enthron'd gods " on " sainted seats."
2. The transformation experienced by those who are foolish and weak enough to be tempted by Comus' words and who, therefore, fall under the power of his liquor and/or his wand.

3. The transformation in the appearance of the Attendant Spirit as he becomes Thyrsis.
4. The transformation in the appearance of Comus as he becomes a harmless villager.
5. The transformation implicit in the Lady's song to Echo.
6. The hypothetical transformation of the virtuous as this process is described by the Elder Brother.
7. The transformation of the Lady into a paralyzed mute.
8. The transformation of Sabrina from a mortal to a surrogate of the gods.

The dramatic vitality inherent in this series of transformations is related to the fact that only with Sabrina's freeing of the Lady from Comus' spell is the series resolved at the level of the action of the masque, and only with the projected free ascent of the Spirit into the sky is the series resolved at the verbal level.

The relation of song to the Lady's problem is finally made explicit by the Spirit. Sabrina can "unlock/The clasping charm" but she must be "right invok't in warbled song" (854). Milton recovered all the potential of the masque form by having the Spirit complement his song by adding "the power of some adjuring verse." As the Lady sang her song to Echo for help, so too here the power of song is enlisted in her behalf. The combination of verse and song is abstractly pleasing, but it is also necessary and probable given the dramatic situation as it has progressed to the climactic scene.

The Spirit sings:

> Sabrina Fair
>   Listen where thou art sitting
> Under the glassy, cool, translucent wave,
>   In twisted braids of Lillies knitting
> The loose train of thy amber-dropping hair; . . .
> (859-863)

Sabrina's "sitting" position radically departs from the present sitting position of the Lady. Sabrina is free; she has not submitted her will to any force. She is the mythological incarnation of freedom. Not only is the free-flowing beauty of her hair ordered beautifully, but there is an implied contrast in this ordering to the knitting of hair that Comus speaks of in his opening speech. Her hair is free, yet restrained. Comus' imitation of this arrangement involves a wild action which leads, paradoxically, to constraint.

As the device continues to turn on its hinge, a central motif makes its verbal and dramatic reappearance. Movement through the drear wood has been horizontal, but this is a time for vertical movement. The Spirit calls on Sabrina to:

> Rise, rise and heave thy rosy head
> From thy coral-pav'n bed. (885-886)

Sabrina does " rise." In answer to the Spirit's summons she naturally appears first as song;[9] and in her song she sings of a scene and an atmosphere which with its blues and greens serves as a contrast to the night scenes and the blankness of Comus' palace and connects her song with the color of the Lady's song to Echo. Taken together, the song of the Lady, the song of the Attendant Spirit, and the song of Sabrina all set the melodramatic world of Comus on edge by imaging a good and pleasant nature.

The " powerful hand " of Sabrina is mysterious precisely because it is the hand of a being so delicate that when she sets her " printless feet " on the cowslip's " velvet head " it does not " bend." Yet her sympathetic magic is so strong, she can instantly free the Lady from enchantment. As the surrogate of the powers of the sea, she is the incarnation of the gentle strength of the free. She is the incarnation of that paradoxical relationship between freedom and restraint which Milton was so concerned with dramatically defining in *Comus*. The free moving Sabrina and the paralyzed Lady face one another (" Brightest Lady look on me "), and it is as a result of the complex verbal framework that Milton has been working with throughout the masque that the scene conveys a sense of power and serenity.

The device has turned: " Sabrina descends, and the Lady rises out of her seat." In a sacramental world, processes are complementary and interchangeable, and in the palace of Comus the activities of the Lady and Sabrina symbolically complement each other. The exact nature of the exchange is mysterious. The results of Sabrina's actions are direct.

In an echo of Comus' appeal to nature's excesses, the Spirit as Thyrsis prays that Sabrina be spared " summer drouth," " singed air," and " October's torrent flood," and talks of Sabrina's " molten crystal "—a phrase which serves to contrast her once again with Comus—this time placing in ironic perspective the " crystal "

[9] For a corroborative but unexpanded view of this passage, see J. W. Saunders, " Milton, Diomede and Amaryllis," *ELH*, XXII (1955), 276-277.

of his enchanted glass. With Sabrina's support the Lady undergoes something akin to apotheosis and is now, and only now, ready
to proceed horizontally on her way home to her father's house.
The Lady must " rise " before moving on her journey, and the
Spirit enjoins her to " fly this cursed place." Then the horizontal
movement resumes, as the Lady and her Brothers, in the company
of Thyrsis, continue on their way to the seat of secular safety,
the palace of the President of Wales.

Milton attended to even the slightest details in *Comus*. Since
the enchantment has been broken, the atmosphere changes; the
stars have been " unmuffl'd " and night loses its more threatening
overtones:

> Come let us haste, the Stars grow high,
> But night sits monarch yet in the mid sky.   (956-957)

With the change of scene to Ludlow town and the President's
castle, the presentation of the children to their father becomes
the center of the dramatic scene. The audience becomes the
fulcrum for the final moments of the masque. As he used the
prologue, so Milton used the formal " presentation "; he made it
an integral part of his masque's dramatic structure.

The rude " shepherds " have their dance, a dance which is the
literal analogue to the supernatural anti-masque performed by
Comus and his monster rout. The revelry of these shepherds is
not evil. It does not involve a perverse imitation of the starry
choir. For this reason it can be easily dispelled by the lyrics of
the song now sung by Thyrsis. There is no drama here because
magic and energy are unnecessary. Milton has thus incorporated
the usual technique for dispelling the antimasque—the verbal
command—into his larger dramatic frame, so that the one approach (the verbally gratuitous) can set off the other (the magical) . The shepherds dance to the kind of rustic music the Lady
and Second Brother initially thought of when they found themselves stranded in the drear wood and before they encountered
Comus and his rout. The ease with which the Spirit handles the
last group of anti-masquers (there is no need for Sabrina) taken
together with the fact that Comus escaped from his palace introduces a note of seriousness into the appearances and disappear-
ances of the anti-masquers that is uncommon. To recapitulate:
the disintegration of the antimasquers (who are *songless*) is
integrally related to the movement of the device and its dramatic

turn on the hinge of the emblem of the paralyzed Lady. The fact that the anti-masquers seem to have been dispelled by the Lady's song to Echo only to return in the scene at Comus' palace dramatically projects the seriousness of the confrontation that is forthcoming. The anti-masquers represent the kind of perversity that only the mysterious Sabrina can threaten. Yet even though Comus escapes, the shepherds, who are the literal extensions of the mythological anti-masquers, can be easily disposed of through *the power of song alone* once their symbolic counterparts have been dispersed. No other masque writer of the period approaches Milton's ingenuity and dramatic skill in his thematic and structural manipulation of the anti-masque.[10]

The fifth song presents (with a " crown of deathless praise ") the three children who, having moved through the drear wood, have " so goodly grown." The crowning of the children is a highly stylized and conventional gesture which contains within itself, because of the phrasal reverberations, an image of what has already been dramatically presented. Thus the " crown " of praise suggests not only Sabrina's " crown," but also the " crown " of those in heaven as they were described by the Spirit in his prologue.

The dances which follow represent the " triumph " of freedom as this has already been dramatically and verbally imaged. They are formal dances of an ordered nature and are, of course, the most overt gestures of what has transpired: what has been defeated, what has been won.

Milton's integration of song and dance in the formal " presentation " scene must be considered with some care. The conventions of the masque called for a final dance, but Milton so handled his device that a dance, rather than a song, is exactly what we should

---

[10] In Jonson's *Pleasure Reconcil'd to Vertue*, for example, the relationship of the masque's main device to its anti-masque involves no suspense, tension or recovery of lost power. The main masque and the anti-masques remain distinct events with little to connect them either thematically or structurally. The points of similarity between Jonson's masque and *Comus* lie in the last scenes of each. In these last scenes, song accumulates and is directly related to dance—both being described in Jonson's masque as " true motion." However, in *Comus*, music and dancing as " true motion " relate directly to the themes of the masque and the verbal patterns which Milton builds up around these themes. In *Pleasure*, although the sense of song and dance as integrated gestures is strongly implied, there is no formal, structural connection between the songs and dances themselves and the main movement of the device. The same could be said for other masques which are often cited as analogous to *Comus* in theme and structure, such as Shirley's *The Triumph of Peace* and Middleton's *The World Tost at Tennis*.

expect from the Lady. After the threat of paralysis and then the temporary experience of paralysis, the Lady would appreciate more fully her physical freedom, and the natural gesture of such an appreciation would be a physical gesture, formally ordered and restrained, but not constrained. The court dance fully corresponds to this formula. The Lady's dance is thus the dramatic quotient of all the various stages of the action, just as the emblem of the paralyzed Lady is the concrete visual embodiment of all the verbal motifs that had been established before its presentation. Because the final, formal dance of the Lady so perfectly concludes the action initiated in the drear wood, the masque has an organic unity that is lacking in most other masques of the period.

The formal unity of the actions surrounding the Lady is completed by her dance. But there is an aesthetic pattern which remains to be completed before the masque can end. To complete the symmetrical structure of *Comus*, Milton ends his masque not with a dance, but with an epilogue. The purpose of the epilogue is to complete the masque by verbally bringing together the contrasting and complementary elements through which he has projected the poem's meaning. As the Lady's dance unifies the previous action through an ordered physical gesture, so the Spirit's epilogue unifies the previous action through an ordered series of words.

In his epilogue, the Spirit recalls and reinforces all that has happened, and reinterprets preceding events in the new light of the various vertical levels of the sky. He verbally imagines a flight to the west, sucks in the liquid air (a final contrast to the air of imbower'd shades), and describes the Garden of Hesperus with its " crisped shades and bow'rs " (an echo of the Second Brother's speech and a penultimate contrast to the " black shades " of Comus' woods). Color returns with greater variety than ever before (" flowers of more mingled hue "), and we are reminded once again of that colorful nature to be found in the songs of Sabrina and the Lady. The Spirit's reference to " elysian dew " picks up and delimits, for the final time, Comus' liquor, while his picture of Adonis' abode relates back to the " flowry cave " in the Echo song. As the Spirit narrates the scene, while Adonis reposes " in slumber soft ":

> on the ground
> Sadly sits th'Assyrian Queen. . . .   (1001-1002)

Roger B. Wilkenfeld   149

This description suggests Comus' Cotytto, another manifestation of the same impulse, and the emblem of the enchanted chair.

The Spirit then moves "far above" to Cupid and Psyche. This is the final mythological equation. The Heavenly pattern of the restrained freedom of the wandering Psyche reinforces and expands the significance of the wandering Lady's similar experience of freedom.

The Attendant Spirit now leaves the earth, but he carries the theme of freedom with him in his verbs, for he tells us that he can "fly," "run," and "soar"; these are particularly appropriate verbs when they are felt in connection with the central emblem of the device. The impression created by this pattern of verbs is reinforced as the Spirit conceptualizes it: "Love Virtue, she alone is free."

The masque ends with a final emphasis on the vertical motif: "Heaven itself would stoop"; the action of the masque has shown Heaven stooping in the form of a "rising" Sabrina, and this paradox returns us to the opening lines of the masque and the sense they convey of heaven's bourne. Through the movement of his device, Milton has shown us that heaven's bourne includes not only the "sphery clime" but the land below the "translucent wave" as well. The lands of both Jove and Neptune are repositories for those guardian angels who come to the aid of distressed virtue. The epilogue swings through an harmonious arc as it verbally images that vision of the world reproduced in the brilliantly stylized dramatic action of *A Maske Presented at Ludlow Castle*.

MILTON'S COUNTERPLOT

BY GEOFFREY HARTMAN

Milton's description of the building of Pandemonium ends with a reference to the architect, Mammon, also known to the ancient world as Mulciber:

> and how he fell
> From Heav'n, they fabl'd, thrown by angry *Jove*
> Sheer o'er the Crystal Battlements: from Morn
> To Noon he fell, from Noon to dewy Eve,
> A Summer's day; and with the setting Sun
> Dropt from the Zenith like a falling Star,
> On *Lemnos* th'Ægæan Isle (*Paradise Lost* I, 740-6).

These verses stand out from a brilliant text as still more brilliant; or emerge from this text, which repeats on several levels the theme of quick or erring or mock activity, marked by a strange mood of calm, as if the narrative's burning wheel had suddenly disclosed a jewelled bearing. Their subject is a Fall, and it has been suggested that Milton's imagination was caught by the anticipation in the Mulciber story of a myth which stands at the center of his epic. Why the " caught " imagination should respond with a pastoral image, evoking a fall gradual and cool like the dying of a summer's day, and the sudden, no less aesthetically distant, dropping down of the star, is not explained. One recalls, without difficulty, similar moments of relief or distancing, especially in the cosmic fret of the first books: the comparison of angel forms lying entranced on the inflamed sea with autumnal leaves on Vallombrosa's shady brooks, or the simile of springtime bees and of the dreaming peasant at the end of Book I, or the applause following Mammon's speech in Book II, likened to lulling if hoarse cadence of winds after a storm, or even the appearance to Satan of the world, when he has crossed Chaos and arrives with torn tackle in full view of this golden-chained star of smallest magnitude.

The evident purpose of the Mulciber story is to help prick inflated Pandemonium, and together with the lines that follow, to emphasize that Mammon's building is as shaky as its architect. This fits in well with the plot of the first two books, a description of the satanic host's effort to build on hell. But the verses on Mulciber also disclose, through their almost decorative character, a second plot, simultaneously expressed with the first, and which may be called the counterplot. Its hidden presence is responsible for the contrapuntal effects of the inserted fable.

The reader will not fail to recognize in Milton's account of the progress of Mulciber's fall the parody of a biblical rhythm: " And the evening and the morning were the (first) day." The thought of creation is present to Milton, somehow associated with this fall. Moreover, the picture of *angry* Jove blends with and gives way to that of *crystal* battlements, and the imperturbability of the summer's day through which the angel drops:

> from Morn
> To Noon he fell, from Noon to dewy Eve,
> A Summer's day;

while in the last part of his descent an image of splendor and effortlessness outshines that of anger or ignominy:

> and with the setting Sun
> Dropt from the Zenith like a falling Star.

In context, of course, this depiction is condemned as mere fabling, and there is nothing splendid or aloof in the way Milton retells the story:

> thus they relate,
> Erring; for he with his rebellious rout
> Fell long before; nor aught avail'd him now
> To have built in Heav'n high Tow'rs; nor did he scape
> By all his Engines, but was headlong sent
> With his industrious crew to build in hell. (746-51)

Yet for a moment, while moving in the charmed land of pagan fable, away from the more literal truth in which he seeks

supremacy over all fable, Milton reveals the overwhelming, if
not autonomous drive of his imagination. Mulciber draws to
himself a rhythm reminiscent of the account of the world's
creation, and his story suggests both God and the creation
undisturbed (Crystal Battlements . . . dewy Eve) by a fall
which is said to occur later than the creation, yet actually
preceded it. Here, surely, is a primary instance of Milton's
automatically involving the idea of creation with that of the
Fall. But further, and more fundamental, is the feeling of the
text that God's anger is not anger at all, rather calm prescience,
which sees that no fall will ultimately disturb the creation,
whther Mulciber's fabled or Satan's real or Adam's universal
Fall.

Milton's feeling for this divine imperturbability, for God's
omnipotent knowledge that the creation will outlive death and
sin, when expressed in such an indirect manner, may be characterized as the counterplot. For it does not often work on the
reader as independent theme or subplot, but lodges in the
vital parts of the overt action, emerging from it like good
from evil. The root-feeling (if feeling is the proper word)
for imperturbable providence radiates from many levels of the
text. It has been given numerous interpretations in the history of criticism, the best perhaps, though impressionistic, by
Coleridge: " Milton is the deity of prescience: he stands *ab
extra* and drives a fiery chariot and four, making the horses
feel the iron curb which holds them in." Satan's fixed mind
and high disdain are perverted reflectors of this same cold
passion, but doomed to perish in the restlessness of hell, and
its compulsive gospel of the community of damnation. So
deep-working is this spirit of the " glassy, cool, translucent
wave," already invoked in *Comus*, that other poets find hard
to resist it, and, like Wordsworth, seek to attain similar virtu-
osity in expressing " central peace, subsisting at the heart Of
endless agitation." Milton's control is such, that even in the
first dramatic account of Satan's expulsion, he makes the steady
flame of God's act predominate over the theme of effort, anger,
and vengefulness: in the following verses " Ethereal Sky "
corresponds to the " Crystal Battlements " of Mulciber's fall,
and the image of a projectile powerfully but steadily thrust
forth (evoked in part by the immediate duplication of stress,

letter and rhythmic patterns) recreates the imperturbability of that other, summer space:

> Him the Almightly Power
> Hurl'd headlong flaming from th'Ethereal Sky
> With hideous ruin and combustion down
> To bottomless perdition, there to dwell
> In Adamantine Chains and penal Fire . . . (44-8)

One of the major means of realizing the counterplot is the simile. Throughout *Paradise Lost*, and eminently in the first two books, Milton has to bring the terrible sublime home to the reader's imagination. It would appear that he can only do this by way of analogy. Yet Milton rarely uses straight analogy, in which the observer and observed remain, relative to each other, on the same plane. Indeed, his finest effects are to employ magnifying and diminishing similes. Satan's shield, for example, is described as hanging on his shoulder like the moon, viewed through Galileo's telescope from Fiesole or in Valdarno (I, 284-91). The rich, elaborate pattern of such similes has often been noted and variously explained. Certain details, however, may be reconsidered.

The similes, first of all, not only magnify or diminish the doings in hell, but invariably put them at a distance. Just as the " Tuscan Artist " sees the moon through his telescope, so the artist of *Paradise Lost* shows hell at considerable remove, through a medium which, while it clarifies, also intervenes between reader and object. Milton varies points-of-view shifting in space and time so skilfully, that our sense of the reality of hell, of its power vis-a-vis man or God, never remains secure. Spirits, we know, can assume any shape they please; and Milton, like Spenser, uses this imaginative axiom to destroy the idea of the simple location of good and evil in the spiritual combat. But despite the insecurity, the abyss momentarily glimpsed under simple event, Milton's main effort in the first books is to make us believe in Satan as a real and terrible agent, yet never as an irresistible power. No doubt at all of Satan's influence: his success is writ large in religious history: which may also be one reason for the epic enumeration of demonic names and place-names in Book I. Nevertheless, even as we are closest to Satan, presented with the hottest view of hell's present and future appeal, all suggestion of irresistible influence must be expunged, if Milton's two means of divine justification, man's free will and God's foreknowledge of the creation's triumph, are to win consent.

These two dominant concepts, expressed through the counter-plot, shed a calm and often cold radiance over all of *Paradise Lost*, issuing equally from the heart of faith and the center of self-determination. The similes must persuade us that man was and is " sufficient to have stood, though free to fall " (III, 99), that his reason and will, however fiercely tempted and besieged, stand on a pinnacle as firm and precarious as that on which the Christ of *Paradise Regained* (IV, 541 ff) suffers his last, greatest, archetypal temptation. They must show the persistence, in the depth of danger, passion or evil, of imperturbable reason, of a power working *ab extra*.

This they accomplish in several ways. They are, for example, marked by an emphasis on place names. It is the *Tuscan* artist who views the moon (Satan's shield) from the top of *Fesole* or in *Valdarno* through his optic glass, while he searches for new Lands, Rivers, Mountains on the spotty globe. Do not the place names serve to anchor this observer, and set him off from the vastness and vagueness of hell, its unnamed and restless geography, as well as from his attempt to leave the earth and rise by science above the lunar world? A recital of names is, of course, not reassuring of itself: no comfort accrues in hearing Moloch associated with *Rabba, Argob, Basan, Arnon*, or sinful Solomon with *Hinnom, Tophet, Gehenna* (I, 397-405). The point is that these places were once neutral, innocent of bloody or holy associations; it is man who has made them what they are, made the proper name a fearful or a hopeful sign (cf. XI, 836-39). Will Valdarno and Fiesole become such by-words as Tophet and Gehenna? At the moment they are still hieroglyphs, words whose ultimate meaning is in the balance. They suggest the inviolate shelter of the created world rather than the incursions of a demonic world. Yet we sense that, if Galileo uses the shelter and Ark of this world to dream of other worlds, paying optical rites to the moon,

Fiesole, Valdarno, even Vallombrosa may yield to the tug of a demonic interpretation and soon become a part of hell's unprotected marl.

Though the figure of the observer *ab extra* is striking in Milton's evocation of Galileo, it becomes more subtly patent in a simile a few lines further on, which tells how the angel forms lay entranced on hell's inflamed sea

> Thick as Autumnal Leaves that strow the Brooks
> In *Vallombrosa,* where th'Etrurian shades
> High overarch't imbow'r; or scatter'd sedge
> Afloat, when with fierce winds *Orion* arm'd
> Hath vext the Red-Sea Coast, whose waves o'erthrew
> *Busiris* and his *Memphian* Chivalry,
> While with perfidious hatred they pursu'd
> The sojourners of *Goshen,* who beheld
> From the safe shore thir floating Carcasses
> And broken Chariot Wheels (302-11)

A finer modulation of aesthetic distance can hardly be found: we start at the point of maximum contrast, with the angels prostrate on the lake, in a region " vaulted with fire " (298), viewed as leaves fallen seasonally on a sheltered brook vaulted by shade; go next to the image of sea-weed scattered by storm, and finally, without break of focus, to the Israelites watching " from the safe shore " the floating bodies and parts of their pursuers. And, as in music, where one theme fading, another emerges to its place, while the image of calm and natural death changes to that of violent and supernatural destruction, the figure of the observer *ab extra* becomes explicit, substituting for the original glimpse of inviolable peace.

Could the counterplot be clearer? A simile intended to sharpen our view of the innumerable stunned host of hell, just before it is roused by Satan, at the same time sharpens our sense of the imperturbable order of the creation, and of the coming storm, and of the survival of man through providence and his safe-shored will. Satan, standing clear of the rout, prepares to vex his legions to new evil:

> on the Beach
> Of that inflamed Sea, he stood and call'd
> His Legions, Angel Forms, who lay intrans't
> Thick as Autumnal Leaves . . .

but the scenes the poet himself calls up mimick hell's defeat before Satan's voice is fully heard, and whatever sought to destroy the calm of autumnal leaves lies lifeless as scattered sedge. The continuity of the similes hinges on the middle image of Orion, which sketches both Satan's power to rouse the fallen host and God's power to scatter and destroy it. In this " plot counterplot " the hand of Satan is not ultimately distinguishable from the will of God.

A further instance, more complex still, is found at the end of Book I. Milton compares the host gathered in the gates of Pandemonium to bees at springtime (768 ff). The wonder of this incongruity has been preserved by many explanations. It is clearly a simile which, like others we have adduced, diminishes hell while it magnifies creation. The bees are fruit-ful, and their existence in the teeth of Satan drowns out the sonorous *hiss* of hell. Their " straw-built Citadel " will survive " bossy " Pandemonium. As Dr. Johnson kicking the stone kicks all excessive idealism, so Milton's bees rub their balm against all excessive demonism. But the irony may not end there. Are the devils not those bees who bring food out of the eater, sweetness out of the strong (Judges 15: 5-19)?

It may also be more than a coincidence that the most famous in this genre of similes describes the bustle of the Carthaginians as seen by storm-exiled Aeneas (*Aeneid* I, 430-40). Enveloped in a cloud by his divine mother, Aeneas looks down from the top of a hill onto a people busily building their city like a swarm of bees at summer's return, and is forced to cry: " O fortunati, quorum iam moenia surgunt! "—o fortunate people, whose walls are already rising! Then Vergil, as if to dispell any impression of despair, adds: *mirabile dictu*, a wonder! Aeneas walks among the Carthaginians made invisible by divine gift.

Here the counterplot thickens, and we behold one of Milton's amazing transpositions of classical texts. Aeneas strives to found Rome, which will outlast Carthage. The bees building in Vergil's text intimate a spirit of creativity seasonally renewed and independent of the particular civilization. The bees in Milton's text represent the same privilege and promise. Aeneas wrapped in the cloud is the observer *ab extra*, the person on the shore, and his impatient cry is of one who desires to build a civilization beyond decay, perhaps even beyond the wrath of the gods. An emergent, as yet invisible figure in Milton's text shares the hero's cry: he has seen Mammon and his troop build Pandemonium, Satan's band swarm triumphant about their citadel: despite this, can the walls of creation outlive Satan as Rome the ancient world?

All this would be putative or extrinsic if based solely on the simile of the bees. For this simile, like the middle image of Orion vexing the Red Sea, is indeterminate in its implications, a kind of visual pivot in a series of images which act in sequence and once more reveal the counterplot. Its indeterminacy is comparable to Milton's previously mentioned use of proper nouns, and his overall stylistic use of the *pivot*, by means of which images and words are made to refer both backwards and forwards, giving the verse period an unusual balance and flexibility. The series in question begins with the trooping to Pandemonium, and we now give the entire modulation which moves through several similes:

> all access was throng'd, the Gates
> And Porches wide, but chief the spacious Hall
> (Though like a cover'd field, where Champions bold
> Wont ride in arm'd, and at the Soldan's chair
> Defi'd the best of *Paynim* chivalry
> To mortal combat or career with Lance)
> Thick swarm'd, both on the ground and in the air,
> Brusht with the hiss of rustling wings. As Bees
> In spring time, when the Sun with *Taurus* rides,
> Pour forth thir populous youth about the Hive
> In clusters; they among fresh dews and flowers
> Fly to and fro, or on the smoothed Plank,
> The suburb of thir Straw-built Citadel,
> New rubb'd with Balm, expatiate and confer
> Thir State affairs. So thick the aery crowd
> Swarm'd and were strait'n'd; till the Signal giv'n,
> Behold a wonder! they but now who seem'd
> In bigness to surpass Earth's Giant Sons
> Now less than smallest Dwarfs, in narrow room
> Throng numberless, like that Pigmean Race
> Beyond the *Indian* Mount, or Faery Elves,
> Whose midnight Revels, by a Forest side
> Or Fountain some belated Peasant sees,
> Or dreams he sees, while over-head the Moon
> Sits Arbitress, and nearer to the Earth
> Wheels her pale course, they on thir mirth and dance

Intent, with jocund Music charm his ear;
At once with joy and fear his heart rebounds. (761-88)

   The very images which marshall the legions of hell to our
view reveal simultaneously that the issue of Satan's triumph
or defeat, his real or mock power, is in the hand of a *secret
arbiter*, whether God and divine prescience or man and free
will. In the first simile the observer *ab extra* is the Soldan,
who as a type of Satan overshadows the outcome of the combat
between pagan and christian warriors in the " cover'd field."
The second simile is indeterminate in tenor, except that it
diminishes the satanic thousands, blending them and their
war-like intents with a picture of natural, peaceful creativity,
Sun and Taurus presiding in place of the Soldan. " Behold a
wonder! " echoes the *mirabile dictu* of Vergil's story, and prepares the coming of a divine observer. The mighty host is seen
to shrink to the size of Pigmies (the third simile), and we know
that these, the " small infantry," as Milton had called them
with a pun reflecting the double perspective of the first books,
can be overshadowed by Cranes (575-6). The verse period
then carries us still further from the main action as the diminished devils are also compared to Faery Elves glimpsed
at their midnight revels by some belated Peasant. From the
presence and pomp of hell we have slowly slipped into a
pastoral.
   Yet does not this moment of stasis hide an inner combat more real than that for which hell is preparing? It
is midnight, the pivot between day and day, and in the
Peasant's mind a similar point of balance seems to obtain.
He is not fully certain of the significance or even reality
of the Fairy ring. Like Aeneas in Hades, who glimpses
the shade of Dido (*Aeneid* VI, 450-5), he " sees, Or dreams
he sees " something barely distinguishable from the pallid
dark, obscure as the new moon through clouds. What
an intensity of calm is here, reflecting a mind balanced on
the critical pivot, as a point of stillness is reached at greatest
remove from the threats and reverberations of hell! But even
as the man stands uncertain, the image of the moon overhead
becomes intense, it has sat there all the time as arbiter, now

wheels closer to the earth, and the Peasant's heart rebounds with a secret intuition bringing at once joy and fear.

The moon, clearly, is a last transformation of the image of the observer *ab extra*, Soldan, Sun and Taurus, Peasant. What was a type of Satan overshadowing the outcome of the real or spiritual combat is converted into a presentment of the individual's naive and autonomous power of discrimination, his free reason, secretly linked with a superior influence, as the moon overhead. The figure of the firmly placed observer culminates in that of the secret arbiter. Yet this moon is not an unambiguous symbol of the secret arbiter. A feeling of the moon's uncertain, changeable nature—incorruptible yet spotty, waxing and waning (I, 284-291; II, 659-666; see also " mooned horns," IV, 978, quoted below) —is subtly present. It reflects this series of images in which the poet constantly suggests, destroys and recreates the idea of an imperturbably transcendent discrimination. The moon that " Sits Arbitress " seems to complete the counterplot, but is only the imperfect sign of a figure not revealed till Book IV. Thus the whole cycle of to and fro, big and small, Pigmies or Elves, seeing or dreaming, far and near, joy and fear, this uneasy flux of couplets, alternatives and reversals, is continued when we learn, in the final lines of Book I, that far within Pandemonium, perhaps as far from consciousness as hell is from the thoughts of the Peasant or demonic power from the jocund, if intent music of the fairy revelers, Satan and the greatest of his Lords sit in their own, unreduced dimensions.

We meet the Peasant once more in *Paradise Lost*, and in a simile which seems to want to outdo the apparent incongruity of all others. At the end of Book IV, Gabriel and his files confront Satan apprehended squatting in Paradise, a toad at the ear of Eve. A heroically contemptuous exchange follows, and Satan's taunts finally so incense the Angel Squadron that they

> Turn'd fiery red, sharp'ning in mooned horns
> Thir Phalanx, and began to hem him round
> With ported Spears, as thick as when a field
> Of *Ceres* ripe for harvest waving bends
> Her bearded Grove of ears, which way the wind

Sways them; the careful Plowman doubting stands
Lest on the threshing floor his hopeful sheaves
Prove chaff. On th'other side *Satan* alarm'd
Collecting all his might dilated stood,
Like *Teneriff* or *Atlas* unremov'd:
His stature reacht the Sky, and on his Crest
Sat horror Plum'd; nor wanted in his grasp
What seem'd both Spear and Shield: now dreadful deeds
Might have ensu'd, nor only Paradise
In this commotion, but the Starry Cope
Of Heav'n perhaps, or all the Elements
At least had gone to rack, disturb'd and torn
With violence of this conflict, had not soon
Th'Eternal to prevent such horrid fray
Hung forth in Heav'n his golden Scales, yet seen
Betwixt *Astrea* and the *Scorpion* sign,
Wherein all things created first he weigh'd,
The pendulous round Earth with balanc'd Air
In counterpoise, now ponders all events,
Battles and Realms . . . (978-1002)

The question of Satan's power does not appear to be academic, at least not at first. The simile which, on previous
occasions, pretended to illustrate hell's greatness but actually
diminished hell and magnified the creation, is used here just
as effectively against heaven. Milton, by dilating Satan, and
distancing the spears of the angel phalanx as ears ready for
reaping, creates the impression of a balance of power between
heaven and hell. Yet the image which remains in control is
neither of Satan nor of the Angels but of the wheatfield, first
as its bearded ears bend with the wind, then as contemplated
by the Plowman. Here the counterplot achieves its most
consummate form. *Paradise Lost* was written not for the sake
of heaven or hell but for the sake of the creation. What is all
the fuss about if not to preserve the " self-balanc't " earth?
The center around which and to which all actions turn is
whether man can stand though free to fall, whether man and
the world can survive their autonomy. The issue may not
therefore be determined on the supernatural level by the direct
clash of heaven and hell, only by these two arbiters: man's free
will, and God's foreknowledge. The ripe grain sways in the
wind, so does the mind which has tended it. Between ripeness and ripeness gathered falls the wind, the threshing floor,

the labour of ancient *ears*, the question of the simultaneity of God's will and man's will. The ears appear to be at the mercy of the wind, what about the thoughts, the " hopeful sheaves " of the Plowman? The fate of the world lies between Gabriel and Satan, but also between the wind and the ripe ears, but also between man and his thoughts. Finally God, supreme arbiter, overbalances the balance with the same pair of golden scales (suspended yet between Virgin and Scorpion) in which the balanced earth weighed at its first creation.

MILTON AND THE PARADOX OF
THE FORTUNATE FALL

BY ARTHUR O. LOVEJOY

To many readers of *Paradise Lost* in all periods the most surprising lines in the poem must have been those in the Twelfth Book in which Adam expresses a serious doubt whether his primal sin—the intrinsic enormity and ruinous consequences of which had elsewhere been so copiously dilated upon—was not, after all, rather a ground for self-congratulation. The Archangel Michael, it will be remembered, has been giving Adam a prophetic relation of the history of mankind after the Fall. This, though for the greater part a most unhappy story, concludes with a prediction of the Second Coming and the Final Judgment, when Christ shall reward

(462)	His faithful and receive them into bliss,
	Whether in Heav'n or Earth, for then the Earth
	Shall all be Paradise, far happier place
	Than this of Eden, and far happier days.
	So spake the Archangel Michael; and then paused,
	As at the world's great period, and our Sire
	Replete with joy and wonder thus replied:
	"O Goodness infinite, Goodness immense,
	That all this good of evil shall produce,
	And evil turn to good—more wonderful
	Than that which by creation first brought forth
(473)	Light out of darkness! Full of doubt I stand,
	Whether I should repent me now of sin
	By me done or occasioned, or rejoice
	Much more that much more good thereof shall spring—
	To God more glory, more good will to men
(478)	From God—and over wrath grace shall abound.

The last six lines are Milton's expression of what may be called the Paradox of the Fortunate Fall. It is a paradox which has at least the look of a formal antinomy. From the doctrinal premises accepted by Milton and implicit in the poem, the two conclusions between which Adam is represented as hesitating were equally inevitable; yet they were mutually repugnant. The Fall could never be sufficiently condemned and lamented; and likewise, when all its consequences were considered, it could never be sufficiently rejoiced over. Adam's eating of the forbidden fruit, many theologians had observed, contained in itself all other sins;[1] as the violation by a rational creature of a command imposed by infinite wisdom, and as the frustration of the divine purpose in the creation of the earth, its sinfulness was infinite; and by it the entire race became corrupted and estranged from God. Yet if it had never occurred, the Incarnation and Redemption could never have occurred. These sublime mysteries would have had no occasion and no meaning; and therefore the plenitude of the divine goodness and power could neither have been exercised nor have become known to men. No devout believer could hold that it would have been better if the moving drama of man's salvation had never taken place; and consequently, no such believer could consistently hold that the first act of that drama, the event from which all the rest of it sprang, was really to be regretted. Moreover, the final state of the redeemed, the consummation of human history, would far surpass in felicity and in moral excellence the pristine happiness and innocence of the first pair in Eden— that state in which, but for the Fall, man would presumably have remained.[2] Thus Adam's sin—and also, indeed, the sins of his posterity which it " occasioned "—were the *conditio sine*

---

[1] So Milton himself in *De doctrina chr.* 1, ch. 11 in *Milton's Prose Wks.*, Bohn ed., 4, p. 258: " What sin can be named, which was not included in this one act? It comprehended at once distrust in the divine veracity, and a proportionate credulity in the assurances of Satan; unbelief; ingratitude; disobedience; gluttony; in the man excessive uxoriousness, in the woman a want of proper regard for her husband, in both an insensibility to the welfare of their offspring, and that offspring the whole human race; parricide; theft, invasion of the rights of others, sacrilege, deceit, presumption in aspiring to divine attributes, fraud in the means employed to attain the object, pride and arrogance."

[2] On this last point, however, there were, in the early Fathers and later theologians, differing opinions; the view that the primeval state was not that in which man was intended to remain, but merely a phase of immaturity to be transcended, had ancient and respectable supporters. Into the history of this view I shall not enter here.

qua non both of a greater manifestation of the glory of God and of immeasurably greater benefits for man than could conceivably have been otherwise obtained.

Necessary—upon the premises of orthodox Christian theology—though this conclusion was, its inevitability has certainly not been always, nor, it may be suspected, usually, apparent to those who accepted those premises; it was a disturbing thought upon which many even of those who were aware of it (as all the subtler theologians must have been) were naturally reluctant to dwell; and the number of theological writers and religious poets who have given it entirely explicit and pointed expression has apparently not been great. Nevertheless it had its own emotional appeal to many religious minds—partly, no doubt, because its very paradoxicality, its transcendence of the simple logic of common thought, gave it a kind of mystical sublimity; between logical contradiction (or seeming contradiction) and certain forms of religious feeling there is a close relation, of which the historic manifestations have never been sufficiently studied. And for writers whose purpose, like Milton's, was a religious interpretation of the entire history of man, the paradox served, even better than the simple belief in a future millennium or celestial bliss, to give to that history as a whole the character, not of tragedy, but of a divine comedy.[3] Not only should the drama have (for the elect—and about the unredeemed the elect were not wont to be greatly concerned) a happy ending, but the happy ending had been implicit in the beginning and been made possible by it. The Paradox of the Fortunate Fall has consequently found recurrent expression in the history of Christian religious thought; the idea was no invention, or discovery, of Milton's. In the present paper, I shall note a few earlier phrasings of the same idea, which it is of interest to compare with Milton's. They may or may not be " sources " of *P. L.* 12. 469-478; they are in any case illustrations of a long tradition lying behind that passage.

---

[3] The application of the phrase here is borrowed from Professor C. A. Moore, *PMLA* 12 (1921). 11.

To Milton-specialists the occurrence of a similar passage in Du Bartas is, of course, well known; but to facilitate comparison it seems worth while to cite the lines here. In the section of the *Seconde Semaine* entitled "The Imposture," after the Creator has pronounced sentence upon Adam, the poet interrupts his narrative to introduce a disquisition of his own, designed to answer the usual complaints against the justice of God in his dealings with Adam and his descendants:

> Here I conceive, that flesh and bloud will brangle,
> And murmuring Reason with th'Almighty wrangle.[4]

The ensuing essay in theodicy is apparently addressed primarily to mankind in general, though the poet sometimes rather confusedly seems, when he uses the second person singular, to be thinking of those whose errors he is refuting, sometimes of Adam, sometimes of departed saints in general, sometimes of all the elect. The lines which concern us are the following:

> For, thou complainest of God's grace, whose Still
> Extracts from dross of thine audacious ill,
> Three unexpected goods; praise for his Name;
> Bliss for thy self; for Satan endless shame:
> Sith, but for sin, *Justice* and *Mercy* were
> But idle names: and but that thou didst erre,
> Christ had not come to conquer and to quell,
> Upon the Cross, Sin, Satan, Death, and Hell;
> Making thee blessèd more since thine offence,
> Then in thy primer happy innocence . . .
> In Earth thou liv'dst then; now in heav'n thou beest:
> Then, thou didst hear God's word; it now thou seest:
> Then pleasant fruits; now, Christ is thy repast:
> Then might'st thou fall; but now thou standest fast.[5]

---

[4] *The Complete Works of Joshua Sylvester*, ed. Grosart (1880), 1. 111. Sylvester's tr., 1611 ed., p. 249.

[5] Grosart 1. 111-2; in 1611 ed., p. 249. The original in Du Bartas, whom Sylvester here follows closely, is as follows:

>   . . . sa grace
> Dont l'alambic extrait de ta rebelle audace
> Trois biens non esperez: sçavoir, gloire pour soy,

Since, as we shall see, the thought was not original with Du Bartas, the passage in *P. L.* 12 is not one of those which can confidently be cited among the evidences of Milton's utilization of *La Semaine.* There is, however, a similarity in one detail which perhaps lends a slight probability to the supposition of a conscious or unconscious reminiscence by Milton of the corresponding passage in the French poet: the fact that both specify three " greater goods " which sprang from the evil inherent in the Fall.[6] Of these, two are identical in both passages —greater " glory " to God, greater benefits conferred by God upon man. The third is different; for the defeat and humiliation of Satan Milton substitutes, as the last happy consequence, the manifestation of the predominance of God's grace over his wrath—religiously a more moving and edifying conception, though less apposite to the plot of Milton's epic of the war between God and the rebel angels.[7] There are two other differ-

---

Vergongne pour Sathan, felicité pour toy.
Veu que sans le peché sa Clemence et Justice
Ne seroient que vains noms; et que sans ta malice
Christ ne fust descendu, qui d'un mortel effort
A vaincu les Enfers, les Pechez, et la Mort,
Et te rend plus heureux mesme apres ton offence,
Qu'en Eden tu n'estois pendant ton innocence . . .
Tu viuois icy-bas, or tu vis sur le Pole.
Dieu parloit avec toy: or tu vois sa Parole.
Tu vivois de doux fruicts: Christ ore est ton repas.
Tu pouvois trebucher: mais or tu ne peux pas.

(*La Seconde Semaine,* Rouen, 1592, p. 53.) It is to be remembered that not only were the poem of Du Bartas, and Sylvester's English version of it, famous and familiar in the 17th century, but also Simon Goulart's prose *Commentaires et Annotations sur la Sepmaine* . . . (1582, 1584) and Thomas Lodge's translation of Goulart: *A learned Summarie of the famous Poeme of William of Saluste, Lord of Bartas, wherein are discovered all the excellent Secrets in Metaphysicall, Physicall, Morall and Historicall Knowledge* . . . , 2 vols., 1637. The 1584 ed. of Goulart in the Harvard University Library does not contain the commentary on *The Second Week,* but the passage corresponding to Du Bartas's lines may be found in Lodge, *ed. cit.,* 2. 69-70: " The Poet expresseth this in the Verse 509, saying. That without sinne the Mercy and Justice of God had not so much been manifested," *etc.* The comparison of this passage of Du Bartas with *P. L.* 12. 468 ff. is not made by G. C. Taylor in *Milton's Use of Du Bartas,* 1934.

[6] This detail is not found in other expressions of the paradox known to me.

[7] This eventual consequence of the Incarnation and Resurrection had, however, been dwelt upon by Milton in *P. L.* 3. 250-8. If in writing the passage in Bk. 12, Milton was recasting that of Du Bartas, the change of the third " good " may be attributable to a desire to avoid repetition.

ences worth noting: (a) Milton gains greater dramatic effect by putting the paradox into the mouth of Adam himself—a ground for this being laid in the device of the preceding recital of the future history of man by the Archangel.[8] (b) In Milton, however, the paradox is not so sharply expressed. Du Bartas puts quite categorically the point that but for the Fall there *could* have been no Incarnation and Redemption and that, " but for sin, Justice and Mercy were but idle names"; Milton's Adam is made to express merely a doubt whether he should repent his sin or " rejoice much more " over its consequences. Yet the logic of the paradox remains clear enough in Milton's lines; Adam could have had no reason for his doubt except upon the assumption that the sin was truly prerequisite to the " much more good " that was to follow—was, in Milton's own significant term, to " spring " from it; and an intelligent reader could hardly have failed to conclude that the doubt was to be resolved in favor of the second alternative.

Du Bartas, however, was not the only poetic precursor of Milton in the use of the paradox. It was peculiarly adapted both to the theme and the style of Giles Fletcher in his most ambitious poem, *The Triumph of Christ.* It naturally occurred to a devout but reflective mind when it dwelt rapturously upon that theme; the more intense the feeling of the sublimity of the redemptive act and the magnitude of the good both inherent in it and resultant from it, the more apparent the impossibility of regarding as merely evil the sin which had evoked it. And to a writer whose poetic method consisted chiefly in the multiplication of conceits and rhetorical antitheses, even when dealing with the gravest articles of his faith, such a paradox naturally had a special attraction. Consequently in *Christ's Triumph over Death* (1610) Fletcher, descanting upon the Passion of Christ in a series of what may be called antithetic parallels between the Fall and the Redemption—the two trees (i. e., the

---

[8] Du Bartas employs the same device of a prophetic recital of subsequent history (*Seconde Semaine*, 1611 ed., p. 293) ; but here the prophet is Adam himself, who tells the story of things to come to Seth, and his prediction abruptly ends with the Deluge. If we were sure that Milton was, in Books 11-12, consciously recasting Du Bartas, the comparison between his and the earlier poet's use of the same group of themes would significantly illuminate the working of Milton's mind in the construction of his poem.

forbidden tree and the cross), the two gardens (Eden and Gethsemane), etc.—introduces the paradox—and converts it into a play upon words:

> Such joy we gained by our parentalls,
> That good, or bad, whither I cannot wiss,
> To call it a mishap, or happy miss
> That fell from Eden and to heav'n did rise.[9]

Fletcher, however, while raising the question clearly, is, like Milton's Adam, ostensibly non-committal about the answer to it; yet it is so put that the reader could hardly remain in doubt about the answer. A fall from Eden which made the greater joys of heaven possible was plainly no " mishap." [10]

The last act of Andreini's *L'Adamo* (1613) has a good deal in common with the last book of *Paradise Lost*, including a long speech by Michael in which, after reproachfully reminding Eve of her guilt—

> Tu cagionera a l'huomo
> E di doglia et di pianto— [11]

he proceeds to a prophecy of the final triumph of grace and of the future bliss to be enjoyed by the first pair and their progeny, both on earth, which will then be like Paradise, and in heaven.[12]

---

[9] *Op. cit.*, stanza 12; in *Giles and Phineas Fletcher: Poetical Works*, ed. F. S. Boas (1908), 1. 61.

[10] The second stanza following might be construed as a more affirmative expression of the paradox:

> Sweet Eden was the arbour of delight,
> Yet in his honey flowres our poyson blew,
> Sad Gethseman the bowre of baleful night
> Whear Christ a health of poyson for us drew;
> Yet all our honey in that poyson grewe.

If the " poyson " in the last two lines is that referred to in the second—i. e., the forbidden fruit, or the consequences of eating it—the final line is a figurative way of asserting once more the dependence of the Redemption upon the Fall. But it is possible that the " poyson " in the penultimate line signifies the Agony in the Garden and that the last line is merely a repetition of this. The former interpretation seems the more likely.

[11] *Op. cit.*, tercentenary ed. E. Allodoli (1913). Act 5, Sc. 9, p. 140, ll. 4122-3; cf. " cagionera " with Milton's " occasioned " in 12. 475, apparently his only use of the word as a verb.

[12] *Ibid.*, p. 143, ll. 4235 ff.: " per la gioia D'esser rapito l'uomo A l'artiglio infernale il tutto gode, E pel diletto sembra Il Cielo in terra, e'n Paradiso il Mondo "; cf. *P. L.* 12. 462-5. The supreme good, however, Andreini, unlike Milton, expressly says, will be the beatific vision: " di Dio . . . il sacrosanto viso, . . . il sommo bel del Paradiso."

Arthur O. Lovejoy

In their response to this archangelic discourse, Andreini's Adam and Eve, like Milton's Adam, expand with gratitude and wonder over the benignant power which can so " unite " good with evil:

> Con la morte, la vita,
> Con la guerra la pace,
> Col perder la Vittoria,
> Con l'error la salute
> E con l'Inferno il Cielo
> Insieme unir, non è poter umano,
> Ma de l'eterno mano
> Omnipotenza summa. Ondè, Signore,
> Ch' Eva trafitta è sana,
> E perdendo trionfa, et vinta hà gloria.[13]

There is in these lines, especially in " perdendo trionfa," an evident adumbration of the paradox, but they hardly give it unequivocal expression.[14]

II

Some of Milton's precursors, then, in the century preceding *Paradise Lost*, had dwelt upon the idea that the Fall had not

---

[13] *Ibid.*, p. 141, ll. 4157 ff.

[14] The later scenes of the fifth act of Salandra's *Adamo Caduto* (1647), especially in a dialogue between two personified divine attributes, Omnipotence and Mercy, dwell upon the happy ending which was to follow the disaster of the Fall; the Incarnation and Atonement are foretold, and, as in Milton, there are devout ejaculations over *la gran Bontade* which is to be made manifest through this outcome; and it is remarked that other attributes of deity—Infinity and Charity—would thereby obtain wider scope for their exercise:

> L'Infinitade
> In compartirsi sin fra Creature.
> Applaudarà la Caritate, mentre
> Verrà più dilatato il suo bel Regno.

But the essence of the paradox—the dependence of the possibility of all this upon the Fall—is not emphasized. In the equally cheerful outlook upon the future with which Vondel's *Lucifer* (1654) concludes, there is no hint of the paradox. That poems about the Fall should be given a happy ending by the introduction, through one device or another, of a prevision of the coming of Christ and the future bliss of the redeemed, may be said to have been a convention of this *genre*; and, as Professor C. A. Moore has pointed out in *PMLA* 12 (1921). 463 ff. the accepted dogma itself made it virtually incumbent upon the author of such a poem to foreshadow the "far happier place, far happier days," which the elect should know. To end upon a tragic note was to depart from both literary and theological orthodoxy. But a recognition of the Paradox of the Fortunate Fall was not a necessary or invariable part of a happy ending.

only been over-ruled for good by the divine beneficence, but had been the indispensable means to the attainment of far greater good for man and—if it may be so put—for God than would have been possible without it. Milton's eighteenth century annotators and editors soon began to point out—though with a characteristic and exasperating neglect to give definite references—that the idea had already been expressed in the patristic period. The earliest suggestion of such a source seems to have been given in J. Richardson's *Explanatory Notes and Remarks on Milton* (1734), in which line 473 is annotated: "*O felix culpa, quae talem ac tantum meruit habere Redemptorem!* 'tis an exclamation of St. Gregory."[15]   Newton and other annotators in the same century were, prudently, still more vague in citation: "He seems to remember the rant of one of the Fathers, *O felix culpa,*" etc.[16] So far as I have observed, no modern editor has given any more precise reference for this yet more striking phrasing of the Paradox of the Fall. An extensive, though not exhaustive, search of the writings of St. Gregory [17] fails to disclose it. But it is to be found in a probably earlier, more noteworthy, and, at least to non-Protestants, more widely familiar source—a passage in the Roman Liturgy.[18] In the service for Easter Even (Holy Saturday) there is a hymn, sung by the deacon in the rite of blessing the paschal candle, which bears the title of *Praeconium* but is better known, from the word with which it opens, as the *Exultet* (*exultet iam angelica turba caelorum*) ; in it, a Catholic writer has remarked, "the language of the liturgy rises into heights to which it is hard to find a parallel in Christian literature."[19] In this rapturous exultation over the mystery of the Redemption the sentence already cited is preceded by another expressing the same paradox yet more pointedly: "*O*

[15] *Op. cit.*, p. 521.
[16] Fourth ed. (1757) of Thomas Newton's ed. of *P. L.*, 2, 429 (note). The parallel is not indicated in the earliest commentary, Patrick Hume's *Annotations on Paradise Lost* (1695)
[17] Richardson's "St. Gregory" presumably refers to Gregory the Great (d. 604), since the citation is in Latin.
[18] For my knowledge of this fact, and for other valued assistance in this section, I am indebted to Professor G. La Piana of Harvard University.
[19] C. B. Walker, in *Catholic Encycl.*, art. "*Exultet.*"

certe necessarium Adae peccatum, quod Christi morte deletum est! O felix culpa, quae talem ac tantum meruit habere redemptorem! " Adam's sin was not only a " happy fault " but " certainly necessary "—necessary to the very possibility of the redemptive act, which, it may be supposed, was by the author of the hymn conceived as itself a necessary, and the central, event in the divine plan of terrestrial history.

The date of composition of the *Exultet* and that of its incorporation in the service of Easter Even can be determined only approximately.[20] It was originally no part of the Roman Liturgy, but appears first in the Gallican, which, as some liturgiologists hold, was probably in existence by the beginning of the fifth century;[21] but the earliest manuscript of this liturgy which includes the hymn in question is of the seventh century.[22] Certain conjectures concerning its authorship have been made, but none is supported by any substantial evidence;[23] in the words of the most careful modern study of the subject, " in the present state of the sources, one must give up the attempt to determine the authorship and even the place of origin of this famous hymn." [24] All that can be said, then, on

[20] For the text of the hymn (in its oldest known form) see Duchesne, *Christian Worship*, 5th ed. (1923), p. 254; Migne, *Patr. Lat.*, 72, col. 269 f. For its history cf. Duchesne, *loc. cit.*: A. Franz, *Die kirchliche Benediktionen im Mittelalter* (1909) 1.519-553; V. Thalhofer and L. Eisenhofer, *Handbuch der katholischen Liturgik* (1912) 1.643 ff.; A. Gastoué, *Les vigiles nocturnes* (1908), p. 18; C. B. Walker, *loc. cit.*; J. Braun, *Liturgisches Handlexikon* (1922), art. "Praeconium paschale." An English version of the entire hymn may be found in I. Schuster, *The Sacramentary* (1925), 2.293-5.

[21] Duchesne, *op. cit.*, p. 86, thinks the hymn may be as early as the middle of the fourth century.

[22] Cf. the liturgiological authorities cited.

[23] Some ancient manuscripts credit it to St. Augustine " when he was deacon," a highly improbable ascription (cf. Thalhofer and Eisenhofer, 1. 644; Franz, 1. 534). It is probably due to the fact that Augustine, as he himself records (*De civ. Dei*, 15. 22), once wrote a short *laus cerei* in verse; but this was not the *Exultet*. It appears to have been originally the custom for the deacon to compose his own *praeconium* for the rite of blessing the Easter candle (Braun, *loc. cit.*), a practice of which the *locus* in Augustine gives probable evidence. One of Migne's editors (H. Menard in *Pat. Lat.*, 78, col. 335) suggests that the hymn may perhaps have been written by St. Ambrose, which is perhaps possible, but incapable of proof. Gastoué's suggestion of St. Ennodius of Pavia (d. 521) as the author appears to be due to a confusion of the *Exultet* with two quite different formulas of benediction composed by that Father (v. *Corp. script. lat. eccles.* 6.415-419).

[24] Franz, *op. cit.*, 1.534.

the question of date, is that the passage which some of Milton's editors have regarded as the probable source of *P. L.* 12. 473 ff. was in liturgical use as early as the seventh and possibly as early as the fourth century, in the churches employing the Gallican sacramentary. It is, however, certain that the popularity of the hymn was so great that it presently drove out, even in the Roman Liturgy—apparently after some hesitancies on the part of the popes—all rival formulas in the rite of blessing the Easter candle. It evidently " owed its triumph," as a Catholic historian of the liturgy has said, "to the fact that it was far superior to all these rivals both in expression and content." [25] In certain medieval missals there are some interesting variations in the wording of the two sentences relevant to the theme of this paper; [26] and it is of interest to note that these sentences were by some ecclesiastical authorities considered dangerous, and were omitted from the hymn—rather generally in German and not infrequently in French and Italian sacramentaries.[27] But with the establishment of liturgical uniformity since the late sixteenth century, both sentences found an accepted and permanent place in the Missal of the Roman Church.

III

That the Protestant religious poets of the sixteenth and seventeenth centuries who gave expression to the Paradox of the Fortunate Fall had heard or read the part of the Catholic liturgy containing the *Exultet* is, of course, possible; but there is no need to suppose them to have done so. It is rather more likely that they—or at all events the earliest of them, Du Bartas—became acquainted with the idea through the reading of one of the Fathers, whose writings still had among Protestant theologians much authority. St. Ambrose, for example, (4th c.) had flatly asserted that Adam's sin " has brought more benefit

[25] Thalhofer and Eisenhofer, *op. cit.*, p. 644.

[26] E. g., in the Missal of Westminster Abbey (ed. Lagg, 1893, 2, 581) the words *et nostrum* follow *Adae peccatum.*

[27] See Franz, 1. 540 f., for examples, of which I cite only one: Hugo, Abbot of Cluny (d. 1109), commanded that these sentences should be "deleted and no longer read, *cum aliquando non bene haberetur ' O felix culpa,' et quod peccatum Adae necessarium esset."*

to us than harm " (*amplius nobis profuit culpa quam nocuit*),[28] and had even permitted himself the more generalized and hazardous apophthegm that "sin is more fruitful than innocence" (*fructuosior culpa quam innocentia*).[29] God "knew that Adam would fall, *in order that* he might be redeemed by Christ (*ut redimeretur a Christo*). *Felix ruina, quae reparatur in melius.*" [30] The identity of the thought and the approximation of the phrasing here to those of the two sentences quoted from the *Exultet* are evident; and it is probable that these Ambrosian passages are the primary source of the expressions of the paradox, alike in that hymn and in Du Bartas, Fletcher and Milton. To the last two the idea may or may not have been transmitted through Du Bartas; [31] or to any of them it is possible that the medium of transmission may have been some later patristic repetition or amplification of the theme. In the century after Ambrose his enunciation of it was echoed, with some weakening, by one of the greatest of the Popes, Leo I, in his *First Sermon on the Lord's Ascension:*

Today we [in contrast with the first of our race] are not only confirmed in the possession of Paradise, but have even penetrated to the higher things of Christ; we have gained more by the ineffable grace of Christ than we had lost by the envy of the Devil.[32]

And in the next century Gregory the Great (d. 604) expressed the paradox with all possible explicitness.[33]

What greater fault than that by which we all die? And what greater goodness than that by which we are freed from death? And certainly, unless Adam had sinned, it would not have behooved our

[28] *De institutione virginis*, ch. 17. 104 (*MPL*, 16. 331).

[29] *De Jacob*, 6. 21 (*MPL*, 14. 607).

[30] *In Ps. XXXIX*, 20 (*MPL*, 14. 1065).

[31] That Du Bartas "used Ambrose's *Hexaemeron*" is said by U. T. Holmes and his associates to be a certainty (*The Works of Du Bartas* (1935), 1. 128); it is improbable that Du Bartas's reading in Ambrose was confined to this writing. Cf. Thibaut de Maisières, *Les poèmes inspirés du début de la Genèse* (1931), p. 26. Milton, however, was acquainted with Ambrose at first hand; cf. *Tetrachordon* in *Prose Works*, Bohn ed. (1848), 3. 418.

[32] *MPL*, 54. 396: ampliora adepti per ineffabilem Christi gratiam quam per diaboli amiseramus invidiam.

[33] Richardson, therefore, was perhaps not wholly wrong in indicating Gregory as a source of the passage in *P. L.*, though in error in attributing the *O felix culpa* to that saint.

Redeemer to take on our flesh. Almighty God saw beforehand that from that evil because of which men were to die, He would bring about a good which would overcome that evil. How wonderfully the good surpasses the evil, what faithful believer can fail to see? Great, indeed, are the evils we deservedly suffer in consequence of the first sin; but who of the elect would not willingly endure still worse evils, rather than not have so great a Redeemer? [34]

IV

In the foregoing examples, the writers who enunciated the paradox, it is evident, usually had chiefly in mind the relation of causal dependence between specific historical events, the Fall and the Redemption; and the argument was that the latter, or consequent, being preponderatingly a good, the former, as its necessary (though not sufficient) cause, must have been preponderatingly a good. Yet the Fall none the less remained, upon orthodox principles, a moral evil. These considerations, taken together, tended to suggest two larger, and awkward, questions. Was it true in general that the existence of moral evils is, from another and more comprehensive point of view, a good? And if, from such a point of view, the Fall was preponderatingly a good, was it not necessary to assume that its occurrence must after all have been in accordance with God's will? These questions, implicit in the notion of the *felix culpa*, were fairly explicitly raised and considered by Augustine; and his answers to both were, at least sometimes, in the affirmative; in other words, he not only accepted the paradox but gave it a more generalized form. Thus in his *Enchiridion ad Laurentium* he writes:

[34] *In Primum Regum Expositiones*, 4. 7; *MPL*, 79. 222: "Quae maior culpa, quam illa, qua omnes morimur? Et quae maior bonitas, quam illa, per quam a morte liberamur? Et quidem nisi Adam peccaret, Redemptorem nostrum carnem suscipere nostram non oporteret. . . Ex illo malo, quo morituri erant, bonum quod malum illum vinceret, omnipotens Deus sese facturum providerat. Cuius profecto boni magnitudo, quis fidelis non videat quam mirabiliter excellat. Magna quippe sunt mala, quae per primae culpae meritum patimur, sed quis electus nollet peiora mala perpeti, quam tantum Redemptorem non habere?" The echo of the last clause in the *Exultet* suggests that the author of the hymn may h̃ave been remembering *both* this passage of Gregory and those of Ambrose; in which case a seventh century date for the hymn, or at least for the part of it which here concerns us, would be indicated. But it is, of course, possible, that Gregory was echoing the *Exultet*.

Although those things that are evil, in so far as they are evil, are not good; nevertheless, it is good that there should be not only goods but evils as well. For unless this—namely, that there be also evils—were not a good, men would under no circumstances fall away from the omnipotent Good; [35]

i. e., neither Adam nor any man would ever have sinned. And again:

The works of God are so wisely and exquisitely contrived that, when an angelic and human creature sins, that is, does, not what God wished it to do, but what itself wishes, yet by that very will of the creature whereby it does what the Creator did not will, it fulfills what he willed—God, as supremely good, putting even evils to good use, for the damnation of those whom he has justly predestined to punishment and for the salvation of those whom he has benignantly predestined to grace.[36]

The greatest of the Latin Fathers was here manifestly skating on rather thin ice. It was always difficult for an acute-minded theologian with a strong sense of the divine sovereignty to admit that Adam's sin had really frustrated the will of God, and had compelled the deity to perform, unwillingly, acts which he would not otherwise have performed; it was therefore not easy, when dealing with these matters, always to avoid the thought that the Fall itself, with its consequences—so happy for the elect—was but a part of the eternal and ineluctable divine purpose for mankind. These passages of Augustine's thus reveal more clearly some of the moral difficulties and metaphysical pitfalls which lay behind the conception of the *felix culpa*—difficulties and pitfalls which Augustine himself cannot be said to have wholly escaped.[37]

[35] *Op. cit.*, ch. 96 (*MPL* 40.276): Quamvis ergo ea quae mala, in quantum mala sunt, non sint bona; tamen ut non solum bona, sed etiam sint et mala, bonum est. Nam nisi esset hoc bonum, ut essent et malla, nullo modo sinerentur ab omnipotente bono.

[36] *Ibid.* ch. 100 (*MPL* 40.279) : Opera domini [sunt] . . . tam sapienter exquisita, ut cum angelica et humana creatura peccasset, id est, non quod ille, sed quod voluit ipsa fecisset, etiam per eamdem creaturae voluntatem, qua factum est quod Creator noluit, impleret ipse quod voluit; bene utens et malis, tamquam summe bonus, ad eorum damnationem quos iuste praedestinavit ad poenam, et ad eorum salutem quos benigne praedestinavit ad gratiam.

[37] Donne in one of his sermons bases upon the authority of Augustine as well as of Scripture a similar remark that matters have been so ordered that sin in general— not specifically the sin of Adam—is made conducive to moral good: " If I cannot

The familiarity of the idea in the fourteenth century is shown by its occurrence both in *The Vision of Piers the Plowman, ca.* 1378, and in Wyclif's *Sermons*. In the former it is put into the mouth of Repentance, after the Seven Deadly Sins have made their confessions: God created man " most like to himself, and afterwards suffered him to sin,"

> And al for the best, as I bileve · what euer the boke telleth,
>   O *felix culpa*! *o necessarium peccatum ade*! *etc.*
> For thourgh that synne thi sone · sent was to this erthe,
> And bicam man of a mayde · mankind to save.[38]

Wyclif in a Christmas sermon preached, perhaps, to his rustic flock at Lutterworth in the early 1380s, did not shrink from the paradox, but on the contrary joined with it a still more sweeping optimism, of very dubious orthodoxy: all things, including sin, are for the best in the best of possible worlds, since all happens in accordance with God's will:

> And so, as many men seien, alle thingis comen for the beste; for alle comen for Goddis ordenance, and so thei comen for God himsilf; and so alle thingis that comen fallen for the beste thing that mai be. Moreover to another witt men seien, that this world is betterid bi everything that fallith therinne, where that it be good or yvel . . . and herfore seith Gregori, that it was a blesful synne that Adam synnede and his kynde, for bi this the world is beterid; but the ground of this goodnesse stondith in grace of Jesus Crist.[39]

find a foundation for my comfort in this subtilty of the Schoole, that sin is nothing, . . . yet I can raise a second step for my consolation in this, that be sin what it will in the nature thereof, yet my sin shall conduce and cooperate to my good. So *Ioseph* saies to his Brethren, *You thought evill against me, but God meant it unto good*: which is not onely good to *Ioseph*, who was not partaker in the evill, but good even to them who meant nothing but evill." What Donne has in mind here at least in part, however, is the more special idea that, after many little sins, a good round sin may be a means of grace, by bringing the sinner to a realization of his own state. " Though it be strangely said, yet I say it, That God's anger is good; so saies S. Augustine, *Audeo dicere*, Though it be boldly said yet must I say it, *Utile est cadere in aliquid manifestum peccatum*, Many sinners would not have been saved if they had not committed some greater sin at last, then before; for, the punishment of that sin, hath brought them to a remorse of all their other sins formerly neglected " (LXXX *Sermons* (1640), p. 171).

[38] B. Ms., *Passus V*, 489 ff., in Skeat, *The Vision of William Concerning Piers the Plowman* (1886).

[39] *Select English Works of John Wyclif*, ed. Thomas Arnold (1869), Sermon XC, 1. 320-321. There is no corresponding passage in the Latin sermon from the same text and for the same festival: *Ioannis Wyclif Sermones*, ed. Loserth (1888) 2. 1 ff.

An interesting late-medieval lyrical poem gives to the paradox a turn not found in any of the other examples here cited; it is presented in its relation to the cult of the Virgin. Since there would have been no Incarnation without the Fall, all that phase of Catholic piety and religious emotion which centers about the figure of the Virgin Mother manifestly owed its possibility to Adam's eating the forbidden fruit. There is also in the poem, if I am not mistaken, a touch of sly humor; the anonymous author hints that poor Adam, to whom not only mankind in general but the Queen of Heaven herself are so deeply indebted, has been rather badly treated. This further inference from the idea of the *felix culpa* would, one may suspect, hardly have been approved by St. Ambrose and St. Gregory. Adam, the poet recalls, lay bound for four thousand winters:

> And all was for an appil,
>   An appil that he tok . . .
> Ne hadde the appil také ben,
>   The appil taken ben,
> Ne haddé never our lady
>   A bene hevené quene.
> Blessed be the time
>   That appil také was.
> Therefore we moun singen
>   ' *Deo gracias.*' [40]

A sixteenth century illustration of the vogue of the concept of the *felix culpa* is to be found in the widely used Latin *Commentary on Genesis* of the Jesuit Benito Pereira (Pererius). The commentator is dilating, *à propos* of Genesis 1, 31, upon the manner in which God transmutes evils— even moral evils (*mala culpae*)—into good.

A signal proof and example of this is exhibited to us in the sin of Adam. How grave this sin was, how far and wide it spread poison and destruction, how severely it was punished, is acknowledged by all men. Yet this so great sin, such is the goodness and power of

---

Wyclif also apparently confused in his memory the *Exultet* and the passage of Gregory above cited, or else believed Gregory to have composed the hymn.

[40] Professor Douglas Bush has kindly brought this poem to my notice. It is printed in Chambers and Sidgwick's *Early English Lyrics* (1907), p. 102, and is believed to have been written in the early fifteenth century.

God, has been wonderfully converted into the greatest good and the most glorious of God's works, namely, the incarnation, passion and death of the Son of God. So that Gregory not unadvisedly or rashly somewhere exclaims, *O felix culpa, quae talem ac tantum meruit habere Redemptorem.*" [41]

Upon the crucial point of the paradox, however—that God could not have performed this *praeclarissimum opus* if Adam had remained innocent—Pereira does not dwell.

V

For a final example, which will bring us back to Milton's century, I will cite one of the most famous and widely read of Catholic devotional works, the *Traité de l'amour de Dieu* of St. Francis de Sales (1616).[42]

The mercy of God [he writes] has been more salutary for the redemption of the race of men than the wretchedness of Adam has been poisonous for its destruction. And so far is it from being true that the sin of Adam has overcome the benevolence (*debonnaireté*) of God, that on the contrary it has served to excite and provoke it: so that, by a gentle and most loving antiperistasis [43] and opposition, that benevolence has been re-invigorated by the presence of

---

[41] *Benedicti Pererii Valentini Commentariorum et disputationum in Genesim tomus primus* (Leyden, 1594), p. 168. Pereira, like Wyclif, it will be observed, either attributes the *Exultet* to St. Gregory or has confused the phrase from the hymn with the dictum of Gregory above cited. The passage is a highly probable source of Richardson's similar error previously noted; and it is a conceivable source of the *locus* in Milton. On the importance of this and similar Renaissance commentaries on Genesis for the background of *P. L.*, see the article of Arnold Williams in *Studies in Philology*, April, 1937, pp. 191-208. But it is to be borne in mind that Pereira's work and the others mentioned by Williams were later than Du Bartas's poem.

[42] The passage is therefore of later date than those cited from Du Bartas and Giles Fletcher.

[43] A technical term of the physics of the period, signifying a process by which a quality or force in a substance is increased or intensified by the action of an opposing quality or force. Milton expresses the same idea in the hymn of the celestial choirs, 7. 613 ff.

> Who seeks
> To lessen thee, against his purpose serves
> To manifest the more thy might: his evil
> Thou usest, and from thence creat'st more good.

The " more good " here, however, is the creation of " this new-made world " and of man, to " repair that detriment " resulting from the defection of the rebel angels—not the Redemption and its consequences.

Arthur O. Lovejoy 179

its adversary: and, so to say, gathering together its forces in order to win the victory, it has caused grace ' to abound more exceedingly where sin abounded.' [44] Therefore the Church, in a holy excess of admiration, exclaims on the Eve of Easter: ' O sin of Adam, truly necessary ' etc. [quotes the two sentences from the *Exultet*]. Of a truth, we can say with that man of ancient times: ' We should be lost (*perdus*) if we had not been lost; ' [45] that is to say, our loss has been our gain, since human nature has received more gifts of grace (*plus de graces*) from its redemption by its Savior than it would ever have received from the innocence of Adam, if he had persevered in it. . . . The redemption of our Lord, touching our miseries, renders them more useful and amiable than the original innocence would ever have been. The Angels, the Savior tells us, ' have more joy over one sinner that repenteth than over ninety-and-nine just persons that need no repentance '; and in the same way, the state of redemption is one hundred times greater in value than the state of innocence.[46]

Here the strangest aspect of the paradox is even more pointedly brought out than by Du Bartas or Milton: not only did the Fall make possible more good for man, but God himself *needed* a fallen race to evoke fully the divine attributes and powers.

VI

It is unlikely that the pre-Miltonic expressions of the Paradox of the Fortunate Fall which I have noted are the only ones to be found in Christian literature from the fourth to the seventeenth centuries, but they pretty certainly include the most important; all but one of them could have been known to Milton at first hand; and they are sufficient to place in its proper historical perspective the passage of the Twelfth Book of *Paradise Lost* cited at the beginning. In that perspective, the passage ceases to be surprising, or indicative of any originality or of any great boldness in Milton's thought. A paradox which had been embraced by Ambrose, Leo the Great, Gregory the Great, Francis de Sales, and Du Bartas, had for at least ten centuries had a place in many missals, and had finally been

[44] *Romans* 5.20. The Pauline text gave a seeming biblical sanction to the paradox, though it does not in fact express the essential point of it.

[45] The reference is to a saying of Themistocles in Plutarch's *Life of Themistocles*, 39.

[46] *Op. cit.*, Bk. 2, ch. 5.

officially adopted by the Roman Church, was, obviously, sufficiently orthodox ; and it had been put more sharply and boldly by at least two of the Doctors of the Church, by the composer of the *Exultet*, by the French mystic, and by the author of *La Semaine*, than by Milton. Though the hint of antinomianism latent in it had made many writers to whom it was probably familiar avoid expressing it, it had nevertheless a recognized and natural place in the treatment of the topic in Christian theology—that of the culmination of the redemptive process in human history—which was also for Milton the culminating theme in his poem. Yet it undeniably placed the story of the Fall, which was the subject of the poem announced at the outset, in a somewhat ambiguous light ; when it was borne in mind, man's first disobedience could not seem the deplorable thing which for the purposes of the poet—and of the theologian—it was important to make it appear. The only solution was to keep the two themes separate. In the part of the narrative dealing primarily with the Fall, the thought that it was after all a *felix culpa* must not be permitted explicitly to intrude ; that was to be reserved for the conclusion, where it could heighten the happy final consummation by making the earlier and unhappy episodes in the story appear as instrumental to that consummation, and, indeed, as its necessary conditions.

ADAM'S FALL

BY RUSSELL E. SMITH, JR.

I

Eve's fall, in both the Christian myth and in Milton's treatment of that myth in *Paradise Lost*, follows from her improper desire to transcend her assigned place in the Divine Hierarchy by means of knowledge. Adam's fall, it is traditionally argued, follows not from a desire to transcend his proper station but from a failure to maintain it. Eve, a creature beneath Adam in the divine order of things, desires to be like God. Adam wrongly chooses Eve instead of God. Eve falls up, and Adam—so to speak—falls down. The possibility that Milton's Adam, like his Eve, is ambitious and aspires upward has not yet been considered in the critical interpretations of the Fall. It is the thesis of this essay that Milton deviates from the traditional explanations of Adam's fall in that his Adam falls for the same reason as does his Eve.

When looking for dramatic preparation for the Fall the natural tendency is to work *backward* through the poem from Book IX. Eve, it is found, first dabbles in self-love when she admires her reflection in the pool (IV. 449-466). And, subsequently, she comments egocentrically on the function of the Cosmos (IV. 657-658). Then she is directly tempted by Satan in her dreams (IV. 797-809). Then Eve equates the bounties of earth and heaven (V. 329-330) and reveals her envy of the angel Raphael. Her last order-violating gesture before the Fall is her insistence that she and Adam work apart in the garden (IX. 205-225).

When we look backward from Book IX Adam's fall is, in terms of the traditional interpretation, scantily prepared for. It is not until far into Book VIII that Adam displays any weakness for Eve. He says to Raphael:

 This essay first appeared in *ELH*, Vol. 35, No. 4 (December 1968).

> yet when I approach
> Her loveliness, so absolute she seems
> And in herself complete, . . . (VIII. 546-548) [1]

This weakness can be found a second and last time when Adam fails in his responsibility as governor of Eden and consents to let Eve work apart from him in the garden. A more dramatically satisfying moment can be found by working *forward* through the poem without worrying about Book IX. If we are able to forget for a time that Adam must fall *down* to Eve, we will be more sensitive to evidence of a different, or seemingly different, weakness in Adam. Adam, like Eve, is directly tempted by forbidden knowledge; and after discussing the crucial Adam-Raphael dialogue, we can consider how such a conclusion affects our interpretation of the Fall.

We may eliminate at the onset the possible suggestion that Adam's five major questions to the angel Raphael serve only the mechanical function of giving the angel an excuse to talk. The problem of intellectual pride and ambition is, after all, at the very center of *Paradise Lost* and it is improbable that Milton would allow his innocent Adam to ask questions about heaven and not account for the theological implications of such curiosity. Is Adam's curiosity proper? We can anticipate that Milton provided a dramatic answer to this question.

Looking at the Adam-Raphael exchange in dramatic terms (treating Adam and Raphael more as individuals than symbols), there are two primary kinds of evidence. First, the successive question-answer episodes are basically parallel in structure, yet sufficiently modified to produce a cumulative effect. In each of his speeches Adam begins by thanking the angel for his visit and assuring him that he (Adam) understands his position in the divine hierarchy and his responsibility as a free agent. Then Adam asks his question. The major cumulative movement is that Adam's questions are increasingly ambitious and his " desire to know " is less and less under rational control. Second, the two elements of the controlling metaphor are food-knowledge, or curiosity-appetite. When Milton describes Adam's intellectual appetite metaphorically, he characterizes it as intemperate, even gluttonous.

[1] All quotations are from *John Milton: Complete Poems and Major Prose*, ed. Merritt Hughes (New York, 1957).

Russell E. Smith, Jr.   183

" To know " is, of course, not in itself wrong. Raphael justifies Adam's preliminary questions on the grounds that a revelation of the " secrets of other worlds " will attest God's magnificence. Since the contemplation of God's goodness and power should be Man's greatest pleasure, the more Adam knows of God the happier he may be. The difference between healthy and unhealthy desire to know is in the origin of the desire. If knowledge is sought for the greater glory of God, the curiosity is praiseworthy. If knowledge is desired as a means of elevating the self, the desire is perverse. Adam does very much " desire to know "; as we begin the discussion the question is whether he desires to know for the right reason.

II

Adam's " sudden " desire to " know of things above this world " comes after and amid explicit warnings against such desire. Satan, in his soliloquy (IV. 505-535), resolved " to excite thir minds with more desire to know," and thereby work the fall of Man. A very few lines later the poem's narrative voice forewarned:

> Sleep on,
> Blest pair; and O yet happiest if ye seek
> No happier state, and know to know no more.
> (IV. 773-775)

The garden scene in Book IV ends with Ithuriel and Zephon finding Satan " squat like a Toad, close at the ear of Eve " (800), telling her that by knowledge she " may ascend to Heav'n ... and see what life the Gods live there, and such live thou " (V. 80-81). These passages still strong in our minds, we come to Adam's first surge of curiosity in the middle of Book V:

> Thus when with meats and drinks they had suffic'd
> Not burd'n'd Nature, sudden mind arose
> In *Adam*, not to let th' occasion pass
> Given him by this great Conference to know
> Of things above his World, and of thir being
> Who dwell in Heav'n, whose excellence he saw
> Transcend his own so far, whose radiant forms
> Divine effulgence, whose high Power so far
> Exceeded human, and his wary speech
> Thus to th' Empyreal Minister he fram'd.   (V. 451-460)

It is only after Adam has eaten Eve's dinner (the best Eden has to offer) that his thoughts are directed elsewhere. " Sudden mind " is the first phrase to draw our attention. Any suddenness in unanxious, unhurried Paradise is noteworthy; something new is going on. Adam's first thoughts are very general. He wonders about " things above his world." Then he makes a specific and personal comparison of himself with the angel. Although each is perfect in his own right, Adam makes the flat statement that in excellence the angel surpasses him. Adam's reaction at this point is primarily one of awe but the potential for jealousy is great.

Of primary interest in this passage, however, is Adam's internal formulation of his first question. His " speech " (a noun implying language which is less than candid) is " wary " and " fram'd." " Wary " can, in obsolete usage, mean timorous and hesitant. Yet, the only other time the word is used in the poem is in the phrase " wary fiend." Similarly, the verb " fram'd " could describe the attempt of a humble and timid Adam to find the right words to address the first angel he has talked with, or it can be taken in the rhetorical sense meaning the careful formulation of language to serve a specific end.

When he does speak, Adam apparently falters and is unable to reveal his interest in " things above this world." On the surface this seems due to a loss of composure:

> Inhabitant with God, now know I well
> Thy favor, in this honor done to Man,
> Under whose lowly roof thou hast voutsaf't
> To enter, and these earthly fruits to taste,
> Food not of Angels, yet accepted so,
> As that more willingly thou couldst not seem
> At Heav'n's high feasts to have fed: yet what compare?
>   (V. 461-467)

Adam has in mind what he wants to say, starts to say it, then (in the first instance of stage fright) drops off into the frustrated " yet what compare? " Not very many lines before, however, Adam and Raphael thoroughly discussed the problem of comparative foods, and Adam seemed confident enough then. He said of Eve's dinner:

> unsavory food perhaps
> To spiritual Natures; only this I know,
> That one Celestial Father gives to all.   (V. 401-403)

Raphael lectured at length on the need of angels for bulky sustenance (V. 404-433), then, with " keen dispatch," dramatically confirmed his angel appetite. For Adam again to raise the question with " fram'd " and " wary " speech is suspect. On the conscious level Adam is afraid to reveal his curiosity, yet at the same time he wants Raphael to talk. Adam may also have an unconscious intention. The " yet what compare? " can be taken as the question of a slightly unsure Adam as he fishes for a boost in morale. " Our best dinner isn't good enough ": such a statement unconsciously reaches for the answer, " Of course it is."

We must remember that Adam has never before had an opportunity to compare himself with a man-like angel. Adam is used to being King. Suddenly he is to Raphael what Eve has been to him—inferior. There is no reason why this should not disturb Adam's sense of equilibrium. If Adam is now reaching for a confirmation of his own worth, he is acting out a desire Milton let Eve as homemaker reveal openly. When gathering food for their dinner Eve anticipated that Raphael " beholding shall confess that here on earth/ God hath dispenst his bounties as in Heav'n " (V. 329-330). Adam is hoping for a similar confession from the angel, a confession implying that in terms of food, at least, his state in Eden is " as good " as Raphael's in Heaven.

Adam asks for a comparison and Raphael responds literally. In essence Raphael says, " Given what you are now, this is the best you can hope for." For Raphael the matter is resolved. Adam has been answered. No further questions are in order.

> Meanwhile enjoy
> Your fill what happiness this happy state
> Can comprehend, incapable of more.   (V. 503-505)

But, Raphael has made it clear that there is a higher happiness. Although it may be unfair to attribute fallen human motivation to the yet innocent Adam, we can anticipate that Raphael's answer would only feed whatever self-doubt Adam has, and stimulate his curiosity accordingly. Milton leaves to Adam the total responsibility for getting the conversation going again. Adam's second speech—because Raphael has said all that needs to be said—is as artificial and awkward as his first. Adam first thanks Raphael for showing the way to God and telling him, Adam, where he stands. Then, very abruptly, Adam forces out second question:

> But say,
> What meant that caution join'd, *if ye be found*

> *Obedient?* can we want obedience then
> To him, or possibly his love desert
> Who form'd us from the dust, and plac'd us here
> Full to the utmost measure of what bliss
> Human desires can seek or apprehend? (V. 512-518)

J. B. Broadbent has noted the "latinate clumsiness" of this and
other speeches in the exchange and has attributed it to Milton's
own hesitancy about discussing the "*secrets of other worlds.*" [2]
In the present framework another possibility suggests itself.
Again Adam is asking a question for which he has an answer. In
his very first speech to Eve he, like Raphael now to him, spelled
out God's command, and eliminated disobedience as a possibility.
The artificiality of "But say, what meant that caution joined"
is Milton's way of drawing attention to Adam's curiosity, and to
Adam's own questioning of his own curiosity. We as readers
feel Adam's discomfort and begin to raise our own doubts about
the propriety of his "desire to know."

After lecturing on free will and its attendant responsibilities,
Raphael alludes to, as a kind of object lesson, the fall of Satan
and the other rebel angels. Although entirely gratuitous, Raphael's
remark serves the dramatic function of giving Adam's free-floating
curiosity a reference point. Adam begins his reply by saying that
the angel's words are received with more delight than Heavenly
music. (The rational Adam should, of course, prefer angels'
words to angels' music.) He then assures Raphael that he understands free will and what is expected of him. Then, for the third
time, there is an abrupt shift in Adam's train of thought. The
transition is the common one from "I understand perfectly," to
"Just one more question, please." I shall begin the quotation well
ahead of the break.

> Yet that we never shall forget to love
> Our maker, and obey him whose command
> Single, is yet so just, my constant thoughts
> Assur'd me and still assure: though what thou tell'st
> Hath past in Heav'n, some doubt within me move,
> But more desire to hear, if thou consent,
> The full relation, which must needs be strange,
> Worthy of Sacred silence to be heard; . . . (V. 550-556)

After the colon the key line is "some doubt within me move/
but more desire to hear." Desire (a nicely ambiguous word)

---

[2] J. B. Broadbent, *Some Graver Subject* (New York, 1960), p. 235.

Russell E. Smith, Jr.   187

overcomes doubt (equally ambiguous). "Doubt" does not refer to "what hath past in Heaven." The conjunction "but" makes clear that Adam doubts the appropriateness of his questions and of his "desire."

For the first time in the poem Adam experiences internal conflict: something inside of him must overcome something else inside of him before he can raise the question. Frank Kermode has said that Milton uses perturbation as an index of fallen nature.[3] Although it would be strong to say that Adam is "perturbed," his present internal experience is of a kind we have seen so far *only* in Satan and Eve.

This time Raphael is hesitant in his reply. He openly questions if not the appropriateness of Adam's curiosity, the appropriateness of his own efforts to satisfy it. "How," Raphael wonders, "unfold the secrets of another world, perhaps not lawful to reveal" (V. 568-569)? Both of Milton's characters have now raised this question, Raphael directly, Adam by implication. Raphael then goes on to tell Adam of the war in Heaven, justifying himself on the grounds that Satan's fall will serve as a warning to Adam and Eve.

III

In Books VII and VIII there is no trace of the shy and hesitant Adam we saw in Book V. After hearing about the war in Heaven Adam asks Raphael about the creation of Heaven and Earth and questions not only the mechanics of creation but God's intentions as well (VII. 54-97). Adam's fifth and last question (VIII. 1-38) is ambitious to the point of being presumptive. Rather than ask Raphael to explain the Cosmos, Adam invites the angel to reason along with him. Adam openly flaunts his new found mental prowess. Since the passage marks the culmination of the series that began with a meek, "yet what compare?" I shall quote it in full:

> When I behold this goodly Frame, this World
> Of Heav'n and Earth consisting, and compute
> Thir magnitudes, this Earth a spot, a grain,
> An Atom with the Firmament compar'd
> And all her number'd Stars, that seem to roll
> Spaces incomprehensible (for such

---

[3] Frank Kermode, "Adam Unparadised," in *The Living Milton*, ed. Frank Kermode (New York, 1961), p. 116.

Thir distance argues and thir swift return
Diurnal) merely to officiate light
Round this opacous Earth, this punctual spot,
One day and night; in all thir vast survey
Useless besides; reasoning I oft admire,
How Nature wise and frugl could commit
Such disproportions, with superfluous hand
So many nobler Bodies to create,
Greater so manifold to this one use,
For aught appears, and on thir Orbs impose
Such restless revolution day by day
Repeated, while the sedentary Earth,
That better might with far less compass move,
Serv'd by more noble than herself, attains
Her end without least motion, and receives,
As Tribute, such a sumless journey brought
Of incorporeal speed, her warmth and light;
Speed, to describe whose swiftness Number fails.

(VIII. 15-38)

The passage contains an impressive array of qualitative adjectives and adverbs: goodly, merely, useless, wise, frugal, superfluous, nobler, greater, better, more noble. Further, we should note Adam's emphasis on his own thought processes: " I behold," " I compute," " I admire," " I compare." As Adam now speculates on the relation of the earth to the Cosmos we cannot help but be reminded of Eve's well known remark:

But wherefore all night long shine these, for whom
This glorious sight, when sleep hath shut all eyes?

(IV. 657-658)

Adam lectured Eve on order after her brief bit of speculation, and now Adam's speculations trigger a lecture on order by Raphael.

Thus, the first generalization to be made about Adam's questions is that they are increasingly ambitious. The second generalization is that his speeches are structurally parallel. Adam's long and bookish recitations of Raphael's lessons always end in the middle of a line with a full stop. In each of the five speeches the full stop is followed by a conjunction (yet, but or though) which both introduces Adam's next question and dramatically undercuts and qualifies what he has just said (' One should never overeat; but I am still hungry '). The lines leading up to the fourth question will serve to illustrate how this transition is made and used (italics mine):

> Great things, and full of wonder in our ears,
> Far differing from this World, thou hast reveal'd
> Divine Interpreter, by favor sent
> Down from the Empryean to forewarn
> Us timely of what might else have been our loss,
> Unknown, which human knowledge could not reach:
> For which to th' infinitely Good we owe
> Immortal thanks, and his admonishment
> Receive with solemn purpose to observe
> Immutably his sovran will, *the end*
> *Of what we are. But since* thou hast voutsaf't
> Gently for our instruction to impart
> Things above Earthly thought, . . .   (VIII. 70-83)

Adam formally, almost ritualistically, protects himself by assuring
Raphael that he is content with what he is and what he knows,
and then dramatically indicates he is not at all content. We come
to anticipate the break in Adam's speeches. Increasingly the
abrupt transitions from proper reasoning to improper curiosity
point up the rift between Adam's intellectual comprehension
of the divine order and his emotional commitment to that order.

IV

The food-knowledge metaphor in *Paradise Lost* extends in
implication beyond forbidden fruit and forbidden knowledge.
Food in general is metaphorically equated with knowledge in
general. The comparison is made explicitly in Raphael's reply to
Adam's question on creation:

> But Knowledge is as food, and needs no less
> Her Temperance over Appetite, to know
> In measure what the mind may well contain,
> Oppresses else with Surfeit, and soon turns
> Wisdom to Folly, as Nourishment to Wind.
>   (VII. 126-130)

Milton uses food as a symbol in two primary ways. First, there
is the apple which symbolizes forbidden knowledge. Second,
there is the other fruit of Eden which symbolizes the general
pre-Fall bounty and delight of Paradise. When describing both
kinds of food Milton uses sensuous adjectives. However, even
though his descriptive terms remain constant, Milton is able
to vary his point of view significantly by shifting emphasis. When
food symbolizes Eden, Milton as narrator emphasizes its general,

its universal desirability. When food is discussed in a context implying or anticipating the Fall, the focus is not on the desirability of the food but on the human desire for it: "this is desirable" compared to "Eve desires this." The first focuses on the object of desire, the second on the desire itself. Thus, the verbs "hunger," "thirst" and "desire"—especially "desire" —can be said to mean unhealthy hunger, thirst, and desire.

Keeping these general principles in mind, note the way Milton characterizes Adam's state of mind just before he asks his question on creation:

> Whence *Adam* soon repeal'd
> The doubts that in his heart arose: and now
> Led on, yet sinless, with desire to know
> What nearer might concern him, how this World
> Of Heav'n and Earth conspicuous first began,
> When, and whereof created, for what cause,
> What within *Eden* or without was done
> Before his memory, as one whose drouth
> Yet scarce allay'd still eyes the current stream,
> Whose liquid murmur heard new thirst excites,
> Proceeded thus to ask his Heav'nly Guest.
>
> (VII. 59-69)

For the second time "desire" and "doubt" are juxtaposed. This time Adam is "led on" by his "desire to know." He is "led on, yet sinless." The only other time in the poem the phrase "yet sinless" is used is to describe Eve as she and Satan arrive at the forbidden tree (IX. 659). The phrase is, like Kermode's "degree of perturbation," a poetic means of marking proximity to the Fall. The phrase serves to draw our attention to the danger inherent in Adam being "led on . . . with desire to know."

I have already mentioned that Adam seeks nothing less than the basic Why? of Creation, so we may pass on to the concluding simile. Adam's desire is explicitly characterized as gluttonous. The verb "eyes" connotes "lust" and "leer." The "liquid murmur" is neutral enough, but since it "new thirst excites" it is the object of intemperate appetite. The phraseology is striking in light of Satan's earlier prophecy: "Hence I will excite thir minds/ with more desire to know." We might also note Satan's statement to Eve from the forbidden tree:

> To satisfy the sharp desire I had
> Of tasting those fair Apples, I resolv'd

> Not to defer; hunger and thirst at once,
> Powerful persuaders, quick'n'd at the scent
> Of that alluring fruit, urg'd me so keen.   (IX. 584-588)

Since Milton is extremely aware of Adam's potential danger he would have made it clear if Adam were reacting to Raphael's words as he should. Similarly, had Milton wished to protect Adam at this point it seems unlikely that he would have lent him a vocabulary belonging primarily to Satan and Eve. Finally, we may contrast the fluidity of the verse of the passage under consideration with the " latinate clumsiness " of Adam's earlier recitations on order, degree and obedience.

The opening fifteen lines of Book VIII furnish a fine example of the " I know; but " transition we have noted before. More important, the passage—prefacing Adam's fifth question—continues the metaphoric equation of intellectual curiosity and physical appetite.

> The Angel ended, and in *Adam's* Ear
> So Charming left his voice, that he a while
> Thought him still speaking, still stood fixt to hear;
> Then as new wak't thus gratefully replied.
> What thanks sufficient, or what recompense
> Equal have I to render thee, Divine
> Historian, who thus largely hast allay'd
> The thirst I had of knowledge, and voutsaf't
> This friendly condescension to relate
> Things else by me unsearchable, now heard
> With wonder, but delight, and, as is due,
> With glory attributed to the high
> Creator; something yet of doubt remains,
> Which only thy solution can resolve.   (VIII. 1-14)

The semi-hypnotic state of the first three lines we might expect of Eve, but not of Adam. It is Adam's ability to reason rightly that makes him superior to Eve. Clearly he is now responding with something other than his distinguishing faculty. Once awake, Adam thanks Raphael for having " largely " satisfied his curiosity. The thirst for knowledge, however, is not so easily quenched. Adam still " eyes the current stream," and launches into his fifth question, the question Raphael will not answer in full.

I skip ahead now to Adam's long concluding recitation of the lesson he has learned from Raphael. In his fifth question Adam took on the task of judging the efficiency of the Cosmos; now he takes over the rôle of schoolmaster. It is Adam who suggests,

Adam's Fall

> Therefore from this high pitch let us descend
> A lower flight, and speak of things at hand
> Useful . . .   (VIII. 198-200)

Adam proposes that Raphael listen to his story. Yet, when he jokingly confesses the reason for making this suggestion we see that Adam's intemperate curiosity is still very much alive:

> till then thou seest
> How subtly to detain thee I devise,
> Inviting thee to hear while I relate,
> Fond, were it not in hope of thy reply: (VIII. 206-209)

After the colon, Adam summarizes his reaction to all that the angel has said:

> For while I sit with thee, I seem in Heav'n,
> And sweeter thy discourse is to my ear
> Than Fruits of Palm-tree pleasantest to thirst
> And hunger both, from labor, at the hour
> Of sweet repast; they satiate, and soon fill,
> Though pleasant, but thy words with Grace Divine
> Imbu'd, bring to thir sweetness no satiety. (VIII. 210-216)

Nothing, perhaps, is more " at hand " than the fruits of Eden. It will be remembered that Adam turned his attention heavenward only after he had eaten Eve's very best dinner. His appetite for Eden is satisfied; his curiosity concerning the world the angel represents cannot be satisfied. Although Adam would from the " high pitch descend " he clearly prefers the happier state, the Heaven he has imaginatively experienced. Adam is not an angel. For him to " seem in Heav'n " is for him to commit imaginatively the *only* sin available to him. Again we recall Satan's words to Eve:

> Ascend to Heav'n, by merit thine, and see
> What life the Gods live there, and such live thou.
>   (V. 80-81)

Adam cannot be " lowly wise " as the angel instructed. By his own admission the words of the angel " bring to thir sweetness no satiety."

The Adam in Adam understands what the angel has said about temperance, and can lecture almost as well as Raphael on the necessity and rightness of the Divine Hierarchy. It is the Eve in Adam that leads him to overstep his bounds. Adam's desire for knowledge is never curbed from within. His last act in Book

VIII is to blurt out the question on angel love-making. To use my already over-worked analogy for a final time: Adam does not push himself away from the table; Raphael removes his plate. And, after the Fall Adam comes to understand that this is what has happened. He says to the angel Michael:

> Greatly instructed I shall hence depart,
> Greatly in peace of thought, and have my fill
> Of knowledge, what this Vessel can contain;
> Beyond which was my folly to aspire.   (XII. 557-560)

V

For my concluding remarks I should like to borrow three observations on the Fall made by Professor Arnold Stein in *Answerable Style*.[4] First, the victory of Evil, if it is to be significant, must be internal. This Adam recognizes on the formal level (V. 117-119). Second, Eve is a part of Adam, his " other half," his " dearer half." When tempted by Eve in Book IX Adam is, symbolically, self-tempted. Third, although Adam is self-tempted, the external tempter (Satan) and the external act of disobedience (eating the apple) are theological and dramatic necessities.

As I have continually implied, Adam as dramatized in his conversation with Raphael is, for want of a better term, a split personality. The Adam in Adam understands that the danger is from within and that the primary threat to his life in Eden is dissatisfaction. The Eve in Adam wants angel-hood and goes after it. When Adam takes the apple from Eve he has, for all intents and purposes, already fallen. All that is needed is the token outward action to symbolize his final acceptance of his " other self," the Eve within as well as without. When he says to Michael that his folly was in desiring knowledge beyond his capacity he is answering for Eve. Similarly, when he complains to the Son that from Eve's hand he " could suspect no ill " he is as much as saying he was unable to see his own internal weakness as he is rationalizing. Raphael warned Adam to " govern well thy appetite, lest Sin/ Surprise thee." That is a fact only experience could make Adam truly understand.

---

[4] Arnold Stein, *Answerable Style* (Minneapolis, 1953), pp. 75-77.

THE SECOND ADAM AND THE CHURCH IN
PARADISE LOST

BY MOTHER MARY CHRISTOPHER PECHEUX, O. S. U.

The relationship of the Unholy Trinity—Satan, Sin, and Death
—to the Holy Trinity in *Paradise Lost* has aroused critical interest
in recent years, and the allegorical characters are now recognized
as artistic and effective components of the poem. There has also
been some discussion of an earthly counterpart of the Trinity,
largely in terms of Eve: she is born from Adam's side, as Sin
from Satan's head; like the Son and Sin, she is made in the image
of the one from whom she proceeds; she embodies the conception
of redeeming love on earth, as the Son does in heaven, while Satan
parodies it by his hate. The third member of the earthly trinity—
less clearly delineated—may be considered either the human race
as a whole or the Promised Seed, the Messiah.[1]

I hope to demonstrate the existence in the poem of a fourth
trinity, which might be styled anagogical or eschatological. Both
the scope of the epic, which reached beyond the end of time, and
the nature of its theme demanded a treatment that would emphasize the complete unfolding of the divine plan in history, whereby
the " loss of Eden " spoken of in the opening invocation is balanced in reality by the qualifying clause, " till one greater Man /
Restore us."[2] I suggest that by presenting this greater man, the
Second Adam, working through his church to effect the redemp-

---

[1] For some discussions of the topic see Cleanth Brooks, " Eve's Awakening," in
Essays in Honor of Walter Clyde Curry (Nashville, 1954), pp. 285-286; Robert A.
Durr, " Dramatic Pattern in *Paradise Lost*," *JAAC*, XIII (1955), 521-522; Robert C.
Fox, " The Allegory of Sin and Death in *Paradise Lost*, *MLQ*, XXIV (1963), 362-363;
Merritt Y. Hughes, ed. *John Milton: Complete Poems and Major Prose* (New York,
1957), p. 177; Maurice Kelley, *This Great Argument* (Princeton, 1941; reprinted
Gloucester, 1962), p. 193; B. Rajan, *Paradise Lost and the Seventeenth Century
Reader* (New York, 1948), pp. 47-48; John Shawcross, " The Balanced Structure of
Paradise Lost, *SP*, LXII (1965), 75; Joseph Summers, *The Muse's Method* (Cam-
bridge, Mass., 1962), p. 48; E. M. W. Tillyard, *Studies in Milton* (New York, 1951),
p. 34.

[2] Citations from *Paradise Lost* in my text are to the Hughes edition cited in n. 1.

This essay first appeared in *ELH*, Vol. 34, No. 2 (June 1967).

tion of the elect, Milton is not only placing the emphasis where he wanted it but is also amplifying his structural trinitarian parallels. An awareness of this fourth trinity explains some apparently inartistic or irrelevant passages in the text and further justifies the allegory of Sin and Death.

The basic element in the parallel is the concept of the church, the bride of Christ, issuing from the side of Christ on the cross, as Eve had come from Adam. A few of the sources from which this analogy was derived, as well as Milton's use of it in his prose writings, will indicate some of its connotations.

The Scriptural basis for the metaphor is found most clearly in the Epistle to the Ephesians:

Husbands, love your wives, as Christ loved the church and gave himself up for her, that he might sanctify her by the washing of water with the word, that the church might be presented before him in splendor, without spot or wrinkle or any such thing, that she might be holy and without blemish. . . . For no man ever hates his own flesh, but nourishes and cherishes it, as Christ does the church. . . . " For this reason a man shall leave his father and mother and be joined to his wife, and the two shall become one." This is a great mystery, and I take it to mean Christ and the church. (v.25-32)[3]

Since St. Paul, in comparing the relationship between Christ and the church to that between husband and wife, quotes the words spoken of marriage in Genesis by Adam, the Christ-church Adam-Eve analogy arises directly and naturally. The detail from St. John's Gospel on the piercing of the side of Christ, the Second Adam, supplied the basis for the refinement of the idea: the church was born from the side of Christ, as Eve from Adam's; Adam's sleep, considered a kind of prophetic ecstasy, corresponded to Christ's death, sleep being an accepted image of death in seventeenth century thought. The typology quickly became a part of traditional exegesis.[4] Thus Tertullian speaks of Adam's " spirit-

[3] In citations from the Bible I have followed the Revised Standard Version, unless otherwise indicated. Since Milton made use of Hebrew, Greek, and Latin texts, as well as of different English translations (see Harris Fletcher, *The Intellectual Development of John Milton*, II [Urbana, 1961], 97-108), it seems that a modern translation based on the King James but with revisions in the light of original texts would ordinarily come closest to Milton's thought.

[4] See the discussion in Arnold Williams, *The Common Expositor* (Chapel Hill, 1948), pp. 86, 88, 234-235. See also the passages from Avitus and Du Bartas cited by Watson Kirkconnell in *The Celestial Cycle* (Toronto, 1952), pp. 5, 58. James Sims, in a different context, notes the connection between Adam and Eve and Christ and his bride, the church; *The Bible in Milton's Epics* (Gainesville, 1962), p. 27.

ual ecstasy, in which he prophesied the sacrament of Christ and the church" and elsewhere explains: "If Adam is a type of Christ, then Adam's sleep is a symbol of Christ's death, and by the wound in the side of Christ was typified the church, who is the true mother of all the living." [5] St Augustine exclaims: "Let our Spouse mount the wood of his bridal chamber. . . . Let him sleep in death, let his side be opened, let the virgin church come forth: as Eve was made from the side of Adam as he slept, so the church was made from the side of Christ hanging on the cross. . . . Rejoice, rejoice, O bride-church, because unless this had been done to Christ, you would not have been formed from him." [6] A contemporary of Milton repeats the analogy: "Adam sleeping Eve is formed: Christ dying the Church is framed. Eve is taken out of Adams side, while he sleepes: out of the second Adams side, while he was in the sleepe of death, issueth the Church." [7]

Milton's concept of the nature of the church is expressed in less poetic and more abstract terms when he treats the subject in the *Christian Doctrine*. He distinguishes between the invisible church (the mystical body of which Christ is the head) and the visible church, or the assembly of those called by God; [8] the church is the twofold kingdom which Christ governs: the kingdom of grace as it exists now, and the kingdom of glory as it will exist in eternity. [9] In other prose works he makes use of various traditional metaphors, including that of the bride. Thus woman is the image and companion of man, "in such wise to be lov'd, as the Church is belov'd of Christ"; the Song of Songs figures the espousals of Christ and the Church; in marriage there should be such love as Christ has for the Church. [10] Similar phrases recur

    [5] *De jejuniis*, iii, in *Patrologia Latina*, ed. Migne, II, 1008; *De anima*, xliii, *ibid.*, 767; see also St. Augustine's commentary on Genesis, *ibid.*, XXXIV, 205-206. The *Patrologia* is hereafter cited as Migne; translations are mine unless otherwise noted.

    [6] *De symbolo ad catechumenos*, vi.15 (Migne, XL, 645).

    [7] Thomas Taylor, *Christ Revealed: or The Old Testament Explained* (London, 1635), p. 7.

    [8] *CD* I.xxiv, xxix, in *The Works of John Milton*, Columbia edition (hereafter cited as *Works*), XVI, 61, 219.

    [9] *CD* I.xv (*Works*, XV, 301). For some discussions of Milton's concept of the church see Michael Fixler, *Milton and the Kingdoms of God* (Evanston, 1964), passim, especially pp. 77-78, 107-108; Kelley (see n. 1), pp. 178-181; Howard Schultz, "Christ and Antichrist in *Paradise Regained*," *PMLA*, LXVII (1952), 790-808, *Milton and Forbidden Knowledge* (New York, 1955), pp. 222-236; "A Fairer Paradise? Some Recent Studies of *Paradise Regained*," *ELH*, XXXII (1965), 275-302.

    [10] *Tetrachordon* (*Works*, IV, 79, 86, 192).

in the " Reason of Church Government ": Christ is the head and husband of his church; if Christ be the church's husband, expecting her to be presented before him a pure unspotted virgin, he shows his tender love to her by prescribing for her his own ways.[11]

Both Milton and his contemporary readers would, then, have been very familiar with the analogy between Adam and Eve and Christ and the church. An examination of the description of Eve's creation in Book VIII of *Paradise Lost* reveals that many of its details seem to have been carefully chosen to bring out the parallel.

Adam begins his account of the event by speaking of the sleep into which he fell. This was, as has been noted, the first aspect of the typology.

> Hee ended, or I heard no more, for now
> My earthly by his Heav'nly overpower'd,
> Which it had long stood under, strain'd to the highth
> In that celestial Colloquy sublime,
> As with an object that excels the sense,
> Dazzl'd and spent, sunk down, and sought repair
> Of sleep, which instantly fell on me, call'd
> By Nature as in aid, and clos'd mine eyes.   (452-459)

It was not, however, an ordinary sleep, for he could see what was happening:

> Mine eyes he clos'd, but op'n left the Cell
> Of Fancy my internal sight, by which
> Abstract as in a trance methought I saw,
> Though sleeping, where I lay, and saw the shape
> Still glorious before whom awake I stood.   (460-464)

Expanding the text in Genesis, " So the Lord God caused a deep sleep to fall upon the man " (ii.21), Milton is making the most of the possible connotations of the " deep sleep " by using both the phrase " in a trance " (suggested by the Greek term) and " though sleeping " (the usual translation of the Latin and Hebrew texts).[12]

The climax is reached in the next lines:

> Who stooping op'n'd my left side, and took
> From thence a Rib, with cordial spirits warm,

---

[11] *Works*, III, 183, 188.

[12] St. Augustine also exploited both words: " illa ecstasis quam Deus immisit in Adam, ut soporatus obdormiret "; *De Gen.* ix.xix.36 (Migne, XXXIV, 408).

And Life-blood streaming fresh; wide was the wound,
But suddenly with flesh fill'd up and heal'd.　　(465-468)

The passage is not one of the most admired in Milton; and the rather gory details cannot be explained on the ground of the necessity of following Genesis, since there the phrase is simply " took one of his ribs " (ii.21). For this Milton has deliberately substituted " op'n'd my left side." Surely we are being directed to the verse in St. John's Gospel: " But one of the soldiers pierced his side with a spear, and at once there came out blood and water " (xix.34). The Vulgate text, followed in the Douay version, offers an even more marked parallel, since it uses the verb " opened " (*aperuit*) instead of " pierced." Milton may have known St. Augustine's exegesis of the text: " The evangelist did not say: he struck his side or he wounded it, or some other word, but he *opened*: so that thus he might indicate that the door of life was opened, whence issued the sacraments of the Church, without which there is no entrance to true life . . . Here the Second Adam bowed his head and slept on the cross that thence might be formed for him a bride, who came forth from his side as he slept." [13] " As a wife was made for Adam from his side while he slept, the Church becomes the property of her dying Saviour, by the sacrament of the blood which flowed from His side after His death." [14] The life-blood streaming from the rib is not, then, the piece of crude literalism it is usually assumed to be: it is a symbol of the grace which comes to men through the church; the birthright " which Christ hath purchas'd for us with his blood " (*RCG* I.iii) ; " that sacred libertie which our Saviour with his own blood purchas'd " (*CP*).[15]

Adam, continuing his narration to Raphael, describes the " Creature . . . Manlike," (in his image) " but different sex " who is formed from his rib but who disappears as his ecstasy ends:

Shee disappear'd, and left me dark, I wak'd
To find her, or for ever to deplore
Her loss, and other pleasures all abjure:
When out of hope, behold her, not far off,
Such as I saw her in my dream, adorn'd
With what all Earth or Heaven could bestow

[13] *Tract. cxx in Joannem* (Migne, XXXV, 1953).
[14] *Contra Faust.*, xii.8 (Migne, XLII, 258); trans. Richard Stothert in *The Nicene and Post-Nicene Fathers*, ist ser., IV (Buffalo, 1887), 186.
[15] *Works*, III, 198; VI, 32.

To make her amiable: On she came,
Led by her Heav'nly Maker, though unseen,
And guided by his voice, nor uninform'd
Of nuptial Sanctity and marriage Rites:
Grace was in all her steps, Heav'n in her Eye,
In every gesture dignity and love.   (478-489)

These lines, as often admired as the preceding ones are condemned, are Milton's expansion of the Biblical statement that God " brought her [the woman] to the man " (Gen. ii.22). They need no vindication. In the light of the bridal imagery which pervades the passage, however, and of the implicit reference to the birth of the church which has just preceded it, there may be an influence from another biblical text using the church-bride metaphor to which a citation by Milton directs us: " The love of Christ towards his invisible and spotless Church is described by the appropriate figure of conjugal love. Rev. xix.7. ' the marriage of the Lamb is come, and his wife hath made herself ready.' "[16] Here, and in Rev. xxi, the church which is to be presented to her husband is prepared and adorned:

Let us rejoice and exult and give him the glory, for the marriage of the Lamb has come, and his Bride has made herself ready . . . And I saw the holy city, new Jerusalem, coming down out of heaven from God, prepared as a bride adorned for her husband; and I heard a great voice from the throne saying, " Behold, the dwelling of God is with men. He will dwell with them, and they shall be his people . . ." Then came one of the seven angels . . . and spoke to me, saying, " Come, I will show you the Bride, the wife of the Lamb." And in the spirit he carried me away to a great, high mountain, and showed me the holy city Jerusalem coming down out of heaven from God. (Rev. xix.7, xxi.2-3, 9-10)

Milton's lines and the biblical text have several elements in common: the adornment of the bride, the voice which leads her, the mention of nuptial sanctity and marriage rites, the general atmosphere of dignity and mystery. Adam's reaction (" I over-joy'd could not forbear aloud ") is an echo of the " Hallelujah "

[16] CD I.xxiv (Works, XVI, 65). Another part of the passage from St. Augustine quoted above (n. 6) also joins imagery from Revelations to that borrowed from Ephesians: " For his side was struck and immediately came forth blood and water, which are the twin sacraments of the church: water, in which the bride is purified: blood, from which is found her dowry. In this blood the holy martyrs, friends of the bridegroom, washed their garments, made them white, came invited to the marriage of the Lamb."

which introduces the passage in Revelations; and the text from Ephesians, with its quotation from Genesis, is reiterated as he makes his prophetic statement:

> I now see
> Bone of my Bone, Flesh of my Flesh, my Self
> Before me: Woman is her Name, of Man
> Extracted; for this cause he shall forgo
> Father and Mother, and to his Wife adhere;
> And they shall be one Flesh, one Heart, one Soul.
>
> (494-499)

As the birth of the church is typologically shown forth by the creation of Eve, its final triumph is hinted at in the description of her marriage. At the last day the Bride of the Lamb will descend from heaven to celebrate her final nuptials, thus fulfilling completely the typological significance of Eve's union with Adam.

And so he leads her to the nuptial bower. It is here, I think, that the third member of the trinity appears, though somewhat tenuously. For the bride is potentially a mother, just as the church is both the bride of Christ and that " Jerusalem which is above . . . which is the mother of us all " (*CD* I.xxiv).[17] The logical counterpart of the Holy Spirit, who in traditional thought is the fruit of the mutual love of the Father and the Son;[18] of Death, who is the fruit of the incestuous union of Satan and Sin; of the Promised Seed, who is to spring from Adam and Eve; should be the members of that visible church of which Milton speaks in the *Christian Doctrine*; of the elect who, forming the kingdom of grace on earth, will one day come into the kingdom of glory. For the spiritual progeny borne by the invisible church to Christ, the marriage supper of the Lamb is the supreme event, the final justification of God's ways.

This idea of spiritual fecundity had been developed at some length in Methodius' *Symposium*. After elaborating the familiar comparison between the sleep and the death of the first and second

---

[17] *Works*, XVI, 61 (paraphrasing Gal. iv.26).

[18] I do not wish to press the analogies between the third persons too far, especially in the light of Milton's views on the Holy Spirit. I think, however, that these views would not prevent him from making some poetic use of more traditional ideas. Even though he rejected the Holy Spirit as a third divine person, he seems to have retained some vestige of the orthodox notion of the Spirit as at least symbolically the bond of love. The descent of the Holy Spirit at the baptism of Christ, for example, is seen as a representation " of the ineffable affection of the Father for the Son " (*CD* I.vi [*Works*, XIV, 367]).

Adam, he explains that the words "Increase and multiply" are fulfilled as the church grows in size and beauty, through the intimate union between her and the Word.

For otherwise the Church could not conceive and bring forth the faithful . . . unless Christ emptied Himself for them too . . . and came down from heaven to die again, and clung to His Spouse the Church, allowing to be removed from His side a power by which all may grow strong who are built upon Him, who have been born by the laver and receive of His flesh and bone, that is, of His holiness and glory. . . . And it is impossible for anyone to participate in the Holy Spirit and to be counted a member of Christ unless again the Word has descended upon him and fallen into the sleep of ecstasy.[19]

Taylor develops the same theme from a slightly different viewpoint:

Eve was no sooner framed but as a pure and innocent spouse she was delivered by God to Adam yet in innocency: so God the Father delivered the Church as a chaste & innocent spouse to be married to the second Adam for ever, to be bone of his bone, and flesh of his flesh. . . . Of Eve marryed to Adam he receives both a Cain and an Abel into his house: so the second Adam hath in his visible Church both elect and reprobates, sound and hypocrites. (p. 7)

At this point in the poem Milton seems content to let the implications of a numerous posterity, present in the scene of the nuptial bower, supply also for the idea of spiritual posterity. The concept is brought out a little more sharply in the earlier description, in Eve's words (her first in the poem), of her first living moments:

> O thou for whom
> And from whom I was form'd flesh of thy flesh,
> And without whom am to no end, my Guide
> And Head, what thou hast said is just and right.
> (IV.440-443)

It may be observed that she is using here the two principal biblical metaphors for the church: the bride (implied in "flesh of thy flesh") and the body united to a head. After relating her experience with the reflection in the lake, she recalls Adam's words, which stress her position as his image and offspring and her role as mother—the middle position in the earthly trinity:

[19] *Convivium Decem Virginum*, iii.8, trans. Herbert Musurillo, in *Ancient Christian Writers*, XXVII (London, 1958), 65-66.

                                hee
Whose image thou art, him thou shalt enjoy
Inseparably thine, to him shalt bear
Multitudes like thyself, and thence be call'd
Mother of human Race:

                        to give thee being I lent
Out of my side to thee, nearest my heart
Substantial Life . . .   (471-475, 483-485)

—type of that life which the Second Adam imparts to the elect.

A fuller development of the concept of spiritual offspring, here perhaps hinted at, occurs near the end of the poem, to which we shall now turn.

As Michael prepares to lead Adam to the hill whence he will see the vision of the future, he remarks in what seems an irrelevant aside:

            let *Eve* (for I have drencht her eyes)
Here sleep below while thou to foresight wak'st,
As once thou slep'st, while Shee to life was form'd.
                                 (XI.367-369)

We have learned to be slow in declaring any line in *Paradise Lost* irrelevant. If we are reminded here of Adam's sleep and Eve's formation, and if a few lines later the Second Adam is mentioned explicitly for the only time in the poem, may it not be that we are being urged to read the panorama of the next book and a half not just as a record of events, not even only as a working out of God's plan in history, but as a history of that church which, existing in promise from the dawn of creation, came into reality at a set moment in history, endures vicissitudes for the rest of time, but blossoms in eternity into the church of glory?

By referring us back to the story of Eve's creation, Milton is equivalently asking us to recall some of its dominant features. It will be remembered that one strand of the tradition emphasized Adam's sleep as a prophetic trance; hence it is fitting that the notion be recalled now, as the full vision of the future is unrolled. The sleep in which he had seen the creation of Eve had been followed by the prophetic statement which St. Paul was to use on the mystery of Christ and the church; now that prophecy is to become more explicit. Milton's care to use the word "trance" in the earlier passage is here justified as well as recalled. Similarly, Henry Ainsworth had remarked, in his annotation on Genesis ii.21, that the Greek term was ecstasy or trance, "which," he added, "the Scriptures shew to have falne also on men, when they did see visions of God . . . In such *deepe-sleepe*, the senses are all bound up. . . ." [20] So Adam now ascends the hill (corresponding to the "great, high mountain" of Revelations) "in the Visions of God," and "enforc't to close his eyes / Sunk down and all his Spirits became intranst" (XI.419-420). The words repeated here from the passage in Book VIII are worth noting: there too Adam "sunk down," "clos'd [his] eyes," and lay "abstract as in a trance." His "internal sight" then had been left open, as now his "inmost seat of mental sight" (418) is strengthened by water from the well of life. Perhaps the later lines which mark the transition from vision to narration are also designed to recall Book VIII:

> but I perceive
> Thy mortal sight to fail; objects divine
> Must needs impair and weary human sense.   (XII.8-10)

So, before, Adam had been dazzled and spent "as with an object that excels the sense."

The relationship between the two scenes, however—Eve's creation and Adam's vision—is not limited to the general concept of prophecy; for it seems clear that in the intention of the poem the world-history of Books XI and XII is a prophecy primarily of the eventual victory of Christ; it is for this reason that we are reminded of the birth of the church before we see its subsequent development.[21] It is, of course, Christ who is the victor, and the church militant owes its triumph to him. But the dimensions of

[20] *Annotations upon the Five Bookes of Moses* (London, 1627), p. 12. Hughes (p. 441) cites the chief epic precedents for the prophecy as well as Biblical parallels. The prophetic books of the Old Testament furnish many possible sources, but Dan. x and xii, both of which refer to the archangel Michael, are perhaps the closest. It is interesting that Todd speaks of Dan. x in a note on Adam's trance in Book VIII (Henry J. Todd, ed. *The Poetical Works of John Milton*, 2d ed. [London, 1809], III, 111). The gloss in the Geneva Bible (1599 ed.) associates the passage (x.14-21) with the church: "For though the Prophet Daniel shoulde ende and cease, yet his doctrine should continue till the comming of Christ, for the comfort of his Church." "For this Angel was appointed for the defence of the Church under Christ, who is the head thereof."

[21] Immediately before the sentence quoted from *Contra Faust*, above (n. 14), St. Augustine enumerates the six ages of world history which Milton seems to have followed; see H. R. MacCallum, "Milton and Sacred History," in *Essays in English Literature from the Renaissance to the Victorian Age*, ed. Millar MacLure and F. M. Watt (Toronto, 1964), pp. 149-168; George W. Whiting, *Milton and This Pendant World* (Austin, 1958), pp. 169-200.

the victory become broader as we see the multitude of the redeemed (and it is a multitude even if only a remnant) rising finally to fill the seats vacated by Satan's followers. Hence the elect—the invisible church—are seen as the final victorious fruit of the union of Christ and his bride-church.

It is here, I suggest, that we find most clearly expressed the function of the third member of the Holy Trinity. Milton's departures from orthodox doctrine on the Holy Spirit did not prevent him from ascribing to it certain essential roles in man's salvation; among the twelve offices which he enumerates are those of effecting regeneration, saving faith, hope, good works, assurance of salvation, and comprehension of spiritual things—[22] all of which are implied in Books XI and XII. Thus it is the work of the third person of the first trinity which ultimately destroys the power of Death, the third person of the second trinity, by elevating the descendants of Adam and Eve, who form the third trinity, to life in the eternal kingdom of glory as trophies of the Second Adam and his church. Taylor's words again are apposite:

Both of them [Adam and Christ] are rootes, both have a posterity . . . Both of them convey that they have unto their posterity . . . As by the first *Adam* sinne, and by sinne *death* came over all men: so by the second *Adam* came *righteousnesse*, and by righteousnesse *life* on all beleevers. . . . In that the Church comes out of Christs side, being in the sleepe of death, as *Eve* out of *Adams* hee sleeping, wee learne to seeke our life in Christs death. That death should be propagated by the sinne of the first *Adam*, was no marvaile: but that life by the death of the second, is an admired mystery. Here is the greatest work of Gods power fetched out of his contrary; of ranke poyson a soveraigne remedy by the most skilfull Physician of hearts.[23]

The future which is revealed to Adam on the hilltop stretches on to the return " of him so lately promis'd to thy aid,/ The Woman's seed " (XII.542-543) , who will raise

> From the conflagrant mass, purg'd and refin'd,
> New Heav'ns, new Earth, Ages of endless date
> Founded in righteousness and peace and love,
> To bring forth fruits Joy and eternal Bliss.   (548-551)

---

[22] I follow here the summary given in Kelley, p. 106, which gathers scattered references on the subject. Cf. his n. 64 on p. 107: Milton " believed that in the salvation of man's soul its work was vital and important."

[23] *Christ Revealed*, pp. 7-8.

The "sum of earthly bliss" which Adam had found in the nuptial bower as the fruit of his union with Eve is subsumed now into the endless joy which the elect share in the spirit of love which is the bond between the Father and the Son. It is Satan with his perverted world of sin which will disappear, and death shall be no more.

So it is that Eve, her spirits soothed to meek submission, can speak her final words, which are reminiscent of her first, for here too she speaks of Adam as her head and guide. Her first recorded words in Paradise had called him her author, flesh of her flesh; her last sentence prophesies the reign of the Second Adam: "By mee the Promis'd Seed shall all restore" (XII.623). Thus the echo of her last word carries us back to the opening of the poem, with its promise of the greater man who would restore the blissful seat. The wheel has come full circle, and the story of Eve's creation has become the story of the end of the world.

Characteristically, Milton has used the typological overtones of his material subtly but none the less effectively. The full force of the Second Adam typology may escape the average twentieth-century reader; yet an awareness of its presence is important for appreciating the tight-knit structure of the poem. Whatever the judgment on the success of the last two books, it is agreed that Milton's theme demanded some indication of Christ's final victory over the adversary Satan—which is, as a matter of fact, the culmination of Michael's narration. But it is not like Milton to leave any thread untied, and, having made use of the Satan-Sin-Death trilogy earlier in the poem, he would be unlikely to drop it now. Though the allegorical characters disappear as personages after Book X, their entities remain throughout XI and XII, as we see supernal grace contending with sinfulness of men. More specifically, I think we can see the church history of these last two books as an exemplification of what the *Christian Doctrine* speaks of as one of the chief roles of Christ as king and mediator: to rule the church and shield it from its enemies, sin and death.[24] The victorious church in particular is contrasted with the second

---

[24] I.xv (*Works*, XV, 301), quoting 1 Cor. xv.26, 54-57, speaks of the victory over death, the law, and sin; cf. Schultz, *Milton and Forbidden Knowledge*, p. 229: the idea that Christ as sole mediator "rules his church and shields it from its enemies— Satan, sin, and death" was common in Reformation Protestant writings. Barbara Lewalski sees the victory over Satan, Sin, and Death accomplished by Christ-Adam-Mankind ("Structure and the Symbolism of Vision in Michael's Prophecy, *PL* XI-XII," *PQ*, XLII [1963], 33-35).

member of the infernal trinity, Sin (we recall that it was from Satan's "left side op'ning wide" [II.755] that she originally sprang), who thus becomes a kind of anti-church—in fact, the kingdom of Antichrist. If this is so, then Milton is not only paralleling Sin and the church in their daughter-wife relationships to Satan and Christ, respectively, but is also providing a parallel metaphor for the church as the new Jerusalem.

Especially significant is the new light in which some of the earlier descriptions are seen if Sin is viewed as the antitype to the church. Possibly, for example, the description when we first meet her in Book II, which certainly owes something to Spenser and to Ovid, has some affinities also with the beast of Revelations, who is there placed in contrast with the Lamb. Exercising the authority of the great dragon, it deceives those who dwell on earth; "its number is six hundred and sixty-six" (Rev. xiii.18) —and the description of Sin ends in line 666.[25] As the keeper of the gate of hell she appears, in any case, as the guardian of the kingdom of antichrist. Her "fatal Key" (725) is the antithesis to the key of the kingdom of heaven:

> this powerful Key
> Into my hand was giv'n, with charge to keep
> These Gates for ever shut, which none can pass
> Without my op'ning.   (774-777)

In St. Matthew's Gospel, Christ says: "And I tell you, you are Peter, and on this rock I will build my church, and the powers of death shall not prevail against it. I will give you the keys of the kingdom of heaven, and whatever you bind on earth shall be bound in heaven, and whatever you loose on earth shall be loosed in heaven" (xvi.18-19). In contrast, after Sin has flung open the infernal doors, the narrator comments, "She op'n'd, but to shut / Excell'd her power" (883-884). To the rock on which the church is built are opposed the "Adamantine Gates" (853) and the bolts and bars "of massy Iron or solid Rock" (878).

In Book III there is a juxtaposition of the third members of the trinities when a reference to the ultimate destruction of Death

[25] Maren-Sofie Røstvig [sic] has called attention to the fact that Comus' chief confrontation speech begins in l. 666 of that poem (*The Hidden Sense*, Norwegian Studies in English, No. 9 [Norway, 1963], p. 67). In "Renaissance Numerology: Acrostics or Criticism?" (*Essays in Criticism*, XVI [1966], 6-21) she notes further that the description of "the beast-like figure of Death" in *PL* II begins with l. 666 (p. 13).

in line 259 is followed by the Son's prediction that he will enter heaven "with the multitude of my redeem'd." The spiritual posterity of the Second Adam are described in terms like Taylor's (with elements of Pauline vocabulary, of course):

> Be thou in *Adam's* room
> The Head of all mankind, though *Adam's* Son.
> As in him perish all men, so in thee
> As from a second root shall be restor'd,
> As many as are restor'd, without thee none.
> His crime makes guilty all his Sons, thy merit
> Imputed shall absolve them who renounce
> Thir own both righteous and unrighteous deeds,
> And live in thee transplanted, and from thee
> Receive new life.   (III.285-94)

The relevance of the Christ-church-elect trinity to that of Satan, Sin, and Death, implied here, is seen more clearly in the commission given by Satan to Sin and Death when he meets them on his return towards Hell:

> My Substitutes I send ye, and Create
> Plenipotent on Earth, of matchless might
> Issuing from mee; on your joint vigor now
> My hold of this new Kingdom all depends,
> Through Sin to Death expos'd by my exploit.   (X.403-407)

The challenge is met when the Church is born:

> this act
> Shall bruise the head of Satan, crush his strength
> Defeating Sin and Death.   (XII.429-431)

The bridge from earth to hell offers another contrast: Death's petrific mace and Gorgonian rigor (X.294, 297) parody the firmness of the rock on which Christ's kingdom is built; the pontifical art by which a "ridge of pendent Rock" is constructed and made fast with "Pins of Adamant" (313, 318) serves the same purpose.[26] The parallel trinities are recalled when Sin greets

---

[26] Simon Trefman has already called attention to the resemblance between Matt. xvi and the bridge of chaos, interpreting it as a demonstration that the prelatical bodies of Anglicanism and especially Roman Catholicism were perverting Christ's meaning ("A Note on the Bridge of Chaos in *Paradise Lost* and Matthew xvi.18-19," *SCN*, XX [Winter 1962-Spring 1963], 62-63). The polemical purpose is probably present, but I think that the more important function of the passage is to underline one of the basic structural elements in the poem by way of a more general contrast between the kingdom of Christ and that of Satan.

Satan as her Parent and declares, " Such fatal consequence unites us three " (364) and again when she addresses Death as " second of *Satan* sprung " (591), recalling the manner of their origin. Many of these examples, of course, are part of the general trinitarian parody and do not demand a reference to the church and anti-church theme, but in the context of the whole they can be said to invite such reference. It is particularly fitting that the last explicit mention of Sin and Death is followed by lines which evoke the image of the New Jerusalem. The Father predicts the final end of the " Hell-hounds," when

> at one sling
> Of thy victorious Arm, well-pleasing Son,
> Both *Sin*, and *Death*, and yawning *Grave* at last
> Through *Chaos* hurl'd, obstruct the mouth of Hell
> For ever, and seal up his ravenous Jaws.
> Then Heav'n and Earth renew'd shall be made pure
> To sanctity that shall receive no stain.   (X.633-639)

And the Son is hailed as the

> Destin'd restorer of Mankind, by whom
> New Heav'n and Earth shall to the Ages rise,
> Or down from Heav'n descend.   (X.646-648)

Although these passages occur before Books XI and XII, their connotations are reflected forward if we see there the struggle between the Kingdom of Christ and the Kingdom of Sin. Moving even farther forward, we can see the theme of the Kingdom forming a significant link between *Paradise Lost* and *Paradise Regained*.

All these implications of the theme of the Second Adam and the church are aspects of the seemingly inexhaustible artistic complexities of *Paradise Lost*. By showing the significance of the terms in which Eve's creation is described, it demonstrates the organic connection between that scene and the narration in Books XI and XII. By adding an eschatological dimension to the divine-infernal-human trinitarian parallels, it intensifies the sense of timelessness which the poem conveys and completes the theme of restoration. Finally, it throws some light on the descriptions of Sin and helps to show that the allegory of Sin and Death is not an excrescence but an integral part of the poem.

NOON-MIDNIGHT AND THE TEMPORAL
STRUCTURE OF *PARADISE LOST*

BY ALBERT R. CIRILLO

I

At the very beginning of his study of the commentaries on Genesis, Arnold Williams makes an observation which puts the narrative aspect of *Paradise Lost* in clear perspective:

The fall of Adam and Eve, who transgressed the will of their Creator by eating of the tree of knowledge, is one of the two crucial points of human history. The reparation of the offense by Christ on the cross is the other. Genesis provides the only account of nearly two thousand years of human life. Hence it serves a double function: it is both sacred and profane history. Culturally, Moses was, the Renaissance believed, the first historian, the first poet, even the first author; and the Book of Genesis was his first work, and consequently the first literary production in history.[1]

Within this double function of sacred and profane history lies the essential core of temporal narrative structure for Milton's poem; for Milton tells us early in the work that he is a poet-prophet similar to Moses, that his poem is to encompass " Mans First Disobedience " and the restoration of the blissful seat by " one greater Man." The account of the lost paradise is thus not merely an historical view of man's earliest years on earth, but a spiritual chronicle of eternal life, a cosmic drama in which God is as important as man, and an assertion of *eternal* providence. Milton is dealing with truths that are at once human, therefore temporal and sequential, and with a higher truth, the eternal plan of God, that encompasses these human ones and is an essential link with man's spiritual origin.

It will be the argument of this reading to demonstrate in detail how Milton has embodied in the very structure of his

---

[1] *The Common Expositor* (Chapel Hill, 1948), p. 3.

narration the paradox of eternity: the effect is that of a double time scheme whereby events that are being expressed in temporal terms—in sequential action—are simultaneously occurring in the eternal present which is the central setting of the poem. The temporal, in this view, is the metaphor for the eternal, and time in its dual aspect becomes a basis of structure.[2] The fall of Satan is related to the elevation of Christ, to the creation of man and the world; the fall of man is related to the crucifixion-redemption, and the crucifixion, in turn, is significant because it *is* the defeat of Satan. Each one of these events must be seen with the other as part of the image of eternal providence.

The well-known and richly suggestive tradition to which this discussion will return is the Platonic Great Year with its eternal noon. For Plato and his commentators the circular image of time was perfectly realized in the theory of the Great Year which was completed and simultaneously renewed when all of the heavenly bodies returned to the same alignment which they had at the moment of creation. The cyclic movement of the Great Year was "all time," the single period of the whole which embraced all of the periods of the planets, thus making the visible world an imitation of the eternal. Since the theory of the Great Year envisioned all of the heavenly bodies in a perfect perpendicular alignment, the temporal image is that of an eternal noon. And virtually every event of thematic importance in *Paradise Lost* occurs at either midnight or noon, polarities that are at once disparate and concordant: the action that apparently oscillates between the two poles really occurs at the single noon imaged in the Great Year.[3]

Our first acquaintance with something approaching a symbolic use of noon together with a hinted juxtaposition of it with midnight comes in the often quoted description of the fall of

[2] See Joseph Anthony Mazzeo, "Light Metaphysics, Dante's 'Convivio' and the letter to Can Grande della Scale," *Traditio*, XIV (1958), 199 for a summary of St. Thomas' discussion of the use of metaphor in scripture and in poetry. The same attitude towards metaphor and scripture may be seen in a seventeenth century context in Thomas Campanella's *The Defense of Galileo* (1622), trans. Grant McColley in *Smith College Studies in History*, Vol. XXII Nos. 3-4 (April-July 1937). See esp. pp. 27-28.

[3] See Plato, *Timaeus*, trans. R. G. Bury, The Loeb Classical Library (London, 1929), pp. 75-83. Proclus' relevant commentary on the Great Year as "all time" is discussed by Francis Macdonald Cornford, *Plato's Cosmology* (New York, 1957), p. 104.

Mulciber. The related images of the falling star and setting sun consign him particularly to the thematic images that surround Satan.

> from Morn
> To Noon he fell, from Noon to dewy Eve,
> A Summers day; and with the setting Sun
> Dropt from the Zenith like a falling Star . . . (I. 742-745) [4]

The almost casual mention of " noon " in this early descriptive passage assumes full importance in retrospect.

As the fall of Satan is related to the fall of man the noon image is deliberately intensified and the Mulciber pattern repeated.[5] It is seen most vividly in Satan's final descent into Hell and his complementary serpentine metamorphosis in Book X. That descent starts paradoxically as an ascent moving north while going down, and reaches its nadir while the sun reaches its Zenith, climaxing the symbolic noon-midnight time scheme of the poem.

This final descent is climactic; but Satan throughout the epic is always associated with images of eclipse which are intimately related to noon and to the falling star of his own decline. These images directed to the metaphoric high noon center produce the pattern which gives the poem a temporal image for eternity. As a metaphoric structure, then, whether the account of the fall is taken as literal history or as Christian myth, *Paradise Lost* illustrates the eternal contemporaneity of the events of Christian history.

The concept of noon for the Renaissance was a richly ambiguous one having an apparent opposite, midnight, to which it was intimately related, but which was no real opposite at all. Noon, according to the history given by the OED, was not only the mid-point of the day but also the time of night which corres-

---

[4] All quotations are from the *Columbia Milton* ed. Frank Allen Patterson, et al. (New York, 1931-42).

[5] By this I mean that Satan's actions as he descends to earth and the scale of being follow the image pattern of Mulciber's fall. Thus, Satan first descends into the garden at noon, is expelled when he is discovered as a toad, and returns as a *dewy* mist at midnight. Goeffrey Hartman, " Milton's Counterplot," *ELH*, XXV (1958), 1-12 interprets the lines on Mulciber's fall as the introduction of a counterplot and of a note of calm reassurance in the midst of the turmoil of the angelic fall. See esp. pp. 2-7. It seems more likely, however, that this description is a precursor of Satan's own literal and metaphoric descent.

ponded to midday—i. e., midnight or the highest point of day or night. Thus, it was a term that figuratively subsumed the meaning of midnight and encompassed both extremes, with evocations of the darkness at noon which occurred at the crucifixion.[6] The ambiguity of noon extended even further to apply to the hour of creation, to the perfect balancing midpoint between day and night.

John Swan in his popular *Speculum Mundi* suggests the spring when the sun is in Aries as the time of creation. If time begins with the creation of the world, as it does for Augustine and the Church Fathers, and if it begins with the sun in Aries in the center of the sky—that is, at noon—then noon becomes the perfect time of the day, the image of eternity.[7] As many commentators pointed out, at noon there was no shadow but constant light which would associate that time with the one truly eternal being, God. Time begins then in a natural cycle at noon. On its appropriate moral level, the order of grace, time begins for the Christian soul at two apparently distinct yet related points: at the fulfillment of the Incarnation, the birth of Christ at midnight and, most particularly, at noon on the day of the crucifixion when the action of redemption was completed and the sun was again in Aries.

It is no accident that Milton has Satan, in the account of his rebellion related by Raphael, defect at midnight and move towards the north. His specific sin, of course, is the often cited one of pride.

> he of the first,
> If not the first Arch-Angel, great in Power,
> In favour and praeeminence, yet fraught
> With envie against the Son of God, that day
> Honourd by his great Father, and proclaimd
> *Messiah* King anointed, could not beare
> Through pride that sight, & thought himself impaird.

---

[6] For a good deal of my information here and for the direction of some of my interpretation I am indebted to Jackson I. Cope's *The Metaphoric Structure of Paradise Lost* (Baltimore, 1962), pp. 130-140. For the history of the word "noon" see esp. p. 135.

[7] Swan, *op. cit.*, 3d. ed. (London, 1665), pp. 8-12, 319. See also Macrobius, *Commentary on the Dream of Scipio*, trans. William Harris Stahl (New York, 1952), p. 179; Dante, *Inferno*, I, 37-40; Batman uppon Bartholome (London, 1582), p. 143 verso; Walter e Teresa Parri, *Anno del Viaggio e Giorno Iniziale della Commedia* (Florence, 1956), pp. 126-7. It was also believed that the sun would be in Aries and at noon at the Last Judgement. See Parri. *op. cit.*, p. 138.

> Deep malice thence conceiving and disdain,
> Soon as midnight brought on the duskie houre
> Friendliest to sleep and silence, he resolv'd
> With all his Legions to dislodge, and leave
> Unworshipt, unobey'd the Throne supream
> Contemptuous, . . .   (V, 659-671)

Satan's sin, conceived at the very moment when he refuses to obey, is a prideful disobedience. The parallel situation in the very center of the poem, "Mans . . . Disobedience," in turn is a sin of pride committed at noon. The circular structure of the poem effects a thematic reconciliation of apparent opposites that transcends the narrative level in which noon and midnight are distinct times for human understanding. Eternity, which exists only for God, and which is a concept not completely understandable in human terms, is paradoxically expanded from its single present point by contracting it to the apparent opposites of midnight and noon. In this context, Satan's fall at midnight is simultaneous with the fall of man at high noon. The common center of two concentric spheres, one of human life, the other, of angelic time, is the sin of disobedience motivated by pride at noon/midnight.[8]

With the significant events in schematic order the whole pattern becomes clearer. On one hand, while Satan sins at midnight he is defeated in heaven by Christ at noon on the third day. The first unsuccessful temptation of Eve is at midnight, and grows to its successful fruition at noon. Satan thus defects at midnight and apparently succeeds at noon as, conversely, man apparently succeeds at midnight but fails at noon. The presentness of all events in eternity brings an even richer imposition of patterns: as Satan sins at midnight in heaven, the beginning of his defeat in eternity is contained in the very same act. Satan's defeat is manifested in the birth of Christ at midnight, an incarnation that is the true fruit of the triunal union parodied in the incarnation of Sin and Death. As man falls at high noon of the ninth day giving Satan an apparent triumph, man is also, in an eternal view, saved at high noon by the crucifixion. Satan's defeat, his true eclipse, begun at the midnight moment of his sin is consummated at the noon death of Christ in the eclipse

---

[8] I refer to St. Thomas' distinction by which eternity is predicated only to God. Angelic time is *aevum*, that mode of existence which has a beginning but no end.

during the crucifixion. This is merely an intensification of another aspect of the eclipse initiated by Christ in heaven at the moment of Satan's midnight rebellion.

> Another now hath to himself ingross't
> All Power, and us eclipst under the name
> Of King anointed, for whom all this haste
> Of midnight march, and hurried meeting here . . .
>   (V, 775-778)

II

As Satan approaches earth and descends into Eden for the first time, his movement is carefully though unobtrusively located at noon. In a passage that is important in the perspective of later developments, the fallen Lucifer has his first confrontation with the sun which " now sat high in his Meridian Towre " (IV, 30). Later in the same book, Uriel, who had been deceived by the great hypocrite in the form of a beautiful angel, tells Gabriel that the unknown spirit has passed his sphere (the sun) at "highth of Noon " (IV, 564). After Satan's expulsion from the garden by the vigilant Gabriel, Raphael is sent by God to warn and instruct Adam. The coming of the warning angel is at the hour of noon (V, 298 ff.). Raphael's evening departure on a warning note (VIII, 630-643) makes way for the return of Satan who, having circled the earth for seven continued nights with the earth always between him and the light, re-enters the garden as a dewy mist at midnight of the eighth day. In contrast to previous tantalizingly muted references to noon, from here on the coming of the noon hour of the ninth day is prepared for with almost overwhelming insistence.

The focal scene in the poem is the temptation and fall of Adam and Eve. Consonant with the central importance of this scene, Milton makes the noon image most prominent. Only as the narrative approaches the actual temptation of Eve do the references to noon increase in number and intensity. It is as if Milton has been insinuating the image in order to bring it before the reader in its full significance at the appropriate narrative climax. Eve, for example, in her first plea to work alone, refers her cessation of labor to noon: " while I / In yonder Spring of Roses intermixt / With Myrtle, find what to redress till Noon "

(IX, 217-219). From this point on in the ninth book the approach of noon is repeatedly stressed.

In the early discussion between Adam and Raphael the heat of noon had already been emphasized.

> voutsafe with us
> Two onely, who yet by sov'ran gift possess
> This spacious ground, in yonder shadie Bowre
> To rest, and what the Garden choicest bears
> To sit and taste, till this meridian heat
> Be over, and the Sun more coole decline.   (V. 365-370)

After Adam and Eve have separated, agreeing to return to the Bower by noon, the serpent tempts Eve through an appeal to her vanity and pride, awakening her appetite not merely for the fruit but for the forbidden knowledge which it represents.

> Mean while the hour of Noon drew on, and wak'd
> An eager appetite, rais'd by the smell
> So savorie of that Fruit, which with desire,
> Inclinable now grown to touch or taste,
> Sollicited her longing eye . . .   (IX, 739-743)

Returning to Adam after her sin, she persuades him to eat of the fruit. Though fully conscious of the wrongness of the deed, he is overcome by the sexual appetite which had been the object of Raphael's final warning.

> he scrupl'd not to eat
> Against his better knowledge, not deceav'd
> But fondly overcome with Femal charm.   (IX, 997-999)

The repetition of noon in this context points to a pattern wherein Satan's first arrival in Eden illustrates a schematic reconciliation of the apparent opposites discussed earlier.

Satan, a midnight figure, joins the light of noon within a framework in which the essence of midnight is the promise of light from the east, the positive light which midnight merely negates. This negative-positive union is apparent as Satan, now a midnight mist, possesses the serpent and waits for the light of morning.

> Like a black mist low creeping, he held on
> His midnight search, where soonest he might finde
> The Serpent: him fast sleeping he found
> In Labyrinth of many round self-rowld,
> His head the midst, well stor'd with suttle wiles:

Not yet in horrid Shade or dismal Den,
Nor nocent yet, but on the grassie Herbe
Fearless unfeard he slept: in at his Mouth
The Devil enterd, and his brutal sense,
In heart or head, possessing soon inspir'd
With act intelligential, but his sleep
Disturbed not, waiting close th' approach of Morn.

(IX, 180-191)

Complementary to this midnight figure from the north and illustrating the reconciliation of the opposites under one symbol, is the physical presence of the sun in Aries in the southern sky at midday. This latter conjunction gave rise to the ambiguity of the word *meridies* which was used equally to mean " south " and/or " noon." [9]

Some of the most important elements in the noon-day temptation are to be found in the body of tradition which gathered around the " noon-day devil," the *daemonio meridiano* of Psalm 90. This passage celebrates the protection given by God to the just man.

Scuto circumdabit te veritas eius;
non timebis a timore nocturno,
a sagitta volante in die,
a negotio perambulante in tenebris,
ab incursu et daemonio meridiano.[10]

Thanks to the researches of Roger Caillois some years ago and to the more recent analysis of them by Fr. Rudolph Arbesmann it is now clear that there was a complex body of interpretation for this passage throughout the Middle Ages and the Renaissance.[11] In addition to this exegetical consensus, the passage invoked a particular religious context in which the noon hour occupied a place of its own. In the East particularly, noon held a position of unique religious importance as the hour that

---

[9] See M. A. Orr, *Dante and the Early Astronomers*, New and Revised Edition (London, 1956), pp. 29-30.

[10] I cite the Vulgate, Psalm 90:5-6. In English translations other than the Douay the Psalm is numbered " ninety-one." For a brief summary of English versions of this passage in Renaissance Bibles see Cope, *Metaphoric Structure*, p. 131 *n*.

[11] Roger Caillois, " Les démons de midi," *Revue de l'Histoire des Religions,* CXV (1937), 142-173; CXVI (1937), 54-83, 143-186. Rudolph Arbesmann, " The ' Daemonum Meridianum' and Greek and Latin Patristic Exegesis," *Traditio,* XIV (1958) 17-31.

divided the day in half at the culminating point of the sun's course through the heavens; it was the moment of greatest heat, least shadow, and greatest light.[12]

Because it is the mid-point between the ascent and descent of the sun, noon is an hour of stillness, a timeless moment during which the course of nature is interrupted. It provides man with his best opportunity to communicate with the eternal world of spirits.[13] As man's closest earthly approach to the eternal, noon assumed the special prominence of the holiest period of the day in the life of religious communities. Because evil spirits and temptations were most likely to occur as a result of the *acedia* and mirages induced by the heat, noon was morally the most dangerous time of the day.[14] The resulting prevalence of *luxuria* and the awakening of the sensual appetite in dreams made mid-day an hour of extreme sexual temptation.[15]

To this body of tradition based primarily on myth and natural conditions commentators on the noon-day devil easily attached profound moral importance. The noon-day devil is the cause of the *acedia* which results in sexual temptation and the consequent deprivation of reason. The mirages of noon contribute to an appearance of good in an actual context of evil. It is thus that St. Jerome knew the noon-day devil as Satan coming to tempt man in the guise of an angel of light.[16]

In virtue of such tradition Milton is able to place the temptation and fall in *Paradise Lost* in clearer perspective. As the symbol for the moment when divine things are most perfectly understood [17] noon may be taken *in bono* because of the eternity symbolized in its zenith of light. Raphael descends at the eternal noon to instruct Adam in his origin and destiny and to warn him of the dangers to which he is now susceptible. On the other hand, temptation too occurs in eternity simultaneously with the

[12] For these points see Arbesmann, 18; Caillois, CXV, 149. See also Isidore of Seville, *Etymologies,* ed. W. M. Lindsay (Oxford, 1911), V, xxx and Ambrose, *Exameron,* ed. Emiliano Pasteris (Turin, 1937), pp. 351-3; Batman, p. 148 verso.

[13] Caillois, CXV, 164; CXVI, 69.

[14] Caillois, CXVI, 146.

[15] *Ibid.,* 150.

[16] See Arbesmann, 26 *n.* Richard of St. Victor, PL, CXCVI, 395 points out that at noon, the moment of greatest light and heat, demons come to us hiding their evil under the form of holiness in order to lead us into perversity by evil counsel.

[17] Arbesmann, 26.

heavenly visitation, just as midnight and noon stand at opposite ends of the axis that makes them one.

Satan, in his first temptation of Eve during her midnight dream, is at her ear in the form of a toad; but the " serenade," if I may use Howard Schultz's term, stirs her imagination to a depiction of him as an angel of light prompting her to eat of the forbidden fruit. The juxtaposition of Satan as a toad in outward reality with the inner illusion provides just the ambiguous contrast implied in the concept of the noon-day devil, and illustrates an important point about the noon-midnight polarity. Temptation occurs in the noon light of eternity, under the positive aspect of good rather than under the negative aspect of midnight evil, because it is of the nature of effective temptation to occur under the appearance of good. Imitating true divinity, Satan must present Eve with that which appears to be good rather than with the mere absence of good. Eve's dream (V, 29ff.) is a prophetic vision of her true temptation with an important symbolic difference: her dream temptation takes place in the deceptive light of the Satanic moon, the false light that must eventually yield to the sun.

> now reignes
> Full Orb'd the Moon, and with more pleasing light
> Shadowie sets off the face of things . . .   (V, 41-43)

Thus the fruit *seemed* much fairer to her midnight fancy than to her noon-day senses (V, 53).

The scene of Eve's final noon temptation has already been suggested as a surrender to more than physical hunger. She participates in *luxuria*, an intemperate appetite for what is in excess of human good, while Adam is led into his sin through his inordinate fondness for her " Femal charm " which anticipates his fall into concupiscence. Concurrently, however, he is guilty of the same prideful aspiration that toppled Satan and Eve. Later he confesses as much to Michael before leaving the garden with a new cognizance of man's limitation in seeking divine knowledge.

> How soon hath thy prediction, Seer blest,
> Measur'd this transient World, the Race of time,
> Till time stand fixt: beyond is all abyss,
> Eternitie, whose end no eye can reach.

> Greatly instructed I shall hence depart,
> Greatly in peace of thought, and have my fill
> Of knowledge, what this Vessel can containe;
> Beyond which was my folly to aspire.   (XII, 553-560)

By deliberately seeking the "test" of temptation, Eve is of her own free will submitting to the dangerous hour of noon and the fraud of the noon-day devil. Adam, after her specious argument, sets her on her way, underscoring the importance of her will.

> But if thou think, trial unsought may finde
> Us both securer then thus warnd thou seemst,
> Go; for thy stay, not free, absents thee more;
> Go in thy native innocence, relie
> On what thou hast of vertue, summon all,
> For God towards thee hath done his part, do thine.
>
>   (IX, 370-375)

Ironically, she soon falls into the practised fraud of Satan, a characteristic of the noon-day devil.[18] This fraud was the very type of attack that Eve had implied she could easily withstand.

> His violence thou fearest not, being such,
> As wee, not capable of death or paine,
> Can either not receave, nor can repell.
> His fraud is then thy fear, which plain inferrs
> Thy equal fear that my firm Faith and Love
> Can by his fraud be shak'n or seduc't;
> Thoughts, which how found they harbour in thy brest
> *Adam*, missthought of her to thee so dear? (IX, 282-289)

As if to emphasize the danger that lies in store particularly at noon, Adam sets that hour as the limit by which she must return to the security of the Bower.

> Oft he to her his charge of quick returne
> Repeated, shee to him as oft engag'd
> To be returnd by Noon amid the Bowre,
> And all things in best order to invite
> Noontide repast, or Afternoons repose.   (IX, 399-403)

Transcending the narrative level, the descent of Satan at noon and his subsequent tempting of Eve is the figurative device for a more universal meaning: the descent of midnight at noon is

---

[18] Richard of St. Victor, *PL*, CXCVI, 395.

the descent of evil into the soul. Noon and midnight are then one—a symbolic darkening of the light of grace. Adam and Eve's temptation and fall places them into the context of the results of sin described in Isaiah 59:10.

We grope for the wall like the blinde, and we grope as if we had no eyes: we stumble at noone day as in the night, we are in desolate places as dead men.   [King James Version]

The noon darkness of their sin and temptation is thus a darkness in the midst of light which is balanced by the act of salvation at noon performed by Satan's conqueror, Christ.

Luxuria, one of the principal vices associated with the noonday devil, was an excessive appetite particularly, though not exclusively, in matters of sex. The extreme forms of this excess are an intemperate desire for knowledge beyond one's bounds, the curiosity that is a species of Satanic pride,[19] and a desire to elevate oneself to the level of divinity because of personal vanity, ambition, and the vain-glory which alienates the mind to forgetfulness of truth.[20]

An ideal traditional context is set for the noon-day temptation within which the association of Satan with the cold north and the obverse association of noon with the warm south, with goodness and light, is illustrated in the first noon-day descent of Satan into the garden. The north wind of sin comes in a meeting of midnight and noon, north and south, darkness and light. This union of opposites is a symbolic preparation for the evil that is to come out of the good of creation; contrariwise, at the moment

[19] For the connection of curiosity with pride see Howard Schultz, *Milton and Forbidden Knowledge* (New York, 1955), pp. 1, 8, 177. Giovanni Lorenzo d'Anania in his *De Natura Daemonum* (Venice, 1589), p. 38 associates curiosity and the noon-day devil with Adam's sin.

[20] Relevant commentary on the various aspects of the noon-day devil and his association with noon-midnight, *luxuria*, *acedia*, and the form of the serpent may be found in Pierre de Lancre, *Tableau de l'Inconstance des Mauvais Anges et Demons, ou il est Amplement Traicté des Sorciers et de la Sorcelerie* (Paris, 1612), fol. 66-67; Robert Bellarmine, *Explanatio in Psalmes* (Rome, 1611), p. 682; Martin Delrio, *Disquisitionum Magicarum* (Venice, 1616), pp. 271-2; Hugh of St. Cher, *In Psalterium universum Davidis Regis, et Prophetae* (Venice, 1754), II, 241verso col. 1-2. For evidence of a popular tradition on the noon-day devil, one might cite Christopher Fowler, *Daemonium Meridianum. Satan at Noon—Antichristian Blasphemie, Anti-scripturall Divelismes, Anti-morall uncleannesse, Evidenced in the light of truth and Punished by the hand of Justice* (London, 1655).

of his apparent noon-day triumph after the fall, the symbol is inverted to display the good that comes out of evil.[21]

In his first address to the sun at noon, Satan had already associated himself with the pride and ambition commentators attached to the noon-day devil (IV, 37-40; 58-61). Satan, who had sinned through his ambition, through his own vanity stemming from pride, comes as the noon-day devil to tempt Eve into the very same sin.

Seeing Eve surrounded, appropriately enough, by the sensual fragrance of roses, a bower of bliss aligned in Milton's simile with the sexual delights of

> Spot more delicious then those Gardens feign'd
> Or of reviv'd *Adonis,* or renownd
> *Alcinous,* host of old *Laertes* Son,
> Or that, not Mystic, where the Sapient King
> Held dalliance with his faire *Egyptian* Spouse.
>
> (IX, 439-443)

Satan's first appeal of fraudulent temptation in this spot of *luxuria,* of sexual dalliance, is to Eve's vanity. Through this he appeals to her pride and ambition to be "A Goddess among Gods, ador'd and serv'd/By angels numberless, thy daily Train" (IX, 547-548). Subtly he shifts his ground to the depiction of the appetizing nature of the fruit.

> Till on a day roaving the field, I chanc'd
> A goodly Tree farr distant to behold
> Loaden with fruit of fairest colours mixt,
> Ruddie and Gold: I nearer drew to gaze;
> When from the boughes a savorie odour blow'n,
> Grateful to appetite, more pleas'd my sense
> Then smell of sweetest Fenel or the Teats
> Of Ewe or Goat dropping with Milk at Eevn,
> Unsuckt of Lamb or Kid, that tend thir play.
> To satisfie the sharp desire I had
> Of tasting those fair Apples, I resolv'd
> Not to deferr; hunger and thirst at once,
> Powerful perswaders, quick'nd at the scent
> Of that alluring fruit, urg'd me so keene. (IX, 575-588)

---

[21] For the association of the east and south with light, heat, and life; north and west with dark, cold, and death see Brendan O'Hehir, *Balanced Opposites in the Poetry of Pope, and the Historical Evolution of the Concept,* Unpublished Dissertation (Johns Hopkins, 1959), p. 167. See also A. B. Chambers, "Goodfriday, 1613. Riding Westward the Poem and the Tradition," *ELH,* XXVIII (1961), 45-6.

What superficially appears to be an appeal to the physical appetite of hunger, is here clearly predicated on the sensuous qualities of the fruit which awaken that desire; but this symbolic luxuriance which arouses desire is next joined by the serpent to a further appeal to Eve's vanity. In a consummation of the temptation of vain-glory perpetrated by the noon-day devil, he tells Eve that after he ate of the fruit it gave him the power to perceive

> . . . all that fair and good in thy Divine
> Semblance, and in thy Beauties heav'nly Ray
> . . . no Fair to thine
> Equivalent or second, which compel'd
> Mee thus, though importune perhaps, to come
> And gaze, and worship thee of right declar'd
> Sovran of Creatures, universal Dame.   (IX, 606-612)

Eve yields to the temptation of vanity and readily allows the serpent to lead her to the tree itself. This is ultimately a journey into his own type of fraud wherein she will justify her action according to the logic of his specious reasoning.[22]

And it is with the approach of the very hour of noon, a symbolic temporal occasion that by now has been woven into the texture of the entire temptation, that Satan makes his final entreaty as the serpentine noon-day devil, the temptation of Eve's prideful ambition to be like God. The appetite aroused at noon does not demand the satisfaction of physical hunger, but the fulfillment of pride and vanity in order to elevate oneself to the level of God.

>   he knows that in the day
> Ye Eate thereof, your Eyes that seem so cleere,
> Yet are but dim, shall perfetly be then
> Op'nd and cleerd, and ye shall be as Gods,
> Knowing both Good and Evil as they know. (IX, 705-709)

Beguiled, in a strong sense metaphorically misled by the fraudulent and specious arguments, Eve finds the conjunction of all of these elements too strong to withstand, and at the precise moment when Eve plucks and eats of the fruit Milton returns

---

[22] St. Thomas gives the significant association of vainglory with pride and the desire for glory: *Summa,* II. ii, Quest. 132.

directly to the noon theme so ominously anticipated a few lines earlier: "Mean while the hour of Noon drew on" (IX, 739). At that time Eve's ears were still ringing with the sound of Satan's persuasive, seemingly reasonable and truthful words. Now the moment is emphatically underscored—" in evil hour / Forth reaching to the Fruit, she pluck'd, she eat "(IX, 780-781).

Adam's fall is essentially the same as Eve's, differing only in degree. He readily yields to Eve's own temptation in full knowledge of his error, not trying to justify it in Satanic rhetoric as Eve had done, but yielding to her illusory charms. The ambiguous appetite which had become, in the noon context, a multifaceted type of *luxuria* symbolized by the fruit and the injunction against eating it—excessive ambition, vanity, and pride—now degenerates into the greatest form of *luxuria*, sensual appetite, as Adam and Eve become subject to fleshly concupiscence.[23] Their inordinate passions are described in a metaphor of the unbalancing of nature as they hide from the noon heat in the shade of the Figtree.

>   nor onely Teares
> Raind at thir Eyes, but high winds worse within
> Began to rise, high Passions, Anger, Hate,
> Mistrust, Suspicion, Discord, and shook sore
> Thir inward State of Mind, calm Region once
> And full of Peace, now tost and turbulent:
> For Understanding rul'd not, and the Will
> Heard not her lore, both in subjection now
> To sensual Appetite, who from beneathe
> Usurping over sovran Reason claimd
> Superior sway . . .   (IX, 1121-1131)

With the breaking of the stillness and balance of noon imaged in the unleashing of the passions in Adam and Eve, the serpent has completed the work of the noon-day devil. In completing his midnight evil at noon in what he regards as his moment of greatest triumph, Satan begins his return to Hell. He has led Adam and Eve into his own sin, a symbolic meeting of his midnight fall with theirs at noon. As his fall through pride contains

---

[23] Ioannis Wierus, *De Praestigiis Daemonum Incantationibus ac veneficiis Libri Sex* (Basel, 1583), col. 21, attributes the fall of the angels to pride and concupiscence, the source of all evils, which led them to try to usurp God's place. See also Ward S. Worden, "Milton's Approach to the Story of the Fall," *ELH*, XV (1948), 299.

theirs, so midnight and noon are joined in one temporal image for eternity.

III

Paralleling this tradition that makes noon most important in the temporal structure is a tributary symbolic aspect of noon which illustrates in another way the circular structure of the action. At the moment of Adam's fall the earth trembles again as it had done when Eve sinned. When the earth shifts from its axis,[24] reflecting the internal disruption of the passions in Adam and Eve, time and its accompanying decay begin.

> Earth trembl'd from her entrails, as again
> In pangs, and Nature gave a second groan,
> Skie lowr'd and muttering Thunder, som sad drops
> Wept at compleating of the mortal Sin
> Original . . .   (IX, 1000-1004; see also X, 668-695)

As we have seen, the cycle of the Great Year, the *magnus annus* of Plato's *Timaeus*, was also associated with noon when the sun was in Aries. Satan's first confrontation with the sun is at noon (Book IV). This meeting, at one and the same time the confrontation of midnight and noon (Satan and Christ as the moon and the sun), coincides with the complex of noon images and presents the same alignment for eclipse and for the Great Year, an alignment that began at the creation. At the fall the Great Year ends only to return again when, in Book X, the sun returns to Aries at noon and Satan is once more in alignment at the opposite pole.[25] Metaphorically, with the renewal of the Great Year at the moment of the crucifixion time begins anew for the Christian soul.

The finest indication that the Great Year is of importance as a temporal symbol in the poem may be seen in connection with Raphael.[26] At his noon descent his resemblance to the Phoenix is made quite explicit.

[24] For an extremely suggestive analysis of the cosmological effect of Adam's sin see Kester Svendsen, *Milton and Science* (Cambridge, Mass., 1956), pp. 70-1.

[25] This alignment was much commented on in connection with Virgil's famous Eclogue IV. See the commentary of Carolus Ruaeus, *P. Virgilii Maronis Opera*, 4th ed. (Hague, 1723), p. 24.

[26] For pointing out the following connection between the Phoenix, noon, Aries, and the Great Year I am indebted to Thomas E. Maresca.

                    Down thither prone in flight
He speeds, and through the vast Ethereal Skie
Sailes between worlds, with steddie wing
Now on the polar windes, then with quick Fann
Winnows the buxom Air; till within soare
Of Towring Eagles, to all the Fowles he seems
A *Phoenix*, gaz'd by all, as that sole Bird
When to enshrine his reliques in the Sun's
Bright Temple, to *Ægyptian Theb's* he flies.
At once on th'Eastern cliff of Paradise
He lights . . .
                    Like *Maia's* son he stood,
And shook his Plumes, that Heavn'ly fragrance filld
The circuit wide. Strait knew him all the Bands
Of Angels under watch; and to his state,
And to his message high in honour rise . . .
                    (V, 266-276; 285-289)

To the traditional Phoenix lore the *Apocalypse* of the Pseudo-Baruch added the significant element that the Phoenix's function was to protect mankind from the heat of the sun by spreading its wings.[27] Raphael's mission is one of warning and protection wherein his broad wings are a symbolic protection for man from the noon-day devil. In addition, the same apocryphal book related the movement of the Phoenix on its outward journey in the morning to the radiation of the sun. The Phoenix returns with the sun's beams in the evening, which, significantly enough, is exactly the same as Raphael's own journey.

The most important connection between Raphael's phoenix-like descent and the Great Year is made by Pliny:

> . . . *Manilius* affirmeth, that the reuolution of the great
> yeare so much spoken of, agreeth just with the life of this
> bird: in which yeare the stars returne againe to their
> first points, and giue significations of times and seasons,
> as at the beginning and withall, that this yeare should
> begin at high noone that very day when the sun entreth
> the signe *Aries*.[28]

It is not difficult to reconstruct the metaphoric texture of the poem: the central temporal locale of noon represents the moment

---

[27] *The Apocalypse of the Pseudo-Baruch* in Jean Hubaux and Maxime Leroy, *Le Mythe du Phénixe dans les littératures grecque et latine* (Paris, 1939), pp. xxvii-xxviii. For further discussion of the Phoenix and Raphael see Svendsen, p. 148.

[28] G. Plinius Secundus, *The Historie of the World*, trans. Philemon Holland (London, 1634), p. 271.

of creation with the sun in mid-heaven in Aries while all of the
planets are in alignment for the Great Year.[29] The Great Year
is the metaphoric perpetual noon that is the image of eternity.
Raphael himself tells us that it is the image of heavenly time;
on the metaphoric " Day " of the Great Year, Christ (the sun)
was elevated in heaven; the rising of the sun in Aries is clearly
a cosmological image of this elevation.

> As yet this world was not, and *Chaos* wilde
> Reignd where these Heav'ns now rowl, where Earth now rests
> Upon her Center pois'd, when on a day
> (For time, though in Eternitie, appli'd
> To motion, measures all things durable
> By present, past, and future) on such day
> As Heav'ns great Year brings forth, th'Empyreal Host
> Of Angels by Imperial summons call'd . . .   (V, 577-584)

As a symbol of harmony before the fall in *Paradise Lost*, the
Great Year ends with the fall at noon, and is renewed with the
defeat of Satan in eternity on his return to Hell when he is in
line with the sun in Aries. The circular, or cyclic, movement is
thus a structural element of the poem as it was for Plato's conception of time and the Great Year.[30] This is what makes the
temporal locale of all of the action of *Paradise Lost* part of the
eternal present under the central image of noon around which all
of the tangential referents form a cluster that always leads back
to the noon axis and hence to eternity. The periodic reconstruc-
tion of the universe that was an essential element of the theory
of the Great Year [31] may be seen as the regeneration of the soul

[29] Pierre Duhem, *Le Systéme du Monde* (Paris, 1913-59), I, 67 notes that in the
theory of the Great Year the planets have the same position that they had at creation. See also the commentary of Chalcidius, *Platonis Timaeus interprete Chalcidio*,
ed. Ioh Wrobel (Lipsius, 1877), pp. 183-4.

[30] Cornford, *Plato's Cosmology*, p. 103.

[31] Ibid., pp. 104, 117. The Great Year was the subject of controversy since it log-
ically led to the postulation of the eternity of the world. Duhem, VII, 443 notes this
controversy and the condemnation of the theory of the Great Year as heretical by
some of the Fathers. I only suggest it here as a poetic myth used metaphorically for
eternity. See also Duhem, VII, 441. Lynn Thorndike, *History of Magic and Experimental Science* (New York, 1923-58), IV, 536 cites Pico della Mirandola's attack on
this theory of the repetition of history. Extensive English discussions of this renewal
aspect of the Great Year were being carried on by Henry More, Ralph Cudworth,
Joseph Glanvill, George Rust and others at the time *Paradise Lost* was being written.
Cf. esp. More's *Immortality of the Soul* (1659), Bk. III, and Glanvill's *Lux Orien-
talis* (1662).

through the coming of grace when, with the eclipse at the crucifixion, the Great Year returns.[32]

Like "noon" itself the image of eclipse has been carefully
patterned throughout the poem so that it works into the alignment of sun and moon imagery climaxed in the scene of Satan's
return to Hell. Satan's association with the moon and with
eclipse appears first in the description of his shield.

> his ponderous shield
> Ethereal temper, massy, large and round,
> Behind him cast; the broad circumference
> Hung on his shoulders like the Moon . . .   (I, 284-287)

Satan here is the original brilliant Lucifer whose light is dimmed
by the interposition of the moon. This image is reinforced later
in the same book by two passages—one concerned with the
meteor and another with eclipse proper. It is of considerable
symbolic importance that the Satanic banner is likened to a
meteor, a flashing falling phenomenon.

> Who forthwith from the glittering Staff unfurld
> Th' Imperial Ensign, which full advanc't
> Shon like a Meteor streaming to the Wind . . . (I, 535-537)

This emblematic ensign is closely followed by a description of
Satan under the gradual diminution of his glory and light, like
an eclipse or a meteor.[33]

> his form had yet not lost
> All her Original brightness, nor appear'd
> Less then Arch Angel ruind, and th' excess
> Of Glory obscur'd: As when the Sun new ris'n
> Looks through the Horizontal misty Air
> Shorn of his Beams, or from behind the Moon
> In dim Eclips disastrous twilight sheds
> On half the Nations, and with fear of change
> Perplexes Monarchs. Dark'n'd so, yet shon
> Above them all th' Arch Angel . . .   (I, 591-600)

---

[32] See Macrobius, pp. 221-2. For the association of the eclipse with the beginning
of the Great Year see Duhem, I, 283 which cites Cicero's *Dream of Scipio*. It is also
well to remember Pliny's conjunction of the sign of Aries with the Phoenix in the
light of the traditional identification of the Phoenix with Christ. Another adumbration
of the temporal pattern of the poem can be seen in the fact that the Phoenix was
believed to have made its last appearance at the time of the crucifixion.

[33] For a suggestive discussion of the eclipse imagery see Svendsen, p. 70.

From the moment of his defection at midnight when he is eclipsed for the first time by Christ (V, 776), the course of Satan as he descends the scale of nature is that of the meteor or moon going into gradual eclipse. Satan's midnight movement is that of defection from God resonating thematically the synonymous value of the terms " eclipse " and " defectum." [34] Satan's gradual descent down the scale of being is imaged in this *defectum*, or gradual eclipse. His association with the descending dragon of the Apocalypse at the beginning of Book IV coincides with the astronomical phenomenon which accompanied comets and which the Renaissance knew as the " dragon."

According to William Fulke, whose *A Most Pleasant Prospect into the Garden of Natural Contemplation* [35] was one of the standard Renaissance handbooks on comets, these " dragons " are a combination of damp vapors and cold air; the " dragon,' he says, has often been associated with the Devil himself.[36] The metaphoric possibility opened up by this belief is evident: coming from the north, where comets were customarily located,[37] Satan partakes of the cold air and vapor of the " dragon," and transforms himself into a mist to enter the garden. Further, the phenomenon of the falling dragon was concomitant with the eclipse of both sun and moon, a point made in Sacrobosco's account of a lunar eclipse.[38] The texture of the continued symbolism of eclipse and falling star is consistent with the narrative.

It is in this context that we must view the most important scene in the poem, Satan's return to Hell after the fall; this scene represents the culmination of his evil, the height of his splendor and, at the same time, his eternal defeat in the climax of his eclipse. His defeat occurs when the sun is at noon in Aries, the final indication of the juxtaposition of events in the simultaneous present of eternity.

[34] See Laurentio Beyerlinck, *Magnum Theatrum Vitae Humane* (Leyden, 1678), III, 46; Isidore of Seville, III, lix.

[35] The complete title is *A Most Pleasant Prospect into the Garden of Naturall Contemplation to behold the naturall causes of all kinde of Meteors*. My references are to the 3d ed. (London, 1640).

[36] Fulke, p. 10recto and verso.

[37] See also Svendsen, pp. 91, 109-111.

[38] Sacrobosco, *The Sphere*, trans. Lynn Thorndike (Chicago, 1949), pp. 141-2. For the position of the sun and moon on the ecliptic paralleling the position of Satan and the Sun, see p. 125. Svendsen, pp. 70-2 discusses the results of the earth's shift on the ecliptic.

At the moment of his return the symbols of noon—the Great Year, the eclipse—are revealed in their fullest implications. The scene is a repetition of Satan's earlier noon *approach* to earth in Book IV. At that time he had paused to fix his sight on the sun.

> Sometimes towards *Eden* which now in his view
> Lay pleasant, his grievd look he fixes sad,
> Sometimes towards Heav'n and the full-blazing Sun,
> Which now sat high in his Meridian Towre . . . (IV, 27-30)

Now, returning to Hell, the midnight figure of the north has an even more explicit confrontation with the image of Christ, the noon figure of the south. Christ sees Satan's fall which fulfills the prophecy of Genesis 3:15, that the seed of the woman will stamp on the serpent.

> So spake this Oracle, then verifi'd
> When *Jesus* son of *Mary* second *Eve*,
> Saw Satan fall like Lightning down from Heav'n,
> Prince of the Aire; then rising from his Grave
> Spoild Principalities and Powers, triumpht
> In open shew, and with ascension bright
> Captivity led captive through the Aire,
> The Realm it self of Satan long usurpt,
> Whom he shall tread at last under our feet . . .
> (X, 182-190)

As Sin and Death build their bridge to the world, they behold Satan returning.

> when behold
> *Satan* in likeness of an Angel bright
> Bewixt the *Centaure* and the *Scorpion* stearing
> His *Zenith*, while the Sun in *Aries* rose . . . (X, 326-329)

Not only does this scene illustrate the complete undoing of all of Satan's actions by Christ, but within these few lines and the succeeding narrative is contained the ultimate concentration of the temporal simultaneity of the noon action. The eternal framework contains all of the action and justifies the ways of God to man showing, from God's standpoint, how the ambiguity of noon/midnight is resolved under the single unambiguous noon of the crucifixion, the symbol of the noon of eternal life.

Satan's descending movement in this scene, from the world to Hell, is along the ecliptic of the now shifted world. In terms of the poetic structure he is travelling both north and west in the traditional directions of evil, between the Scorpion and Sagittarius, while at the same time the sun is rising directly opposite in Aries properly consigned to the east and the coming of light. The sun, once more at its meridian height in Aries (significantly the sign of the Ram) was in mid-sky in the south.[39] For both Batman and Ficino the sun in the sign of Aries was an indication of the hope of life, of the coming fortune of the whole world.[40] This promise of rebirth, of the hope of life, occurs for the Christian with Christ's suffering and death as Picinello points out in connecting the ascent of the sun in Aries with the time of crucifixion and with spiritual rebirth through Christ's merits.[41] Just as the original sin of Adam and Eve had cosmic effects, shifting the earth from its axis and causing a rumble in the universe, so nature responds at the crucifixion with an answering cosmic effect—an earthquake and eclipse—restoring, on the level of grace, the balance broken in both grace and nature at the original fall.[42]

What this scene presents, then, is one of the basic paradoxes of the poem under the noon aspect of eternal presentness. At the same time as Satan is returning north towards his midnight sin, he is reaching *his* meridian height, a nadir which is, for him, a noon at midnight; his height of splendor is a descent into darkness, to a midnight meridian. At the other pole, the sun is rising in Aries to its meridian height at noon: Christ, through his elevation on the cross at noon, is completing the eclipse of Satan begun at the midnight fall in heaven. Satan's triumph is thus a defeat in eternity wherein the ambiguity of the apparent polarity of noon and midnight is resolved in a *single* eternal noon. Further, the scene fulfills Christ's prophecy to Satan articulated

[39] For a discussion of direction according to Aristotle's *De Coelo* see John Freccero, "Dante's Pilgrim in a Gyre," *PMLA*, LXXVI (1961), 170-1. For the association of Aries with the east see Batman, pp. 124verso-125verso.

[40] Batman, p. 134verso; Ficino, *Liber de Sole* in *Opera Amnia*, ed. M. Sancipriano (Turin, 1959), I. 2, fol. 966. D. Philippo Picinello, *Mundus Symbolicus* (Cologne, 1688), I, 28 col. 1 associates Christ with the divine sun and rebirth. On 27 col. 2 Picinello draws an analogy between the Incarnation and the entrance of the sun into Aries.

[41] Picinello, I, 27 col. 2, 28 col. 1.

[42] Chambers, "Goodfriday," 49-50.

in *Paradise Regained*: "Know'st thou not that my rising is thy fall, / And my promotion will be thy destruction?" (III, 201-202).

Satan returns to Hell in the form of the noon-day devil, that is, as an angel of light (X, 327). His eclipse occurs ironically in the symbolic form of his triumph. This resolves a further ambiguity in which Satan as the moon is also an angel of light, and is thus the false sun eclipsed at the crucifixion. At the same time the astronomical symbolism remains valid, for he is opposite the sun in position of lunar eclipse. As Christ is crucified, the ultimate eclipse of Satan is fully realized not only in his descent towards midnight but in his actual and final unwilling transformation into the serpent. His full glory, earlier obscured by his moon-like shield, by his aspect of a falling star and eclipsed sun, has now degenerated to that of the hissing serpent.

> till supplanted down he fell
> A monstrous Serpent on his Belly prone,
> Reluctant, but in vaine, a greater power
> Now rul'd him, punisht in the shape he sin'd,
> According to his doom . . .   (X, 513-517)

With the approach of the sun into Aries all of the noon references converge in order that time may be seen as the metaphor for eternity. At creation the sun was in the middle of the sky in Aries making noon the first and most perfect time; [43] it is in Aries at the fall of man; it is in Aries at the crucifixion, the beginning of the time of grace, and this is the metaphoric renewal of the Great Year. To an age which could see Christ's crucifixion as taking place in the same spot where the tree from which Adam and Eve ate the forbidden fruit stood, and at the same time of day as Adam sinned, [44] the scene of Satan's return to Hell would

[43] See Macrobius, p. 179.
[44] For the location of the cross at the site of the Tree of Knowledge in poetic tradition see Donne's "Hymn to God my God, in my sickness," 11. 21-2. The whole question of the time of the cruicifixion was the subject of some discussion. See Matt. 27:45, Mark 15:25 and Cornelius à Lapide, *Commentarius in Quatuor Evangelia* (Antwerp, 1695), pp. 535 col. 2-536 col. 1; p. 616 col. 1. See also Hugh of St. Cher, *In Evangelia secundum Matthaeum, Lucam, Marcum, & Joannem* (Venice, 1703) VI, pp. 122recto col. 2, 270recto col.2; John Diodati, *Pious Annotations Upon the Holy Bible,* 2nd ed. (London, 1648), pp. 45, 52, 119. On the miraculous nature of the eclipse commentators agreed. See Sacrobosco, p. 142; Cornelius, *Evangelia,* p. 536 col. 1-2. The planetary conjunctions are the same as they are for Satan and the sun at the moment

be an ideal image of the eternity of fall and redemption, of the opposition between Satan and Christ which is in effect, no real opposition at all. Satan, imitating good, has attempted a deceptive parody of the divine. The result of his succesful temptation has been only his own final eclipse.

In a poetic incarnation Milton creates his poem to justify God's eternal providence. He must submit eternity to time in an imitation of the Incarnation, the central fact of eternal providence; and in an imitation of that history which is both sacred and profane, he must demonstrate that midnight and noon are polarities only for man, the temporal being who must understand the eternal through temporal symbols. This divine providence presented in temporal terms reflects the Christian universality at the heart of Milton's poetic myth. If the fall happened at a moment in history, it is perpetually present in Christian lives; if the Incarnation was a historical event, it is co-present with the redemption which it implies. Time, developed through the basic transcendent symbol of noon, significantly contributes to structure the whole poem and is the basic metaphor, making the poem through its depiction of physical battle, of ascent and descent, a temporal image of the eternal epic of good versus evil. It is an exemplum of the divine lesson that what is given in time be healing for eternity.[45]

_____

of his return to Hell in the form of an angel of light. Thus Satan as the fading Lucifer who has become associated with the dependent light of the moon is now the false light—the moon in the guise of the sun—eclipsed by the true sun of Christ.

[45] *Noon* has a similar value in *Samson Agonistes*. In addition to the central setting of the action at noon, the whole concept of Samson's psychological drama involves the darkness of midnight and eclipse (11. 80-109). For Samson the pattern entails a movement out of the midnight darkness of despair into the noon light of grace which penetrates, and ultimately subsumes that darkness (151-163). His three temptations (sloth, lust, and wrath) all occur within the noon framework. The chorus makes the important connection between high noon and the sin of pride (682-686) thus aligning Samson's sin with that of Adam and Eve. Not only does the messenger's account of Samson's death clearly locate the action at high noon (1612) but it also points to the fact that this is the moment of Samson's closest communion with God, the moment when the actual light of noon becomes the inner light which overcomes his midnight darkness of sin and despair (1635-1638). After this account the chorus significantly invokes the comparison of Samson with the Phoenix (1687-1707). The culmination of the drama thus draws us back to the Christ-Phoenix-noon relationship which is so significant in *Paradise Lost*.

PATHOS AND KATHARSIS IN SAMSON AGONISTES

BY MARTIN MUELLER

The Aristotelian critics of *Samson Agonistes* have never succeeded in freeing themselves from the influence of Dr. Johnson. For two hundred years critics have either followed his complaint that the play lacked a "middle" or they have attempted to prove that *Samson Agonistes* is a psychological drama and that it is foolish to expect a probable or necessary sequence of outward events in a drama of this kind. Such criticism has been useful, but it has not answered Dr. Johnson's complaint: it has merely declared it irrelevant. In this paper I shall once more apply the critical terms of the *Poetics* to *Samson Agonistes*, but I shall argue that the crucial problem lies not in the "probability and necessity" of the play but in its *pathos*, the deed of violence which constitutes the catastrophe. Milton's tragedy differs from those Greek tragedies which one might call Aristotelian in that the catastrophe has no immediate bearing on any human relations but is only meaningful as the final event in the relationship of Samson and God. For this reason the "probability and necessity" of the play cannot be the laws that govern human events; we must instead discover the necessity that connects the events of the tragedy under the aspect of that relationship. In Aristotle's theory the *pathos*—if it is tragic—arouses pity and fear and effects a katharsis of these emotions. We may expect that the tragic quality of *Samson Agonistes*—and with it Milton's concept of katharsis—will not remain unaffected by the play's peculiar *pathos*.

Aristotle discusses *pathos* in chapter XIV of the *Poetics*:

Let us define then, which kinds of acts appeal to people as horrible and which as pitiable. Now such acts must necessarily be done to one another by persons who are bound by natural ties of affection, or are enemies, or are neither. Well then, if by an enemy to an enemy, there is nothing pathetic either in the doing or in the intention, except at the actual moment of the deed; nor if by persons who are neither; but when the painful deed is done in the context of close family relationships, for example when a brother kills or intends to kill a brother, or a son a father, or a mother a son, or a son a mother, or does something else of that kind—those are the acts one should look for . . . (14. 53b 15-22).

Aristotle goes on to discuss how the tragic potential inherent in a *pathos* can be increased by the device of *anagnorisis*. Thus *anagnorisis* distinguishes plays in which the *pathos* is represented in a straightforward manner (simple tragedy) from plays in which the full horror of the deed is crystallised in the moment of recognition (complex tragedy). It is clear that by Aristotelian standards Milton's play is not even a good simple tragedy. Samson kills his enemies: What is tragic about that? It is possible to imagine the plot of a Samson drama in which the Philistines would be given a chance to recognise what was happening to them. But such an *anagnorisis* would not be the recognition of a tragic situation which radically alters the relationship of the characters involved (*Poetics* 11. 52a 30); it would merely be the realisation that the tables are turned: the underlying relationship of irreconcilable hatred would not be affected by it. The same is true of *Samson Agonistes*: the *pathos* of Milton's tragedy involves a situation which Aristotle expressly condemns as untragic.

The relations of Samson and the Philistines, then, cannot constitute the tragic centre of the play. But neither do any other human relations, for Samson deliberately severs his connexions with his fellowmen; when he leaves the stage he has done with Manoa, Dalila, and the Danites. Milton isolates his Samson from humanity to such a degree that in Aristotelian terms his *pathos* appears to be not merely untragic, but positively antitragic. And yet, there were potentially tragic situations in Samson's human relations. By making Dalila Samson's wife Milton invited a tragic conflict comparable to that of Corneille's *Horace*. In the Dalila scene he even pursues this conflict for a while: Samson's infatuation is gradually revealed as a tragic dilemma in which he was caught between the duty to his country and his overwhelming passion for Dalila—a situation which she shamelessly exploited. But Samson explicitly resolves this conflict; in the end it has no bearing on the catastrophe (*S. A.* ll. 876-881; 885-888).

The notorious lack of a " middle " in *Samson Agonistes* is only a symptom of the lack of a tragic *pathos*. If there is no human relationship that enters into the *pathos*; if in fact all human relations are expressly rejected by the hero, how can he be judged in human terms? His visitors can provoke Samson, but their influence on him is restricted to setting in motion a process that follows its own logic irrespective of their intentions. Samson is indifferent to the "probability and necessity" of this world and his actions cannot be measured by them.

If we wish to justify the play as a tragedy we have to find that relationship which is crucially affected by the *pathos* of the play and in turn lends to it a tragic quality. Now for Samson the only thing that matters is his relationship with God; the Aristotelian critic of *Samson Agonistes* should therefore attempt to apply Aristotle's critical terms to that relationship; the drama's necessity as well as the hero's tragedy must be sought here, if anywhere.

For the greater part of the play it seems as if God had abandoned Samson; it is only with the "rousing motions" after the Hebrew officer's first exit that He indicates His continued care for Samson. We may accordingly divide the play into two parts: part one in which Samson appears abandoned, and part two in which he is once more accepted into the service of God. This division corresponds roughly to Samson's actions on and off stage. The two parts are linked by the scene in which the Hebrew officer summons Samson to the Festival. Now there is a curious inconsistency about this summons. From the officer's words we gather that a sudden whim made the Philistines call for Samson (1314, 1343) and the semi-chorus at the end (1675-79) gives a similar impression. But in the messenger's report, when the first horror has subsided and the sum of Samson's life is about to be drawn, the summons is represented very differently, for the messenger had heard rumours early in the morning that Samson would appear at the Festival (1600). How are the two accounts to be reconciled? The first part of the play had shown "the unification of a mind": a series of slightly related incidents brought about that Samson, who when we first saw him was "carelessly diffused" (118), regained his faith.[1] The process was essentially human and testified to the strength of Samson's will.

---

[1] I borrow the phrase from Una Ellis-Fermor, *The Frontiers of Drama* (London, 1946), p. 27.

When he was ready God gave him a sign that He would employ him again in His service. But the messenger's speech makes it plain that God had decided on this sign long before Samson was ready. He knew before, and indeed set, the goal towards which Samson struggled with only partial understanding. For a long time it looks as if God's plan and Samson's struggle were independent of each other; they meet only in the end. God's grace manifests itself long before Samson is aware of it, in the choice of time and place for Samson's vindication, in the gathering of the largest audience for his final *agon* and the blinding of the Philistines at the right moment. But he deliberately withholds the appointment of the protagonist until the very last minute and this delay constitutes Samson's last and greatest test. For it must still be determined whether Samson is worthy of the role he has been chosen for, and proof of his worthiness can only consist in a decision of his free will. When Samson refuses to attend the Festival at the Philistines' bidding, he makes this decision. It leads to an impasse, at which point the "rousing motions" remove all obstacles: Samson's struggle has finally been integrated into God's design.

The illumination is so sudden that neither Samson nor the Chorus fully understands its significance. This emphasis on suddenness has a number of reasons. It is welcome in a play that had moved sluggishly so far: as the audience watches the officer bid Samson make haste it knows that decisive events are in the offing. The sudden whim of the Philistines illustrates their *hubris*. But the chief reason for this abrupt acceleration of a sluggish pace is that it expresses an experience: God may not act at all for a long time, but when He acts He does so with speed. The very speed of His intervention at first suggests some discontinuity, but this apparent discontinuity is in truth pivotal in the structure of the action and in retrospect the necessity of the total design becomes clear. Hence the messenger's speech, which looks back on the whole tragedy, represents Samson's appearance before the Philistines as part of a design planned long before. One may say that in *Samson Agonistes* a teleological nexus replaces the causal nexus of probability and necessity which Aristotle demands in the *Poetics*: at the end of a seemingly loose plot it is shown that the events did fulfil a supreme design.

The relationship of such a teleological nexus to the dramatic probability of the *Poetics* may be illustrated by a look at the beginning of *Samson Agonistes*, which is and is not a good *archê* in an Aristotelian sense. Milton's play embraces an action of greater scope than most Greek tragedies; his purpose is no less than to give a complete account of Samson's life. The problem is as formidable as the problem of the choice of a suitable plot for the *Iliad* and Milton deserves Aristotle's praise of Homer:

He did not attempt to deal even with the Trojan war in its entirety, though it was a whole with a definite beginning and end—through a feeling apparently, that it was too long a story to be taken in at one view, or if not that, too complicated from the variety of incident in it. As it is, he has singled out one section of the whole; many of the other incidents, however, he brings in as episodes, using the Catalogue of the Ships, for instance . . . (*Poetics* 23. 59a 30-36).[2]

Milton, too, chose a short span of Samson's life which would be "easy to take in at one view" (*eusunoptos*) but managed to represent the whole biography of Samson by a judicious choice of episodic flashbacks. The beginning of *Samson Agonistes* is indeed a very pure *archê*; it interrupts a long monotonous period of hard work undistinguished by events of any kind; it is almost self-explanatory and leads shortly to a decisive event. On the other hand, there is little suspense. The quarrel between Agamemnon and Achilles, the beacon signal, and the plague in Thebes all are violent disruptions of order that forebode some critical event. In comparison the *archê* of *Samson Agonistes* seems slack. Again this apparent deficiency is integral to the play. The Chorus note with surprise that extraordinary things happened on a day set apart for rest. They realise this the moment before the Hebrew officer delivers his summons and the unification of Samson's mind and God's plan of vindication are to be joined in the catastrophe (1297-99). Retrospectively, the *archê* too assumes another significance; it is fully justified only by the revelation of a teleological design.

If we interpret the play as the re-establishment of a sacred

[2] Aristotle's distinction between the beginning of the story and the beginning of the epic here refutes M. E. Grenander's contention that the beginning of *S. A.* is Samson's earlier state of glory referred to in the play ("*Samson's* Middle, Aristotle, and Dr. Johnson," *UTQ*, XXIV, 1955, 377-389). Aristotle always distinguishes between plot and story; if he did not do so, his insistence on the choice of a proper beginning would be meaningless, since the Greek dramatist who worked with traditional myths could not choose the beginning of the *story*.

relationship between God and Samson and maintain that a teleological nexus replaces the probability of Aristotelian drama, we may have answered Dr. Johnson's charge, but the last possibility of a tragic conflict seems to have vanished. What could be less tragic than the fulfilment of the will of God? And yet, the circumstances of Samson's death are a source of terror and bewilderment to the Chorus and to Manoa. They repeatedly express a sense of frustration that bears a striking resemblance to the reaction of the critic who blames the play for lacking suspense, coherence, probability, or whatever else the notorious term "middle" may stand for. They are puzzled at first that nothing happens and then that everything happens at once. The second semi-chorus with its imagery of delay and sudden outburst of violent action gives powerful expression to this bewilderment, and still labouring under the shock of the news of Samson's death the Chorus exclaim:

> O dearly bought revenge, yet glorious!
> Living or dying thou hast fulfill'd
> The work for which thou was foretold
> To *Israel*, and now li'st victorious
> Among thy slain self-kill'd
> Not willingly, but tangl'd in the fold
> Of dire necessity, whose law in death conjoin'd
> Thee with thy slaughter'd foes in number more
> Than all thy life had slain before.   (1660-69)

How are the words "tangl'd in the fold of dire necessity" compatible with the revelation of a teleological design? If we take them merely as adding a Greek flavour to a Christian play about Samson Triumphant, we should be accusing Milton of poor writing, but if we take them seriously, are we not accusing him of blasphemy?

The answer to this question is further complicated by Milton's extraordinary reticence about salvation and eternity. According to Una Ellis-Fermor the drama shows a "steady psychological progression from despair through heroic conflict upwards to exultation and the final assumption into beatitude"; but hardly anywhere do we catch a glimpse of the beatific vision that in Milton's other works transcends the suffering of the here and now.[3] Although he never grew tired of insisting that they were "unex-

---

[3] *The Frontiers of Drama*, p. 32.

pressive" or *inenarrabile*, Milton often depicted the raptures of heaven in ecstatic language. But in *Samson Agonistes* he was for once silent. Compare the spiritual crises in *Paradise Lost* and *Samson Agonistes*. Discussions between God and Christ on Man's fall and redemption through Grace frame the representation of the Fall. It is expressly stated that it is "prevenient grace" which softens the hearts of Adam and Eve and enables them to pray and be pardoned (*P.L.* XI, 3). At the end of the tenth book Adam's and Eve's resolution to pray is repeated verbatim (except for a change in pronouns), a Homeric device Milton does not elsewhere employ (1087-92, 1099-1104). Finally, the Fall occurs in a universe that despite immeasurable sufferings may look forward to the blissful vision of a new and eternal heaven. In *Samson Agonistes* pardon and mercy are rare words. When Manoa hears the Philistines' shout of death he exclaims:

> Mercy of Heav'n! what hideous noise was that?   (1509)

and there are other passages (520, 1169-72) that discourage the hope that pardon and grace may alter the conditions of this world. Black curtains on all sides prevent the eye from perceiving anything beyond temporal sufferings, and all hopes to the contrary are inexorably crushed. But there can and must be no doubt that "all is best." The ultimate good of the reunion of God and Samson must not be called in question even though it will remain shrouded in mystery forever.

Between the revelation of God's plan as something ultimately good and the horror and bewilderment it causes in the survivors, there remains a tension, an element of terror and fear, that cannot be explained but has to be accepted. This sense of incongruity is heightened rather than allayed by looking at the plan from Samson's perspective. Samson's development should be seen in terms of his *hamartia* and *katharsis*. In the *Poetics hamartia* is probably an element of plot, the condition of ignorance that leads to the fatal deed; it is the opposite of *anagnorisis*, which is the realisation of the deed. In the ideal complex tragedy *anagnorisis* coincides with *peripeteia*: the hero's awareness of his situation suddenly makes him either "happy" or "unhappy." Such a sudden shift is necessarily absent from *Samson Agonistes*, since it is irreconcilable with the theme of slow and painful recovery.

There is no opposition of *hamartia* and *anagnorisis*, but one might speak of a concept of progressive *hamartia*: as Samson becomes gradually aware of his failure, his attitude towards it changes. Thus the concept of *hamartia* that one gains from an analysis of the play is closely related to Aristotle's use of the term in the *Nicomachean Ethics* (book V, ch. 8). Samson's progressive notion of his *hamartia* reflects a change of consciousness. What he first sees as an involuntary accident becomes in his mind a voluntary act of injustice due to wicked intention. But the classical concept of *hamartia* cannot account for Samson's spiritual regeneration; it can only serve to describe the preparatory process that makes it possible. The regeneration itself should be understood as a *katharsis*, if by *katharsis* we mean the purgation of the hero. Such an interpretation strays rather far from Aristotle, but it is supported by the evidence of the play. There is clearly some connexion between Milton's medical interpretation of *katharsis* in the preface and his extensive use of medical imagery in the play itself.[4] This imagery suggests strongly that it is Samson who is to be healed or purged.

Samson's increasing self-awareness is seen in his changing attitude towards his strength. At the beginning of the play he is inclined to think of it as something physical, almost a magic charm hung in his hair. Harapha, who is like the unregenerate Samson in so many other ways follows him in this too. Samson's

> God, when he gave me strength, to show withal
> How slight the gift was, hung it in my hair.   (59-60)

is echoed by Harapha:

> . . . some Magician's Art
> Arm'd three or charm'd thee strong, which thou from Heaven
> Feign'd'st at thy birth was giv'n thee in thy hair
> (1133-35)

But Samson has meanwhile developed a more profound view of his gift: it is the corollary of a special relationship, a secret at

[4] For a discussion of Milton's theory of *katharsis* in the preface to *Samson Agonistes* see Paul Selin, "Sources of Milton's Catharsis: A Reconsideration," *JEGP*, LX (1961), 712-730, and M. Mueller, "Sixteenth-Century Italian Criticism and Milton's Theory of Catharsis," *SEL*, VI (1966), 139-150.

once mysterious and clear, translucently obscure. He reaches this understanding of his calling through a clearer realisation of what his betrayal involved. Manoa and the Chorus see Samson's fall simply as something shameful in the eyes of the enemy and their own country; Samson comes to consider it base and shameful before God. Milton makes much of Samson's betrayal of a secret because it involved a *hamartia* entirely dependent on the free will. In Judges the secret is a *donnée* about which the chronicler does not greatly bother; he takes it for granted that no one would reveal important information to the enemy. Nor is there any mention of a secret in Numbers where the Nazarite's code is described. Milton's Samson, however, is an initiate who receives a secret under pledge of vow and under the seal of silence. Milton may have been thinking of the Eleusinian mysteries and the case of Aeschylus who was accused of having betrayed them but was acquitted when he was able to prove that he had done it without realising it (*Nicomachean Ethics*, III, i). Aristotle uses this case as an illustration for his theory that the intention, not the deed, determines the nature of a crime. Samson comes to precisely the same conclusion and is therefore unable to acquit himself; he can no longer consider his crime an act of inconsiderate rashness as he used to; it is the folly of deliberate wrongdoing against better knowledge and experience, for his marriage to the woman of Timna should have been a warning to him in his dealings with Dalila. And as his attitude towards his failure changes, so the realisation of his loss becomes more profound. It is not the loss of strength, power, and fame that torments him, but the loss of that unique relationship with God which he has wilfully forfeited. The progress Samson has made is measured by the spirited reply he makes to Harapha's charges:

> I know no spells, use no forbidden Arts;
> My trust is in the living God who gave me
> At my Nativity this strength, diffus'd
> No less through all my sinews, joints and bones,
> Than thine, while I preserv'd these locks unshorn,
> The pledge of my unviolated vow.   (1139-44)

Milton's drama is so intellectual that it often approaches the nature of a debate, but in the end it transcends the limits of the intellect and beyond these limits direct expression must yield to metaphor. The decisive discontinuity in *Samson Agonistes*, the change from reason to faith, is accompanied by a change from argument to image. Samson's final regeneration cannot be attributed to the strength of his will alone: it is a process of katharsis of which he is unaware until the end. This katharsis is expressed in a complex of images of pollution and purgation in which medical imagery plays a special role.

Samson's damp, filthy, verminous, and foul-smelling prison serves as a highly thematic setting for the play. His clothes are part of this setting. Like the joined hands in *Paradise Lost*, they constitute a minor and almost trivial motif, which allows us to trace accurately the development of the main theme. At the first sight of Samson the Chorus are repelled by the squalor about him:

> . . . ill-fitted weeds
> O'erworn and soil'd   (121-122)

Allusions to his clothes recur toward the end. Harapha considers Samson an untouchable, the very opposite of a Nazarite:

> To combat with a blind man I disdain,
> And thou hast need much washing to be toucht.
> (1106-07)

The Hebrew officer concludes his summons with the promise that he will see Samson "heart'n'd and fresh clad" (1317), and the messenger finally reports that Samson was clad in the state livery of a public servant (1616).

There is in these images an ironical contrast between inward and outward purity. While it is right to see in the washed and newly dressed figure a new Samson, it is also true to say that the new Samson had been hiding underneath his rags. The contrast goes further. Samson's pure acts, his first marriage and his appearance at the Festival, are impure in the eyes of the law, but legal purity, though ultimately transcended, may be a proof of inward regeneration. Samson regains his status as a Nazarite by his initial refusal to attend the impure Philistine Festival. His obedience to the law is a sort of purification, which is not yet the final *katharsis*, but points towards it. Samson, outwardly a pariah, has inwardly regained legal purity. On the other hand, this legal purity is formal and to that extent outward. Once Samson has satisfied its requirements he is allowed to transcend it. He regains his legal status in one way, only to reject it in another, and his legal purification adumbrates that state of mind which enables him in the end to go beyond it.

The mystery of the Nazarite's intimate communion with the divinity is never explicitly stated but hinted at in the seeming digression about Samson's abstinence from wine (541-558). The difference between purity and impurity is the difference between water and wine. Impurity is disorder and excitement. "The dancing ruby sparkling, outpoured" contrasts with the limpid tranquillity of the "cool crystalline stream." The liquor is "turbulent" whereas the brook has direction and flows "towards the Eastern ray." The water Samson drank when he was pure combined clarity with the freshness of juice and the goodness of milk. Samson usually and very properly dwells on the sordidness of his past; here he is tempted to look back even further to a past he is about to regain. That water is used as a symbol of regeneration in the play is proved by the irony in the expression of Manoa's hopes:

> But God who caus'd a fountain at thy prayer
> From the dry ground to spring, thy thirst to allay
> After the brunt of battle, can as easy
> Cause light again within thy eyes to spring,
> Wherewith to serve him better than thou hast;
>
> (581-585)

This glimpse of the future is followed by a head-long plunge into the corruption of the present. Samson's great monody should be read against the evocation of purity which the water imagery produces. The monody abounds in medical images that resume the motif of the first lines where Samson felt amends at breathing the "breath of heaven, pure and sweet" instead of "unwholesome draught." The contrast between "ease" and "disease" reflects in more particular, medical terms that of purity and impurity. Before Manoa left Samson he had asked the Chorus to be Samson's physician and soothe him with healing words (605). Earlier the Chorus had confidently expressed that

> . . . apt words have power to suage
> The tumors of a troubl'd mind,
> And are as Balm to fester'd wounds.   (184-186)

But Samson's case is hopeless. At the play's opening he had complained that he found

> Ease to the body some, none to the mind
> From restless thoughts, that like a deadly swarm
> Of Hornets arm'd, no sooner found alone,
> But rush upon me thronging and present
> Times past, what once I was and what am now.
>
> (18-22)

Now his thoughts have become "tormentors arm'd with deadly stings"; they "exasperate, exulcerate, and raise dire inflammation" (623-626). Samson's impurity had first been expressed by words that suggest primarily defilement of the surface, such as "foul," "defile," "pollute," "unclean," "stain," and "blot," but the disease of his corruption goes deeper: words like "rankle," "gangrene," "fester," "tumour," "exulcerate," probe beneath the surface to the very core. It is possible at the end to wash off Samson's superficial impurity with "lavers pure and cleansing herbs" (1727), but "no cooling herb or med'cinal liquor can assuage" "dire inflammation" (626 f.). A fair surface may hide such corruption for a while, but it will end in "black mortification" and there is no remedy but "death's benumbing Opium" (630), which is itself as impure as the wine that made the Philistine lords "insensate left or to sense reprobate" (1685). In his darkest hour Samson comes to think of himself as a gangrened limb to be amputated; God's nursling, the sacred plant (362), is now totally blighted (633-651). Human medicine cannot help; Samson needs—in Eliot's phrase—the "sharp compassion" of a healer who "tempers" things in his own way (S.A. 670).

The monody implies that the purifying power of water has failed. Only the violence of fire can heal Samson, since fire alone can penetrate below the surface. This is the meaning of the second semi-chorus, in which the image of the holocaust is equated with that of the Phoenix (1697-1707). There is no better comment on this passage than the lines from Eliot's "Little Gidding":

> The dove descending breaks the air
> With flame of incandescent terror
> Of which the tongues declare
> The one discharge from sin and error.
> The only hope, or else despair
> > Lies in the choice of pyre or pyre—
> > To be redeemed from fire by fire.

The fulfilment of God's design and of Samson's *katharsis* is a holocaust, the burnt offering Samson makes of himself. The metaphor applies not so much to his final act as to his whole life. Immediately after Samson's exit the Chorus invoke the angel who "rode up in flames" after announcing Samson's conception (1431-35). One of Samson's most urgent questions in the *prologos* had been:

> O wherefore was my birth from Heaven foretold
> Twice by an Angel, who at last in sight
> Of both my Parents all in flames ascended
> From off the Altar, where an Off'ring burn'd,
> As in a fiery column charioting
> His Godlike presence, and from some great act
> Or benefit reveal'd to *Abraham's* race?   (22-29)

It has finally been answered.

Far from supporting an interpretation which makes *Samson Agonistes* a drama of salvation that ends with the hero's "assumption into beatitude" the images of the Phoenix and the holocaust increase the tension and perplexity which the revelation of the teleological design had caused. About any kind of immortality other than that of fame the poet is silent. No "unexpressive nuptial songs" welcome Samson; instead of rapturous hymns the only music of the tragedy is "sweet lyric song" (1737). This is not altogether due to the Old Testament setting of the play as one may see from the radiant optimism of Psalm 51 and its apostrophe of shining purity. The Psalm is sung by a man conscious of his sinfulness who desires to be purified. His hopes to attain purity make him exuberant in affirmation. He prays for "joy and gladness" and promises to "sing aloud" of "His righteousness." But the crucial point is that in this Psalm the sacrifice of blood is replaced by the sacrifice of the contrite heart. Thus the psalmist can contrast death, pain, and sacrifice with the bliss of salvation. In *Samson Agonistes* these elements are combined, inextricably interwoven and "tangled in the fold of dire necessity."

The *katharsis* of Samson, his reconciliation with God, is a complex, problematic, and mysterious solution of the drama, which is not without its own very bitter and deeply felt sense of tragedy. But there remains the more conventional *katharsis* of the audience. In Milton's play the audience's reaction is integrated into the drama since Manoa and the Chorus are the spectators of a tragic event and experience that purgation which Renaissance criticism considered the ultimate end of poetry. This purgation of the audience is chiefly represented in the purgation of Manoa, which deserves special attention since in it Milton attempts to resolve or mitigate the harshness and perplexity that attend Samson's death. As in the case of Samson, Manoa's purgation is a process that occurs within a little drama of its own. One can speak of a Manoa sub-plot in *Samson Agonistes*, consisting of the ransom intrigue, a beautiful plan, too clever by half, which falls through in the end. The counterpoint of a seemingly loose and simple action that is fulfilled and a subtle, complex intrigue that is foiled is important to the dramatic structure of the play. That it is a deliberate device can hardly be doubted if one considers the close attention Milton paid to the details of the Manoa plot in the "argument" of his play, particularly since the Dalila and Harapha episodes are summed up in the brief statement: "who meanwhile is visited by other persons." An account of Manoa's *katharsis*, then, must proceed from an analysis of the structure of the scenes in which he is on stage.

It has always been taken for granted that the end of *Samson Agonistes* is modelled on *Oedipus Coloneus*, but the very obviousness of this debt has obscured some important differences that may explain Manoa's role in the play. When Oedipus leaves the stage, the action is over; in fact, the play's action had never been anything but the turmoil that disrupted anew the peace which Oedipus thought he had found in the sanctuary of the Eumenides. When Samson leaves the stage, the action is about to begin. A similar difference exists between the catastrophes: Samson's is an act of violence, that of Oedipus simply a coming to an end. Milton had to cope with a problem very different from that of Sophocles. The latter could proceed immediately from the exit of Oedipus to the messenger's report since Oedipus' transfiguration, the subject of that report, was in outline known to the audience who had heard it mentioned in the *prologos* and throughout the play. In *Samson Agonistes* the mere report of the messenger would fail to integrate the catastrophe into the play because it would not refer to, or confirm, any expectations raised in the course of the action. Some kind of link is needed which connects Samson's exist with the messenger's entrance and this link is provided by the second Manoa scene. The scene, for which there is no parallel in the *Coloneus*, is a representation of Samson's death. The audience that hears the two shouts which interrupt Manoa's conversation with the Chorus is a first-hand witness of some dreadful event. In Aristotelian terms it is a dramatic mimesis; it may be vague, but it is more immediate than the circumstantial second-hand evidence provided by the messenger. Ostensibly Manoa's return resumes the ransom intrigue begun in the first Manoa scene; the contrast with the real purpose of the scene is one of the most poignant ironies in the play.

The scene should be interpreted as a little complex tragedy with Manoa as the tragic hero, Samson's death as the *pathos*, and the messenger's arrival as the *peripeteia* through *anagnorisis*.[5] There is a dislocation in this structure, since the *pathos* is neither done nor suffered by the tragic hero. But at least it concerns a close relation and it does bring about in Manoa a change from happiness to unhappiness. The scene is almost certainly modelled on the *peripeteia* of the *Oedipus Tyrannus*. There the entrance of the messenger from Corinth is preceded by a prayer of Iocaste to Apollo in which she asks for the deliverance of Oedipus from his apprehensions (911-923). The messenger's news of the death of Polybus causes in Iocaste a febrile euphoria; she exclaims: "Where are you now, divine prognostications?" (946 ff.). But Oedipus remains still apprehensive; the message has not freed him from the fear about his mother (990). So the messenger proceeds to tell the story of Oedipus' birth. The scene is a peculiar form of a dialogue between three persons: only the third, silent character understands. And as Oedipus conceives a short-

---

[5] The traditional interpretation of *anagnorisis* and *peripeteia* in *S. A.* should be rejected. Neither Samson's illumination (rousing motions) nor his sudden decision to go with the officer qualifies. The illumination is not a "recognition," but simply a confirmation of what S. had said to Harapha shortly before (1139-45; 1168-77); besides, it does not bring about a critical change to friendship or enmity in his relationship with anybody. Nor is his compliance with the officer's request a *peripeteia*, since no circumstances are changed radically by it; only a minor obstacle for the catastrophe is removed. Tillyard—*Milton* (London, 1946), p. 343—had applied Vahlen's interpretation to *S. A.*, which saw in *peripeteia* a frustration of purpose. Bywater's refutation of this theory in his commentary is now generally accepted; see D. W. Lucas, "Pity, Terror, and *Peripeteia*," *CQ*, LVI (1962), 52-60. Milton makes *peripeteia* the subject of a rather grim literary joke. One meaning of *agonistes* is 'actor' and S. groups himself with "jugglers and dancers, antics, mummers, mimics" and other performers when he refuses to go to the Festival (1323-25). The tragic actor is not mentioned in this catalogue, but the place of Samson's final per-

lived hope that the oracle may not be true after all, Iocaste is plunged into deepest misery. Her exit is misinterpreted both by the Chorus and by Oedipus, who now rises to a final gesture of unwitting presumption and calls himself the child of fortune (1080 f.). Overcoming their initial apprehensions, the Chorus pursue his thought and speculate on the possibility of divine birth. But the shepherd's words soon destroy all hopes and Oedipus is revealed as the culprit:

> Alas! All out! All known, no more concealment
> O Light! May I never look on you again, . . .   (1182 f.)

The Manoa scene follows a very similar pattern, although the parallel is a little blurred by the fact that Manoa and the Chorus do not consistently parallel Iocaste and Oedipus. But if one disregarded the characters and charted the movement of the two scenes, the resulting curves would be almost exactly alike. Manoa's cheerful confidence in the eventual success of his negotiations resembles Iocaste's elation after the first words of the messenger. He is rejuvenated by the anticipation of happiness. Even the Philistines suddenly appear in a friendly light; Manoa calls some of them generous, civil, and magnanimous (1466-71). At this moment the Philistines' first shout is heard, which is the sign that God's plan has entered its critical stage, but now Manoa, too, reveals his plan—a desperate and foolish competition. And as the imminent disaster looms larger and larger Manoa's imagination envisages a happy end. The ransom is already a fact; the sacrifice of all of Manoa's riches is overshadowed by the noble vision of the heroic Samson waiting for some great task to perform. The growth of Samson's hair must be an earnest of further divine favours, and what greater favour could there be than the restoration of eyesight? The Chorus consider this reasonable, but Manoa's reply is interrupted by

---

formance is a "spacious theatre" (1605) and he appears before an audience whom he duly delights (1642). But then he offers to give an encore that "with amaze shall strike all who behold" (1645), that is, he will fulfil the requirement for a good tragedy, which should cause *admiratio*, a major critical term of the period, roughly equivalent of Aristotle's *ekplêktikon* and *thaumaston* (*Poetics*, 9.52 a 4; 14.54 a 4). Then he proceeds to draw the audience into his tragedy, or, to put the matter with Daniel Heinsius: *subito et* praeter expectationem . . . *in contrarium mutatio apparet quam* peripetiam *maximus virorum Aristoteles vocavit* (*De Tragoediae Constitutione Liber*, Leyden, 1643, p. 48).

the second noise. . . . Here we reach the stage of Iocaste's exit: a sign of some dreadful turn of events has been given. In Sophocles' play the king's imperious will brushes away all fearful apprehensions, but neither Manoa nor the Danites possess the boldness of Oedipus: they dare neither hope nor fear. Manoa immediately suspects the worst, but the Chorus attempts to reassure him. As in the *Tyrannus*, there is a slight reversal here: with Iocaste's exit Oedipus changes from anxiety to presumption; so Manoa changes from confidence to fear whereas the Chorus, who had been sceptical, are now willing to assert the possibility of a miracle. The messenger arrives and through a series of misunderstandings the truth is held back until it can no longer be concealed:

> Then take the worst in brief, Samson is dead.   (1570)

In both scenes the revelation of truth is delayed as long as possible and the tension during this delay is increased by raising the hero to giddy heights of expectation before plunging him into misery: the catastrophe crushes the artificial hopes that had seemed so reasonable. The characters live in a state of such blindness that suddenly the marvellous seems possible and even necessary. At the crises of the *Tyrannus* and *Samson Agonistes* a miracle is hoped for, whether it be the sudden revelation of divine birth or the restoration of eyesight. Because hopes had been raised, the truth is all the more disastrous, particularly in *Samson Agonistes* where the catastrophe appears much more "amazing" and less reasonable than the miracle one had hoped for. It is easy to reproach Manoa for his silly illusions, but one should realise that they are reasonable and justified in the world he lives in.

It has often been remarked that the superhuman strength and determination of Samson preclude our feeling pity or terror at his death. He is not sufficiently "like us" and by rejecting his father's help as well as a reconciliation with his wife he has made this unambiguously clear. To reflect the tragedy of Samson in that of Manoa, then, seems an inspired solution. For Manoa's feelings for Samson are very human, and his cruel disillusion cannot fail to rouse pity and terror. In *Samson Agonistes* tragic feeling in an Aristotelian sense is aroused through the realisation of the *pathos* of a *philos*.

The tragedy of Manoa is complex as opposed to the simple drama of Samson. This can be explained on the grounds of dramatic economy. The play is long and interest might flag, particularly after the exit of the protagonist, who alone can command attention by himself. The resort to a more immediately gripping style is an excellent device for holding the audience. The Manoa drama accelerates the Samson drama and crystallises the tragic potential of the catastrophe in the *peripeteia* and *anagnorisis* of Manoa. But if it serves to emphasise the harshness of Samson's death, it also represents a return to quiet acceptance and "sweet lyric song" in which the healing power of poetry is exemplified. During this return Manoa undergoes a profound change which may be called his *katharsis*. The nature of this process and its function in the play as a whole may be illuminated by Goethe's fruitful misunderstanding of Aristotle's definition of tragedy.[6] Goethe turned indignantly against a theory that measured a tragedy "by the effect and, which is more, by the remote effect that it might have on the spectator." He interprets Aristotle as saying that a tragedy after a course of events that involve the characters in pity and fear ends with the "balancing and reconciling of these passions" on the stage. *Katharsis* is the *aussöhnende Abrundung*, which is in fact a requirement not only of drama but of all poetry. In tragedy it is usually brought about by a human sacrifice or its surrogate (Abraham, Agamemnon), but irrespective of the method it is imperative for a complete tragedy to end on a note of reconciliation.

In this interpretation of *katharsis* as a state of equilibrium achieved at the end of the work, we find a striking agreement between Goethe and Milton. The attempt to achieve a harmony or *aussöhnende Abrundung* in spite of terrible discords of conflict and doubt, is discernible in Milton as early as "Lycidas" and fully developed in *Paradise Lost*. In *Samson Agonistes* the reconciliation is made possible by the "dislocation" in the structure of the Manoa tragedy, which is not a real tragedy. From the tragic impression, the horror of the first news, the play moves towards the quiet realisation that "all is best." Manoa recog-

---

[6] "Nachlese zu Aristoteles' Poetik," *Artemis Gedenkausgabe* (Zürich, 1949), XIV, 709-712. A discussion of the essay is found in Max Kommerell, *Lessing und Aristoteles* (Frankfurt, 1940, rptd. 1957), pp. 258-262.

nises his foolish ignorance—a *hamartia* closer to Greek thought than Samson's sin, and from the horror of the extraordinary he returns to human wisdom which, conscious of its limitations, attempts to cope with the extraordinary. The sudden eruption of a tragic disaster tests Manoa no less than Samson was tested, and like his son, he proves himself worthy of his trial.

The death of Samson is harsh and contains in it an abyss that opens more widely the more desperately one tries to bridge it. But Milton's art demands such a bridge, whether one calls it *katharsis* or "mitigation." A. S. P. Woodhouse has written that Samson's personal tragedy is ultimately mitigated in the wider context of Christian doctrine.[7] But in some ways the perspective narrows rather than broadens at the end of the tragedy. The mitigation of the tragic sense is expressed in the change which Manoa undergoes, but his "calm of mind" and "new acquist of experience" are accompanied by a deliberate limitation and a resigned resolution to be "lowly wise." He cannot be expected to resolve all difficulties and he knows it. There remains some tension between the "uncontrollable intent," the "unsearchable dispose" and the quiet affirmation that "all is best." There may not be cause for lamentation, but there is no cause for the psalmist's joy and gladness either. The tragedy is mitigated because it is accepted, not because it is resolved. The state of *katharsis* retains an element of ambiguity: on the one hand it is "calm of mind, all passion spent"; on the other hand it is "new acquist of true experience," an insight into the perplexing ways of dire necessity, which willing acceptance can mitigate but the terror of which it can never entirely remove.

---

[7] "Tragic Effect in *Samson Agonistes*," *UTQ*, XXVIII (1959), 205-223.

NATURAL SCIENCE AND FIGURATIVE DESIGN IN *SAMSON AGONISTES*

BY LEE SHERIDAN COX

Samson's destruction of the Philistines is described as elemental cataclysm. Samson shakes the massy pillars " as with the force of winds and waters pent " and the roof falls with a " burst of thunder " on the " flower " of Philistia (1646-56).[1] But the image of the elemental force that is Samson remains with us most vividly, not as earthquake, wind, or water, but as fire. The angel who predicted Samson's greatness had " all in flames ascended / From off the Altar, where an Off'ring burn'd, / As in a fiery column charioting / His Godlike presence, and from some great act / Or benefit reveal'd to *Abraham's* race " (23-29). Samson's " great act " takes place in the theater of the Philistines, and both the essential character of the deed and the imagery describing it recall the nature of the angel's performance. Samson, like the angel, manifests himself in " Off'ring "; and in the last image used for him, the phoenix image, we have the implication that Samson, like the angel, flourishes in fire, that he is so purified in spirit that he is become a " Godlike presence."

Milton does not use element imagery only to comment on and link such crucial passages as these describing the prediction and the thing predicted. " If we look but on the nature of elementall and mixt things, we know they cannot suffer any change of one kind, or quality into another without the struggl of contrarieties," Milton says.[2] In *Samson Agonistes*, he leads the reader to " look . . . on the nature of elementall and mixt things "; and he defines Samson's change from one quality into another by way of analogy between Samson and a whole universe of elemental and mixed things. He invests the matter of Samson's rebirth with the magnitude of cosmological movements. Moreover, in defining a

---

[1] The text cited is *The Works of John Milton,* ed. F. A. Patterson *et al.* (New York, 1931-38), I, Pt. 2.

[2] *The Reason of Church-government urg'd against Prelaty,* in *Works,* III, Pt. 1, 223.

natural universe wherein there is ever a " struggl of contrarieties," where different elements may bear the same face, where each element reveals a two-fold nature, he leads the reader to consider a universal climate of ambiguity, ambivalence, and paradox, of diversity and unity, of conflict and harmony, within which human choice must operate. He thus illuminates the difficulties arising from the changing appearance of truth and falsehood, the problem springing from the double nature of the thought, the word, the act, from which both good and evil can come, as " from out the rinde of one apple tasted . . . the knowledge of good and evill as two twins cleaving together leapt forth into the World." [3] And he thus clarifies the nature of the final choice, which results in Samson " victorious . . . self-kill'd " (1663-64).

Milton's selection of image is determined by a large pattern of thought, a pattern dependent on a Renaissance habit of thinking in metaphor, of seeing correspondence between man and everything in the worlds outside man; though he uses correspondence in a manner unlike that of his predecessors and contemporaries, he reflects and depends on prevalent habits of mind and prevalent conceptions of universal harmony. In the following study, I propose to show that Milton, with craft and individuality, employs a ready-made symbolism, a popular metaphorical frame of reference for the moral question, and that a perception of his figurative design is essential to an understanding of his meaning and to an appreciation of his art.

I

The metaphorical pattern in *Samson Agonistes* is tightly woven, and to get at Milton's increasingly complicated comment, it is necessary first to isolate the obvious, to note what he chooses to emphasize in his poetic use of the elements of water, earth, air, and fire. In the first lines of the drama, he points to certain characteristics of the elements by way of air imagery. The elements may be free or imprisoned (8) ; they may be wholesome or unwholesome (9-10) ; one element may exhibit the peculiar quality of another: the air dissolves the sense of words (176-177). The imagery also insists that the wholesomeness in the element air springs from the same source as the wholesomeness in another element—for example, fire; in the following phrase, there is not

[3] *Areopagitica*, in *Works*, IV, 310.

only the implication of equation between two elements (fire and water), but also the declaration that fire and air come from the same source: " The breath of Heav'n fresh-blowing, pure and sweet, / [Is] With day-spring born " (10-11). The suggestions in this imagery are continued in the re-employment of significant adjectives: here, " fresh " is applied to air which is the breath of Heaven, and later to water, the " fresh current " which " flow'd . . . pure, / With touch aetherial of Heav'ns fiery rod " (547-549); still later, the " sourse of consolation from above " is described as " secret refreshings, that repair [man's] strength " (664-665). Also, the air imagery suggests that whatever exists within the climate of the elements may improperly reflect their nature: " Windy joy," says Manoa, " proves / Abortive as the first-born bloom of spring " (1574-76).

The ideas expressed in the poetic manipulation of the references to air appear in the references to water. Imprisoned air is " close and damp "; the linking of " damp " with " close " and " imprison'd " air suggests the two-fold nature of the element: though water may spring in Heaven, it is also the element of Dagon, the Sea-Idol (13). Again, the interrelation of the elements is reiterated in allusions to liquids: the liquid grape " fills with fumes " (552); wine fires (1418-19); the current flows with the touch of fire (547-549). In paradox and ambiguity, Milton reiterates the idea that good or evil is potential in a liquid element: it may be " pure " and at the same time " mixt," its essential oneness and wholesomeness defined by a life-giving quality within: the fountain that flows " translucent, pure, / With touch aetherial " is " clear " but " milkie "—such a liquid refreshes. But a turbulent liquor fills with fumes, and to be drunk with wine is to be " drunk with Idolatry " (1670). The liquid-figures suggest that the elements may equate properly, but they must at the same time observe their own proper qualities: a liquid that fills with fumes or fires with zeal, an air that is close, lacks its proper quality. Nor can a misapprehension of a " mixt thing " or the use of it lead to anything but unwholesomeness: it is " madness, to think use of strongest wines / And strongest drinks our chief support in health " (553-554). The implications in the emphasis on sameness, difference, and ambivalence in the element imagery are, as we shall note in more detail later, carried over in an emphasis on sameness, difference, and ambivalence in the senses.

Samson exchanges a vow for " a word, a tear " (200-201): the implications in the element imagery lead the reader to consider the difference between the two sounds, the vow and the word; the linking of the product of the tongue and the eye; and the linking of wrong sound and salty water.

The same pattern of comment appears in the fire imagery. Frequently, light or fire equates, in a sense, with water: " God who caus'd a fountain at [Samson's] prayer / From the dry ground to spring, [his] thirst to allay / . . . can as easie / Cause light again within [his] eies to spring." Again, the peculiar qualities of one element are found in another: the angel does not chariot on land or ascend in air; he chariots up in flame. The fire imagery also repeats the comment that the same element may be good or evil: virtue is fiery (1690); but a man can blaze like a petty God (528-529), and a people can be " insolent, unquenchable " (1422), so that only fire of a greater sort can overcome such fire. Not only is the element good or evil, but also good and evil can operate in it: breasts can be inflamed to valour (1739), but they can be fired with unholy zeal (1419-20).

Earth as evil appears in the references to " soil," a word used in connection with references to the unregenerate. Samson is first seen in " slavish habit . . . o're worn and soild " (122-123), a line linking earth imagery with imprisonment. Again, when the old warriors defeated by God's champion " grovling soild thir crested helmets in the dust " (141), earth imagery evokes a picture of degradation and fall. Samson, blind in Gaza, occupies a " land of darkness " in more ways than one. And in this phrase appears also an equation of the elements of earth and fire, although at the same time in this land of darkness a bank has choice of " Sun or shade." The poetic use of the element earth also suggests good operating in it or its products: the Chorus comes from " *Zora's* fruitful Vale "; and when the blood is washed from Samson's body, it is done, not only with lavers pure, but also with cleansing herbs (1727). Moreover, this element which may be good or evil is itself a passageway for a force operating in a life-giving way within it, even when it is itself sterile: God causes a fountain to spring from dry ground.

Milton, setting the stage for human drama, is employing familiar general notions about man, the world, and the universe. 1) The ambivalence of each element reflects conflict between good and evil, an unavoidable condition in the human theater of action. And this ambivalence in external nature may furnish comment on human nature, since man is made of the elements and supported by the elements. 2) The corrupt element is characterized by a failure to exhibit its proper qualities, to observe order. 3) The equation of different elements reflects a universal unity and dynamism. Man's life is conditioned, not only by the fact that he inhabits a world where natural elements conflict with unnatural elements, but also by the fact that he lives in a world marked by a natural flux and change: the proper elements, operating properly, are contrary to one another, yet feed one another; fight, yet are constantly in a state of transformation one into the other. It is not in the nature of man made of the elements to remain in a static state. He inhabits a condition of change. 4) The elements have their source in one great Power, which may transmute evil into good, but which is consistently reflected in the element properly exhibiting its proper qualities. So Milton sets the stage for Samson by placing him in a world where conflict between good and evil is inevitable, struggle between good and better is inevitable, and observance of order is the key to ascent.

II

The posing of alternatives and options by way of the ambivalence and paradox revealed in the element imagery appears again in the imagery of storm, wherein all the elements operate. Dalila says that Samson is " more deaf / To prayers, then winds and seas, yet winds to seas / Are reconcil'd at length, and Sea to Shore " (960-962); but then she refers to his anger as an " eternal tempest never to be calm'd." Harapha is called a storm (1061) and " another kind of tempest " (1063). The Chorus warns Samson that if he does not accompany the officer, he may expect another message, " more Lordly thund'ring then [he] well [will] bear " (1350-53); yet the Chorus has just used a storm image in a description of God's judgment (1284). When the messenger reports Samson's great act, he describes it in element and storm imagery; and it is linked to the earlier suggestion of divine tempest by the repetition of the word " amaze " (cf. 1286, 1645). The Semi-chorus repeats the storm image; it also links Samson's act to the earlier description of God's judgment (" winged expedition ") when it says that Samson " as an Eagle / His cloudless thunder bolted on thir heads " (1695-96).

The comment developing in the earth, water, air, and fire images is supplemented by the imagery of storm, which vividly reiterates the emphasis on the condition of strife which is man's native habitat, but which at the same time defines divergent or disparate conditions. Samson, a man on the way to regeneration, exhibits the stormy working of the elements; but the unregenerate Harapha is a tempest, too, albeit " another kind of tempest." The judgment of the Philistine lords who honor Dagon is defined by way of the storm image; but so is God's judgment. And at the climax of the play the act of Samson, who has reassumed the image of God, is pictured as storm. Storm is thus evoked to define the struggle between good and evil, order and chaos (Samson and Dalila; Samson and Harapha; Samson and the Philistines); to define the chaos in Harapha and the Philistine lords, wherein the stormy passions are given free rein and evil contends with evil; and to define the victorious struggle of the will over the senses, the stormy transmutation as the contrary elements strive against one another, feed one another, and are purified. Basic Renaissance conceptions of the perpetual struggle between order and chaos and of change within order are delineated in this imagery. And the presence of paradox and ambivalence in the storm imagery underlines the difficulty of choice. Not only are there several kinds of storm; even struggle and reconcilement are, in a sense, equated: air is eventually reconciled to water, water to earth; yet there may be eternal tempest.

We have seen the kind of multiple comment the imagery effects when man is likened to one element or to a natural phenomenon composed of all the elements. This comment is expanded (and the complexity of the condition within which man's understanding, will, and choice operate is amplified) by Milton's likening a man to an object largely supported by a specific element—to a plant in the earth, a ship on the water, a bird in the air.

Samson is likened to a plant: Manoa says that the angel " Ordain'd [Samson's] nurture holy, as of a Plant; / Select, and Sacred, Glorious for a while, / The miracle of men " (362-364). Dalila is called " a fair flower surcharg'd with dew " (728), and woman is called " a thorn . . . a cleaving mischief " (1037-39). At the beginning of the play, Samson's defeated enemies who have fallen in the dust are described as "the flower of *Palestin*" (144), and at the end of the play the storm which occurs in the Philistine theater destroys "the flower" of the Philistian cities (1654-55). The plant image is evoked for all men when the Chorus speaks of "mortal seed" (1439). And the physical and emotional qualities and attributes of men are referred to in plant imagery: the cutting of Samson's hair is a "fatal harvest" (1024); manhood is defined in the figure, "a grain of manhood" (408); Manoa's joy is like "the first-born bloom of spring" (1576); and Samson speaks of his youth and strength as a flower (938).

The plant imagery becomes more significant when considered in conjunction with the other images defining man as something supported by a specific element. Both Samson and Dalila are described as steerers of ships: the Chorus says, "What Pilot so expert but needs must wreck / Embarqu'd with such a Stearsmate at the Helm?" (1044-45). And the same image is evoked for the Chorus, who are first seen as "stearing" toward Samson (111). Moreover, Samson and Dalila and Harapha are also pictured as ships or as possessors of something described in ship imagery: Samson laments that he has "shipwrack't / [The] Vessel trusted to [him] from above / Gloriously rigg'd" (198-200); Dalila is a "thing of Sea or Land" (710) and is "like a stately Ship" (714); Harapha bears a "fraught" (1075), is called a "bulk" (1238), and is blown by a wind (1070), as the "floating" Dalila (1072) is "courted by all the winds" (719).

Again, men are described as creatures whose element is the air. The Chorus likens the "common rout" of men to the "summer flie" (674-676). Samson, who before his downfall "flew" on a whole host of the enemy (262), is likened at the end of the poem, when he is regenerated, to a winged dragon, an eagle, and a phoenix (1692-99). Milton's continuing preoccupation with correspondences and unity in diversity is observable in this imagery. Just as a man may be a plant (yet have physical, emotional, and intellectual qualities which are like plants), may be a ship (yet be a feeling pilot), he may be a creature which inhabits the element air and at the same time have qualities or attributes described as creatures operating in this element: Samson's restless thoughts are "like a deadly swarm / Of Hornets" (19-20).

The plant, the ship, and the winged-creature images enable Milton to explore the relation between the microcosm and the geocosm. By the plant imagery he can comment on the inseparable relation between the external elements and individual growth. Though a man composed of the elements is liable by the very nature of his composition to change, he is also affected by the elements outside himself: they enable him to thrive. By way of the ship imagery Milton can link this growth with voyaging: man is enabled by the elements to attain a particular end. The images of flying creatures connect this growth, this journey, with flight and ascension: man is enabled by the elements to rise. The evocation of life and growth, journey, and ascent in connection with one specific element attests to the importance of each element, as well as to their interaction. It might perhaps be argued that a plant in the earth, a bird in the air, are more properly related to a fish in the sea than to a ship. But Milton avoids an image related to Dagon, the fish-diety; and the implications of journey afforded by the familiar ship-figure amplify the pattern of growth and flight.

The emphasis on alternatives in being, choice, and action is continued by these images. A plant may be a miracle or a mischief. A ship may be a " bulk without spirit " or a vessel still aware that a bank has choice of sun or shade; it may be courted by all the winds, blown by the winds, or responsive to "the breath of Heav'n fresh-blowing " (10). A flying creature may be of little wing power and short-lived; or growing in knowledge of the nature of God, who himself operates in winged expedition, the winged creature may change from dragon to eagle to phoenix and live " ages of lives." Secondly, the emphasis on similarity in dissimilarity, on the presence of a great unifying, harmonizing force in all things, continues. Like the element whose purity and freshness finds its source in a divine Element, so these objects supported by the elements find their power to come from a divine wholesomeness: the strength in the seed is imparted from Heaven; the vessel, gloriously rigged, is entrusted " from above." Moreover, as with the elements which can equate one with the other, the plant in the earth and the vessel in the sea and the bird in the air are all one. Man contains within himself all elements and all samples of creation. A man is air, is a winged thing in air, and has thoughts which are winged things in air. And one of these objects can be defined in the light of the other. If the element in a man is evil, he is incapable of flying high or long, he is a stinging thing—self-destructive, and he engenders hornets. But the process works in reverse: if a man's thoughts are renewed in wisdom, he is an eagle, a phoenix—self-perpetuating, and he is made of the purest of elements. There is an underscoring of the oneness of thought, body, and element. At the same time the persistent emphasis on flux and gradation is continued in the growth, journey, and flight images. Though the other characters in the drama may he shown as inhabiting the earth, the sea, and the air, only Samson is likened to a creature which inhabits fire. Other men are revealed as having fire working within them, for either good or evil; but only a man purified of evil can live in fire. Samson, like the phoenix, flames into life; like the angel, he manifests himself in God's element.

III

Milton turns the prospective two ways. He studies man by seeking in him characteristics of the geocosm and the macrocosm; he studies the external world by seeking in it a human nature. Repeatedly, he ascribes to the elements human senses and attributes: the winds and seas are deaf; the sun is silent; divine fire is a glance. Or turning the prospective the other way, he describes words as fuel for flame. The figurative method fosters a continually expanding figurative view of the human condition. If the elements hear or are deaf, speak or are mute, see or are blind; if the element is a seeing, a hearing, a speaking; if seeing, hearing, speaking are fuel for the elements, then it must follow that man (who is earth and a plant in the earth and a container of the flower joy) is potentially a seeing, something that moves in an element of seeing, and an increaser of that seeing.

Milton's manipulation of the figurative language persistently emphasizes the linking of the elements and the senses, the assessment of one by way of metaphorical definitions of the other. The senses are described as if they are earth or air or fire or water: the sight is " easie to be quench't " (95); the sense of sound can be dissolved (176-177). Just as a man may be defined as a single element, he may be defined as a single sense: Samson is a gaze (34, 567); Harapha is a tongue (1066); Dalila is a voice (1065); the Philistine lords are an ear (921). Just as an element may exhibit the attributes of a man, a thing apprehended by the senses may take on the characteristics of human nature:

a scent is a harbinger; noise walks; odours visit. Just as there is an equating of the elements or a substituting of one element for another, there is an equating of the senses or a substituting of one sense for another. When Samson declares that the sun is silent, there is the suggestion that he equates the senses of sight and hearing. He grieves that sight is not diffused as feeling through all the body, so that one " might look at will through every pore " (93-97); later, he substitutes feeling for seeing: " Thou shalt see, or rather . . . feel, whose God is strongest " (1154-55). And in a phrase recalling the Scriptural use of the word " tasting," Samson substitutes tasting for seeing (and suggests the equation of both with the sense of touch): " The way to know were not to see but taste " (1091). Finally, just as one element is defined by way of the peculiar quality of another element, so one sense is shown operating in the fashion peculiar to another sense or human quality: the Chorus tells Manoa that it " thirst[s] to hear " (1456); Samson is told not to look for a voice (1065); tidings pierce the ear (1568); the officer comes, " speed in his look " (1304).

Although many of these figures, being the stuff of poetry, might appear in any poem, there is a development in the thought by means of them, quite aside from their individual function. In the element imagery we have seen the repeated suggestion that the elements may equate or may substitute one for the other: lacking light, which is " almost life it self " (91), a man may be refreshed by the " clear milkie juice " (550), which is also light. The consistent linking of the element and the sense and the figurative equation of the senses implies that the sense of sight gone, another sense may convey the life-giving element of light, that by hearing or tasting a man may see.

Moreover, Milton's comment on diversity and ambivalence in the elements, as well as unity, his figurative suggestion of moral alternatives, is further extended by the interplay of element and sense images. There are an outward and an inward light (160-162), the physical blindness of Samson and his spiritual blindness (418-419), the " blindness internal " of the Philistines and the " inward eyes " of the regenerated hero (1686-89). The suggestion that the pure element properly exhibits its proper qualities is extended in the suggestion that there must be proper use of the element and proper assessment of each of the means of sight.

If Samson prizes improperly the physical sense, if the physical loss is what he most complains (67), then he is spiritually blind. And physical sight, without the safeguard of spiritual sight, opens the door to evil in the element involved. Dalila tells Samson, " Though sight be lost, / Life yet hath many solaces, enjoy'd / Where other senses want not their delights / At home . . . / Exempt from many a care and chance to which / Eye-sight exposes daily men abroad " (914-919). But if eye-sight exposes men to care and chance, so do the other senses. A subscription to Dalila's philosophy is a subscription to disorder. The sense imagery implies that spiritual blindness, ultimate care and chance, can come by way of any of the senses; but so can a renewal of vision and solace.

The sound and silence imagery, the deafness and hearing imagery, enrich and amplify the developing comment on alternatives and the difficulty of choice. At first glance, it would appear that silence, in this drama of a man who talked too much, stands for good, sound for evil. We read that silence is a " sacred trust " (428), that love combats in silence (863-864). And sound is defined in terms of the " popular noise " of the Philistines celebrating their idol (16), of a swarm of restless thoughts (19) or a swarm of counterfeit friends (192), of the open mouths of idolists and atheists (452-453), of the unregenerate " chaunting thir Idol " (1672), of scandal brought to Israel (453-454), of evil tidings (1567), of the thundering of the proud Philistines. " Blood, death, and deathful deeds " are in noise (1513); noise is destructive—it tears the sky (1472); garrulity is a crime (490-491). Harapha, the boaster, is a noise—a tongue; Dalila, the traitress, is a noise—a voice; Samson, the traitor, is a noise—a blab. The military imagery depicts a struggle between the " good " silence and the " evil " sound: silence is a fort (236); Dalila attacks Samson by way of " tongue-batteries " and " blandisht parlies " (403-404); Samson is vanquished by a " peal of words " (235); the sound of a name renews an assault (331); and Dalila describes the solicitations of the magistrates, the priest who was " ever at [her] ear," as " assaults " and " sieges " (845-846).

Yet the imagery also insists that good may work in sound and evil in silence. " The Sun . . . is dark / And silent," says Samson when he has lost both physical and spiritual vision;

here, silence is equated with lack of light, and sound with light: the first "great Word" was "let there be light." Noise is defined in terms of God's "prime decree" (85), of divine prediction (23, 472-473), of the thunder of God's judgment (1696), of Samson's vow (378-379), of "apt words" (184), of "healing words" (605), of "sweet Lyric Song" (1737). And the military imagery shows that defense does not lie always in silence: Jephtha, by argument, defended Israel (283-285).

Milton thus reiterates in the sound and silence imagery the idea of ambivalence in all things and of the two-fold nature of alternatives. One must perceive (Dalila does not) that fame is "double-fac't" as well as "double-mouth'd" (971). One must learn that the right word, expressed in terms of knowledge and truth, leads to life; but lack of knowledge of the same word may lead to death: men can die "without Reprieve adjudg'd to death, / For want of well pronouncing *Shibboleth*" (288-289). And for the wrong word, one does not exchange the right silence: one does not "for a word, a tear, / . . . [divulge] the secret gift of God" (200-201). For the right silence may equate with the right sound: "The deeds themselves, though mute, spoke loud the dooer" (248).

Milton's comment in the sense imagery falls consistently into the pattern we have been tracing. There are an inward and an outward ear, two kinds of exercise of the sense of hearing. Both a deaf and an open ear may be right, may be wrong. "*Israel's* Governours, and Heads of Tribes . . . persisted deaf, and would not seem to count [as] things worth notice" the acts which God did "singly by [Samson]" (242-250). Deaf to God's call, they came to love bondage more than liberty. Yet an open ear may invite bondage. Dalila does not doubt that the ear of the Philistine lords will be open to certain proposals, and if Samson's ear is open to these same proposals, a hearing will inaugurate return to "worse" bondage. Dalila says that Samson is deaf; but he is deaf only to the wrong sound. His ear is open to her prayer for forgiveness, though he is deaf to her prayer to return to him. Samson is learning to "fence [his] ear against . . . sorceries" (937),[4] to be deaf in the right way, to hear in the right way, an act which presupposes right perception of the sound. Harapha says that his ears are "unus'd [to] hear . . .

---

[4] See Kester Svendsen, *Milton and Science* (Cambridge, Massachusetts, 1956), p. 166.

dishonours " (1231-32), but they are unused to hear truth. And misnaming the sound, he is deaf. Only Samson, Manoa, and the Chorus exhibit the workings of a spiritual hearing, an imitation of God, " whose ear is ever open; and his eye / Gracious to re-admit the suppliant " (1172-73). Thus, the sound and hearing imagery continues to emphasize the need for right assessment of the element received by the senses and the need for proper use of and differentiation between the physical and the spiritual senses, while at the same time suggesting that they feed one another.

The seventeenth-century poet often explored the relation between the senses and the soul by way of prison imagery. Andrew Marvell says, " O who shall, from this Dungeon, raise / A Soul inslav'd so many wayes? / With bolts of Bones, that fetter'd stands / In Feet; and manacled in Hands. / Here blinded with an Eye; and there / Deaf with the drumming of an Ear." Milton does not suggest that the body is inevitably the dungeon of the soul; and he does not separate the health and freedom of the body and of the soul as Marvell does in the words of the Soul (" Constrain'd not only to indure / Diseases, but, whats worse, the Cure: / And ready oft the Port to gain, / Am Shipwrackt into Health again "). He does, like Marvell, conventionally juxtapose sense and imprisonment images, but his figurative comment is far more complicated than that in the lines quoted above.

Physically, there are several kinds of a limitation of freedom; the two-fold helplessness of Samson, in chains and in blindness, is expressed in the phrase " Prison within Prison " (153). But when the Chorus says that "inward light . . ./ Puts forth no visual beam " (162-163), the phrase " Prison within Prison " acquires another meaning. We know that the element which does not properly exhibit its proper qualities is " imprison'd "; similarly, spiritual bondage is co-existent with spiritual blindness. Samson is both spiritually and physically blind, both spiritually and physically in chains. Moreover, Milton equates Samson's imprisonment with death, a death which is not physical: the Chorus says to Samson, "Thou art become . . ./ The Dungeon of thy self " (155-156), and Samson has lamented, " My self, my Sepulcher, a moving Grave " (102). The lines imply that the self is imprisoned, dead, by its own victory.

When the self becomes a " sepulcher," there is always in Renaissance thought an implication of an upset of order, an upset often defined by way of a misuse of the senses. The physical and spiritual imprisonment of Samson has been effected, in part at least, by Dalila, whose " bond slave " Samson was before the Philistines chained him. And Milton repeatedly connects references to Dalila with a slavery and imprisonment imagery and repeatedly develops this imagery in relation to sense images. Samson, on being praised by the Chorus as one temperate in drink, says, " What boots it at one gate to make defence, / And at another to let in the foe " (560-561). Again and again, Dalila is defined as the foe, is described by way of trap and imprisonment imagery, of snares, trains, gins, toils. When she appears before Samson, she most appropriately trails a " damsel train behind " (721). Her " fair fallacious looks " are a snare (532-533); her " honied words " are bait (1066); the " trains " are venereal (533); this " inchanting voice " (1065) is an accomplished snare (230). Such imagery reveals that Samson has been trapped by way of the senses of sight, taste, touch, and hearing. Even Dalila's golden scent, the " Amber sent of ordorous perfume " (720), implies a trap when joined to Samson's contention that *she* conceived treason by the " sent " of gold (389-391).[5] Milton does not use a scent of flowers to define the trap potential in the sense of smell: he uses the product of the whale, commonly in beast lore a figure for Satan; he uses an odor which suggests that Dalila, this " thing of Sea or Land," is primarily a thing of the evil element in which the fish-god reigns. So the sense and the prison images are fused in descriptions of Dalila. Her " warbling charms " are trains, gins, toils; so is her " fair enchanted cup " (932-934). In the latter metonymy is a reiteration of an idea we have seen before—that the element may signify degradation, slavery, imprisonment; in conjunction with a sense imagery, the figure suggests the danger inherent in misapprehension and misuse of the element.

The sense imagery then defines the result of a failure in the understanding or the will: trap, prison, death. And it defines the nature of a corrupting away from freedom and life. The " bait "

[5] Ambergris and honey, both used in descriptions of Dalila, are ingredients used by alchemists to get water to dissolve gold (see Svendsen, *Milton and Science*, p. 125). The currency-payment imagery is most important in the drama; and if there is in these words a hint connecting Dalila with alchemy and the effort to get potable gold, the elixir of life, such an evocation affords ironic comment on the incident of Samson's temptation and betrayal.

of Dalila's " honied words " makes Samson turn " drone " (567). The references to Dalila's warbling charms and her enchanted cup recall Circe, who turned sense-indulging men to beasts; and Samson, in chains, is " put to the labour of a Beast." All those in the drama who misapprehend the element which comes by way of the sense or who wilfully misuse the sense are described in words identifying them as not properly human. The worshippers of the fish-god are " inhuman " (109); Dalila is a " thing "; Samson in the toils of Dalila is a " tame Weather." [6]

The imagery also implies that the human being who through misuse of the senses has forfeited his own proper place in the scheme of things and has become something less than man can harm only the sinful. The scorpion-figure, which is used for Dalila, is traditionally an image for lechery; [7] but the Scorpion of Lechery can harm only the lecherous, and the figure is also suggested for Samson (360). The beast imagery suggests the general nature of the sinner, the peculiar sensuality into which the sinner declines, and the vulnerability of the sinful. It also suggests the powerlessness of evil against good. The Chorus, referring to men who fall, says that their " carkasses " are prey for " dogs and fowls " (693-694). Later, Dalila is called a hyena (748), a dog-like creature and " a cruel beast . . . [which] reseth on dead men, and taketh their carcase out of the earth, and devoureth them "; [8] still later, the Philistines, who " regorg'd of Bulls and Goats " (1671) call for the erstwhile wether, are called " Fowl " (1695). But although Samson has been prey for scorpion and summer fly, when the hyena and the fowls appear in the drama, he is no longer vulnerable to them, for he is no longer a dead man.

Milton, then, implies that a proper use of the senses is bound up with freedom and life and that a misuse of the senses, a sin

[6] The word *wether* would appear to have been chosen because of the fleece-shearing connotations; but Milton does not choose *lamb* or *sheep*, the word *wether* having many other associations which make it an evocative image for Samson: the wether is a castrated ram (*OED*, Wether, 1) and a figure used for a eunuch (*OED*, Wether, 1, b). In beast lore, the ram is said to have " great strength passing other sheepe," Stephen Batman, *Batman uppon Bartholome* (London, 1582), p. 339; and it is connected with the " gotebucke," which " is verie wanton . . . whose eyes for insatiate lust thereof, turneth in his head," John Maplet, *A Greene Forest . . . Reprinted from the Edition of 1567* (London, 1930), p. 148. The wether is related to a figure used for a chief or leader, " mostly contemptuous " (*OED*, Bel-wether, 2), and used opprobriously for a " clamorous person, one ready to give mouth " (*OED*, Bel-wether, 3, a).

[7] See Svendsen, *Milton and Science*, pp. 149-150.

[8] Anglicus Bartholomew, *Medieval Lore*, ed. Robert Steele (London, 1893), p. 130.

against order, inevitably results in an imprisonment characterized by death and decay. And this prison is the hide of a beast, as man's spirit corrupts and he assumes a beast nature. By his choice and manipulation of the beast images, Milton can, as we have seen, comment in various ways on the nature of the corruption. When Dalila is called a hyena, one particular meaning of the image pinpoints Dalila's error: according to the beast lore still prevalent in Milton's time, "It is [the hyena's] kind to change sex, for he is now found male, and now female, and is therefore an unclean beast";[9] awareness of this lore recalls to mind the fact that Dalila had assumed the prerogative of the man in desiring mastery over Samson. So in a large sense the moral implication in the choice of beast image for Dalila is that she is not properly woman, that a misuse of the senses or the will reveals a beast nature; more specifically, she is shown to exhibit the peculiar nature of the hyena, the scorpion, the adder. And not only are Samson's state and sin defined by the wether, the scorpion, the worm, and the drone images,[10] but also Samson is thus shown to be an anomaly, a corruption in and a corrupter of order. By his manipulation of the sense, beast, and restraint images, Milton defines the danger consequent upon the initial sin against order, the downward movement once the first step down is taken, the continual closing in of the prison and the continual diminishing of the human nature: Dalila's erstwhile "bond slave" eventually grinds for the Philistines "among the Slaves and Asses"; and Samson sees himself as changing from "tame Wether" to something "inferior to the vilest . . . / Of man or worm." The individual consequence of choice consistently suggests universal cause and consequence: man is subject to the universal law of order; but he can choose to increase the universal store of good or of evil.

Implicit in the figurative comment on the nature, result, and effect of a sin against order is, as we have seen, a comment on the

---

[9] Bartholomew, *Medieval Lore*, p. 130.

[10] Drones are "without sting, as it were unperfect Bees" (*Batman uppon Bartholome*, p. 368). Later, the dragon-figure is used for Samson, and according to beast lore, the dragon "grieveth with . . . stinging" (*Batman uppon Bartholome*, pp. 360-361). The contrast between the drone and the dragon images furnishes graphic illustration of the change in Samson. It should perhaps be noted that when the beast image suggests a virtuous quality or a characteristic which is, in the general context of the drama, to be desired, then the image does not imply a movement contrary to order.

nature, result, and effect of an observance of order. But the figurative language also, as we have seen, explicitly defines the latter. " A grain of manhood well resolv'd / Might easily have shook off all [Dalila's] snares," says Samson (408-409). If a man holds to " manhood," if he properly exercises the qualities that differentiate him from the beast, if he exerts his will, reason, and understanding to control his senses, he is not subject to trap or corruption.

Milton thus points to the freedom consequent on proper restraint as he points to the restraint consequent on improper freedom. Images of restraint illustrate the result of sin: toil, gin, snare, prison follow on improper exercise of sense and will. But images of restraint also define proper conduct: the right silence is itself a " Seal " (49). True freedom is bound up with an observance of order, a law not apparent to the Philistines, who " with blindness internal struck " invite their own ruin. The " Fowl " are " insensate left, or to sense reprobate " (1685). Lack of feeling and abandonment to feeling may be two extremes; but insofar as both reflect a breach of order, they equate. (Even in such apparently casual phrases we see Milton's preoccupation with similarity in alternatives, with the ambiguity and paradox that are a condition of existence, a condition which makes choice difficult but which also furnishes guide lines to understanding and choice.) The man who " with inward eyes illuminated " submits himself to order possesses a creative freedom and, paradoxically, may prove " vigorous most / When most unactive deem'd " (1704-05). Samson, in chains, eventually relearns that a man is, by the very nature of being, both fettered and free, but that he, by the gift of will, is allowed the choice of determining the nature and scope of both that fettering and that freedom. " My heels are fetter'd, but my fist is free," Samson says to Harapha (1235); and the speech symbolically establishes the victory of the will over the senses which had once fettered it.

IV

We have traced the development of the premise that the freedom and life inherent in order is manifest in the man who properly observes the qualities of manhood. There still remains the problem of remedy for the man who has fallen into disorder and has thus chained and diminished the reason, the understanding, and the will. Milton defines this condition of disorder, not only in beast and restraint images, but also in an imagery of disease; and by way of a juxtaposition of disorder and disease, he explores the great question of remedy for fallen man in cosmic terms.[11]

The Chorus refers to Samson's " Sores " (184), to his " fester'd wounds " (186), to the " tumors of a troubl'd mind " (185). Samson says that his griefs are like a " lingring disease " (618), like " wounds " that " ranckle, and fester, and gangrene, / To black mortification " (620-622); his thoughts " raise dire inflammation " (625-626); torment finds a secret passage " to th' inmost mind " and " on her purest spirits prey, / As on entrails, joints, and limbs, / With answerable pains " (611-615). Samson may be blind and bound, but the imagery insists that the great trouble is an internal disorder. And this inward malady is described in words which evoke the external elements and which continue the emphasis noted in the element, storm, and sense images on ambivalence and paradox. Samson's sickness is characterized by both blackness and flame; and though lack of fire is connected with mortification, presence of flame is dire. When Samson is described as a flower, the implication is that health or corruption may come to man by way of the elements; when the image of storm is used for man, he is the elements and exhibits their positive or negative quality. In the disease imagery the same comment is observable: man is made of the elements which may either flourish or corrupt; at the same time, they are something external to him which bear a relation to his health. But " no cooling herb / Or medcinal liquor can asswage / Nor breath of Vernal Air " can allay the " dire inflammation " (626-628). Samson's disease is of a cosmic nature; the elements in him are corrupt; and the fact that nature cannot, by itself, right itself applies to Samson.

The pointing to physical and spiritual correspondences may be aesthetic habit to Milton, as to other Renaissance writers; the figurative pattern in *Samson* may imply that one comes to self-

[11] Svendsen, *Milton and Science*, pp. 193-194, says, " The dialectic of disease and remedy so frequently met in Milton's prose issues from such postulates as the cosmic correspondence of man with the great world and the inescapable equation of disease with disorder, health with harmony and unity. . . . The insistent analogy between the law of nature and the law of God is expressed so heavily in medical-anatomical images as to become almost a myth in itself in *Doctrine of Divorce*."

knowledge, to knowledge of external creation, to knowledge of God through a contemplation of universal order and unity; Samson's physical ills may be both consequent on and reflective of spiritual ills. But none of this precludes Milton's insistence on the need for a proper discrimination between the physical and the spiritual. And Samson initially reveals considerable confusion in his assessment of disease and cure. Describing a disorder of mind and spirit, he sees it as " immedicable," an inflammation which nothing in the physical universe can relieve; but then he sees physical death as cure for this incurable spiritual malady: " Deaths . . . Opium [is] my only cure " (610-630). He links a sense of God's desertion with loss of physical sight and physical freedom, and calls them all " evils " which are " remediless "; then, he immediately names physical death as remedy for all: " speedy death, / The close of all my miseries, and the balm " (641-651). There is here no proper discrimination between spiritual and physical ills; and Samson's understanding darkened, he cannot properly relate disease and cure. In a constant play of irony and paradox, Milton suggests the need for knowledge if one is to find the way to remedy. It is ironic that Samson—defined repeatedly as a dead man, calling himself a " moving Grave," and lamenting the impossibility of cure—should see death as cure. It is doubly ironic that his words are true, though not in the sense in which he uses them. By difference as well as analogy between the spiritual and the physical disease and death, Milton points to the contrast and eventually the parallel between what Samson knows and what he needs to know. In Samson's informed choice, in part, lie balm and remedy. And when he eventually says to Harapha, " Nothing from thy hand / Fear I incurable," he is manifesting a larger comprehension of disease and cure, for the physical death that he once saw as cure is now something that is itself curable.

Besides saying that a man cannot initiate his own redemption and that, at the same time, his understanding is adjunct to ultimate remedy, Milton figuratively defines the source of remedy for the man whose condition may appear " remediless." We have seen in the element images that a great controlling power may conjure life from sterility, may cause water to spring from dry ground. This, in the light of the persistent microcosm-macrocosm equation, suggests that a man, however dry of spirit, can be regenerated by a spring of living waters; however imprisoned, can be freed by God's call and God's grace: there are " secret refreshings " that can " repair his strength "; there are " rousing motions " from the prime mover that can invest immobility and death with its own creative dynamism.

Against grace, Milton would have the reader weigh and consider the remedies suggested by Samson's visitors. The Chorus sees cure in " counsel," in " apt words "; but in the light of the imagery, man's counsel cannot penetrate the imprisoned ear, unless God's Word is operating in it, is calling the sinner to hearken. Dalila's remedy is intercession with the Philistine rulers to the end that the blind man may enjoy the " solaces " of the " other senses "; but the imagery suggests that remedy does not lie in either a wrong speaking or an inordinate prizing of the senses, and offsetting the possibly " favorable ear " of the Philistine lords is the ever " open ear " of Israel's Lord. The Officer thinks that Samson by " compliance " will win favor and perhaps freedom; but the imagery implies that wrong use of the will results in loss of the will and consequently of freedom. Manoa thinks that remedy may be found in ransom paid to the Philistines, a remedy which partakes of the nature of gift, since Manoa is willing to " forgo " all his patrimony for Samson's redemption (1482). Thus, remedy, in Manoa's eyes, lies in gold, which is both ransom and gift; and later he is again to see remedy in a price paid when he says that Samson's death has paid his ransom and bought his freedom. In a remarkable fusion of image and idea, Milton develops in the complex gold-payment imagery illuminating relationships between the remedy ransom and the remedy grace, which is termed " the gift of God." [12]

Early in the play, a money image is used to symbolize falsehood: a false species of friend is " counterfeit coin " (189). And gold is a currency for counterfeit action: Dalila, conceiving treason by the scent of gold, sells the one she should have cherished, an act which she describes as the yielding of " private respects " to " public good," duty, truth, and virtue (867-870). Thus, money and payment are linked with a misuse of the senses and the will, with corruption, and with a sin against order. Also, money and payment images are used to describe punishment. Samson tells Harapha that he had paid his " underminers in thir

[12] *The Christian Doctrine,* in *Works,* XV, 393.

coin " (1204); the imagery suggests that the nature of the money and payment is determinable by the nature of the one paid, and Samson, who has trafficked in betrayal, is also paid in his own coin. The nature of money and payment is also determinable by the nature of the payer: valuing things of the sense, Samson is, blind and captive, " paying [a] rigid score " (432-433). If the payer does not value the currency, such payment need not be punishment; on the other hand, there is a currency, the value of which is absolute and the loss of which is not limited: when Samson pays for an " amber sent " with a " holy secret," he must " pay on [his] punishment " (489).

An imagery of counterfeit coin and counterfeit transactions, of payment which invites or reflects corruption, as well as of payment which is fitting punishment, conjoined with a persistent emphasis on Manoa's hope that a payment of gold will be *remedial* (481-486; 516-518; 601-604; 1453-54; 1457-71; 1476-84), forces the reader to be aware of multiple image and idea in the currency and payment references. There is a currency for an action of falsehood, lechery, greed, and treachery, a coin which is legal tender within a system of wrong values and wrong choice. And there is a currency for an action of love, wherein value and choice are defined in terms of selflessness: " I shall chuse / To live the poorest in my Tribe, then richest, / And he in that calamitous prison left " (1478-80), says Manoa, who is willing to give his " whole inheritance " for Samson's freedom. Manoa's proposed payment, characterized by love and givingness, corresponds to God's remedy, for a consideration of what makes this " Fathers timely care " current recalls the fact that grace, the ultimate remedy, is a free gift.

The comment in the currency-payment imagery and in the two-fold view of remedy as ransom and gift informs the descriptions of Samson's " great act." Death pays Samson's ransom (1572-73); but the nature of this currency and payment varies with the nature of those involved in the transaction. Renewed in strength, Samson again pays his " underminers in thir coin." He pays them in an undermining; he pays them in coin of the sense, in which they have chosen to place highest value, in the heavy pillars of the theater where they honor Dagon and disorder. Components of the figurative pattern which we have traced are fused in the description of the Philistines—flower and fowl, clamourous, drunk, blind, sick—and in the description of the disorder which they, in disorder (1675-76), invite on themselves —earthquake and storm. And so components of the moral comment in the developing structure of conceit and extended metaphor are bound together in this ironic evocation of payment. Worshipping things of the sense, the Philistines are vulnerable to things of the sense; choosing sense rather than spirit, they lose in physical death all that they value; choosing disorder, they reap disorder. And though material ruin is mere reflection of a spiritual ruin which they choose with " hearts . . . jocund and sublime " (1669), physical death is a currency and a payment which is rigid punishment for the Philistines.

The same currency and payment is remedy and life for Samson. For Samson pays God in God's own coin. Payment to the Philistines in coin legal tender to them requires an undermining; but to pay God in his own coin requires a rising above sense limitations, a faith, a selflessness; for God's remedy and ransom is a gift of love, a free offering. Moreover, thematic implications on the nature of true remedy are expressed figuratively when the angel, revealing " his Godlike presence " in a " fiery column," ascends in flames " from off the Altar, where an Offr'ing burn'd ": God manifests himself in offerings. Early in the play, Manoa speaks of offerings to avert God's " further ire " (519-520); but at the end of the play, by the gift of grace God has " quit [Samson] all his debt." Yet Samson, in imitation of God, acts in faith, makes a gift of himself; and his " fierie vertue rouz'd / . . . into sudden flame " (1690-91), he assumes the image of God. The place of feast to honor Dagon becomes an altar to God, and Samson, the offering, paying God in his own gold, " as in a fiery column [chariots] / His Godlike presence."

Samson has said that there is nothing incurable in Harapha's fist; the imagery in the passages decribing the event in the theater implies that there is, for Samson, nothing incurable in the fall of the " massie Pillars." The use of " flower " to describe the Philistines and of " massie " to describe their building recalls that the same words, used to the same end, appear in an earlier description of a feat of strength by Samson at a time when he is linked with one " whom the Gentiles feign to bear up Heav'n " (144-150). By the reiteration of an imagery of earth and matter for the Philistines and their creations; the evocation of a giant who bore up heaven, a description peculiarly appropriate to Samson's "great act"; the reminder of the prediction, the "fiery column," in the fire imagery used for the thing predicted—by such devices Milton reinforces and extends his metaphysical comment and evokes a play of idea and imagination on the question of Samson's "suicide" and the Philistines' invitation of their own ruin: the "fiery column" as opposed to the "massie Pillars" suggests the purity of one who bears up Heaven and the impurity of those who bear up Dagon, the invulnerable spirit and the vulnerable matter, and the victory of spirit over the once death-dealing senses. Sense and matter cannot affect the health of one who manifests himself in fire.

Milton's figurative structure, culminating in the descriptions of Samson's triumph, is a masterly exhibition of the poetic practice possible when certain lofty concepts and a certain lore are common property. Given interchangeable symbols in fire, the purest of elements, and gold, the purest of metals; given a popular scientific lore wherein fire is "the renewer of all thing, and warden of kinde . . . for he overcommeth all things, that he worketh in, and chaungeth it," [13] wherein gold is alchemically the mixture of the elements in proper proportion and health the same perfect proportion of elements in the human body, Milton evokes such ideas when he uses the fire image to develop the theme of remedy and ransom and to conclude his figurative exposition of the purity, health, and order which is God. Given a popular natural lore wherein the dragon is a creature who "reeseth up into the aire" and "setteth the ayre on fire," who "devour[s] beasts and fowles," and who has "right sharp sight"; wherein the eagle is a creature in whom "the vertue of sight is most mightye," who can behold "the Sunne . . . without anye blemishing of eyen," and who is capable of renewal, for "she is taught by kinde, to seeke a well of springing water . . . and the dimnesse of her eien is wiped away and purged, and she taketh againe her might and strength "; wherein the phoenix is a creature who grows from "a little worme . . . gendered of [her own] ashes," [14] Milton skilfully puts such figures to many uses: they symbolize Samson's renewal in strength, vision, and life, and develop the general comment on the nature of regeneration; they mark the difference

[13] *Batman uppon Bartholome*, p. 155.
[14] *Batman uppon Bartholome*, pp. 360-361, 177, 183.

between the spiritual nature of Samson and that of the sick, blind " Fowl "; they artfully conclude a pattern of beast imagery which begins with Samson as " worm " and " drone "; they suggest spiritual change at the moment of the deed, a transformation in line with the details of the birth of the phoenix, as from a worm, Samson " taketh feathers, and is shapen and turned into a bird." [15] Milton chooses images with multiple associations, all applicable to his pattern of moral comment, and fits them into a complex figurative design. The progression of winged-figures echoes the progression in Samson's act as a movement of earth (mountain), air (winds), water, and eventually fire, a description which evokes the lore of elemental transmutation and which, like the images of dragon, eagle, and phoenix, suggests Samson's spiritual metamorphosis.

In short, Milton's use of a ready-made symbolism is remarkably discriminating, complex, and coherent. At the beginning of the drama, Samson is shown led by a " guiding hand " to a place which has " choice of Sun or shade." However limited in the context of the opening situation this line may be, it has, in the light of subsequent image and event, great implications. Through wrong choice, Samson has fallen into a land of darkness; repeatedly, we are to see him faced with the figurative choice of sun or shade; we are to see him renewed, through the help of a guiding hand, in reason and freedom of choice; and finally we are to see the choice in the opening figurative alternatives resolved and defined in the concluding fire imagery, when renewed in strength, vision, and health, Samson imitates God. Though literal event appears to be a choice of shade and disorder brought on those " in order rang'd," what is shade to the Philistines is sun to Samson. And choosing sun, he becomes invulnerable to darkness.

A close study of Milton's imagery reveals a careful craftsman, whose emphasis is on the vision, not the sound, upon the idea, not the word. Beneath the smooth surface rhetoric of his poetry lies a complex structure of metaphor and symbol, a figurative comment which illuminates Samson's struggle and victory and which, in itself, constitutes a definitive philosophic comment on everyman's conduct and life.

[15] *Batman uppon Bartholome,* p. 183.

DESPAIR AND "PATIENCE AS THE TRUEST FORTITUDE" IN *SAMSON AGONISTES*

BY WILLIAM O. HARRIS

Two choral passages in *Samson Agonistes,* whose themes are complementary and whose positions are balanced early and late in the drama's structure, deserve somewhat closer scrutiny than is usually given them. For, as I hope to show, they reflect the doctrinal concept which informs the play—the concept of Patience as the highest manifestation of Fortitude, that particular cardinal virtue traditionally opposed to the terrible sin of *tristitia* and despair, which Don Cameron Allen has shown to be the cause of Samson's inner struggle.[1] The concept is a theologically precise one which evolved from Cicero through patristic literature into scholastic and, later, Christian humanistic commentary. Furthermore, the association of Samson with it is attested by strong iconographical tradition. This religious heritage Milton transmuted into poetic drama just as he rendered theology into epic form in *Paradise Lost.*

As an initial step in understanding this theme in the drama, it might be well to read again the two key passages in the light of Milton's statements elsewhere on patience and fortitude. The first of the choral passages is spoken in response to Samson's outcry of deepest despair after Manoa has visited him:

> Many are the sayings of the wise
> In antient and in modern books enroll'd;
> Extolling Patience as the truest fortitude;
> And to the bearing well of all calamities,
> All chances incident to mans frail life
> Consolatories writ
> With studied argument, and much perswasion sought

---

[1] "The Idea as Pattern: Despair and *Samson Agonistes*," in *The Harmonious Vision: Studies in Milton's Poetry* (Baltimore, 1954), pp. 71-94. See also John M. Steadman, "'Faithful Champion': the Theological Basis of Milton's Hero of Faith," *Anglia,* LXXVII (1959), 19-20.

This essay first appeared in *ELH,* Vol. 30, No. 2 (June 1963).

Lenient of grief and anxious thought,
But with th' afflicted in his pangs thir sound
Little prevails, or rather seems a tune,
Harsh, and of dissonant mood from his complaint,
Unless he feel within
Some sourse of consolation from above;
Secret refreshings, that repair his strength,
And fainting spirits uphold (652-666).[2]

The passage can provoke many questions. Do the Danites reject the validity of the " sayings of the wise " or merely observe the sufferer's inability to profit from them? Is it implied that patience can be triumphant after " he feel[s] within / Some sourse of consolation from above "? Does the Chorus utter Truth; or are the Danites, as participants in the drama, deceived and shortsighted? These questions must eventually be answered; but, for the moment, I would pose one of more limited scope: In what sense is patience, " the truest fortitude "? The implication of the superlative is that there is a lesser fortitude.

This implication the second choral refrain makes more explicit. After Harapha departs, the Chorus sings,

Oh how comely it is and how reviving
To the Spirits of just men long opprest!
When God into the hands of thir deliverer
Puts invincible might
To quell the mighty of the Earth, th' oppressour,
The brute and boist'rous force of violent men
Hardy and industrous to support
Tyrannic power, but raging to pursue
The righteous and all such as honour Truth;
He all thir Ammunition
And feats of War defeats
With plain Heroic magnitude of mind
And celestial vigour arm'd,
Thir Armories and Magazins contemns,
Renders them useless, while
With winged expedition
Swift as the lightning glance he executes
His errand on the wicked, who surpris'd
Lose thir defence distracted and amaz'd.
　　But patience is more oft the exercise
Of Saints, the trial of thir fortitude,

---

[2] Quotations from Milton are taken from *The Works of John Milton*, ed. F. A. Patterson (New York, 1931-38)—hereafter cited as " Columbia edition."

Making them each his own Deliverer,
And Victor over all
That tyrannie or fortune can inflict,
Either of these is in thy lot,
Samson, with might endu'd
Above the Sons of men; but sight bereav'd
May chance to number thee with those
Whom Patience finally must crown   (1268-1296).

Two alternate modes of human triumph are poised in balance. And of the two, at least among God's saints, " patience is more oft . . . the trial of thir fortitude." The alternative, of course, is the gloriously active battling performed by God's champion, whose chief virtue is " Heroic magnitude of mind "—or *magnanimitas*, the hallmark of all epic heros, all renaissance courtiers. Is this, for all the Danites' enthusiasm, the lesser fortitude complementary to patience, as implied in the earlier passage?

Milton's own views found elsewhere would confirm that it is. For instance, pausing in Book IX of *Paradise Lost* to justify the unique subject chosen for his epic, he rejects what had been " hitherto the onely Argument / Heroic deem'd " (that is, the triumphant deeds of " fabl'd Knights / In Battels feign'd ") and chooses instead " the better fortitude / Of Patience and Heroic Martydom / Unsung " (28-33). Not only is the concept explicitly affirmed, but in this case the speaker is Milton himself, not a Chorus which might merely be speaking as *dramatis persona*. Also undeniably Miltonic is the insight of Adam in Book XII " that suffering for Truth's sake / Is fortitude to highest victorie " (569-70). Such passages indicate the degree of Milton's assent to the choral pairing of magnanimity and patience as manifestations for fortitude, with patience the greater of the two.

However, to consider the concept as a purely Miltonic one is as erroneous as assuming it to be merely an outburst of the Danite Chorus. For, as I hope to show, it was a traditionally Christian pattern of ethical thought, known and rendered dramatic by Milton in keeping with his usual creative method. For example, the theme which John F. Danby elucidates in Sidney's *Arcadia*[3] provides a very close parallel to the ideas expressed

[3] The quotations throughout this paragraph are drawn in sequence from Danby's *Poets on Fortune's Hill: Studies in Sidney, Shakespeare, Beaumont & Fletcher* (London, 1952), pp. 47-70.

by the Chorus. Recalling the passage in the *Apologie* in which
Sidney says that Ulysses' various trials "are but exercises of
patience and magnanimity," Danby finds a balancing of these
two virtues as the architectonic principle underlying the *Arcadia*. There are "two separate but related spheres in the Sidneain
universe . . . One is the sphere of magnanimity, the other the
sphere for the exercise of patience . . . Patience and magnanimity . . . are opposite and yet complementary." Thus, continues
Danby, "Magnanimity is Virtue in its aspect of successful command: when Fortune is compelled to be the well-waiting hand-
maid. Patience is Virtue in its aspect of sufferance rather than
control: when Fortune is frowning." Consequently, when Philoclea and Pamela are imprisoned, "the captivity episode portray
[sic] their heroism in the sphere where only patience can be
operative . . . just as the episodes that have led up to it have
Musidorus and Pyrocles as their heroes and portrays [sic] the
masculine qualities of heroic magnanimity, courage, endurance,
and command." Similarly, in Sidney's original plan, the knights
themselves are imprisoned in the climactic episode; and Pyrocles,
tempted to despair and suicide, is saved by Philoclea's urging of
patient acceptance of God's time. "Thus," comments Danby,
"The princes learn patience, too, in this last trial of manhood
and add a further (and Christian) virtue to 'magnanimitie.' They
conduct themselves in their capivity 'like men indeed, fortifying
courage with the true rampire of patience, [and] did so endure
that they did rather appear governors of necessity, than serv-
ants of fortune'" The plan of the *Arcadia*, then, suggests that
patience is "the prime virtue, man's prime necessity too" in
that, beyond magnanimity, it "leans on and demands the transcendent."

The same ethical pattern may be found in the writings of
another Christian humanist, Lodowick Bryskett, who bases his
plan of princely instruction in *A Discourse of Civill Life* (London, 1606) upon the four cardinal virtues, culminating with an
extensive treatment of fortitude, of which he says there are two
kinds. The species which serves as "a spurre to pricke men forward in defense of just and honest causes" is precisely that
which Milton's Chorus exults to in the opening of the second
ode. However, continues Bryskett, "there is a kind of fortitude
that hath no need of any such spurre of anger . . . And this is

that blessed virtue which never suffereth a man to fall from the height of his minde, being called by some men patience: who will not onely haue her to be a vertue separate from the four principal vertues, but also that she should be aboue them. But this opinion of theirs is not well grounded, since in truth she is but a branch of fortitude " (p. 88). This insistence that patience, for all its excellence, is yet subsumed along with its complement within the cardinal virtue of fortitude does not mean that Bryskett considers the two species equal. For he goes on to say of patience that "who so beareth stoutly aduersities, deserueth greater commendation and praise then they which ouercome their enemies, or by force win cities or countries, or otherwise defend their owne " (p. 89).

The vitality of this ethical concept among Christian humanists during the English renaissance is amply testified to by such expressions of it. However, its pervasiveness through centuries of European thought can be more easily gauged by noticing its reflection in iconographic and emblematic works. A particularly revealing example is that provided by the *Fior di Virtu*, in which each virtue is treated in a separate chapter including an analysis, a woodcut emblem, a compendium of classical quotations, and a fitting narrative *exemplum*. In such a chapter upon fortitude appears the familiar dictum that there are two concepts which alone " are truly fortitude and are real virtues "—" courage, or audacity of character " and "patience, enabling us patiently to endure all adversity and all distress." Among the classical references appended is one: " Cicero says of the virtue called fortitude: 'Man must be brave in battle and patient in adversity.' " [4] Actually Cicero never says it quite so explicitly, though the idea is certainly important in both the *De officiis* and *De inventione*. The allusion is a helpful one in understanding the genesis, and tracing the evolution, of this dichotomy implicit in Milton's poem and the works of his fellow Christian humanists.

However, I would postpone its consideration to notice first the iconography associated with the doctrine in the *Fior di Virtu*. For, accompanying the passage as to the dual attributes

[4] *The Florentine Fior di Virtu of 1491*, trans. Nicholas Fersin [sic] ([Philadelphia], 1953), p. 75.

which alone " are truly fortitude " is an exemplifying woodcut depicting Samson pulling down the temple.[5] Further, the narrative exemplum which concludes the chapter is that of Samson's life, emphasizing especially the temple episode.[6] This identification of Milton's hero with the virtue of fortitude so prominent in the choral passages actually reflects the traditional iconography for that virtue throughout the middle ages and the renaissance.[7] That the tradition remained strong in Milton's own age is suggested by its perpetuation in such emblem collections as those by Ripa and Bocchi[8] and by the use made of it by a theologian like Polanus,[9] whose influence upon Milton is known.

The *Fior di Virtu*, then, while it certainly should not itself be thought any influence upon Milton's conception of Samson and fortitude, does draw together iconographical and ethical heritages which seem reflected in the drama. The allusion to Cicero noticed earlier in the *Fior*, for instance, takes one to the source from which the magnanimity-patience dichotomy evolved. In the *De inventione* Cicero, defining and subdividing each of the four cardinal virtues, says that " fortitudo est considerata periculorum susceptio et laborum perpessio " (ii. 163) and classifies its parts as being magnificence, confidence, patience, and perserverance. As early as St. Augustine the passage was absorbed into Christian ethical literature,[10] but it was Thomas Aquinas who

[5] *Ibid.*   [6] *Ibid.*, pp. 76-77.

[7] Émile Mâle, *L'Art religieux de la fin du moyen âge en France: Etude sur l'iconographie du moyen âge et sur ses sources d'inspiration*, 4th ed. (Paris, 1931), p. 322. Raimònd van Marle, *Iconographie de l'art profane au moyen-age et à la renaissance et la décoration des desmeures* (Le Harve, 1932), I, 67-69. Louis Réau, *Iconographie de l'art Crétien* (Paris, 1955), I, 189.

[8] See, for example, Cesare Ripa, *Iconologia, overo descrittione di diversi imagini cauate dell' antichita, & de propria inventione* (Rome, 1603), p. 165 [sic]; or symbol XXII in the first book of Achille Bocchi's *Symbolicarvm quaestionum de universo genere quas serio ludebat* (Bologna, 1555), pp. XLIIII-XLV.

[9] Amandus Polanus, *The Substanec* [sic] *of Christian Religion*, trans. Thomas Wilcocks (London, 1600), p. 515. In his essay, " Miltonic Tragedy and Christian Vision " in *The Tragic Vision and the Christian Faith*, ed. Nathan A. Scott, Jr. (New York, 1957), T. S. K. Scott-Craig suggests but never documents the influence of Polanus and Wolleb in helping to form Milton's concepts of Fortitude and Patience as exemplified in Samson (pp. 104-105).

[10] *De diversis quaestionibus lxxxiii*, xxi, 1, in *PL*, XL, 21. For a study of the absorption and modification of all the cardinal virtues by Christianity, see Otto Zöckler, *Die Tugendlehre des Christentums* (Gutersloh, 1904), to which might well be added an admirable unpubl. thesis (Mt. Holyoke, 1941) by Catharine Haines, " The Four Greek Virtues from Socrates to Bonaventure."

modified the inherited concept so that it became the one reflected in the *Fior*, and later in the works of Sidney, Bryskett, and Milton. For, completely without warrant other than his Aristotelian inclinations, St. Thomas substituted "magnanimity" for Cicero's "confidence" and then schematized the dualism of Cicero's definition of fortitude by labeling magnanimity and magnificence as virtues of "aggression" and patience and perserverance as those of "endurance."[11]

Within the context of this Stoic idea becoming transformed into Christian ethics, another modification—or, more accurately, an accretion—was taking place. Fortitude came to be considered the bulwark against the terrible sin of *tristitia* and despair, which D. C. Allen has shown to be the temptation Samson nearly succumbs to in Milton's drama. As early as the sixth century, Julianus Pomerius held that the cardinal virtue of fortitude could "drive out the cowardice of despair," by which he meant the "despair of God's gift whereby we are strengthened."[12] Hrabanus Maurus and others borrowed and perpetuated the idea[13] until, in the prolific septenaries of the middle ages, the standard *remedium* for the sin of *tristitia* or *accidia* came to be fortitude.[14] And finally, the ultimate popularization came when lay manuals

[11] *Summa Theologica*, II-II, Q 128. Though apparently neither so influential nor so exact in his schematizing, Abelard actually anticipated St. Thomas by observing "Fortitudo duabus partibus videtur comprehendi, magnanimitate scilicet et tolerantia" (from *Dialogus inter philosophorum, Iudaeum et Christianum* as cited in Odon Lottin, *Psychologie et morale aux XIIe et XIIIe Siecle* [Louvain, 1942-54], III, 187n). In passing, it is also worth noting the continuing pressure of Aristotelian *magnanimitas* to dominate the concept. In his commentary on the *De inventione* (Venice, 1563), Nascimbeni insists that *magnitudo animi* is the genus, *fortitudo* and *patientia* the species (p. 125v).

[12] *The Contemplative Life,* trans. Sister Mary Suelzer, in *Ancient Christian Writers*, IV, ed. Johannes Quasten and Joseph C. Plumpe (Westminster, Md., 1947), p. 148. (*PL*, LIX, 504-505).

[13] *PL*, CXII, 1337-38; CV, 675. For the question of influence, see M. L. W. Laistner, "The Influence during the Middle Ages of the Treatise 'De vita contemplativa' and Its Surviving Manuscripts," *Miscellanea Giovanni Mercati,* II (1949), 349-351, and the unpubl. diss. (Univ. of North Carolina, 1950) by Father John B. Dwyer, "The Tradition of Medieval Manuals of Instruction in the Poems of John Gower," p. 270.

[14] Septenaries are so numerous and so repetitious, at least on this point, that to cite even representative ones would border on the excessive; but Hugo of St. Victor, because of the influence of his pioneer work, and St. Bonaventure, because of the culminating effect of his synthesis, both deserve mention. For the former, see *De quinque septenis seu septenariis,* i and iv (*PL*, CLXXV, 405 and 409), and *De sacramentis,* II: XIII.ii (*PL*, CLXXVI, 527); for the latter, see Jean-François Bonnefoy, *Le Saint-Esprit et ses dons selon saint Bonaventure* in *Étude de Philosophie Médiévale,* X, ed Etienne Gilson (Paris, 1929), pp. 220-221.

William O. Harris   283

of instruction incorporated the idea. Thus Chaucer's Parson, deriving his sermon from such manuals, offers "fortitudo or strengthe" as the *remedium* against "Accidie," which leads to "wanhope, that is despair of the mercy of God, that comth . . . somtyme of to muche drede, ymaginynge that he hath doon so muche synne that it wol nat availlen hym, though he wolde repenten hym and forsake synne," and, consequently, whose end is *"tristicia"* whereof it "comth that a man is anoyed of his owene lif." [15]

Finally, it is not surprising that, in the light of the magnanimity-patience dualism examined earlier, the attribute of fortitude which often assumed the burden of this opposition to despair or *tristitia* was that of patience. For example, in a versified treatment of the virtues Hrabanus Maurus includes the following couplet entitled *De fortitudine patientiae*:

> Fortiter adversa virtus patientia suffert,
> Victrix confidens tristia cunctu fugat.[16]

Similarly, Acquinas says that "endurance" as one of the attributes of fortitude is necessary "ne . . . animus frangatur *per tristitiam*, et decidat a sua magnitudine. Et quantum ad hoc [Cicero] ponit patientiam." [17] It is not surprising, then, that Sidney in the *Arcadia* should depict Pyrocles' despair and attempted suicide as "an extreme falling away from the frame of patience" [18] or that, in *King Lear*, Edgar should counter his father's suicidal despair with the admonition to "bear free and patient thoughts" (IV. vi. 80). Finally, to cite Milton's own "better teacher," the Redcrosse Knight, after his encounter with Despair, goes to the House of Holiness where still he was "Greevd with remembrance of his wicked wayes, / And prickt with anguish of his sinnes so sore, / That he desirde to end his wretched dayes" until Caelia went "To fetch a Leach, the which had great insight / In that disease of grieved conscience, / And well could cure the same. His name was Patience" (I. x. 21-23).

Thus, the Christian literary and iconographical heritage that

---

[15] *The Complete Works of Chaucer*, ed. Fred N. Robinson, 2nd ed. (Boston, 1957), pp. 250-251.

[16] *PL*, CXII, 1632.

[17] *Summa Theologica*, II-II, Q 128. Actually, Cicero says nothing at all about *tristitia;* St. Thomas is expressing a purely Christian idea.

[18] Danby, p. 66.

Milton knew so thoroughly suggests that fortitude, universally exemplified by Samson, consisted of an active sphere of magnanimous deeds and a more exalted sphere of patient endurance, the latter often assuming the task of resisting the ultimate despair of God's mercy. Read against this background, the two choral passages on patience in *Samson Agonistes* have far more thematic significance than has been accorded them. I shall conclude by interpreting them in this context.

The Danites prepare us from the play's beginning for a Samson caught in the snares of *tristitia*, describing him " As one past hope, abandon'd / And by himself given over " (120-21). Their estimate, for all its later justification, is as yet too bleak; for Samson's contrition serves at the beginning as a healthy antidote to excessive quarreling with God's justice;

> Yet stay, let me not rashly call in doubt
> Divine Prediction; what if all foretold
> Had been fulfilld but through mine own default,
> Whom have I to complain of but my self? (43-46)

Thus, when Manoa comes, petulantly accusing God, Samson replies again:

> Appoint not heavenly disposition, Father,
> Nothing of all these evils hath befall'n me
> But justly; I my self have brought them on,
> Sole Author I, sole cause (373-76).

However, this time in resisting the temptation represented by his father he proclaims his guilt at great length, " ymaginynge," as Chaucer's Parson would say, "that he hath doon so muche synne that it wol not availlen hym, though he wolde repenten hym." Inevitably he sinks into *tristitia*, resolved to let " oft-invocated death / Hast'n the welcom end of all my pains " (575-76). Seeking "deaths benumming Opium as [his] only cure " and testifying to " swounings of despair / And sense of Heav'ns desertion " (630-32), he reaches the nadir of *tristitia* with the anguished outcry:

> Nor am I in the list of them that hope;
> Hopeless are all my evils, all remediless;
> This one prayer yet remains, might I be heard,
> No long petition, speedy death,
> The close of all my miseries, and the balm (647-51).

The first of the two choral refrains on patience occurs immediately and appropriately in response to this despair. Yet critics of our day are inclined to pass over the lines without comment,[19] while one at least has rather dismissed them as containing mere "platitudes about patience."[20] But, as noted earlier, almost identical praise of patience as the highest fortitude is to be found in other passages clearly representing the poet's own views. To these might surely be added that personification of Patience who replies to prevent the murmur of the near-despairing Milton writhing in blind isolation from God's purposes for his life. These instances are not platitudinous; neither then are likely to be the words offered by Samson's countrymen at the point of his greatest despair. In some sense, the choral passage must represent the poet's own Christian belief.

On the other hand, the Danites who recall the doctrine at so fitting a moment have themselves no faith in its efficacy in this case, concluding that it " little prevails, or rather seems a tune / Harsh, and of dissonant mood . . ." And we who read the play isolated from its doctrinal presuppositions are inclined to applaud this " common sense " observation [21] and to accept their view as representing truth within the drama. Before too easy acceptance of this interpretation, however, it might be well to recall that the remainder of their ode at this point consists of the extended challenge of God's justice, a passage as ironic as any in the drama. Overmastered by their sympathy for Samson in his degradation, they flail blindly at the encompassing wisdom of Jehovah. Is it not reasonable that the opening portion of this ode, the lines on patience, be read in the same ironic light? Rather than men whose " common sense " leads them to perceive the inadequacy of traditional teachings at one moment and then to expose in the next the limitations of their human vision before the mysteries of Gôd, are they not throughout the ode ironically critical of truths their grief for Samson will not let them see?

The subtlety of Milton's diction and syntax in framing the Danites' rejection of patience suggests that he does intend that

---

[19] Tillyard, pp. 341 and 347; Allen, p. 87; and A. S. P. Woodhouse, "Tragic Effect in *Samson Agonistes*," *University of Toronto Quarterly*, XXVIII (1959), 210, for example, all ignore the lines though each comments upon the remainder of the ode.
[20] Parker, p. 39. [21] *Ibid.*, p. 147.

rejection to contain a truth ironically unapparent to them but implicit in the drama of which they are a part. Their first evaluation of the virtue is that, though much proclaimed, it "little prevails" when a man is actually in torment. But so assertive a judgment is immediately supplanted by a less certain one. It "a little prevails, or rather seems . . . ." That its "*seems* a tune /Harsh, and of dissonant mood" to the afflicted does not mean that it is so of itself. Finally, there is the "unless" which foreshadows the very event upon which the drama turns: "Unless he feel within / Some sourse of consolation from above." Of course, the Chorus itself is not so much expressing hope for such heavenly grace as it is suggesting its absence at the present, their quarrel with Heaven's treatment of Samson spilling over into the great challenge of divine justice which concludes the ode. But present along with the appearance of things to them is the reality only the play itself unfolds. The first ode on "Patience as the truest fortitude" has suggested this traditional *remedium* to *tristitia* at the very moment of Samson's deepest despair and has ironically balanced the Chorus's rejection of it with a foreshadowing of ultimate victory through patience and divine sustenance.

The second choral passage is equally strategic in its location and significant in its meaning. For it occurs just after Samson's first recovery from despair through renewed patience and just prior to the influx of heavenly grace which the earlier passage had foreshadowed.

Whatever prototypes we may variously see embodied in the character of Harapha, at one crucial moment at least he speaks a part long traditional in English literature—the tempter to ultimate despair of God's forgiveness. In words reminiscent of those urged by characters in Spenser, Marlowe, Skelton and numerous others employing the tradition,[22] he says to a Samson already endangered by *tristitia*, "Presume not on thy God, what e're he be, / Thee he regards not, owns not, hath cut off / Quite from his people . . ." (1156-58).

---

[22] Thorough studies of this tradition have been made by Frederic Ives Carpenter, "Spenser's Cave of Despair: an Essay in Literary Comparison," *MLN*, XII (1897), 257-273; Harold Golder, "Bunyan's Giant Despair," *JEGP*, XXX (1931), 361-365; and Samuel C. Chew, *The Virtues Reconciled: an Iconographic Study* (Toronto, 1947), pp. 110-118.

With an assurance unlike anything he had expressed before, however, Samson repulses the temptation. At the play's beginning, he had accepted his guilt and rejected Manoa's questioning of God's treatment of him. Pushed to excess, this honest self-knowledge had led him into wanhope. But now, before the heathen taunts, while continuing to confess his sinfulness, he balances contrition with faith in God's ultimate forgiveness:

> . . . these evils I deserve and more,
> Acknowledge them from God inflicted on me
> Justly, yet despair not of his final pardon
> Whose ear is ever open; and his eye
> Gracious to re-admit the suppliant (1169-73).

Similarly, his attitude toward death has undergone change. No longer invoking it, praying for it, he patiently awaits it and, in that calmer mood, comes so near an understanding as to foreshadow unknowingly the triumphal catastrophe:

> But come what will, my deadliest foe will prove
> My speediest friend, my death to rid me hence,
> The worst that he can give, to me the best.
> Yet so it may fall out, because thir end
> Is hate, not help to me, it may with mine
> Draw thir own ruin who attempt the deed (1262-67).

At this moment when the first signs of Samson's regeneration through patience coincide with the momentary return of his vigor as God's former champion, the second and fuller of the pertinent odes is sung. Both attributes of fortitude, the heroic aggressiveness of magnanimity and the martyring endurance of patience, are weighed. The striking thing, though, is the paradoxical contrast between the clear enthuisasm of the Danites for one and the endorsement their words give to the other. The exultant ring and sustained jubilation of their paean, " Oh how comely it is and how reviving" when to God's oppressed appears His champion " With plain Heroic magnitude of mind / And celestial vigour arm'd," modulates to the minor-keyed and brief, " But patience is more oft the exercise / Of Saints, the trial of thir fortitude . . ." Their preference for the former is implicit in this contrast of tone. Yet it is the latter which parallels Milton's views in *Paradise Lost*, IX, and his espousal of " the heavenly Fortitude of Martyrdome" in *Of Reformation*.[23] Such analogues notwithstanding, the fervor of the Danite vision of a conquering hero so appeals to a reader's imagination that we come away with something of Tillyard's impression that "the Chorus sings the glory of the 'plain Heroic magnitude of mind' leading to action, but not without mentioning the other state when action is denied and every saint must be his own deliverer merely" (p. 348). We are inclined to sense the "merely" in the resigned voices of Samson's countrymen; but here, as before, we must distinguish between the human attitudes of these *dramatis personae* and the truths ironically expressed in their reluctance. Victory through patience was to Milton the nobler triumph, though we and the Danites may feel otherwise.

Similarly, a proper balance seems hard for us to maintain before the choral conclusion:

> Either of these is in thy lot,
> *Samson*, with might endu'd
> Above the Sons of men; but sight bereav'd
> May chance to number thee with those
> Whom Patience finally must crown (1292-96).

One critic says of these lines, as Tillyard says of the preceding ones, that Samson may be God's invincible champion or "he may simply have to bear his lot with patience."[24] The pathos of "simply having to bear" without tangible victory may accurately characterize the tone of the speakers and may be what leads Douglas Bush to say "The chorus forecast is of course wrong."[25] But while the Chorus may be wrong in its under-

[23] Columbia edition, III, 11.

[24] M. E. Grenander, "*Samson's* Middle: Aristotle and Dr. Johnson," *University of Toronto Quarterly*, XXIV (1955), 387.

[25] *Major British Writers*, ed. G. B. Harrison (New York, 1954), I, 517n. Few are as forthright as Mr. Bush in commenting on the lines. J. Holly Hanford, in "*Samson Agonistes* and Milton in Old Age," *Studies in Shakespeare, Milton, and Donne by Members of the English Department of the University of Michigan* (New York, 1925), comments on the triumphal opening lines and then adds that the Danites "are, of course, like Samson himself, still blind to what is to come, and they go on to sing of patience as the final crown of saints" (p. 176). Later, however, he relates the drama to Milton's advocacy in *PL*, IX, of "the better fortutude / Of Patience" (pp. 177-178). Similarly, there seems a note of condescension when Arnold Stein says, "Though either of these may be Samson's destiny, the Chorus believes that his hope lies with patience. It is a reasonable guess." (*Heroic Knowledge* [Minneapolis, 1957], p. 185). However, his later comments on patience (pp. 188, 197, 201) suggest that

standing of patience, its " forecast " is ironically right. For the victory which Milton's Samson struggles for and has just begun to win is the one within—a victory over despair, whose antidote is patience, the higher attribute of fortitude, that cardinal virtue which Samson and his column had come to symbolize by Milton's age.

The consummation of that spiritual victory (upon which then is wrought the physical one) comes with the sudden influx of heavenly grace which calls from Samson his first confident assurance:

> Be of good courage, I begin to feel
> Some rouzing motions in me which dispose
> To something extraordinary my thoughts (1381-83).

As ironically foreshadowed in the earlier ode, that " source of consolation from above: / Secret refreshings, that repair his strength, / and fainting spirits uphold " does indeed come to ease the seeming harshness of the patience Samson has turned to in his *tristitia*. Hereafter his words and actions reflect an inner calm unknown before so that, with the messenger's description, we last see him standing " patient and undaunted " (1623), praying or meditating with his reconciled God before the final act of terrible vengeance.

the Chorus had been right to some degree. To my knowledge, Michael Krouse alone holds unequivocally that the Chorus is right in its prediction (*Milton's Samson and the Christian Tradition* [Princeton, 1949], pp. 15-16, 98n).